Man and his Symbols

Man and his Symbols

Carl G. Jung

and M.-L. von Franz, Joseph L. Henderson, Jolande Jacobi, Aniela Jaffé

Aldus Books • Jupiter Books • London

Editor: Carl G. Jung

and after his death M.-L. von Franz

Co-ordinating Editor: John Freeman

Aldus Editors

Text: Douglas Hill

Design: Michael Kitson

Assistants: Marian Morris, Gilbert Doel, Michael Lloyd

Research: Margery MacLaren

Advisers: Donald Berwick, Norman MacKenzie

ISBN 0-904-04124-7

Printed and bound in Spain by TONSA, San Sebastian

Introduction: John Freeman

The origins of this book are sufficiently unusual to be of interest, and they bear a direct relation to its contents and what it sets out to do. So let me tell you just how it came to be written.

One day in the spring of 1959 the British Broadcasting Corporation invited me to interview for British television Dr. Carl Gustav Jung. The interview was to be done "in depth." I knew little enough at that time about Jung and his work, and I at once went to make his acquaintance at his beautiful lakeside home near Zurich. That was the beginning of a friendship that meant a great deal to me and, I hope, gave some pleasure to Jung in the last years of his life. The television interview has no further place in this story, except that it was accounted successful and that this book is by an odd combination of circumstances an end-product of that success.

One man who saw Jung on the screen was Wolfgang Foges, managing director of Aldus Books. Foges had been keenly interested in the development of modern psychology since his childhood, when he lived near the Freuds in Vienna. And as he watched Jung talking about his life and work and ideas, Foges suddenly reflected what a pity it was that, while the general outline of Freud's work was well known to educated readers all over the Western world, Jung had never managed to break through to the general public and was always considered too difficult for popular reading.

Foges, in fact, is the creator of *Man and his Symbols*. Having sensed from the TV screen that a warm personal relation existed between Jung and myself, he asked me whether I would join him in trying to persuade Jung to set out some of his more important and basic ideas in language and at a length that would be intelligible and interesting to non-specialist adult readers. I jumped at the idea and set off once more to Zurich, determined that I could convince Jung of the value and importance of such a work. Jung listened to me in his garden for two hours almost without interruption—and then said nò. He said it in the nicest possible way, but with great firmness; he had never in the past tried to popularize his work, and he wasn't sure that he could successfully do so now; anyway, he was old and rather tired and not keen to take on such a long commitment about which he had so many doubts.

Jung's friends will all agree with me that he was a man of most positive decision. He would weigh up a problem with care and without

9

hurry; but when he did give his answer, it was usually final. I returned to London greatly disappointed, but convinced that Jung's refusal was the end of the matter. So it might have been, but for two intervening factors that I had not foreseen.

One was the pertinacity of Foges, who insisted on making one more approach to Jung before accepting defeat. The other was an event that, as I look back on it, still astonishes me.

The television program was, as I have said, accounted successful. It brought Jung a great many letters from all sorts of people, many of them ordinary folk with no medical or psychological training, who had been captivated by the commanding presence, the humor, and the modest charm of this very great man, and who had glimpsed in his view of life and human personality something that could be helpful to them. And Jung was very pleased, not simply at getting letters (his mail was enormous at all times) but at getting them from people who would normally have no contact with him.

It was at this moment that he dreamed a dream of the greatest importance to him. (And as you read this book, you will understand just how important that can be.) He dreamed that, instead of sitting in his study and talking to the great doctors and psychiatrists who used to call on him from all over the world, he was standing in a public place and addressing a multitude of people who were listening to him with rapt attention and *understanding what he said.* . . .

When, a week or two later, Foges renewed his request that Jung should undertake a new book designed, not for the clinic or the philosopher's study, but for the people in the market place, Jung allowed himself to be persuaded. He laid down two conditions. First, that the book should not be a single-handed book, but the collective effort of himself and a group of his closest followers, through whom he had attempted to perpetuate his methods and his teaching. Secondly, that I should be entrusted with the task of co-ordinating the work and resolving any problems that might arise between the authors and the publishers.

Lest it should seem that this introduction transgresses the bounds of reasonable modesty, let me say at once that I was gratified by this second condition—but within measure. For it very soon came to my knowledge that Jung's reason for selecting me was essentially that he regarded me as being of reasonable, but not exceptional, intelligence and without the slightest serious knowledge of psychology. Thus I was to Jung the "average reader" of this book; what I could understand would be intelligible to all who would be interested; what I boggled at might possibly be too difficult or obscure for some. Not unduly flattered by this estimate of my role, I have none the less scrupulously insisted (sometimes, I fear, to the exasperation of the authors) on having every paragraph written and, if necessary, rewritten to a degree of clarity and directness that enables me to say with confidence that this book in its entirety is designed for and addressed to the general reader, and that the complex subjects it deals with are treated with a rare and encouraging simplicity.

After much discussion, the comprehensive subject of this book was agreed to be Man and his Symbols; and Jung himself selected as his collaborators in the work Dr. Marie-Louise von Franz of Zurich, perhaps his closest professional confidante and friend; Dr. Joseph L. Henderson of San Francisco, one of the most prominent and trusted of American Jungians; Mrs. Aniela Jaffé of Zurich, who, in addition to being an experienced analyst, was Jung's confidential private secretary and his biographer; and Dr. Jolande Jacobi, who after Jung himself is the most experienced author among Jung's Zurich circle. These four people were chosen partly because of their skill and experience in the particular subjects allocated to them and partly because all of them were completely trusted by Jung to work unselfishly to his instructions as members of a team. Jung's personal responsibility was to plan the structure of the whole book, to supervise and direct the work of his collaborators, and himself to write the keynote chapter, "Approaching the Unconscious."

The last year of his life was devoted almost entirely to this book, and when he died in June 1961, his own section was complete (he finished it, in fact, only some 10 days before his final illness) and his colleagues' chapters had all been approved by him in draft. After his death, Dr. von Franz assumed over-all responsibility for the completion of the book in accordance with Jung's express instructions. The subject matter of *Man and his Symbols* and its outline were therefore laid down— and in detail—by Jung. The chapter that bears his name is his work and (apart from some fairly extensive editing to improve its intelligibility to the general reader) nobody else's. It was written, incidentally, in English. The remaining chapters were written by the various authors to Jung's direction and under his supervision. The final editing of the complete work after Jung's death has been done by Dr. von Franz with a patience, understanding, and good humor that leave the publishers and myself greatly in her debt.

Finally as to the contents of the book itself:

Jung's thinking has colored the world of modern psychology more than many of those with casual knowledge realize. Such familiar terms, for instance, as "extravert," "introvert," and "archetype" are all Jungian concepts—borrowed and sometimes misused by others. But his overwhelming contribution to psychological understanding is his concept of the unconscious—not (like the unconscious of Freud) merely a sort of glory-hole of repressed desires, but a world that is just as much a vital and real part of the life of an individual as the conscious, "cogitating" world of the ego, and infinitely wider and richer. The language and the "people" of the unconscious are symbols, and the means of communications dreams.

Thus an examination of Man and his Symbols is in effect an examination of man's relation to his own unconscious. And since in Jung's view the unconscious is the great guide, friend, and adviser of the conscious, this book is related in the most direct terms to the study of human beings and their spiritual problems. We know the unconscious and communicate with it (a two-way service) principally by dreams; and all through this book (above all in Jung's own chapter) you will find a quite remarkable emphasis placed on the importance of dreaming in the life of the individual.

It would be an impertinence on my part to attempt to interpret Jung's work to readers, many of whom will surely be far better qualified to understand it than I am. My role, remember, was merely to serve as a sort of "intelligibility filter" and by no means as an interpreter. Nevertheless, I venture to offer two general points that seem important to me as a layman and that may possibly be helpful to other non-experts. The first is about dreams. To Jungians the dream is not a kind of standardized cryptogram that can be decoded by a glossary of symbol meanings. It is an integral, important, and personal expression of the individual unconscious. It is just as "real" as any other phenomenon attaching to the individual. The dreamer's individual unconscious is communicating with the dreamer alone and is selecting symbols for its purpose that have meaning to the dreamer and to nobody else. Thus the interpretation of dreams, whether by the analyst or by the dreamer himself, is for the Jungian psychologist an entirely personal and individual business (and sometimes an experimental and very lengthy one as well) that can by no means be undertaken by rule of thumb.

The converse of this is that the communications of the unconscious are of the highest importance to the dreamer—naturally so, since the unconscious is at least half of his total being—and frequently offer him advice or guidance that could be obtained from no other source. Thus, when I described Jung's dream about addressing the multitude, I was not describing a piece of magic or suggesting that Jung dabbled in fortune telling. I was recounting in the simple terms of daily experience how Jung was "advised" by his own unconscious to reconsider an inadequate judgment he had made with the conscious part of his mind.

Now it follows from this that the dreaming of dreams is not a matter that the well-adjusted Jungian can regard as simply a matter of chance. On the contrary, the ability to establish communications with the unconscious is a part of the whole man, and Jungians "teach" themselves (I can think of no better term) to be receptive to dreams. When, therefore, Jung himself was faced with the critical decision whether or not to write this book, he was able to draw on the resources of both his conscious and his unconscious in making up his mind. And all through this book you will find the dream treated as a direct, personal, and meaningful communication to the dreamer—a communication that uses the symbols common to all mankind, but that uses them on every occasion in an entirely individual way that can be interpreted only by an entirely individual "key."

The second point I wish to make is about a particular characteristic of argumentative method that is common to all the writers of this book —perhaps to all Jungians. Those who have limited themselves to living entirely in the world of the conscious and who reject communication with the unconscious bind themselves by the laws of conscious, formal life. With the infallible (but often meaningless) logic of the algebraic equation, they argue from assumed premises to incontestably deduced conclusions. Jung and his colleagues seem to me (whether they know it or not) to reject the limitations of this method of argument. It is not that they ignore logic, but they appear all the time to be arguing to the unconscious as well as to the conscious. Their dialectical method is itself symbolic and often devious. They convince not by means of the narrowly focused spotlight of the syllogism, but by skirting, by repetition, by presenting a recurring view of the same subject seen each time from a slightly different angle—until suddenly the reader who has never been aware of a single, conclusive moment of proof finds that he has unknowingly embraced and taken into himself some wider truth.

Jung's arguments (and those of his colleagues) spiral upward over his subject like a bird circling a tree. At first, near the ground, it sees only a confusion of leaves and branches. Gradually, as it circles higher and higher, the recurring aspects of the tree form a wholeness and relate to their surroundings. Some readers may find this "spiraling" method of argument obscure or even confusing for a few pages—but not, I think, for long. It is characteristic of Jung's method, and very soon the reader will find it carrying him with it on a persuasive and profoundly absorbing journey.

The different sections of this book speak for themselves and require little introduction from me. Jung's own chapter introduces the reader to the unconscious, to the archetypes and symbols that form its language and to the dreams by which it communicates. Dr. Henderson in the following chapter illustrates the appearance of several archetypal patterns in ancient mythology, folk legend, and primitive ritual. Dr. von Franz, in the chapter entitled "The Process of Individuation," describes the process by which the conscious and the unconscious within an individual learn to know, respect, and accommodate one another. In a certain sense this chapter contains not only the crux of the whole book, but perhaps the essence of Jung's philosophy of life: Man becomes whole, integrated, calm, fertile, and happy when (and only when) the process of individuation is complete, when the conscious and the unconscious have learned to live at peace and to complement one another. Mrs. Jaffé, like Dr. Henderson, is concerned with demonstrating, in the familiar fabric of the conscious, man's recurring interest in—almost obsession with—the symbols of the unconscious. They have for him a profoundly significant, almost a nourishing and sustaining, inner attraction—whether they occur in the myths and fairy tales that Dr. Henderson analyzes or in the visual arts, which, as Mrs. Jaffé shows, satisfy and delight us by a constant appeal to the unconscious.

Finally, I must say a brief word about Dr. Jacobi's chapter, which is somewhat separate from the rest of the book. It is in fact an abbreviated case history of one interesting and successful analysis. The value of such a chapter in a book like this is obvious; but two words of warning are nevertheless necessary. First, as Dr. von Franz points out, there is no such thing as a typical Jungian analysis. There can't be, because every dream is a private and individual communication, and no two dreams use the symbols of the unconscious in the same way. So every Jungian analysis is unique—and it is misleading to consider this one, taken from Dr. Jacobi's clinical files (or any other one there has ever been), as "representative" or "typical." All one can say of the case of Henry and his sometimes lurid dreams is that they form one true example of the way in which the Jungian method may be applied to a particular case. Secondly, the full history of even a comparatively uncomplicated case would take a whole book to recount. Inevitably, the story of Henry's analysis suffers a little in compression. The references, for instance, to the *I Ching* have been somewhat obscured and lent an unnatural (and to me unsatisfactory) flavor of the occult by being presented out of their full context. Nevertheless, we concluded—and I am sure the reader will agree—that, with the warnings duly given, the clarity, to say nothing of the human interest, of Henry's analysis greatly enriches this book.

I began by describing how Jung came to write *Man and his Symbols*. I end by reminding the reader of what a remarkable—perhaps unique —publication this is. Carl Gustav Jung was one of the great doctors of all time and one of the great thinkers of this century. His object always was to help men and women to know themselves, so that by self-knowledge and thoughtful self-use they could lead full, rich, and happy lives. At the very end of his own life, which was as full, rich, and happy as any I have encountered, he decided to use the strength that was left him to address his message to a wider public than he had ever tried to reach before. He completed his task and his life in the same month. This book is his legacy to the broad reading public.

Contents

1   Approaching the unconscious

Carl G. Jung

The importance of dreams

Man uses the spoken or written word to express the meaning of what he wants to convey. His language is full of symbols, but he also often employs signs or images that are not strictly descriptive. Some are mere abbreviations or strings of initials, such as UN, UNICEF, or UNESCO; others are familiar trade marks, the names of patent medicines, badges, or insignia. Although these are meaningless in themselves, they have acquired a recognizable meaning through common usage or deliberate intent. Such things are not symbols. They are signs, and they do no more than denote the objects to which they are attached.

What we call a symbol is a term, a name, or even a picture that may be familiar in daily life, yet that possesses specific connotations in addition to its conventional and obvious meaning. It implies something vague, unknown, or hidden from us. Many Cretan monuments, for instance, are marked with the design of the

double adze. This is an object that we know, but we do not know its symbolic implications. For another example, take the case of the Indian who, after a visit to England, told his friends at home that the English worship animals, because he had found eagles, lions, and oxen in old churches. He was not aware (nor are many Christians) that these animals are symbols of the Evangelists and are derived from the vision of Ezekiel, and that this in turn has an analogy to the Egyptian sun god Horus and his four sons. There are, moreover, such objects as the wheel and the cross that are known all over the world, yet that have a symbolic significance under certain conditions. Precisely what they symbolize is still a matter for controversial speculation.

Thus a word or an image is symbolic when it implies something more than its obvious and immediate meaning. It has a wider "unconscious" aspect that is never precisely defined or

fully explained. Nor can one hope to define or explain it. As the mind explores the symbol, it is led to ideas that lie beyond the grasp of reason. The wheel may lead our thoughts toward the concept of a "divine" sun, but at this point reason must admit its incompetence; man is unable to define a "divine" being. When, with all our intellectual limitations, we call something "divine," we have merely given it a name, which may be based on a creed, but never on factual evidence.

Because there are innumerable things beyond the range of human understanding, we constantly use symbolic terms to represent concepts that we cannot define or fully comprehend. This is one reason why all religions employ symbolic language or images. But this conscious use of symbols is only one aspect of a psychological fact of great importance: Man also produces symbols unconsciously and spontaneously, in the form of dreams.

It is not easy to grasp this point. But the point must be grasped if we are to know more about the ways in which the human mind works. Man, as we realize if we reflect for a moment, never perceives anything fully or comprehends anything completely. He can see, hear, touch, and taste; but how far he sees, how well he hears, what his touch tells him, and what he tastes depend upon the number and quality of his senses. These limit his perception of the world around him. By using scientific instruments he can partly compensate for the deficiencies of his senses. For example, he can extend the range of his vision by binoculars or of his hearing by electrical amplification. But the most elaborate apparatus cannot do more than bring distant or small objects within range of his eyes, or make faint sounds more audible. No matter what instruments he uses, at some point he reaches the edge of certainty beyond which conscious knowledge cannot pass.

Left, three of the four Evangelists (in a relief on Chartres Cathedral) appear as animals: The lion is Mark, the ox Luke, the eagle John. Also animals are three of the sons of the Egyptian god Horus (above, *c.* 1250 B.C.). Animals, and groups of four, are universal religious symbols.

In many societies, representations of the sun express man's indefinable religious experience. Above, a decoration on the back of a throne belonging to the 14th-century B.C. Egyptian pharaoh Tutankhamen is dominated by a sun disk; the hands at the end of the rays symbolize the sun's life-giving power. Left, a monk in 20th-century Japan prays before a mirror that represents the divine Sun in the Shinto religion.

Right, tungsten atoms seen with a microscope that magnifies 2,000,000 times. Far right, the spots in center of picture are the farthest visible galaxies. No matter how far man extends his senses, limits to his conscious perception remain.

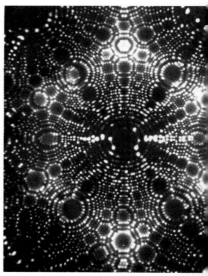

There are, moreover, unconscious aspects of our perception of reality. The first is the fact that even when our senses react to real phenomena, sights, and sounds, they are somehow translated from the realm of reality into that of the mind. Within the mind they become psychic events, whose ultimate nature is unknowable (for the psyche cannot know its own psychical substance). Thus every experience contains an indefinite number of unknown factors, not to speak of the fact that every concrete object is always unknown in certain respects, because we cannot know the ultimate nature of matter itself.

Then there are certain events of which we have not consciously taken note; they have remained, so to speak, below the threshold of consciousness. They have happened, but they have been absorbed subliminally, without our conscious knowledge. We can become aware of such happenings only in a moment of intuition or by a process of profound thought that leads to a later realization that they must have happened; and though we may have originally ignored their emotional and vital importance, it later wells up from the unconscious as a sort of afterthought.

It may appear, for instance, in the form of a dream. As a general rule, the unconscious aspect of any event is revealed to us in dreams, where it appears not as a rational thought but as a symbolic image. As a matter of history, it was the study of dreams that first enabled psychologists to investigate the unconscious aspect of conscious psychic events.

It is on such evidence that psychologists assume the existence of an unconscious psyche —though many scientists and philosophers deny its existence. They argue naïvely that such an assumption implies the existence of two "subjects," or (to put it in a common phrase) two personalities within the same individual. But this is exactly what it does imply—quite correctly. And it is one of the curses of modern man that many people suffer from this divided personality. It is by no means a pathological symptom; it is a normal fact that can be observed at any time and everywhere. It is not merely the neurotic whose right hand does not know what the left hand is doing. This predicament is a symptom of a general unconsciousness that is the undeniable common inheritance of all mankind.

Man has developed consciousness slowly and laboriously, in a process that took untold ages to reach the civilized state (which is arbitrarily dated from the invention of script in about 4000 B.C.). And this evolution is far from complete, for large areas of the human mind are still shrouded in darkness. What we call the "psyche" is by no means identical with our consciousness and its contents.

Whoever denies the existence of the unconscious is in fact assuming that our present knowledge of the psyche is total. And this belief is clearly just as false as the assumption that we know all there is to be known about the natural universe. Our psyche is part of nature, and its enigma is as limitless. Thus we cannot define either the psyche or nature. We can merely state what we believe them to be and describe, as best we can, how they function. Quite apart, therefore, from the evidence that medical research has accumulated, there are strong grounds of logic for rejecting statements like "There is no unconscious." Those who say such things merely express an age-old "misoneism" —a fear of the new and the unknown.

There are historical reasons for this resistance to the idea of an unknown part of the human psyche. Consciousness is a very recent acquisition of nature, and it is still in an "experimental" state. It is frail, menaced by specific dangers, and easily injured. As anthropologists have noted, one of the most common mental derangements that occur among primitive people is what they call "the loss of a soul"—which means, as the name indicates, a noticeable disruption (or, more technically, a dissociation) of consciousness.

Among such people, whose consciousness is at a different level of development from ours, the "soul" (or psyche) is not felt to be a unit. Many primitives assume that a man has a "bush soul" as well as his own, and that this bush soul is incarnate in a wild animal or a tree, with which the human individual has some kind of psychic identity. This is what the distinguished French ethnologist Lucien Lévy-Brühl called a "mystical participation." He later retracted this term under pressure of adverse criticism, but I believe that his critics were wrong. It is a well-known psychological fact that an individual may have such an unconscious identity with some other person or object.

This identity takes a variety of forms among primitives. If the bush soul is that of an animal, the animal itself is considered as some sort of brother to the man. A man whose brother is a crocodile, for instance, is supposed to be safe when swimming a crocodile-infested river. If the bush soul is a tree, the tree is presumed to have something like parental authority over the individual concerned. In both cases an injury to the bush soul is interpreted as an injury to the man.

In some tribes, it is assumed that a man has a number of souls; this belief expresses the feeling of some primitive individuals that they each consist of several linked but distinct units. This means that the individual's psyche is far from being safely synthesized; on the contrary, it threatens to fragment only too easily under the onslaught of unchecked emotions.

While this situation is familiar to us from the studies of anthropologists, it is not so irrelevant to our own advanced civilization as it might seem. We too can become dissociated and lose

"Dissociation" means a splitting in the psyche, causing a neurosis. A famous fictional example of this state is *Dr. Jekyll and Mr. Hyde* (1886) by the Scots author R. L. Stevenson. In the story Jekyll's "split" took the form of a physical change, rather than (as in reality) an inner, psychic state. Left, Mr. Hyde (from the 1932 film of the story)—Jekyll's "other half."

Primitive people call dissociation "loss of a soul"; they believe that a man has a "bush soul" as well as his own. Right, a Nyanga tribesman of west central Africa wearing a mask of the hornbill—the bird that he identifies with his bush soul.

Far right, telephonists on a busy switchboard handle many calls at once. In such jobs people "split off" parts of their conscious minds to concentrate. But this split is controlled and temporary, not a spontaneous, abnormal dissociation.

our identity. We can be possessed and altered by moods, or become unreasonable and unable to recall important facts about ourselves or others, so that people ask: "What the devil has got into you?" We talk about being able "to control ourselves," but self-control is a rare and remarkable virtue. We may think we have ourselves under control; yet a friend can easily tell us things about ourselves of which we have no knowledge.

Beyond doubt, even in what we call a high level of civilization, human consciousness has not yet achieved a reasonable degree of continuity. It is still vulnerable and liable to fragmentation. This capacity to isolate part of one's mind, indeed, is a valuable characteristic. It enables us to concentrate upon one thing at a time, excluding everything else that may claim our attention. But there is a world of difference between a conscious decision to split off and temporarily suppress a part of one's psyche, and a condition in which this happens spontaneously, without one's knowledge or consent and even against one's intention. The former is a civilized achievement, the latter a primitive "loss of a soul," or even the pathological cause of a neurosis.

Thus, even in our day the unity of consciousness is still a doubtful affair; it can too easily be disrupted. An ability to control one's emotions that may be very desirable from one point of view would be a questionable accomplishment from another, for it would deprive social intercourse of variety, color, and warmth.

It is against this background that we must review the importance of dreams—those flimsy, evasive, unreliable, vague, and uncertain fantasies. To explain my point of view, I should like to describe how it developed over a period of years, and how I was led to conclude that dreams are the most frequent and universally accessible source for the investigation of man's symbolizing faculty.

Sigmund Freud was the pioneer who first tried to explore empirically the unconscious background of consciousness. He worked on the general assumption that dreams are not a matter of chance but are associated with conscious thoughts and problems. This assumption was not in the least arbitrary. It was based upon the

conclusion of eminent neurologists (for instance, Pierre Janet) that neurotic symptoms are related to some conscious experience. They even appear to be split-off areas of the conscious mind, which, at another time and under different conditions, can be conscious.

Before the beginning of this century, Freud and Josef Breuer had recognized that neurotic symptoms—hysteria, certain types of pain, and abnormal behavior—are in fact symbolically meaningful. They are one way in which the unconscious mind expresses itself, just as it may in dreams; and they are equally symbolic. A patient, for instance, who is confronted with an intolerable situation may develop a spasm whenever he tries to swallow: He "can't swallow it." Under similar conditions of psychological stress, another patient has an attack of asthma: He "can't breathe the atmosphere at home." A third suffers from a peculiar paralysis of the legs: He can't walk, i.e. "he can't go on any more." A fourth, who vomits when he eats, "cannot digest" some unpleasant fact. I could cite many examples of this kind, but such physical reactions are only one form in which the problems that trouble us unconsciously may express themselves. They more often find expression in our dreams.

Any psychologist who has listened to numbers of people describing their dreams knows that dream symbols have much greater variety than the physical symptoms of neurosis. They often consist of elaborate and picturesque fantasies. But if the analyst who is confronted by this dream material uses Freud's original technique of "free association," he finds that dreams

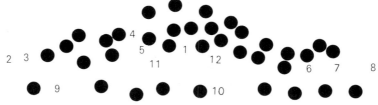

1 Sigmund Freud (Vienna)
2 Otto Rank (Vienna)
3 Ludwig Binswanger (Kreuzlingen)
4 A. A. Brill

5 Max Eitingon (Berlin)
6 James J. Putnam (Boston)
7 Ernest Jones (Toronto)
8 Wilhelm Stekel (Vienna)

9 Eugen Bleuler (Zürich)
10 Emma Jung (Küsnacht)
11 Sandor Ferenczi (Budapest)
12 C. G. Jung (Küsnacht)

can eventually be reduced to certain basic patterns. This technique played an important part in the development of psychoanalysis, for it enabled Freud to use dreams as the starting point from which the unconscious problem of the patient might be explored.

Freud made the simple but penetrating observation that if a dreamer is encouraged to go on talking about his dream images and the thoughts that these prompt in his mind, he will give himself away and reveal the unconscious background of his ailments, in both what he says and what he deliberately omits saying. His ideas may seem irrational and irrelevant, but after a time it becomes relatively easy to see what it is that he is trying to avoid, what unpleasant thought or experience he is suppressing. No matter how he tries to camouflage it, everything he says points to the core of his predicament. A doctor sees so many things from the seamy side of life that he is seldom far from the truth when he interprets the hints that his patient produces as signs of an uneasy conscience. What he eventually discovers, unfortunately, confirms his expectations. Thus far, nobody can say anything against Freud's theory of repression and wish fulfillment as apparent causes of dream symbolism.

Freud attached particular importance to dreams as the point of departure for a process of "free association." But after a time I began to feel that this was a misleading and inadequate use of the rich fantasies that the unconscious produces in sleep. My doubts really began when a colleague told me of an experience he had during the course of a long train journey in Russia. Though he did not know the language and could not even decipher the Cyrillic script, he found himself musing over the strange letters in which the railway notices were written, and he fell into a reverie in which he imagined all sorts of meanings for them.

One idea led to another, and in his relaxed mood he found that this "free association" had stirred up many old memories. Among them he was annoyed to find some long-buried disagreeable topics—things he had wished to forget and had forgotten *consciously*. He had in fact arrived at what psychologists would call his "complexes"—that is, repressed emotional themes that can cause constant psychological disturbances or even, in many cases, the symptoms of neurosis.

This episode opened my eyes to the fact that it was not necessary to use a dream as the point of departure for the process of "free association" if one wished to discover the complexes of a patient. It showed me that one can reach the center directly from any point of the compass. One could begin from Cyrillic letters, from

Left, many of the great pioneers of modern psychoanalysis, photographed at a Congress of Psychoanalysis in 1911 at Weimar, Germany. The key, below left, identifies some of the major figures.

Right, the "inkblot" test devised by the Swiss psychiatrist Hermann Rorschach. The shape of the blot can serve as a stimulus for free association; in fact, almost any irregular free shape can spark off the associative process. Leonardo da Vinci wrote in his *Notebooks*: "It should not be hard for you to stop sometimes and look into the stains of walls, or ashes of a fire, or clouds, or mud or like places, in which . . . you may find really marvelous ideas."

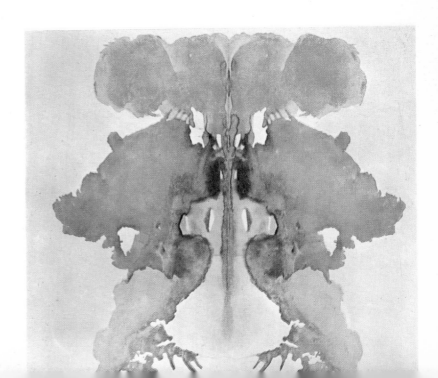

meditations upon a crystal ball, a prayer wheel, or a modern painting, or even from casual conversation about some quite trivial event. The dream was no more and no less useful in this respect than any other possible starting point. Nevertheless, dreams have a particular significance, even though they often arise from an emotional upset in which the habitual complexes are also involved. (The habitual complexes are the tender spots of the psyche, which react most quickly to an external stimulus or disturbance.) That is why free association can lead one from any dream to the critical secret thoughts.

At this point, however, it occurred to me that (if I was right so far) it might reasonably follow that dreams have some special and more significant function of their own. Very often dreams have a definite, evidently purposeful structure, indicating an underlying idea or intention—though, as a rule, the latter is not immediately comprehensible. I therefore began to consider whether one should pay more attention to the actual form and content of a dream, rather than allowing "'free'" association to lead one off through a train of ideas to complexes that could as easily be reached by other means.

This new thought was a turning point in the development of my psychology. It meant that I gradually gave up following associations that led far away from the text of a dream. I chose to concentrate rather on the associations to the dream itself, believing that the latter expressed something specific that the unconscious was trying to say.

The change in my attitude toward dreams involved a change of method; the new tech-

nique was one that could take account of all the various wider aspects of a dream. A story told by the conscious mind has a beginning, a development, and an end, but the same is not true of a dream. Its dimensions in time and space are quite different; to understand it you must examine it from every aspect—just as you may take an unknown object in your hands and turn it over and over until you are familiar with every detail of its shape.

Perhaps I have now said enough to show how I came increasingly to disagree with "free" association as Freud first employed it: I wanted to keep as close as possible to the dream itself, and to exclude all the irrelevant ideas and associations that it might evoke. True, these could lead one toward the complexes of a patient, but I had a more far-reaching purpose in mind than the discovery of complexes that cause neurotic disturbances. There are many other means by which these can be identified: The psychologist, for instance, can get all the hints he needs by using word-association tests (by asking the patient what he associates to a given set of words, and by studying his responses). But to know and understand the psychic life-

Two different possible stimuli of free association: the whirling prayer wheel of a Tibetan beggar (left), or a fortune teller's crystal ball (right, a modern crystal gazer at a British fair).

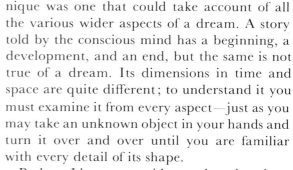

process of an individual's whole personality, it is important to realize that his dreams and their symbolic images have a much more important role to play.

Almost everyone knows, for example, that there is an enormous variety of images by which the sexual act can be symbolized (or, one might say, represented in the form of an allegory). Each of these images can lead, by a process of association, to the idea of sexual intercourse and to specific complexes that any individual may have about his own sexual attitudes. But one could just as well unearth such complexes by day-dreaming on a set of indecipherable Russian letters. I was thus led to the assumption that a dream can contain some message other than the sexual allegory, and that it does so for definite reasons. To illustrate this point:

A man may dream of inserting a key in a lock, of wielding a heavy stick, or of breaking down a door with a battering ram. Each of these can be regarded as a sexual allegory. But the fact that his unconscious for its own purposes has chosen one of these specific images— it may be the key, the stick, or the battering ram—is also of major significance. The real task is to understand *why* the key has been preferred to the stick, or the stick to the ram. And sometimes this might even lead one to discover that it is not the sexual act at all that is represented, but some quite different psychological point.

From this line of reasoning, I concluded that only the material that is clearly and visibly part of a dream should be used in interpreting it. The dream has its own limitation. Its specific

form itself tells us what belongs to it and what leads away from it. While "free" association lures one away from that material in a kind of zigzag line, the method I evolved is more like a circumambulation whose center is the dream picture. I work all around the dream picture and disregard every attempt that the dreamer makes to break away from it. Time and time again, in my professional work, I have had to repeat the words: "Let's get back to your dream. What does the *dream* say?"

For instance, a patient of mine dreamed of a drunken and disheveled vulgar woman. In the dream, it seemed that this woman was his wife, though in real life his wife was totally different. On the surface, therefore, the dream was shockingly untrue, and the patient immediately rejected it as dream nonsense. If I, as his doctor, had let him start a process of association, he would inevitably have tried to get as far away as possible from the unpleasant suggestion of his dream. In that case, he would have ended with one of his staple complexes—a complex, possibly, that had nothing to do with his wife— and we should have learned nothing about the special meaning of this particular dream.

One of the countless symbolic or allegorical images of the sexual act is a deer hunt: Right, a detail from a painting by the 16th-century German artist Cranach. The sexual implication of the deer hunt is underlined by a medieval English folk song called "The Keeper":
The first doe that he shot at he missed,
And the second doe he trimmed he kissed,
And the third ran away in a young man's heart,
She's amongst the leaves of the green O.

A key in a lock *may* be a sexual symbol—but not invariably. Left, a section of an altarpiece by the 15th-century Flemish artist Campin. The door was intended to symbolize hope, the lock to symbolize charity, and the key to symbolize the desire for God. Below, a British bishop during the consecration of a church carries out a traditional ceremony by knocking on the church door with a staff—which is obviously not a phallic symbol but a symbol of authority and the shepherd's crook. No individual symbolic image can be said to have a dogmatically fixed, generalized meaning.

The "anima" is the female element in the male unconscious. (It and the "animus" in the female unconscious are discussed in Chapter 3.) This inner duality is often symbolized by a hermaphroditic figure, like the crowned hermaphrodite, above right, from a 17th-century alchemical manuscript. Right, a physical image of man's psychic "bisexuality": a human cell with its chromosomes. All organisms have two sets of chromosomes—one from each parent.

What, then, was his unconscious trying to convey by such an obviously untrue statement? Clearly, it somehow expressed the idea of a degenerate female who was closely connected with the dreamer's life; but since the projection of this image on to his wife was unjustified and factually untrue, I had to look elsewhere before I found out what this repulsive image represented.

In the Middle Ages, long before the physiologists demonstrated that by reason of our glandular structure there are both male and female elements in all of us, it was said that "every man carries a woman within himself." It is this female element in every male that I have called the "anima." This "feminine" aspect is essentially a certain inferior kind of relatedness to the surroundings, and particularly to women, which is kept carefully concealed from others as well as from oneself. In other words, though an individual's visible personality may seem quite normal, he may well be concealing from others—or even from himself—the deplorable condition of "the woman within."

That was the case with this particular patient: His female side was not nice. His dream was actually saying to him: "You are in some respects behaving like a degenerate female," and thus gave him an appropriate shock. (An example of this kind, of course, must not be taken as evidence that the unconscious is concerned with "moral" injunctions. The dream was not telling the patient to "behave better," but was simply trying to balance the lopsided nature of his conscious mind, which was maintaining the fiction that he was a perfect gentleman throughout.)

It is easy to understand why dreamers tend to ignore and even deny the message of their dreams. Consciousness naturally resists anything unconscious and unknown. I have already pointed out the existence among primitive peoples of what anthropologists call "misoneism," a deep and superstitious fear of novelty. The primitives manifest all the reactions of the wild animal against untoward events. But "civilized" man reacts to new ideas in much the same way, erecting psychological barriers to protect himself from the shock of facing something new. This can easily be observed in any individual's reaction to his own dreams when obliged to admit a surprising thought. Many pioneers in philosophy, science, and even literature have been victims of the innate conservatism of their contemporaries. Psychology is one of the youngest of the sciences; because it attempts to deal with the working of the unconscious, it has inevitably encountered misoneism in an extreme form.

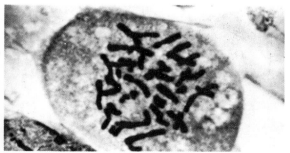

Past and future in the unconscious

So far, I have been sketching some of the principles on which I approached the problem of dreams, for when we want to investigate man's faculty to produce symbols, dreams prove to be the most basic and accessible material for this purpose. The two fundamental points in dealing with dreams are these: First, the dream should be treated as a fact, about which one must make no previous assumption except that it somehow makes sense; and second, the dream is a specific expression of the unconscious.

One could scarcely put these principles more modestly. No matter how low anyone's opinion of the unconscious may be, he must concede that it is worth investigating; the unconscious is at least on a level with the louse, which, after all, enjoys the honest interest of the entomologist. If somebody with little experience and knowledge of dreams thinks that dreams are just chaotic occurrences without meaning, he is at liberty to do so. But if one assumes that they are normal events (which, as a matter of fact, they are), one is bound to consider that they are either causal—i.e. that there is a rational cause for their existence—or in a certain way purposive, or both.

Let us now look a little more closely at the ways in which the conscious and unconscious contents of the mind are linked together. Take an example with which everyone is familiar. Suddenly you find you cannot remember what you were going to say next, though a moment ago the thought was perfectly clear. Or perhaps you were about to introduce a friend, and his name escaped you as you were about to utter it. You say you cannot remember; in fact, though, the thought has become unconscious, or at least momentarily separated from consciousness. We find the same phenomenon with our senses. If we listen to a continuous note on the fringe of audibility, the sound seems to stop at regular intervals and then start again. Such oscillations are due to a periodic decrease and increase in one's attention, not to any change in the note.

But when something slips out of our consciousness it does not cease to exist, any more than a car that has disappeared round a corner has vanished into thin air. It is simply out of sight. Just as we may later see the car again, so we come across thoughts that were temporarily lost to us.

Thus, part of the unconscious consists of a multitude of temporarily obscured thoughts, impressions, and images that, in spite of being lost, continue to influence our conscious minds.

A man who is distracted or "absent-minded" will walk across the room to fetch something. He stops, seemingly perplexed; he has forgotten what he was after. His hands grope about among the objects on the table as if he were sleepwalking; he is oblivious of his original purpose, yet he is unconsciously guided by it. Then he realizes what it is that he wants. His unconscious has prompted him.

If you observe the behavior of a neurotic person, you can see him doing many things that he appears to be doing consciously and purposefully. Yet if you ask him about them, you will discover that he is either unconscious of them or has something quite different in mind. He hears and does not hear; he sees, yet is blind; he knows and is ignorant. Such examples are so common that the specialist soon realizes that unconscious contents of the mind behave as if they were conscious and that you can never be sure, in such cases, whether thought, speech, or action is conscious or not.

It is this kind of behavior that makes so many physicians dismiss statements by hysterical patients as utter lies. Such persons certainly produce more untruths than most of us, but "lie" is scarcely the right word to use. In fact, their mental state causes an uncertainty of

behavior because their consciousness is liable to unpredictable eclipse by an interference from the unconscious. Even their skin sensations may reveal similar fluctuations of awareness. At one moment the hysterical person may feel a needle prick in the arm; at the next it may pass unnoticed. If his attention can be focused on a certain point, the whole of his body can be completely anesthetized until the tension that causes this blackout of the senses has been relaxed. Sense perception is then immediately restored. All the time, however, he has been unconsciously aware of what was happening.

The physician can see this process quite clearly when he hypnotizes such a patient. It is easy to demonstrate that the patient has been aware of every detail. The prick in the arm or the remark made during an eclipse of consciousness can be recalled as accurately as if there had been no anesthesia or "forgetfulness." I recall a woman who was once admitted to the clinic in a state of complete stupor. When she recovered consciousness next day, she knew who she was but did not know where she was, how or why she had come there, or even the date. Yet after I had hypnotized her, she told me why she had fallen ill, how she had got to the clinic, and who had admitted her. All these details

MONKEYANA.

AM I
A
MAN AND
A
BROTHER?

"Misoneism," an unreasoning fear and hatred of new ideas, was a major block to public acceptance of modern psychology. It also opposed Darwin's theories of evolution—as when an American schoolteacher named Scopes was tried in 1925 for teaching evolution. Far left, at the trial, the lawyer Clarence Darrow defending Scopes; center left, Scopes himself. Equally anti-Darwin is the cartoon, left, from an 1861 issue of Britain's magazine Punch. Right, a light-hearted look at misoneism by the American humorist James Thurber, whose aunt (he wrote) was afraid that electricity was "leaking all over the place."

could be verified. She was even able to tell the time at which she had been admitted, because she had seen a clock in the entrance hall. Under hypnosis, her memory was as clear as if she had been completely conscious all the time.

When we discuss such matters, we usually have to draw on evidence supplied by clinical observation. For this reason, many critics assume that the unconscious and all its subtle manifestations belong solely to the sphere of psychopathology. They consider any expression of the unconscious as something neurotic or psychotic, which has nothing to do with a normal mental state. But neurotic phenomena are by no means the products exclusively of disease. They are in fact no more than pathological exaggerations of normal occurrences; it is only because they are exaggerations that they are more obvious than their normal counterparts. Hysterical symptoms can be observed in all normal persons, but they are so slight that they usually pass unnoticed.

Forgetting, for instance, is a normal process, in which certain conscious ideas lose their specific energy because one's attention has been deflected. When interest turns elsewhere, it leaves in shadow the things with which one was previously concerned, just as a searchlight lights up a new area by leaving another in darkness. This is unavoidable, for consciousness can keep only a few images in full clarity at one time, and even this clarity fluctuates.

But the forgotten ideas have not ceased to exist. Although they cannot be reproduced at will, they are present in a subliminal state—just beyond the threshold of recall—from which they can rise again spontaneously at any time, often after many years of apparently total oblivion.

I am speaking here of things we have consciously seen or heard, and subsequently forgotten. But we all see, hear, smell, and taste many things without noticing them at the time, either because our attention is deflected or because the stimulus to our senses is too slight to leave a conscious impression. The unconscious, however, has taken note of them, and such subliminal sense perceptions play a significant part in our everyday lives. Without our realizing it, they influence the way in which we react to both events and people.

An example of this that I found particularly revealing was provided by a professor who had been walking in the country with one of his pupils, absorbed in serious conversation. Suddenly he noticed that his thoughts were being interrupted by an unexpected flow of memories from his early childhood. He could not account for this distraction. Nothing in what had been said seemed to have any connection with these memories. On looking back, he saw that he had been walking past a farm when the first of these childhood recollections had surged up in his mind. He suggested to his pupil that they

In cases of extreme mass hysteria (which was in the past called "possession"), the conscious mind and ordinary sense perception seem eclipsed. Left, the frenzy of a Balinese sword dance causes the dancers to fall into trances and, sometimes, to turn their weapons against themselves. Right, rock and roll music in its heyday seemed to induce an almost comparable trance-like excitement.

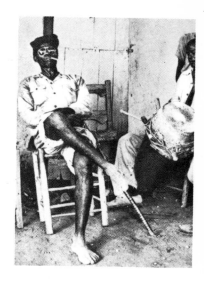

Among primitives, "possession" implies that a god or demon has taken over a human body. Above left, a Haitian woman collapses in a religious ecstasy. Above center and right, Haitians possessed by the god Ghede, who is invariably manifested in this position, legs crossed, cigarette in mouth.

Left, a religious cult in Tennessee, U.S.A., today, whose ceremonies include the handling of poisonous snakes. Hysteria is induced by music, singing, and hand clapping; then the people pass the snakes from hand to hand. (Sometimes participants are fatally bitten.)

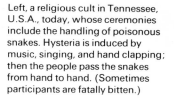

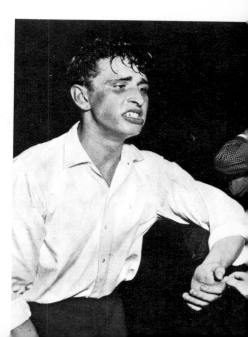

should walk back to the point where the fantasies had begun. Once there, he noticed the smell of geese, and instantly he realized that it was this smell that had touched off the flow of memories.

In his youth he had lived on a farm where geese were kept, and their characteristic smell had left a lasting though forgotten impression. As he passed the farm on his walk, he had noticed the smell subliminally, and this unconscious perception had called back long-forgotten experiences of his childhood. The perception was subliminal, because the attention was engaged elsewhere, and the stimulus was not strong enough to deflect it and to reach consciousness directly. Yet it had brought up the "forgotten" memories.

Such a "cue" or "trigger" effect can explain the onset of neurotic symptoms as well as more benign memories when a sight, smell, or sound recalls a circumstance in the past. A girl, for instance, may be busy in her office, apparently in good health and spirits. A moment later she develops a blinding headache and shows other signs of distress. Without consciously noticing

it, she has heard the foghorn of a distant ship, and this has unconsciously reminded her of an unhappy parting with a lover whom she has been doing her best to forget.

Aside from normal forgetting, Freud has described several cases that involve the "forgetting" of disagreeable memories—memories that one is only too ready to lose. As Nietzsche remarked, where pride is insistent enough, memory prefers to give way. Thus, among the lost memories, we encounter not a few that owe their subliminal state (and their incapacity to be voluntarily reproduced) to their disagreeable and incompatible nature. The psychologist calls these *repressed* contents.

A case in point might be that of a secretary who is jealous of one of her employer's associates. She habitually forgets to invite this person to meetings, though the name is clearly marked on the list she is using. But, if challenged on the point, she simply says she "forgot" or was "interrupted." She never admits—not even to herself—the real reason for her omission.

Many people mistakenly overestimate the role of willpower and think that nothing can

The toy cars forming the Volkswagen trade-mark in this advertisement may have a "trigger" effect on a reader's mind, stirring unconscious memories of childhood. If these memories are pleasant, the pleasure may be associated (unconsciously) with the product and brand name.

happen to their minds that they do not decide and intend. But one must learn to discriminate carefully between intentional and unintentional contents of the mind. The former are derived from the ego personality; the latter, however, arise from a source that is not identical with the ego, but is its "other side." It is this "other side" that would have made the secretary forget the invitations.

There are many reasons why we forget things that we have noticed or experienced; and there are just as many ways in which they may be recalled to mind. An interesting example is that of cryptomnesia, or "concealed recollection." An author may be writing steadily to a preconceived plan, working out an argument or developing the line of a story, when he suddenly runs off at a tangent. Perhaps a fresh idea has occurred to him, or a different image, or a whole new sub-plot. If you ask him what prompted the digression, he will not be able to tell you. He may not even have noticed the change, though he has now produced material that is entirely fresh and apparently unknown to him before. Yet it can sometimes be shown convincingly that what he has written bears a striking similarity to the work of another author —a work that he believes he has never seen.

I myself found a fascinating example of this in Nietzsche's book *Thus Spake Zarathustra*, where the author reproduces almost word for word an incident reported in a ship's log for the year 1686. By sheer chance I had read this seaman's yarn in a book published about 1835 (half a century before Nietzsche wrote); and when I found the similar passage in *Thus Spake Zarathustra*, I was struck by its peculiar style, which was different from Nietzsche's usual language. I was convinced that Nietzsche must also have seen the old book, though he made no reference to it. I wrote to his sister, who was still alive, and she confirmed that she and her brother had in fact read the book together when he was 11 years old. I think, from the context, it is inconceivable that Nietzsche had any idea that he was plagiarizing this story. I believe that fifty years later it had unexpectedly slipped into focus in his conscious mind.

In this type of case there is genuine, if unrealized, recollection. Much the same sort of thing may happen to a musician who has heard a peasant tune or popular song in childhood and finds it cropping up as the theme of a symphonic movement that he is composing in adult life. An idea or an image has moved back from the unconscious into the conscious mind.

What I have so far said about the unconscious is no more than a cursory sketch of the nature and functioning of this complex part of the human psyche. But it should have indicated the kind of subliminal material from which the symbols of our dreams may be spontaneously produced. This subliminal material can consist of all urges, impulses, and intentions: all perceptions and intuitions; all rational or irrational thoughts, conclusions, inductions, deductions, and premises; and all varieties of feeling. Any or all of these can take the form of partial, temporary, or constant unconsciousness.

Such material has mostly become unconscious because—in a manner of speaking— there is no room for it in the conscious mind. Some of one's thoughts lose their emotional energy and become subliminal (that is to say, they no longer receive so much of our conscious attention) because they have come to seem uninteresting or irrelevant, or because there is some reason why we wish to push them out of sight.

It is, in fact, normal and necessary for us to "forget" in this fashion, in order to make room in our conscious minds for new impressions and ideas. If this did not happen, everything we experienced would remain above the threshold of consciousness and our minds would become impossibly cluttered. This phenomenon is so widely recognized today that most people who know anything about psychology take it for granted.

But just as conscious contents can vanish into the unconscious, new contents, which have never yet been conscious, can *arise* from it. One may have an inkling, for instance, that something is on the point of breaking into consciousness—that "something is in the air," or that one "smells a rat." The discovery that the unconscious is no mere depository of the past, but is also full of germs of future psychic situations and ideas, led me to my own new approach to psychology. A great deal of controversial discussion has arisen around this point. But it is a fact that, in addition to memories from a long-distant conscious past, completely new thoughts and creative ideas can also present themselves from the unconscious — thoughts and ideas that have never been conscious before. They grow up from the dark depths of the mind like a lotus and form a most important part of the subliminal psyche.

We find this in everyday life, where dilemmas are sometimes solved by the most surprising new propositions; many artists, philosophers, and even scientists owe some of their best ideas to inspirations that appear suddenly from the unconscious. The ability to reach a rich vein of such material and to translate it effectively into philosophy, literature, music, or scientific discovery is one of the hallmarks of what is commonly called genius.

We can find clear proof of this fact in the history of science itself. For example, the French mathematician Poincaré and the chemist Kekulé owed important scientific discoveries (as they themselves admit) to sudden pictorial "revelations" from the unconscious. The so-called "mystical" experience of the French philosopher Descartes involved a similar sudden revelation in which he saw in a flash the "order of all sciences." The British author Robert Louis Stevenson had spent years looking for a story that would fit his "strong sense of man's double being," when the plot of *Dr. Jekyll and Mr. Hyde* was suddenly revealed to him in a dream.

Later I shall describe in more detail how such material arises from the unconscious, and I shall examine the form in which it is expressed. At the moment I simply want to point out that the capacity of the human psyche to produce such new material is particularly significant when one is dealing with dream symbolism, for I have found again and again in my professional work that the images and ideas that dreams contain cannot possibly be explained solely in terms of memory. They express new thoughts that have never yet reached the threshold of consciousness.

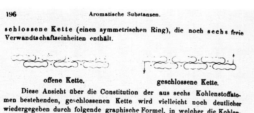

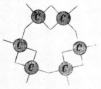

The 19th-century German chemist Kekulé, researching into the molecular structure of benzene, dreamed of a snake with its tail in its mouth. (This is an age-old symbol: left, a representation of it from a third-century B.C. Greek manuscript.) He interpreted the dream to mean that the structure was a closed carbon ring — as on the page, far left, from his *Textbook of Organic Chemistry* (1861).

Right, an ordinary European highway with a familiar sign that means "look out for animals crossing." But the motorists (their shadows appear in the foreground as they leave their car) see an elephant, a rhinoceros, even a dinosaur. This painting of a dream (by the modern Swiss artist Erhard Jacoby) accurately depicts the apparently illogical, incoherent nature of dream imagery.

The function of dreams

I have gone into some detail about the origins of our dream life, because it is the soil from which most symbols originally grow. Unfortunately, dreams are difficult to understand. As I have already pointed out, a dream is quite unlike a story told by the conscious mind. In everyday life one thinks out what one wants to say, selects the most telling way of saying it, and tries to make one's remarks logically coherent. For instance, an educated person will seek to avoid a mixed metaphor because it may give a muddled impression of his point. But dreams have a different texture. Images that seem contradictory and ridiculous crowd in on the dreamer, the normal sense of time is lost, and commonplace things can assume a fascinating or threatening aspect.

It may seem strange that the unconscious mind should order its material so differently from the seemingly disciplined pattern that we can impose on our thoughts in waking life. Yet anyone who stops for a moment to recall a dream will be aware of this contrast, which is in fact one of the main reasons why the ordinary person finds dreams so hard to understand. They do not make sense in terms of his normal waking experience, and therefore he is inclined either to disregard them or to confess that they baffle him.

Perhaps it may be easier to understand this point if we first realize the fact that the ideas with which we deal in our apparently disciplined waking life are by no means as precise as we like to believe. On the contrary, their meaning (and their emotional significance for us) becomes more imprecise the more closely we examine them. The reason for this is that anything we have heard or experienced can become subliminal—that is to say, can pass into the unconscious. And even what we retain in

our conscious mind and can reproduce at will has acquired an unconscious undertone that will color the idea each time it is recalled. Our conscious impressions, in fact, quickly assume an element of unconscious meaning that is psychically significant for us, though we are not consciously aware of the existence of this subliminal meaning or of the way in which it both extends and confuses the conventional meaning.

Of course, such psychic undertones differ from one person to another. Each of us receives any abstract or general notion in the context of the individual mind, and we therefore understand and apply it in our individual ways. When, in conversation, I use any such terms as "state," "money," "health," or "society," I assume that my listeners understand more or less the same thing as I do. But the phrase "more or less" makes my point. Each word means something slightly different to each person, even among those who share the same cultural background. The reason for this variation is that a general notion is received into an individual context and is therefore understood and applied in a slightly individual way. And the difference of meaning is naturally greatest when people have widely different social, political, religious or psychological experiences.

As long as concepts are identical with mere words, the variation is almost imperceptible and plays no practical role. But when an exact definition or a careful explanation is needed, one can occasionally discover the most amazing variations, not only in the purely intellectual understanding of the term, but particularly in its emotional tone and its application. As a rule, these variations are subliminal and therefore never realized.

One may tend to dismiss such differences as redundant or expendable nuances of meaning that have little relevance to everyday needs. But the fact that they exist shows that even the most matter-of-fact contents of consciousness have a penumbra of uncertainty around them. Even the most carefully defined philosophical or mathematical concept, which we are sure does not contain more than we have put into it, is nevertheless more than we assume. It is a

psychic event and as such partly unknowable. The very numbers you use in counting are more than you take them to be. They are at the same time mythological elements (for the Pythagoreans, they were even divine); but you are certainly unaware of this when you use numbers for a practical purpose.

Every concept in our conscious mind, in short, has its own psychic associations. While such associations may vary in intensity (according to the relative importance of the concept to our whole personality, or according to the other ideas and even complexes to which it is associated in our unconscious), they are capable of

Le temps n'a point de rive. 1930-39. Oil on canvas, 39⅜" x 32". *Collection, The Museum of Modern Art New York*

On these pages, further examples of the irrational, fantastic nature of dreams. Above left, owls and bats swarm over a dreaming man in an etching by the 18th-century Spanish artist Goya.

Dragons or similar monsters are common dream images. Left, a dragon pursues a dreamer in a woodcut from *The Dream of Poliphilo*, a fantasy written by a 15th-century Italian monk, Francesco Colonna.

Above, a painting entitled *Time is a River without Banks* by the modern artist Marc Chagall. The unexpected association of these images—fish, violin, clock, lovers—has all the strangeness of a dream.

41

The mythological aspect of ordinary numbers appears in Mayan reliefs (top of page, *c.* A.D. 730), which personify numerical divisions of time as gods. The pyramid of dots, above, represents the *tetraktys* of Greek Pythagorean philosophy (sixth century B.C.). It includes four numbers —1, 2, 3, 4—making a total of 10. Both four and 10 were worshiped as divinities by the Pythagoreans.

changing the "normal" character of that concept. It may even become something quite different as it drifts below the level of consciousness.

These subliminal aspects of everything that happens to us may seem to play very little part in our daily lives. But in dream analysis, where the psychologist is dealing with expressions of the unconscious, they are very relevant, for they are the almost invisible roots of our conscious thoughts. That is why commonplace objects or ideas can assume such powerful psychic significance in a dream that we may awake seriously disturbed, in spite of having dreamed of nothing worse than a locked room or a missed train.

The images produced in dreams are much more picturesque and vivid than the concepts and experiences that are their waking counterparts. One of the reasons for this is that, in a dream, such concepts can express their unconscious meaning. In our conscious thoughts, we restrain ourselves within the limits of rational statements—statements that are much less colorful because we have stripped them of most of their psychic associations.

I recall one dream of my own that I found difficult to interpret. In this dream, a certain man was trying to get behind me and jump on my back. I knew nothing of this man except that I was aware that he had somehow picked up a remark I had made and had twisted it into a grotesque travesty of my meaning. But I could not see the connection between this fact and his attempt in the dream to jump on me. In my professional life, however, it has often happened that someone has misrepresented what I have said—so often that I have scarcely bothered to wonder whether this kind of misrepresentation makes me angry. Now there is a certain value in keeping a conscious control over one's emotional reactions; and this, I soon realized, was the point the dream had made. It had taken an Austrian colloquialism and translated it into a pictorial image. This phrase, common enough in ordinary speech, is *Du kannst mir auf den Buckel steigen* (You can climb on my back), which means "I don't care what you say about me." An American equivalent, which could easily appear in a similar dream, would be "Go jump in the lake."

One could say that this dream picture was symbolic, for it did not state the situation directly but expressed the point indirectly by means of a metaphor that I could not at first understand. When this happens (as it so often does) it is not deliberate "disguise" by a dream; it simply reflects the deficiencies in our understanding of emotionally charged pictorial language. For in our daily experience we need to state things as accurately as possible, and we have learned to discard the trimmings of fantasy both in our language and in our thoughts—thus losing a quality that is still characteristic of the primitive mind. Most of us

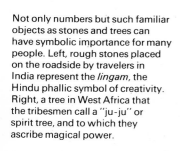

Not only numbers but such familiar objects as stones and trees can have symbolic importance for many people. Left, rough stones placed on the roadside by travelers in India represent the *lingam*, the Hindu phallic symbol of creativity. Right, a tree in West Africa that the tribesmen call a "ju-ju" or spirit tree, and to which they ascribe magical power.

have consigned to the unconscious all the fantastic psychic associations that every object or idea possesses. The primitive, on the other hand, is still aware of these psychic properties; he endows animals, plants, or stones with powers that we find strange and unacceptable.

An African jungle dweller, for instance, sees a nocturnal creature by daylight and knows it to be a medicine man who has temporarily taken its shape. Or he may regard it as the bush soul or ancestral spirit of one of his tribe. A tree may play a vital part in the life of a primitive, apparently possessing for him its own soul and voice, and the man concerned will feel that he shares its fate. There are some Indians in South America who will assure you that they are Red Arara parrots, though they are well aware that they lack feathers, wings, and beaks. For in the primitive's world things do not have the same sharp boundaries they do in our "rational" societies.

What psychologists call psychic identity, or "mystical participation," has been stripped off our world of things. But it is exactly this halo of unconscious associations that gives a colorful and fantastic aspect to the primitive's world. We have lost it to such a degree that we do not recognize it when we meet it again. With us such things are kept below the threshold; when they occasionally reappear, we even insist that something is wrong.

I have more than once been consulted by well-educated and intelligent people who have had peculiar dreams, fantasies, or even visions, which have shocked them deeply. They have assumed that no one who is in a sound state of mind could suffer from such things, and that anyone who actually sees a vision must be pathologically disturbed. A theologian once told me that Ezekiel's visions were nothing more than morbid symptoms, and that, when Moses and other prophets heard "voices" speaking to them, they were suffering from hallucinations. You can imagine the panic he felt when something of this kind "spontaneously" happened to him. We are so accustomed to the apparently rational nature of our world that we can scarcely imagine anything happening that cannot be explained by common sense. The primitive man confronted by a shock of this kind would not doubt his sanity; he would think of fetishes, spirits, or gods.

Yet the emotions that affect us are just the same. In fact, the terrors that stem from our elaborate civilization may be far more threatening than those that primitive people attribute to demons. The attitude of modern civilized man sometimes reminds me of a psychotic patient in my clinic who was himself a doctor. One morning I asked him how he was. He replied that he had had a wonderful night disinfecting the whole of heaven with mercuric chloride, but that in the course of this thoroughgoing sanitary process he had found no trace of God. Here we see a neurosis or something worse. Instead of God or the "fear of God," there is an anxiety neurosis or some kind of phobia. The emotion has remained the same, but its object has changed both its name and nature for the worse.

Left, a witch doctor from Cameroon wearing a lion mask. He isn't pretending to be a lion; he is convinced that he *is* a lion. Like the Nyanga tribesman and his bird mask (p. 25), he shares a "psychic identity" with the animal— an identity that exists in the realm of myth and symbolism. Modern "rational" man has tried to cut himself off from such psychic associations (which nevertheless survive in the unconscious); to him, a spade is a spade and a lion is only what the dictionary (right) says it is.

620   liquefy

ail, or **lion**, lī'*ən*, *n.* a large, fierce, tawny, loud-roaring
ı part animal of the cat family, the male with shaggy
gment mane: (*fig.*) a man of unusual courage: (*astron.*)
inding the constellation or the sign Leo: any object of
ecome interest, esp. a famous or conspicuous person
ge, an much sought after (from the lions once kept in
inked: the Tower, one of the sights of London): **an old**
(*elect.*) Scots coin, with a lion on the obverse, worth 74
coils: shillings Scots (James VI.):—*fem.* **li'oness.**—*ns.*
escrib- **li'oncel**, **li'oncelle**, **li'onel**, (*her.*) a small lion
certain used as a bearing; **li'onet**, a young lion; **li'on-**
ɔ'tion, **heart**, one with great courage.—*adj.* **li'on-**
em of **heart'ed.**—*n.* **li'on-hunter**, a hunter of lions:
issing one who runs after celebrities.—*v.t.* **li'onise**, to
series treat as a lion or object of interest: to go around
ɔrm in the sights of: to show the sights to.—*n.* **li'onism**,
[Prob. lionising: lion-like appearance in leprosy.—*adjs.*
ı (pl.), **li'on-like**, **li'only**.—**lion's provider**, the jackal,
supposed to attend upon the lion, really his hanger-
Shak.) on; **lion's share**, the whole or greater part;

45

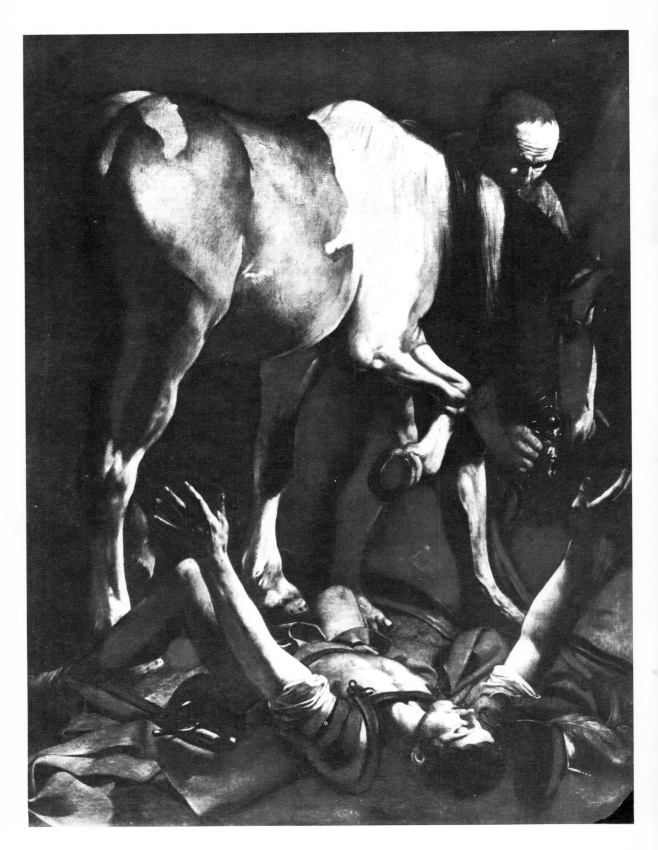

Left, St. Paul struck down by the impact of his vision of Christ (in a painting by the 16th-century Italian artist Caravaggio).

Above, Javanese farmers sacrifice a cock to protect their fields from spirits. Such beliefs and practices are fundamental in primitive life.

Above, in a modern sculpture by Britain's Jacob Epstein, man is seen as a mechanized monster—perhaps an image of today's "evil spirits."

I recall a professor of philosophy who once consulted me about his cancer phobia. He suffered from a compulsive conviction that he had a malignant tumor, although nothing of the kind was ever found in dozens of X-ray pictures. "Oh, I know there is nothing," he would say, "but there *might* be something." What was it that produced this idea? It obviously came from a fear that was not instilled by conscious deliberation. The morbid thought suddenly overcame him, and it had a power of its own that he could not control.

It was far more difficult for this educated man to make an admission of this kind than it would have been for a primitive to say that he was plagued by a ghost. The malign influence of evil spirits is at least an admissible hypothesis in a primitive culture, but it is a shattering experience for a civilized person to admit that his troubles are nothing more than a foolish prank of the imagination. The primitive phenomenon of *obsession* has not vanished; it is the same as ever. It is only interpreted in a different and more obnoxious way.

I have made several comparisons of this kind between modern and primitive man. Such comparisons, as I shall show later, are essential to an understanding of the symbol-making propensities of man, and of the part that dreams play in expressing them. For one finds that many dreams present images and associations that are analogous to primitive ideas, myths, and rites. These dream images were called "archaic remnants" by Freud; the phrase suggests that they are psychic elements surviving in the human mind from ages long ago. This point of view is characteristic of those who regard the unconscious as a mere appendix of consciousness (or, more picturesquely, as a trash can that collects all the refuse of the conscious mind).

Further investigation suggested to me that this attitude is untenable and should be discarded. I found that associations and images of this kind are an integral part of the unconscious, and can be observed everywhere—whether the dreamer is educated or illiterate, intelligent or stupid. They are not in any sense lifeless or meaningless "remnants." They still function, and they are especially valuable (as Dr. Henderson shows in a later chapter of this book) just because of their "historical" nature. They form a bridge between the ways in which we consciously express our thoughts and a more primitive, more colorful and pictorial form of

expression. It is this form, as well, that appeals directly to feeling and emotion. These "historical" associations are the link between the rational world of consciousness and the world of instinct.

I have already discussed the interesting contrast between the "controlled" thoughts we have in waking life and the wealth of imagery produced in dreams. Now you can see another reason for this difference: Because, in our civilized life, we have stripped so many ideas of their emotional energy, we do not really respond to them any more. We use such ideas in our speech, and we show a conventional reaction when others use them, but they do not make a very deep impression on us. Something more is needed to bring certain things home to us effectively enough to make us change our attitude and behavior. This is what "dream language" does; its symbolism has so much psychic energy that we are forced to pay attention to it.

There was, for instance, a lady who was well known for her stupid prejudices and her stubborn resistance to reasoned argument. One could have argued with her all night to no effect; she would have taken not the slightest notice. Her dreams, however, took a different line of approach. One night, she dreamed she was attending an important social occasion. She was greeted by the hostess with the words: "How nice that you could come. All your friends are here, and they are waiting for you." The hostess then led her to the door and opened it, and the dreamer stepped through—into a cowshed!

This dream language was simple enough to be understood even by a blockhead. The woman would not at first admit the point of a dream that struck so directly at her self-importance; but its message nevertheless went home, and after a time she had to accept it because she could not help seeing the self-inflicted joke.

Such messages from the unconscious are of greater importance than most people realize. In our conscious life, we are exposed to all kinds of influences. Other people stimulate or depress us, events at the office or in our social life distract us. Such things seduce us into following ways that are unsuitable to our individuality. Whether or not we are aware of the effect they have on our consciousness, it is disturbed by and exposed to them almost without defense. This is especially the case with a person whose extraverted attitude of mind lays all the emphasis upon external objects, or who harbors feelings of inferiority and doubt concerning his own innermost personality.

The more that consciousness is influenced by prejudices, errors, fantasies, and infantile wishes, the more the already existing gap will widen into a neurotic dissociation and lead to a more or less artificial life, far removed from healthy instincts, nature, and truth.

Left, two further visualizations of spirits: Top, hellish demons descend on St. Anthony (a painting by the 16th-century German artist Grünewald). Below, in the center panel of a 19th-century Japanese triptych, the ghost of a murdered man strikes down his killer.

Ideological conflict breeds many of modern man's "demons." Right, a cartoon by America's Gahan Wilson depicts the shadow of the former Russian leader Khrushchev as a monstrous death-machine. Far right, a cartoon from the Russian magazine Krokodil shows "colonialism" as a demonic wolf being driven into the sea by the flags of various independent African nations.

The general function of dreams is to try to restore our psychological balance by producing dream material that re-establishes, in a subtle way, the total psychic equilibrium. This is what I call the complementary (or compensatory) role of dreams in our psychic make-up. It explains why people who have unrealistic ideas or too high an opinion of themselves, or who make grandiose plans out of proportion to their real capacities, have dreams of flying or falling. The dream compensates for the deficiencies of their personalities, and at the same time it warns them of the dangers in their present course. If the warnings of the dream are disregarded, real accidents may take their place. The victim may fall downstairs or may have a motor accident.

I remember the case of a man who was inextricably involved in a number of shady affairs. He developed an almost morbid passion for dangerous mountain climbing, as a sort of compensation. He was seeking "to get above himself." In a dream one night, he saw himself stepping off the summit of a high mountain into empty space. When he told me his dream, I instantly saw his danger and tried to emphasize the warning and persuade him to restrain himself. I even told him that the dream fore-

shadowed his death in a mountain accident. It was in vain. Six months later he "stepped off into space." A mountain guide watched him and a friend letting themselves down on a rope in a difficult place. The friend had found a temporary foothold on a ledge, and the dreamer was following him down. Suddenly he let go of the rope, according to the guide, "as if he were jumping into the air." He fell upon his friend, and both went down and were killed.

Another typical case was that of a lady who was living above herself. She was high and mighty in her daily life, but she had shocking dreams, reminding her of all sorts of unsavory things. When I discovered them, she indignantly refused to acknowledge them. The dreams then became menacing, and full of references to the walks she used to take by herself in the woods, where she indulged in soulful fantasies. I saw her danger, but she would not listen to my many warnings. Soon afterwards, she was savagely attacked in the woods by a sexual pervert; but for the intervention of some people who heard her screams, she would have been killed.

There was no magic in this. What her dreams had told me was that this woman had a secret longing for such an adventure—just as

the mountain climber unconsciously sought the
satisfaction of finding a definite way out of his
difficulties. Obviously, neither of them expected
the stiff price involved: She had several bones
broken, and he paid with his life.

Thus dreams may sometimes announce certain situations long before they actually happen.
This is not necessarily a miracle or a form of
precognition. Many crises in our lives have a
long unconscious history. We move toward
them step by step, unaware of the dangers that
are accumulating. But what we consciously fail
to see is frequently perceived by our unconscious, which can pass the information on
through dreams.

Dreams may often warn us in this way; but
just as often, it seems, they do not. Therefore,
any assumption of a benevolent hand restrain-
ing us in time is dubious. Or, to state it more
positively, it seems that a benevolent agency is
sometimes at work and sometimes not. The
mysterious hand may even point the way to
perdition; dreams sometimes prove to be traps,
or appear to be so. They sometimes behave like
the Delphic oracle that told King Croesus that
if he crossed the Halys River he would destroy
a large kingdom. It was only after he had been
completely defeated in battle after the crossing

51

that he discovered that the kingdom meant by the oracle was his own.

One cannot afford to be naïve in dealing with dreams. They originate in a spirit that is not quite human, but is rather a breath of nature—a spirit of the beautiful and generous as well as of the cruel goddess. If we want to characterize this spirit, we shall certainly get closer to it in the sphere of ancient mythologies, or the fables of the primeval forest, than in the consciousness of modern man. I am not denying that great gains have resulted from the evolution of civilized society. But these gains have been made at the price of enormous losses, whose extent we have scarcely begun to estimate. Part of the purpose of my comparisons between the primitive and the civilized states of man has been to show the balance of these losses and gains.

Primitive man was much more governed by his instincts than are his "rational" modern descendants, who have learned to "control" themselves. In this civilizing process, we have increasingly divided our consciousness from the deeper instinctive strata of the human psyche, and even ultimately from the somatic basis of the psychic phenomenon. Fortunately, we have not lost these basic instinctive strata; they remain part of the unconscious, even though they may express themselves only in the form of dream images. These instinctive phenomena—one may not, incidentally, always recognize them for what they are, for their character is symbolic—play a vital part in what I have called the compensating function of dreams.

For the sake of mental stability and even physiological health, the unconscious and the conscious must be integrally connected and thus move on parallel lines. If they are split apart or "dissociated," psychological disturbance follows. In this respect, dream symbols are the essential message carriers from the instinctive to the rational parts of the human mind, and their interpretation enriches the poverty of consciousness so that it learns to understand again the forgotten language of the instincts.

Of course, people are bound to query this function, since its symbols so often pass un-

noticed or uncomprehended. In normal life, the understanding of dreams is often considered superfluous. I can illustrate this by my experience with a primitive tribe in East Africa. To my amazement, these tribesmen denied that they had any dreams. But through patient, indirect talks with them I soon found that they had dreams just like everyone else, but that they were convinced their dreams had no meaning. "Dreams of ordinary men mean nothing," they told me. They thought that the only dreams that mattered were those of chiefs and medicine men; these, which concerned the welfare of the tribe, were highly appreciated. The only drawback was that the chief and the medicine man both claimed that they had ceased having meaningful dreams. They dated this change from the time that the British came to their country. The district commissioner—the British official in charge of them—had taken over the function of the "great dreams" that had hitherto guided the tribe's behavior.

When these tribesmen conceded that they did have dreams, but thought them meaningless, they were like the modern man who thinks that a dream has no significance for him simply because he does not understand it. But even a civilized man can sometimes observe that a dream (which he may not even remember) can alter his mood for better or worse. The dream

has been "comprehended," but only in a subliminal way. And that is what usually happens. It is only on the rare occasions when a dream is particularly impressive or repeats itself at regular intervals that most people consider an interpretation desirable.

Here I ought to add a word of warning against unintelligent or incompetent dream analysis. There are some people whose mental condition is so unbalanced that the interpretation of their dreams can be extremely risky; in such a case, a very one-sided consciousness is cut off from a correspondingly irrational or "crazy" unconscious, and the two should not be brought together without taking special precautions.

And, speaking more generally, it is plain foolishness to believe in ready-made systematic guides to dream interpretation, as if one could simply buy a reference book and look up a particular symbol. No dream symbol can be separated from the individual who dreams it, and there is no definite or straightforward interpretation of any dream. Each individual varies so much in the way that his unconscious complements or compensates his conscious mind that it is impossible to be sure how far dreams and their symbols can be classified at all.

It is true that there are dreams and single symbols (I should prefer to call them "motifs") that are typical and often occur. Among such motifs are falling, flying, being persecuted by dangerous animals or hostile men, being insufficiently or absurdly clothed in public places, being in a hurry or lost in a milling crowd, fighting with useless weapons or being wholly defenseless, running hard yet getting nowhere. A typical infantile motif is the dream of growing infinitely small or infinitely big, or being transformed from one to the other—as you find it, for instance, in Lewis Carroll's *Alice in Wonderland.* But I must stress again that these are motifs that must be considered in the context of the dream itself, not as self-explanatory ciphers.

The recurring dream is a noteworthy phenomenon. There are cases in which people have dreamed the same dream from childhood into the later years of adult life. A dream of this kind is usually an attempt to compensate for a particular defect in the dreamer's attitude to life; or it may date from a traumatic moment that has left behind some specific prejudice. It may also sometimes anticipate a future event of importance.

I myself dreamed of a motif over several years, in which I would "discover" a part of my house that I did not know existed. Sometimes it was the quarters where my long-dead parents lived, in which my father, to my surprise, had a laboratory where he studied the comparative

Left, a photograph of Jung (fourth from the right) in 1926 with the tribesmen of Mt. Elgon, Kenya. Jung's firsthand study of primitive societies led to many of his most valuable psychological insights.

Right, two dream books—one from 20th-century Britain and the other from ancient Egypt (the latter is among the oldest written documents extant, c. 2000 B.C.). Such ready-made, rule-of-thumb interpretation of dreams is worthless; dreams are highly individualized, and their symbolism cannot be pigeonholed.

anatomy of fish and my mother ran a hotel for ghostly visitors. Usually this unfamiliar guest wing was an ancient historical building, long forgotten, yet my inherited property. It contained interesting antique furniture, and toward the end of this series of dreams I discovered an old library whose books were unknown to me. Finally, in the last dream, I opened one of the books and found in it a profusion of the most marvelous symbolic pictures. When I awoke, my heart was palpitating with excitement.

Some time before I had this particular last dream of the series, I had placed an order with an antiquarian bookseller for one of the classic compilations of medieval alchemists. I had found a quotation in literature that I thought might have some connection with early Byzantine alchemy, and I wished to check it. Several weeks after I had had the dream of the unknown book, a parcel arrived from the bookseller. Inside was a parchment volume dating from the 16th century. It was illustrated by fascinating symbolic pictures that instantly reminded me of those I had seen in my dream. As the rediscovery of the principles of alchemy came to be an important part of my work as a pioneer of psychology, the motif of my recurring dream can easily be understood. The house, of course, was a symbol of my personality and its conscious field of interests; and the unknown annex represented the anticipation of a new field of interest and research of which my conscious mind was at that time unaware. From that moment, 30 years ago, I never had the dream again.

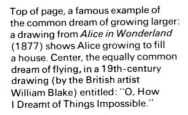

Top of page, a famous example of the common dream of growing larger: a drawing from *Alice in Wonderland* (1877) shows Alice growing to fill a house. Center, the equally common dream of flying, in a 19th-century drawing (by the British artist William Blake) entitled: "O, How I Dreamt of Things Impossible."

The analysis of dreams

I began this essay by noting the difference between a sign and a symbol. The sign is always less than the concept it represents, while a symbol always stands for something more than its obvious and immediate meaning. Symbols, moreover, are natural and spontaneous products. No genius has ever sat down with a pen or a brush in his hand and said: "Now I am going to invent a symbol." No one can take a more or less rational thought, reached as a logical conclusion or by deliberate intent, and then give it "symbolic" form. No matter what fantastic trappings one may put upon an idea of this kind, it will still remain a sign, linked to the conscious thought behind it, not a symbol that hints at something not yet known. In dreams, symbols occur spontaneously, for dreams happen and are not invented; they are, therefore, the main source of all our knowledge about symbolism.

But symbols, I must point out, do not occur solely in dreams. They appear in all kinds of psychic manifestations. There are symbolic thoughts and feelings, symbolic acts and situations. It often seems that even inanimate objects co-operate with the unconscious in the arrangement of symbolic patterns. There are numerous well-authenticated stories of clocks stopping at the moment of their owner's death; one was the pendulum clock in the palace of Frederick the Great at Sans Souci, which stopped when

the king died. Other common examples are those of a mirror that breaks, or a picture that falls, when a death occurs; or minor but unexplained breakages in a house where someone is passing through an emotional crisis. Even if skeptics refuse to credit such reports, stories of this kind are always cropping up, and this alone should serve as ample proof of their psychological importance.

There are many symbols, however (among them the most important), that are not individual but *collective* in their nature and origin. These are chiefly religious images. The believer assumes that they are of divine origin—that they have been revealed to man. The skeptic says flatly that they have been invented. Both are wrong. It is true, as the skeptic notes, that religious symbols and concepts have for centuries been the object of careful and quite conscious elaboration. It is equally true, as the believer implies, that their origin is so far buried in the mystery of the past that they seem to have no human source. But they are in fact "collective representations," emanating from primeval dreams and creative fantasies. As such, these images are involuntary spontaneous manifestations and by no means intentional inventions.

This fact, as I shall later explain, has a direct and important bearing upon the interpretation of dreams. It is obvious that if you assume the

Inanimate objects sometimes seem to "act" symbolically: left, the clock of Frederick the Great, which stopped when its owner died in 1786.

Symbols are produced spontaneously from the unconscious (though they may later be consciously elaborated). Right, the *ankh*, ancient Egypt's symbol of life, the universe, and man. By contrast, the airways insignia (far right) are consciously contrived signs, not symbols.

dream to be symbolic, you will interpret it differently from a person who believes that the essential energizing thought or emotion is known already and is merely "disguised" by the dream. In the latter case, dream interpretation makes little sense, for you find only what you already know.

It is for this reason that I have always said to my pupils: "Learn as much as you can about symbolism; then forget it all when you are analyzing a dream." This advice is of such practical importance that I have made it a rule to remind myself that I can never understand somebody else's dream well enough to interpret it correctly. I have done this in order to check the flow of my own associations and reactions, which might otherwise prevail over my patient's uncertainties and hesitations. As it is of the greatest therapeutic importance for an analyst to get the particular message of a dream (that is, the contribution that the unconscious is making to the conscious mind) as accurately as possible, it is essential for him to explore the content of a dream with the utmost thoroughness.

I had a dream when I was working with Freud that illustrates this point. I dreamed that I was in "my home," apparently on the first floor, in a cosy, pleasant sitting room furnished in the manner of the 18th century. I was astonished that I had never seen this room before, and began to wonder what the ground floor was like. I went downstairs and found the place was rather dark, with paneled walls and heavy

furniture dating from the 16th century or even earlier. My surprise and curiosity increased. I wanted to see more of the whole structure of this house. So I went down to the cellar, where I found a door opening onto a flight of stone steps that led to a large vaulted room. The floor consisted of large slabs of stone and the walls seemed very ancient. I examined the mortar and found it was mixed with splinters of brick. Obviously the walls were of Roman origin. I became increasingly excited. In one corner, I saw an iron ring on a stone slab. I pulled up the slab and saw yet another narrow flight of steps leading to a kind of cave, which seemed to be a prehistoric tomb, containing two skulls, some bones, and broken shards of pottery. Then I woke up.

If Freud, when he analyzed this dream, had followed my method of exploring its specific associations and context, he would have heard a far-reaching story. But I am afraid he would have dismissed it as a mere effort to escape from a problem that was really his own. The dream is in fact a short summary of my life, more specifically of the development of my mind. I grew up in a house 200 years old, our furniture consisted mostly of pieces about 300 years old, and mentally my hitherto greatest spiritual adventure had been to study the philosophies of Kant and Schopenhauer. The great news of the day was the work of Charles Darwin. Shortly before this, I had been living with the still medieval concepts of my parents, for

Right, Jung's mother and father. Jung's interest in ancient religion and mythology drew him away from the religious world of his parents (his father was a pastor) — as shown by the dream, discussed on this page, that he had while working with Freud. Far right, Jung at Burghölzli Hospital, Zürich, where he worked in 1900 as a psychiatrist.

whom the world and men were still presided over by divine omnipotence and providence. This world had become antiquated and obsolete. My Christian faith had become relative through its encounter with Eastern religions and Greek philosophy. It is for this reason that the ground floor was so still, dark, and obviously uninhabited.

My then historical interests had developed from an original preoccupation with comparative anatomy and paleontology while I was working as an assistant at the Anatomical Institute. I was fascinated by the bones of fossil man, particularly by the much discussed *Neanderthalensis* and the still more controversial skull of Dubois' *Pithecanthropus*. As a matter of fact these were my real associations to the dream; but I did not dare to mention the subject of skulls, skeletons, or corpses to Freud, because I had learned that this theme was not popular with him. He cherished the peculiar idea that I anticipated his early death. And he drew this conclusion from the fact that I had shown much interest in the mummified corpses in the so-called Bleikeller in Bremen, which we visited together in 1909 on our way to take the boat to America.

Thus I felt reluctant to come out with my own thoughts, since through recent experience I was deeply impressed by the almost unbridgeable gap between Freud's mental outlook and background and my own. I was afraid of losing his friendship if I should open up to him about

my own inner world, which, I surmised, would look very queer to him. Feeling quite uncertain about my own psychology, I almost automatically told him a lie about my "free associations" in order to escape the impossible task of enlightening him about my very personal and utterly different constitution.

I must apologize for this rather lengthy narration of the jam I got into through telling Freud my dream. But it is a good example of the difficulties in which one gets involved in the course of a real dream analysis. So much depends upon the personal differences between the analyst and the analyzed.

I soon realized that Freud was looking for some incompatible wish of mine. And so I suggested tentatively that the skulls I had dreamed of might refer to certain members of my family whose death, for some reason, I might desire. This proposal met with his approval, but I was not satisfied with such a "phoney" solution.

While I was trying to find a suitable answer to Freud's questions, I was suddenly confused by an intuition about the role that the subjective factor plays in psychological understanding. My intuition was so overwhelming that I thought only of how to get out of this impossible snarl, and I took the easy way out by a lie. This was neither elegant nor morally defensible, but otherwise I should have risked a fatal row with Freud—and I did not feel up to that for many reasons.

My intuition consisted of the sudden and most unexpected insight into the fact that my dream meant *myself, my* life and *my* world, my whole reality against a theoretical structure erected by another, strange mind for reasons and purposes of its own. It was not Freud's dream, it was mine; and I understood suddenly in a flash what my dream meant.

This conflict illustrates a vital point about dream analysis. It is not so much a technique that can be learned and applied according to the rules as it is a dialectical exchange between two personalities. If it is handled as a mechanical technique, the individual psychic personality of the dreamer gets lost and the therapeutic problem is reduced to the simple ques-

tion: Which of the two people concerned—the analyst or the dreamer—will dominate the other? I gave up hypnotic treatment for this very reason, because I did not want to impose my will on others. I wanted the healing processes to grow out of the patient's own personality, not from suggestions by me that would have only a passing effect. My aim was to protect and preserve my patient's dignity and freedom, so that he could live his life according to his own wishes. In this exchange with Freud, it dawned on me for the first time that before we construct general theories about man and his psyche we should learn a lot more about the real human being we have to deal with.

The individual is the only reality. The further we move away from the individual toward abstract ideas about *Homo sapiens*, the more likely we are to fall into error. In these times of social upheaval and rapid change, it is desirable to know much more than we do about the individual human being, for so much depends upon his mental and moral qualities. But if we are to see things in their right perspective, we need to understand the past of man as well as his present. That is why an understanding of myths and symbols is of essential importance.

The problem of types

In all other branches of science, it is legitimate to apply a hypothesis to an impersonal subject. Psychology, however, inescapably confronts you with the living relations between two individuals, neither of whom can be divested of his subjective personality, nor, indeed, depersonalized in any other way. The analyst and his patient may set out by agreeing to deal with a chosen problem in an impersonal and objective manner; but once they are engaged, their whole personalities are involved in their discussion. At this point, further progress is possible only if mutual agreement can be reached.

Can we make any sort of objective judgment about the final result? Only if we make a comparison between our conclusions and the standards that are generally valid in the social milieu to which the individuals belong. Even then, we must take into account the mental equilibrium (or "sanity") of the individual concerned. For the result cannot be a completely collective leveling out of the individual to

An assertive extravert overpowers a withdrawn introvert in a cartoon by America's Jules Feiffer. These Jungian terms for human "types" are not dogmatic: For instance, Gandhi, right, was both an ascetic (introvert) and a political leader (extravert). An individual—any face in the crowd (far right)—can only *more or less* be categorized.

adjust him to the "norms" of his society. This would amount to a most unnatural condition. A sane and normal society is one in which people habitually disagree, because general agreement is relatively rare outside the sphere of instinctive human qualities.

Disagreement functions as a vehicle of mental life in society, but it is not a goal; agreement is equally important. Because psychology basically depends upon balanced opposites, no judgment can be considered to be final in which its reversibility has not been taken into account. The reason for this peculiarity lies in the fact that there is no standpoint above or outside psychology that would enable us to form an ultimate judgment of what the psyche is.

In spite of the fact that dreams demand individual treatment, some generalities are necessary in order to classify and clarify the material that the psychologist collects by studying many individuals. It would obviously be impossible to formulate any psychological theory, or to teach it, by describing large numbers of separate cases without any effort to see what they have in common and how they differ. Any general characteristic can be chosen as a basis. One can, for instance, make a relatively simple distinction between individuals who have "extraverted" personalities and others who are "introverted." This is only one of many possible generalizations, but it enables one to see immediately the difficulties that can arise if the analyst should happen to be one type and his patient the other.

Since any deeper analysis of dreams leads to the confrontation of two individuals, it will obviously make a great difference whether their types of attitude are the same or not. If both belong to the same type, they may sail along happily for a long time. But if one is an extravert and the other an introvert, their different and contradictory standpoints may clash right away, particularly when they are unaware of

their own type of personality, or when they are convinced that their own is the only right type. The extravert, for instance, will choose the majority view; the introvert will reject it simply because it is fashionable. Such a misunderstanding is easy enough because the value of the one is the non-value of the other. Freud himself, for instance, interpreted the introverted type as an individual morbidly concerned with himself. But introspection and self-knowledge can just as well be of the greatest value and importance.

It is vitally necessary to take account of such differences of personality in dream interpretation. It cannot be assumed that the analyst is a superman who is above such differences, just because he is a doctor who has acquired a psychological theory and a corresponding technique. He can only imagine himself to be superior in so far as he assumes that his theory and technique are absolute truths, capable of embracing the whole of the human psyche. Since such an assumption is more than doubtful, he cannot really be sure of it. Consequently, he will be assailed by secret doubts if he confronts the human wholeness of his patient with a theory or technique (which is merely a hypothesis or an attempt) instead of with his own living wholeness.

The analyst's whole personality is the only adequate equivalent of his patient's personality. Psychological experience and knowledge do not amount to more than mere advantages on the side of the analyst. They do not keep him outside the fray, in which he is bound to be tested just as much as his patient. Thus it matters a good deal whether their personalities are harmonious, in conflict, or complementary.

Extraversion and introversion are just two among many peculiarities of human behavior. But they are often rather obvious and easily recognizable. If one studies extraverted individuals, for instance, one soon discovers that they differ in many ways from one another, and that being extraverted is therefore a superficial and too general criterion to be really characteristic. That is why, long ago, I tried to find some further basic peculiarities—peculiarities that might serve the purpose of giving some order to the apparently limitless variations in human individuality.

I had always been impressed by the fact that there are a surprising number of individuals who never use their minds if they can avoid it, and an equal number who do use their minds, but in an amazingly stupid way. I was also surprised to find many intelligent and wideawake people who lived (as far as one could make out) as if they had never learned to use their sense organs: They did not see the things before their eyes, hear the words sounding in their ears, or notice the things they touched or tasted. Some lived without being aware of the state of their own bodies.

The "compass" of the psyche—another Jungian way of looking at people in general. Each point on the compass has its opposite: for a "thinking" type, the "feeling" side would be least developed. ("Feeling" here means the faculty of weighing and evaluating experience—in the way that one might say "I *feel* that is a good thing to do," without needing to analyze or rationalize the "why" of the action.) Of course, there is overlapping in each individual: In a "sensation" person the thinking or the feeling side could be almost as strong (and "intuition," the opposite, would be weakest).

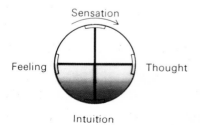

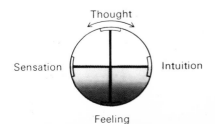

There were others who seemed to live in a most curious condition of consciousness, as if the state they had arrived at today were final, with no possibility of change, or as if the world and the psyche were static and would remain so forever. They seemed devoid of all imagination, and they entirely and exclusively depended upon their sense-perception. Chances and possibilities did not exist in their world, and in "today" there was no real "tomorrow." The future was just the repetition of the past.

I am trying here to give the reader a glimpse of my own first impressions when I began to observe the many people I met. It soon became clear to me, however, that the people who used their minds were those who *thought*—that is, who applied their intellectual faculty in trying to adapt themselves to people and circumstances. And the equally intelligent people who did not think were those who sought and found their way by *feeling*.

"Feeling" is a word that needs some explanation. For instance, one speaks of "feeling" when it is a matter of "sentiment" (corresponding to the French term *sentiment*). But one also applies the same word to define an opinion; for example, a communication from the White House may begin: "The President feels . . . ." Furthermore, the word may be used to express an intuition: "I had a feeling as if . . . ."

When I use the word "feeling" in contrast to "thinking," I refer to a judgment of value— for instance, agreeable or disagreeable, good or bad, and so on. Feeling according to this definition is not an emotion (which, as the word conveys, is involuntary). *Feeling* as I mean it is (like thinking) a *rational* (i.e. ordering) function, whereas intuition is an *irrational* (i.e. perceiving) function. In so far as intuition is a "hunch," it is not the product of a voluntary act; it is rather an involuntary event, which depends upon different external or internal circumstances instead of an act of judgment. Intuition is more like a sense-perception, which is also an irrational event in so far as it depends essentially upon objective stimuli, which owe their existence to physical and not to mental causes.

These four functional types correspond to the obvious means by which consciousness obtains its orientation to experience. *Sensation* (i.e. sense-perception) tells you that something exists; *thinking* tells you what it is; *feeling* tells you whether it is agreeable or not; and *intuition* tells you whence it comes and where it is going.

The reader should understand that these four criteria of types of human behavior are just four viewpoints among many others, like will power, temperament, imagination, memory, and so on. There is nothing dogmatic about them, but their basic nature recommends them as suitable criteria for a classification. I find them particularly helpful when I am called upon to explain parents to children and husbands to wives, and vice versa. They are also useful in understanding one's own prejudices.

Thus, if you want to understand another person's dream, you have to sacrifice your own predilections and suppress your prejudices. This is not easy or comfortable, because it means a moral effort that is not to everyone's taste. But if the analyst does not make the effort to criticize his own standpoint and to admit its relativity, he will get neither the right information about, nor sufficient insight into, his patient's mind. The analyst expects at least a certain willingness on the patient's part to listen to his opinion and to take it seriously, and the patient must be granted the same right. Although such a relationship is indispensable for any understanding and is therefore of self-evident necessity, one must remind oneself again and again that it is more important in therapy for the patient to understand than for the analyst's theoretical expectations to be satisfied. The patient's resistance to the analyst's interpretation is not necessarily wrong; it is rather a sure sign that something does not "click." Either the patient has not yet reached the point where he understands, or the interpretation does not fit.

In our efforts to interpret the dream symbols of another person, we are almost invariably hampered by our tendency to fill in the unavoidable gaps in our understanding by projection—that is, by the assumption that what the analyst perceives or thinks is equally perceived or thought by the dreamer. To overcome this source of error, I have always insisted on the importance of sticking to the context of the particular dream and excluding all theoretical assumptions about dreams in general—except for the hypothesis that dreams in some way make sense.

It will be clear from all I have said that we cannot lay down general rules for interpreting dreams. When I suggested earlier that the over-all function of dreams seems to be to compensate for deficiencies or distortions in the conscious mind, I meant that this assumption opened up the most promising approach to the nature of *particular* dreams. In some cases you can see this function plainly demonstrated.

One of my patients had a very high opinion of himself and was unaware that almost everyone who knew him was irritated by his air of moral superiority. He came to me with a dream in which he had seen a drunken tramp rolling in a ditch—a sight that evoked from him only the patronizing comment: "It's terrible to see how low a man can fall." It was evident that the unpleasant nature of the dream was at least in part an attempt to offset his inflated opinion of his own merits. But there was something more to it than this. It turned out that he had a brother who was a degenerate alcoholic. What the dream also revealed was that his superior attitude was compensating the brother, as both an outer and an inner figure.

In another case I recall, a woman who was proud of her intelligent understanding of psychology had recurring dreams about another woman. When in ordinary life she met this woman, she did not like her, thinking her a vain and dishonest intriguer. But in the dreams the woman appeared almost as a sister, friendly and likeable. My patient could not understand why she should dream so favorably about a person she disliked. But these dreams were trying to convey the idea that she herself was "shadowed" by an unconscious character that resembled the other woman. It was hard for my patient, who had very clear ideas about her own personality, to realize that the dream was telling her about her own power complex and

her hidden motivations—unconscious influences that had more than once led to disagreeable rows with her friends. She had always blamed others for these, not herself.

It is not merely the "shadow" side of our personalities that we overlook, disregard, and repress. We may also do the same to our positive qualities. An example that comes to mind is that of an apparently modest and self-effacing man, with charming manners. He always seemed content with a back seat, but discreetly insisted on being present. When asked to speak he would offer a well-informed opinion, though he never intruded it. But he sometimes hinted that a given matter could be dealt with in a far superior way at a certain higher level (though he never explained how).

In his dreams, however, he constantly had encounters with great historical figures, such as Napoleon and Alexander the Great. These dreams were clearly compensating for an inferiority complex. But they had another implication. What sort of man must I be, the dream was asking, to have such illustrious callers? In this respect the dreams pointed to a secret meg-

alomania, which offset the dreamer's feeling of inferiority. This unconscious idea of grandeur insulated him from the reality of his environment and enabled him to remain aloof from obligations that would be imperative for other people. He felt no need to prove—either to himself or to others—that his superior judgment was based on superior merit.

He was, in fact, unconsciously playing an insane game, and the dreams were seeking to bring it to the level of consciousness in a curiously ambiguous way. Hobnobbing with Napoleon and being on speaking terms with Alexander the Great are exactly the kind of fantasies produced by an inferiority complex. But why, one asks, could not the dream be open and direct about it and say what it had to say without ambiguity?

I have frequently been asked this question, and I have asked it myself. I am often surprised at the tantalizing way dreams seem to evade definite information or omit the decisive point. Freud assumed the existence of a special function of the psyche, which he called the "censor." This, he supposed, twisted the dream images and made them unrecognizable or misleading in order to deceive the dreaming consciousness about the real subject of the dream. By concealing the critical thought from the dreamer, the "censor" protected his sleep against the shock of a disagreeable reminiscence. But I am skeptical about the theory that the dream is a guardian of sleep; dreams just as often disturb sleep.

It rather looks as if the approach to consciousness has a "blotting-out" effect upon the subliminal contents of the psyche. The subliminal state retains ideas and images at a much lower level of tension than they possess in consciousness. In the subliminal condition they lose clarity of definition; the relations between them are less consequential and more vaguely analogous, less rational and therefore more "incomprehensible." This can also be observed in all dreamlike conditions, whether due to fatigue, fever, or toxins. But if something happens to endow any of these images with greater tension, they become less subliminal and, as they come close to the threshold of consciousness, more sharply defined.

Left, a down-and-out alcoholic in a New York slum (from the 1955 film *On the Bowery*). Such a figure might appear in the dreams of a man who felt himself to be superior to others. In this way his unconscious would be compensating for his conscious mind's onesidedness.

Right, *The Nightmare*, painted by the 18th-century Swiss-born artist Henry Fuseli. Almost everyone has been awakened, upset, or disturbed by his dreams; our sleep does not appear to be protected from the contents of the unconscious.

It is from this fact that one may understand why dreams often express themselves as analogies, why one dream image slides into another, and why neither the logic nor the time scale of our waking life seems to apply. The form that dreams take is natural to the unconscious because the material from which they are produced is retained in the subliminal state in precisely this fashion. Dreams do not guard sleep from what Freud called the "incompatible wish." What he called "disguise" is actually the shape all impulses naturally take in the unconscious. Thus, a dream cannot produce a definite thought. If it begins to do so, it ceases to be a dream because it crosses the threshold of consciousness. That is why dreams seem to skip the very points that are most important to the conscious mind, and seem rather to manifest the "fringe of consciousness," like the faint gleam of stars during a total eclipse of the sun.

We should understand that dream symbols are for the most part manifestations of a psyche that is beyond the control of the conscious mind. Meaning and purposefulness are not the prerogatives of the mind; they operate in the whole of living nature. There is no difference in principle between organic and psychic growth. As a plant produces its flower, so the psyche creates its symbols. Every dream is evidence of this process.

So, by means of dreams (plus all sorts of intuitions, impulses, and other spontaneous events), instinctive forces influence the activity of consciousness. Whether that influence is for better or for worse depends upon the actual contents of the unconscious. If it contains too many things that normally ought to be conscious, then its function becomes twisted and prejudiced; motives appear that are not based upon true instincts, but that owe their existence and psychic importance to the fact that they have been consigned to the unconscious by repression or neglect. They overlay, as it were, the normal unconscious psyche and distort its natural tendency to express basic symbols and motifs. Therefore it is reasonable for a psychoanalyst, concerned with the causes of a mental disturbance, to begin by eliciting from his patient a more or less voluntary confession and realization of everything that the patient dislikes or fears.

This is like the much older confession of the Church, which in many ways anticipated modern psychological techniques. At least this is the general rule. In practice, however, it may work the other way round; overpowering feelings of inferiority or serious weakness may make it very difficult, even impossible, for the patient to face fresh evidence of his own inadequacy. So I have often found it profitable to begin by giving a positive outlook to the patient; this provides a helpful sense of security when he approaches the more painful insights.

Take as an example a dream of "personal exaltation" in which, for instance, one has tea with the queen of England, or finds oneself on intimate terms with the pope. If the dreamer is not a schizophrenic, the practical interpretation of the symbol depends very much upon his present state of mind—that is, the condition of his ego. If the dreamer overestimates his own value, it is easy to show (from the material produced by association of ideas) how inappropriate and childish the dreamer's intentions are, and how much they emanate from childish wishes to be equal to or superior to his parents. But if it is a case of inferiority, where an all-pervading feeling of worthlessness has already overcome every positive aspect of the dreamer's personality, it would be quite wrong to depress him still more by showing how infantile, ridiculous, or even perverse he is. That would cruelly increase his inferiority, as well as cause an unwelcome and quite unnecessary resistance to the treatment.

There is no therapeutic technique or doctrine that is of general application, since every case that one receives for treatment is an individual in a specific condition. I remember a patient I once had to treat over a period of nine years.

Right, the heroic dreams with which Walter Mitty (in the 1947 film of James Thurber's story) compensates his sense of inferiority.

I saw him only for a few weeks each year, since he lived abroad. From the start I knew what his real trouble was, but I also saw that the least attempt to get close to the truth was met by a violent defensive reaction that threatened a complete rupture between us. Whether I liked it or not, I had to do my best to maintain our relation and to follow his inclination, which was supported by his dreams and which led our discussion away from the root of his neurosis. We ranged so widely that I often accused myself of leading my patient astray. Nothing but the fact that his condition slowly but clearly improved prevented me from confronting him brutally with the truth.

In the 10th year, however, the patient declared himself to be cured and freed from all his symptoms. I was surprised because theoretically his condition was incurable. Noticing my astonishment, he smiled and said (in effect): "And I want to thank you above all for your unfailing tact and patience in helping me to circumvent the painful cause of my neurosis. I am now ready to tell you everything about it.

If I had been able to talk freely about it, I would have told you what it was at my first consultation. But that would have destroyed my rapport with you. Where should I have been then? I should have been morally bankrupt. In the course of 10 years I have learned to trust you; and as my confidence grew, my condition improved. I improved because this slow process restored my belief in myself. Now I am strong enough to discuss the problem that was destroying me."

He then made a devastatingly frank confession of his problem, which showed me the reasons for the peculiar course our treatment had had to follow. The original shock had been such that alone he had been unable to face it. He needed the help of another, and the therapeutic task was the slow establishment of confidence, rather than the demonstration of a clinical theory.

From cases like this I learned to adapt my methods to the needs of the individual patient, rather than to commit myself to general theoretical considerations that might be inapplicable

The Madhouse, painted by Goya. Note the "king" and the "bishop" on the right. Schizophrenia often takes the form of "personal exaltation."

in any particular case. The knowledge of human nature that I have accumulated in the course of 60 years of practical experience has taught me to consider each case as a new one in which, first of all, I have had to seek the individual approach. Sometimes I have not hesitated to plunge into a careful study of infantile events and fantasies; at other times I have begun at the top, even if this has meant soaring straight into the most remote metaphysical speculations. It all depends on learning the language of the individual patient and following the gropings of his unconscious toward the light. Some cases demand one method and some another.

This is especially true when one seeks to interpret symbols. Two different individuals may have almost exactly the same dream. (This, as one soon discovers in clinical experience, is less uncommon than the layman may think.) Yet if, for instance, one dreamer is young and the other old, the problem that disturbs them is correspondingly different, and it would be obviously absurd to interpret both dreams in the same way.

An example that comes to my mind is a dream in which a group of young men are riding on horseback across a wide field. The dreamer is in the lead and he jumps a ditch full of water, just clearing this hazard. The rest of the party fall into the ditch. Now the young man who first told me this dream was a cautious, introverted type. But I also heard the same dream from an old man of daring character, who had lived an active and enterprising life. At the time he had this dream, he was an invalid who gave his doctor and nurse a great deal of trouble; he had actually injured himself by his disobedience of medical instructions.

It was clear to me that this dream was telling the young man what he *ought* to do. But it was telling the old man what he actually was still *doing*. Whereas it encouraged the hesitant young man, the old man was in no such need of encouragement; the spirit of enterprise that still flickered within him was, indeed, his greatest trouble. This example shows how the interpretation of dreams and symbols largely depends upon the individual circumstances of the dreamer and the condition of his mind.

As this museum display shows, the fetus of man resembles those of other animals (and thus provides an indication of man's physical evolution). The psyche, too, has "evolved"; and some contents of modern man's unconscious resemble products of the mind of ancient man. Jung termed these products *archetypal* images.

The archetype in dream symbolism

I have already suggested that dreams serve the purpose of compensation. This assumption means that the dream is a normal psychic phenomenon that transmits unconscious reactions or spontaneous impulses to consciousness. Many dreams can be interpreted with the help of the dreamer, who provides both the associations to and the context of the dream image, by means of which one can look at all its aspects.

This method is adequate in all ordinary cases, such as those when a relative, a friend, or a patient tells you a dream more or less in the course of conversation. But when it is a matter of obsessive dreaming or of highly emotional dreams, the personal associations produced by the dreamer do not usually suffice for a satisfactory interpretation. In such cases, we have to take into consideration the fact (first observed and commented on by Freud) that elements often occur in a dream that are not individual and that cannot be derived from the dreamer's personal experience. These elements, as I have previously mentioned, are what Freud called "archaic remnants"—mental forms whose presence cannot be explained by anything in the individual's own life and which seem to be aboriginal, innate, and inherited shapes of the human mind.

Just as the human body represents a whole museum of organs, each with a long evolutionary history behind it, so we should expect to find that the mind is organized in a similar way. It can no more be a product without history than is the body in which it exists. By "history" I do not mean the fact that the mind builds itself up by conscious reference to the past through language and other cultural traditions. I am referring to the biological, prehistoric, and unconscious development of the mind in archaic man, whose psyche was still close to that of the animal.

This immensely old psyche forms the basis of our mind, just as much as the structure of our body is based on the general anatomical pattern of the mammal. The trained eye of the anatomist or the biologist finds many traces of this original pattern in our bodies. The experienced investigator of the mind can similarly see the analogies between the dream pictures of modern man and the products of the primitive mind, its "collective images," and its mythological motifs.

Just as the biologist needs the science of comparative anatomy, however, the psychologist cannot do without a "comparative anatomy of the psyche." In practice, to put it differently, the psychologist must have a sufficient experience not only of dreams and other products of unconscious activity, but also of mythology in its widest sense. Without this equipment, nobody can spot the important analogies; it is not possible, for instance, to see the analogy between a case of compulsion neurosis and that of a classical demonic possession without a working knowledge of both.

My views about the "archaic remnants," which I call "archetypes" or "primordial images," have been constantly criticized by people who lack a sufficient knowledge of the psychology of dreams and of mythology. The term "archetype" is often misunderstood as meaning certain definite mythological images or motifs. But these are nothing more than conscious representations; it would be absurd to assume that such variable representations could be inherited.

The archetype is a tendency to form such representations of a motif—representations that can vary a great deal in detail without losing their basic pattern. There are, for instance, many representations of the motif of the hostile brethren, but the motif itself remains the same. My critics have incorrectly assumed that I am dealing with "inherited representations," and on that ground they have dismissed the idea of the archetype as mere superstition. They have

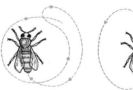

Man's unconscious archetypal images are as instinctive as the ability of geese to migrate (in formation); as ants' forming organized societies; as bees' tail-wagging dance (above) that communicates to the hive the exact location of a food source.

A modern professor had a "vision" exactly like a woodcut in an old book that he had never seen. Right, the book's title page; and another woodcut, symbolizing the male and female principles united. Such archetypal symbols arise from the psyche's age-old collective basis.

failed to take into account the fact that if archetypes were representations that originated in our consciousness (or were acquired by consciousness), we should surely understand them, and not be bewildered and astonished when they present themselves in our consciousness. They are, indeed, an instinctive *trend*, as marked as the impulse of birds to build nests, or ants to form organized colonies.

Here I must clarify the relation between instincts and archetypes: What we properly call instincts are physiological urges, and are perceived by the senses. But at the same time, they also manifest themselves in fantasies and often reveal their presence only by symbolic images. These manifestations are what I call the archetypes. They are without known origin; and they reproduce themselves in any time or in any part of the world—even where transmission by direct descent or "cross fertilization" through migration must be ruled out.

I can remember many cases of people who have consulted me because they were baffled by their own dreams or by their children's. They were at a complete loss to understand the terms of the dreams. The reason was that the dreams contained images that they could not relate to anything they could remember or could have passed on to their children. Yet some of these patients were highly educated: A few of them were actually psychiatrists themselves.

I vividly recall the case of a professor who had had a sudden vision and thought he was insane. He came to see me in a state of complete panic. I simply took a 400-year-old book from the shelf and showed him an old woodcut depicting his very vision. "There's no reason for you to believe that you're insane," I said to him. "They knew about your vision 400 years ago." Whereupon he sat down entirely deflated, but once more normal.

A very important case came to me from a man who was himself a psychiatrist. One day he brought me a handwritten booklet he had received as a Christmas present from his 10-year-old daughter. It contained a whole series of dreams she had had when she was eight. They made up the weirdest series of dreams that I have ever seen, and I could well understand why the father was more than just puzzled by them. Though childlike, they were uncanny, and they contained images whose origin was wholly incomprehensible to the father.

Here are the relevant motifs from the dreams:
1. "The evil animal," a snakelike monster with many horns, kills and devours all other animals. But God comes from the four corners, being in fact four separate gods, and gives rebirth to all the dead animals.

2. An ascent into heaven, where pagan dances are being celebrated; and a descent into hell, where angels are doing good deeds.

3. A horde of small animals frightens the dreamer. The animals increase to a tremendous size, and one of them devours the little girl.

4. A small mouse is penetrated by worms, snakes, fishes, and human beings. Thus the mouse becomes human. This portrays the four stages of the origin of mankind.

5. A drop of water is seen, as it appears when looked at through a microscope. The girl sees that the drop is full of tree branches. This portrays the origin of the world.

6. A bad boy has a clod of earth and throws bits of it at everyone who passes. In this way all the passers-by become bad.

7. A drunken woman falls into the water and comes out renewed and sober.

8. The scene is in America, where many people are rolling on an ant heap, attacked by the ants. The dreamer, in a panic, falls into a river.

9. There is a desert on the moon where the dreamer sinks so deeply into the ground that she reaches hell.

10. In this dream the girl has a vision of a luminous ball. She touches it. Vapors emanate from it. A man comes and kills her.

11. The girl dreams she is dangerously ill. Suddenly birds come out of her skin and cover her completely.

12. Swarms of gnats obscure the sun, the moon, and all the stars, except one. That one star falls upon the dreamer.

In the unabridged German original, each dream begins with the words of the old fairy

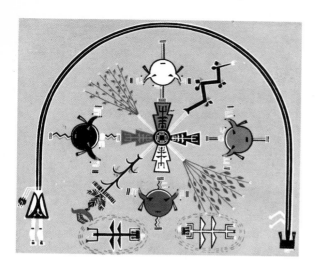

Parallels to archetypal motifs in
the girl's first dream (p. 70):
Left, from Strasbourg Cathedral,
Christ crucified on Adam's grave—
symbolizing the theme of rebirth
(Christ as the second Adam). In
a Navaho sand painting, above, the
horned heads are the four corners
of the world. In Britain's royal
coronation ceremony, the monarch
(right, Queen Elizabeth II in 1953)
is presented to the people at the
four doors of Westminster Abbey.

tale: "Once upon a time. . . ." By these words
the little dreamer suggests that she feels as if
each dream were a sort of fairy tale, which she
wants to tell her father as a Christmas present.
The father tried to explain the dreams in
terms of their context. But he could not do so,
for there seemed to be no personal associations
to them.

The possibility that these dreams were conscious elaborations can of course be ruled out
only by someone who knew the child well
enough to be absolutely sure of her truthfulness.
(They would, however, remain a challenge to
our understanding even if they were fantasies.)
In this case, the father was convinced that the
dreams were authentic, and I have no reason to
doubt it. I knew the little girl myself, but this
was before she gave her dreams to her father,
so that I had no chance to ask her about them.
She lived abroad and died of an infectious
disease about a year after that Christmas.

Her dreams have a decidedly peculiar character. Their leading thoughts are markedly philosophic in concept. The first one, for instance, speaks of an evil monster killing other animals, but God gives rebirth to them all through a divine *Apokatastasis*, or restitution. In the Western world this idea is known through the Christian tradition. It can be found in the Acts of the Apostles III:21: "[Christ] whom the heaven must receive until the time of restitution of all things. . . ." The early Greek Fathers of the Church (for instance, Origen) particularly insisted upon the idea that, at the end of time, everything will be restored by the Redeemer to its original and perfect state. But, according to St. Matthew XVII:11, there was already an old Jewish tradition that Elias "truly shall first come, and restore all things." I Corinthians xv:22 refers to the same idea in the following words: "For as in Adam all die, even so in Christ shall all be made alive."

One might guess that the child had encountered this thought in her religious education.

But she had very little religious background. Her parents were Protestants in name; but in fact they knew the Bible only from hearsay. It is particularly unlikely that the recondite image of *Apokatastasis* had been fully explained to the girl. Certainly her father had never heard of this mythical idea.

Nine of the 12 dreams are influenced by the theme of destruction and restoration. And none of these dreams shows traces of specific Christian education or influence. On the contrary, they are more closely related to primitive myths. This relation is corroborated by the other motif—the "cosmogonic myth" (the creation of the world and of man) that appears in the fourth and fifth dreams. The same connection is found in I Corinthians xv:22, which I have just quoted. In this passage too, Adam and Christ (death and resurrection) are linked together.

The general idea of Christ the Redeemer belongs to the world-wide and pre-Christ theme of the hero and rescuer who, although he has

Above, the hero-god Raven (of the Haida Indians of America's Pacific Coast) in the belly of a whale—corresponding to the "devouring monster" motif in the girl's first dream (p. 70).

The girl's second dream—of angels in hell and demons in heaven—seems to embody the idea of the relativity of morality. The same concept is expressed in the dual aspect of the fallen angel who is both Satan, the devil, and (right) Lucifer, the resplendent bringer of light. These opposites can also be seen in the figure of God, far right (in a drawing by Blake): He appears to Job, in a dream, with a cloven hoof like a demon's.

been devoured by a monster, appears again in a miraculous way, having overcome whatever monster it was that swallowed him. When and where such a motif originated nobody knows. We do not even know how to go about investigating the problem. The one apparent certainty is that every generation seems to have known it as a tradition handed down from some preceding time. Thus we can safely assume that it "originated" at a period when man did not yet know that he possessed a hero myth; in an age, that is to say, when he did not yet consciously reflect on what he was saying. The hero figure is an archetype, which has existed since time immemorial.

The production of archetypes by children is especially significant, because one can sometimes be quite certain that a child has had no direct access to the tradition concerned. In this case, the girl's family had no more than a superficial acquaintance with the Christian tradition. Christian themes may, of course, be represented by such ideas as God, angels, hea-

ven, hell, and evil. But the way in which they are treated by this child points to a totally non-Christian origin.

Let us take the first dream of the God who really consists of four gods, coming from the "four corners." The corners of what? There is no room mentioned in the dream. A room would not even fit in with the picture of what is obviously a cosmic event, in which the Universal Being himself intervenes. The quaternity (or element of "fourness") itself is a strange idea, but one that plays a great role in many religions and philosophies. In the Christian religion, it has been superseded by the Trinity, a notion that we must assume was known to the child. But who in an ordinary middle-class family of today would be likely to know of a divine quaternity? It is an idea that was once fairly familiar among students of the Hermetic philosophy in the Middle Ages, but it petered out with the beginning of the 18th century, and it has been entirely obsolete for at least 200 years. Where, then, did the little girl pick it up?

With Dreams upon my bed thou scarest me & affrightest me with Visions

From Ezekiel's vision? But there is no Christian teaching that identifies the seraphim with God.

The same question may be asked about the horned serpent. In the Bible, it is true, there are many horned animals—in the Book of Revelation, for instance. But all these seem to be quadruped, although their overlord is the dragon, the Greek word for which (*drakon*) also means serpent. The horned serpent appears in 16th-century Latin alchemy as the *quadricornutus serpens* (four-horned serpent), a symbol of Mercury and an antagonist of the Christian Trinity. But this is an obscure reference. So far as I can discover, it is made by only one author; and this child had no means of knowing it.

In the second dream, a motif appears that is definitely non-Christian and that contains a reversal of accepted values—for instance, pagan dances by men in heaven and good deeds by angels in hell. This symbol suggests a relativity of moral values. Where did the child find such a revolutionary notion, worthy of Nietzsche's genius?

These questions lead us to another: What is the compensatory meaning of these dreams, to which the little girl obviously attributed so much importance that she presented them to her father as a Christmas present?

If the dreamer had been a primitive medicine man, one could reasonably assume that they represent variations of the philosophical themes of death, of resurrection or restitution, of the origin of the world, the creation of man, and the relativity of values. But one might give up such dreams as hopelessly difficult if one tried to interpret them from a personal level. They undoubtedly contain "collective images," and they are in a way analogous to the doctrines taught to young people in primitive tribes when they are about to be initiated as men. At such times they learn about what God, or the gods, or the "founding" animals have done, how the world and man were created, how the end of the world will come, and the meaning of death. Is there any occasion when we, in Christian civilization, hand out similar instructions? There is: in adolescence. But many people begin to think again of things like this in old age, at the approach of death.

The little girl, as it happened, was in both these situations. She was approaching puberty and, at the same time, the end of her life. Little or nothing in the symbolism of her dreams

The little girl's dreams (p. 70) contain symbols of creation, death, and rebirth, which resemble the teachings given to adolescents in primitive initiation rituals. Left, the end of a Navaho ceremony: A girl, having become a woman, goes into the desert to meditate.

Death and rebirth symbolism also appears in dreams at the end of life, when the approach of death casts a shadow before it. Right, one of Goya's last paintings: The strange creature, apparently a dog, that emerges from the dark can be interpreted as the artist's foreshadowing of his death. In many mythologies dogs appear as guides to the land of the dead.

points to the beginning of a normal adult life, but there are many allusions to destruction and restoration. When I first read her dreams, indeed, I had the uncanny feeling that they suggested impending disaster. The reason I felt like that was the peculiar nature of the compensation that I deduced from the symbolism. It was the opposite of what one would expect to find in the consciousness of a girl of that age.

These dreams open up a new and rather terrifying aspect of life and death. One would expect to find such images in an aging person who looks back upon life, rather than to be given them by a child who would normally be looking forward. Their atmosphere recalls the old Roman saying, "Life is a short dream," rather than the joy and exuberance of its springtime. For this child's life was like a *ver sacrum vovendum* (vow of a vernal sacrifice), as the Roman poet puts it. Experience shows that the unknown approach of death casts an *adumbratio* (an anticipatory shadow) over the life and dreams of the victim. Even the altar in Christian churches represents, on the one hand, a tomb and, on the other, a place of resurrection—the transformation of death into eternal life.

Such are the ideas that the dreams brought home to the child. They were a preparation for death, expressed through short stories, like the tales told at primitive initiations or the *Koans* of Zen Buddhism. This message is unlike the orthodox Christian doctrine and more like ancient primitive thought. It seems to have originated outside historical tradition in the long-forgotten psychic sources that, since prehistoric times, have nourished philosophical and religious speculation about life and death.

It was as if future events were casting their shadow back by arousing in the child certain thought forms that, though normally dormant, describe or accompany the approach of a fatal issue. Although the specific shape in which they express themselves is more or less personal, their general pattern is collective. They are found everywhere and at all times, just as animal instincts vary a good deal in the different species and yet serve the same general purposes. We do not assume that each new-born animal creates its own instincts as an individual acquisition, and we must not suppose that human individuals invent their specific human ways with every new birth. Like the instincts, the collective thought patterns of the human mind are innate and inherited. They function, when the occasion arises, in more or less the same way in all of us.

Emotional manifestations, to which such thought patterns belong, are recognizably the same all over the earth. We can identify them even in animals, and the animals themselves understand one another in this respect, even though they may belong to different species. And what about insects, with their complicated symbiotic functions? Most of them do not even know their parents and have nobody to teach them. Why should one assume, then, that man is the only living being deprived of specific instincts, or that his psyche is devoid of all traces of its evolution?

Naturally, if you identify the psyche with consciousness, you can easily fall into the erroneous idea that man comes into the world with a psyche that is empty, and that in later years it contains nothing more than what it has learned by individual experience. But the psyche is more than consciousness. Animals have little consciousness, but many impulses and reactions that denote the existence of a psyche; and primitives do a lot of things whose meaning is unknown to them.

You may ask many civilized people in vain for the real meaning of the Christmas tree or of the Easter egg. The fact is, they do things without knowing why they do them. I am inclined to the view that things were generally done first and that it was only a long time afterward that somebody asked why they were done. The medical psychologist is constantly confronted with otherwise intelligent patients who behave in a peculiar and unpredictable way and who have no inkling of what they say or do. They are suddenly caught by unreasonable moods for which they themselves cannot account.

Superficially, such reactions and impulses seem to be of an intimately personal nature, and so we dismiss them as idiosyncratic behavior. In fact, they are based upon a preformed and ever-ready instinctive system that is characteristic of man. Thought forms, universally understandable gestures, and many attitudes follow a pattern that was established long before man developed a reflective consciousness.

It is even conceivable that the early origins of man's capacity to reflect come from the painful consequences of violent emotional clashes. Let me take, purely as an illustration of this point, the bushman who, in a moment of anger and disappointment at his failure to catch any fish, strangles his much beloved only son, and is then seized with immense regret as he holds the little dead body in his arms. Such a man might remember this moment of pain for ever.

We cannot know whether this kind of experience was actually the initial cause of the development of human consciousness. But there is no doubt that the shock of a similar emotional experience is often needed to make people wake up and pay attention to what they are doing. There is a famous case of a 13th-century Spanish hidalgo, Raimon Lull, who finally (after a long chase) succeeded in meeting the lady he admired at a secret rendezvous. She silently opened her dress and showed him her breast, rotten with cancer. The shock changed Lull's life; he eventually became an eminent theologian and one of the Church's greatest missionaries. In the case of such a sudden change one can often prove that an archetype has been at work for a long time in the unconscious, skillfully arranging circumstances that will lead to the crisis.

Such experiences seem to show that archetypal forms are not just static patterns. They are dynamic factors that manifest themselves in impulses, just as spontaneously as the instincts. Certain dreams, visions, or thoughts can suddenly appear; and however carefully one investigates, one cannot find out what causes them. This does not mean that they have no cause; they certainly have. But it is so remote or obscure that one cannot see what it is. In

Some dreams seem to predict the future (perhaps due to unconscious knowledge of future possibilities); thus dreams were long used as divination. In Greece the sick would ask the healing god Asklepios for a dream indicating a cure. Left, a relief depicts such a dream cure: A snake (the god's symbol) bites a man's diseased shoulder and the god (far left) heals the shoulder. Right, Constantine (an Italian painting c. 1460) dreaming before a battle that was to make him Roman Emperor. He dreamed of the cross, a symbol of Christ, and a voice said: "In this sign conquer." He took the sign as his emblem, won the battle, and was thus converted to Christianity.

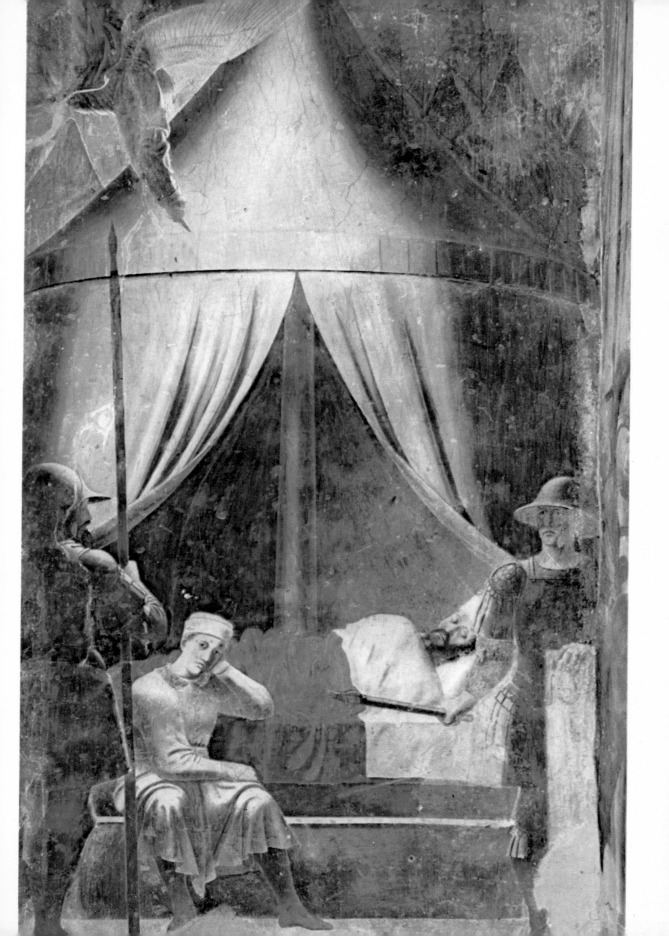

such a case, one must wait either until the dream and its meaning are sufficiently understood, or until some external event occurs that will explain the dream.

At the moment of the dream, this event may still lie in the future. But just as our conscious thoughts often occupy themselves with the future and its possibilities, so do the unconscious and its dreams. There has long been a general belief that the chief function of dreams is prognostication of the future. In antiquity, and as late as the Middle Ages, dreams played their part in medical prognosis. I can confirm by a modern dream the element of prognosis (or precognition) that can be found in an old dream quoted by Artemidorus of Daldis, in the second century A.D. A man dreamed that he saw his father die in the flames of a house on fire. Not long afterwards, he himself died in a *phlegmone* (fire, or high fever), which I presume was pneumonia.

It so happened that a colleague of mine was once suffering from a deadly gangrenous fever —in fact, a *phlegmone*. A former patient of his, who had no knowledge of the nature of his doctor's illness, dreamed that the doctor died in a great fire. At that time the doctor had just entered a hospital and the disease was only beginning. The dreamer knew nothing but the bare fact that his doctor was ill and in a hospital. Three weeks later, the doctor died.

As this example shows, dreams may have an anticipatory or prognostic aspect, and anybody trying to interpret them must take this into consideration, especially where an obviously meaningful dream does not provide a context

sufficient to explain it. Such a dream often comes right out of the blue, and one wonders what could have prompted it. Of course, if one knew its ulterior message, its cause would be clear. For it is only our consciousness that does not yet know; the unconscious seems already informed, and to have come to a conclusion that is expressed in the dream. In fact, the unconscious seems to be able to examine and to draw conclusions from facts, much as consciousness does. It can even use certain facts, and anticipate their possible results, just because we are *not* conscious of them.

But as far as one can make out from dreams, the unconscious makes its deliberations instinctively. The distinction is important. Logical analysis is the prerogative of consciousness; we select with reason and knowledge. The unconscious, however, seems to be guided chiefly by instinctive trends, represented by corresponding thought forms—that is, by the archetypes. A doctor who is asked to describe the course of an illness will use such rational concepts as "infection" or "fever." The dream is more poetic. It presents the diseased body as a man's earthly house, and the fever as the fire that is destroying it.

As the above dream shows, the archetypal mind has handled the situation in the same way as it did in the time of Artemidorus. Something that is of a more or less unknown nature has been intuitively grasped by the unconscious and submitted to an archetypal treatment. This suggests that, instead of the process of reasoning that conscious thought would have applied, the archetypal mind has stepped in and taken over

In a dream quoted from Artemidorus on this page, a burning house symbolizes a fever. The human body is often represented as a house: Left, from an 18th-century Hebrew encyclopedia, the body and a house are compared in detail—turrets as ears, windows as eyes, a furnace as stomach, etc. Right, in a cartoon by James Thurber, a henpecked husband sees his home and his wife as the same being.

the task of prognostication. The archetypes thus have their own initiative and their own specific energy. These powers enable them both to produce a meaningful interpretation (in their own symbolic style) and to interfere in a given situation with their own impulses and their own thought formations. In this respect, they function like complexes; they come and go very much as they please, and often they obstruct or modify our conscious intentions in an embarrassing way.

We can perceive the specific energy of archetypes when we experience the peculiar fascination that accompanies them. They seem to hold a special spell. Such a peculiar quality is also characteristic of the personal complexes; and just as personal complexes have their individual history, so do social complexes of an archetypal character. But while personal complexes never produce more than a personal bias, archetypes create myths, religions, and philosophies that influence and characterize whole nations and epochs of history. We regard the personal complexes as compensations for one-sided or faulty attitudes of consciousness; in the same way, myths of a religious nature can be interpreted as a sort of mental therapy for the sufferings and anxieties of mankind in general—hunger, war, disease, old age, death.

The universal hero myth, for example, always refers to a powerful man or god-man who vanquishes evil in the form of dragons, serpents, monsters, demons, and so on, and who liberates his people from destruction and death. The narration or ritual repetition of sacred texts and ceremonies, and the worship of such a figure with dances, music, hymns, prayers, and sacrifices, grip the audience with numinous emotions (as if with magic spells) and exalt the individual to an identification with the hero.

If we try to see such a situation with the eyes of a believer, we can perhaps understand how the ordinary man can be liberated from his personal impotence and misery and endowed (at least temporarily) with an almost superhuman quality. Often enough such a conviction will sustain him for a long time and give a certain style to his life. It may even set the tone of a whole society. A remarkable instance of this can be found in the Eleusinian mysteries, which were finally suppressed at the beginning of the seventh century of the Christian era. They expressed, together with the Delphic oracle, the essence and spirit of ancient Greece. On a much greater scale, the Christian era itself owes its name and significance to the antique mystery of the god-man, which has its roots in the archetypal Osiris-Horus myth of ancient Egypt.

It is commonly assumed that on some given occasion in prehistoric times, the basic mythological ideas were "invented" by a clever old philosopher or prophet, and ever afterward "believed" by a credulous and uncritical people. It is said that stories told by a power-seeking priesthood are not "true," but merely "wishful thinking." But the very word "invent" is derived from the Latin *invenire*, and means to "find" and hence to find something by "seeking" it. In the latter case the word itself hints at some foreknowledge of what you are going to find.

The energy of archetypes can be focused (through rituals and other appeals to mass emotion) to move people to collective action. The Nazis knew this, and used versions of Teutonic myths to help rally the country to their cause. Far right, a propaganda painting of Hitler as a heroic crusader; right, a solstice festival celebrated in summer by the Hitler Youth, a revival of an ancient pagan festival.

Top, a child's painting of Christmas
includes the familiar tree decorated
with candles. The evergreen tree is
connected with Christ through the
symbolism of the winter solstice
and the "new year" (the new aeon of
Christianity). There are many links
between Christ and the tree symbol:
The cross is often seen as a tree,
as in a medieval Italian fresco,
left, of Christ crucified on the tree
of knowledge. Candles in Christian
ceremonies symbolize divine light, as
in the Swedish festival of St. Lucia
(above), where girls wear crowns of
burning candles.

Let me go back to the strange ideas contained in the dreams of the little girl. It seems unlikely that she sought them out, since she was surprised to find them. They occurred to her rather as peculiar and unexpected stories, which seemed noteworthy enough to be given to her father as a Christmas present. In doing so, however, she lifted them up into the sphere of our still living Christian mystery—the birth of our Lord, mixed with the secret of the evergreen tree that carries the new-born Light. (This is the reference of the fifth dream.)

Although there is ample historical evidence for the symbolic relation between Christ and the tree symbol, the little girl's parents would have been gravely embarrassed had they been asked to explain exactly what they meant by decorating a tree with burning candles to celebrate the nativity of Christ. "Oh, it's just a Christmas custom!" they would have said. A serious answer would require a far-reaching dissertation about the antique symbolism of the dying god, and its relation to the cult of the Great Mother and her symbol, the tree—to mention only one aspect of this complicated problem.

The further we delve into the origins of a "collective image" (or, to express it in ecclesiastical language, of a dogma), the more we uncover a seemingly unending web of archetypal patterns that, before modern times, were never the object of conscious reflection. Thus, paradoxically enough, we know more about mythological symbolism than did any generation before our own. The fact is that in former times men did not reflect upon their symbols; they lived them and were unconsciously animated by their meaning.

I will illustrate this by an experience I once had with the primitives of Mount Elgon in Africa. Every morning at dawn, they leave their huts and breathe or spit into their hands, which they then stretch out to the first rays of the sun, as if they were offering either their breath or their spittle to the rising god—to *mungu*. (This Swahili word, which they used in explaining the ritual act, is derived from a Polynesian root equivalent to *mana* or *mulungu*. These and similar terms designate a "power" of extraordinary efficiency and pervasiveness, which we should call divine. Thus the word *mungu* is their equivalent for Allah or God.) When I asked them what they meant by this act, or why they did it, they were completely baffled. They could only say: "We have always done it. It has always been done when the sun rises." They laughed at the obvious conclusion that the sun is *mungu*. The sun indeed is not *mungu* when it is above the horizon; *mungu* is the actual moment of the sunrise.

What they were doing was obvious to me, but not to them; they just did it, never reflecting on what they did. They were consequently unable to explain themselves. I concluded that they were offering their souls to *mungu*, because the breath (of life) and the spittle mean "soul-substance." To breathe or spit upon something conveys a "magical" effect, as, for instance, when Christ used spittle to cure the blind, or where a son inhales his dying father's last breath in order to take over the father's soul. It is most unlikely that these Africans ever, even in the remote past, knew any more about the meaning of their ceremony. In fact, their ancestors probably knew even less, because they were even more profoundly unconscious of their motives and thought less about their doings.

Goethe's Faust aptly says: "*Im Anfang war die Tat* [In the beginning was the deed]." "Deeds" were never invented, they were done; thoughts, on the other hand, are a relatively late discovery of man. First he was moved to deeds by unconscious factors; it was only a long time afterward that he began to reflect upon the causes that had moved him; and it took him a very long time indeed to arrive at the preposterous idea that he must have moved himself—his mind being unable to identify any other motivating force than his own.

We should laugh at the idea of a plant or an animal inventing itself, yet there are many people who believe that the psyche or mind invented itself and thus was the creator of its own existence. As a matter of fact, the mind has grown to its present state of consciousness as an acorn grows into an oak or as saurians developed into mammals. As it has for so long been developing, so it still develops, and thus we are moved by forces from within as well as by stimuli from without.

These inner motives spring from a deep source that is not made by consciousness and is not under its control. In the mythology of earlier times, these forces were called *mana*, or spirits, demons, and gods. They are as active today as they ever were. If they conform to our wishes, we call them happy hunches or impulses and pat ourselves on the back for being smart fellows. If they go against us, then we say that it is just bad luck, or that certain people are against us, or that the cause of our misfortunes must be pathological. The one thing we refuse to admit is that we are dependent upon "powers" that are beyond our control.

It is true, however, that in recent times civilized man has acquired a certain amount of will power, which he can apply where he pleases. He has learned to do his work efficiently without having recourse to chanting and drumming to hypnotize him into the state of doing. He can even dispense with a daily prayer for divine aid. He can carry out what he proposes to do, and he can apparently translate his ideas into action without a hitch, whereas the primitive seems to be hampered at each step by fears, superstitions, and other unseen obstacles to action. The motto "Where there's a will, there's a way" is the superstition of modern man.

Yet in order to sustain his creed, contemporary man pays the price in a remarkable lack of introspection. He is blind to the fact that, with all his rationality and efficiency, he is possessed by "powers" that are beyond his control. His gods and demons have not disappeared at all; they have merely got new names. They keep him on the run with restlessness, vague apprehensions, psychological complications, an insatiable need for pills, alcohol, tobacco, food —and, above all, a large array of neuroses.

Two examples of belief in the "magical" quality of breath: Below left, a Zulu witch doctor cures a patient by blowing into his ear through a cow's horn (to drive the spirits out); below, a medieval painting of the creation depicts God breathing life into Adam. Right, in a 13th-century Italian painting, Christ heals a blind man with spittle—which, like breath, has long been believed to have a life-giving ability.

The soul of man

What we call civilized consciousness has steadily separated itself from the basic instincts. But these instincts have not disappeared. They have merely lost their contact with our consciousness and are thus forced to assert themselves in an indirect fashion. This may be by means of physical symptoms in the case of a neurosis, or by means of incidents of various kinds, such as unaccountable moods, unexpected forgetfulness, or mistakes in speech.

A man likes to believe that he is the master of his soul. But as long as he is unable to control his moods and emotions, or to be conscious of the myriad secret ways in which unconscious factors insinuate themselves into his arrangements and decisions, he is certainly not his own master. These unconscious factors owe their existence to the autonomy of the archetypes. Modern man protects himself against seeing his own split state by a system of compartments. Certain areas of outer life and of his own behavior are kept, as it were, in separate drawers and are never confronted with one another.

As an example of this so-called compartment psychology, I remember the case of an alcoholic who had come under the laudable influence of a certain religious movement, and, fascinated by its enthusiasm, had forgotten that he needed a drink. He was obviously and miraculously cured by Jesus, and he was correspondingly displayed as a witness to divine grace or to the efficiency of the said religious organization. But after a few weeks of public confessions, the novelty began to pale and some alcoholic refreshment seemed to be indicated, and so he drank again. But this time the helpful organization came to the conclusion that the case was "pathological" and obviously not suitable for an intervention by Jesus, so they put him into a clinic to let the doctor do better than the divine healer.

This is an aspect of the modern "cultural" mind that is worth looking into. It shows an

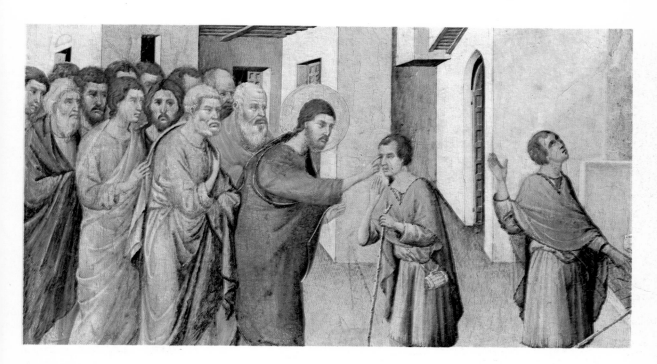

alarming degree of dissociation and psychological confusion.

If, for a moment, we regard mankind as one individual, we see that the human race is like a person carried away by unconscious powers; and the human race also likes to keep certain problems tucked away in separate drawers. But this is why we should give a great deal of consideration to what we are doing, for mankind is now threatened by self-created and deadly dangers that are growing beyond our control. Our world is, so to speak, dissociated like a neurotic, with the Iron Curtain marking the symbolic line of division. Western man, becoming aware of the aggressive will to power of the East, sees himself forced to take extraordinary measures of defense, at the same time as he prides himself on his virtue and good intentions.

What he fails to see is that it is his own vices, which he has covered up by good international manners, that are thrown back in his face by the communist world, shamelessly and methodically. What the West has tolerated, but secretly and with a slight sense of shame (the diplomatic lie, systematic deception, veiled threats), comes back into the open and in full measure from the East and ties us up in neurotic knots. It is the face of his own evil shadow that grins at Western man from the other side of the Iron Curtain.

It is this state of affairs that explains the peculiar feeling of helplessness of so many people in Western societies. They have begun to realize that the difficulties confronting us are moral problems, and that the attempts to answer them by a policy of piling up nuclear arms or by economic "competition" is achieving little, for it cuts both ways. Many of us now understand that moral and mental means would be more efficient, since they could provide us with psychic immunity against the ever-increasing infection.

"Our world is dissociated like a neurotic." Left, the Berlin Wall.

But all such attempts have proved singularly ineffective, and will do so as long as we try to convince ourselves and the world that it is only *they* (i.e. our opponents) who are wrong. It would be much more to the point for us to make a serious attempt to recognize our own shadow and its nefarious doings. If we could see our shadow (the dark side of our nature), we should be immune to any moral and mental infection and insinuation. As matters now stand, we lay ourselves open to every infection, because we are really doing practically the same thing as *they*. Only we have the additional disadvantage that we neither see nor want to understand what we ourselves are doing, under the cover of good manners.

The communist world, it may be noted, has one big myth (which we call an illusion, in the vain hope that our superior judgment will make it disappear). It is the time-hallowed archetypal dream of a Golden Age (or Paradise), where everything is provided in abundance for everyone, and a great, just, and wise chief rules over a human kindergarten. This powerful archetype in its infantile form has gripped them, but it will never disappear from the world at the mere sight of our superior point of view. We even support it by our own childishness, for our Western civilization is in the grip of the same mythology. Unconsciously, we cherish the same prejudices, hopes, and expectations. We too believe in the welfare state, in universal peace, in the equality of man, in his eternal human rights, in justice, truth, and (do not say it too loudly) in the Kingdom of God on Earth.

The sad truth is that man's real life consists of a complex of inexorable opposites—day and night, birth and death, happiness and misery, good and evil. We are not even sure that one will prevail against the other, that good will overcome evil, or joy defeat pain. Life is a battleground. It always has been, and always will be; and if it were not so, existence would come to an end.

It was precisely this conflict within man that led the early Christians to expect and hope for an early end to this world, or the Buddhists to

85

Every society has its idea of the archetypal paradise or golden age that, it is believed, once existed and will exist again. Left, a 19th-century American painting embodies the idea of a past utopia: It shows William Penn's treaty with the Indians in 1682 occurring in an ideal setting where all is harmony and peace. Below left, a reflection of the idea of a utopia yet to come: A poster in a Moscow park shows Lenin leading the Russian people toward the future.

Above, the Garden of Eden, depicted as a walled (and womb-like) garden in a 15th-century French painting and showing the expulsion of Adam and Eve. Right, a "golden age" of primitive naturalness is pictured in a 16th-century painting by Cranach (entitled *Earthly Paradise*). Far right, the 16th-century Flemish artist Brueghel's *Land of Cokaygne*, a mythical land of sensual delights and easy living (stories of which were widely popular in medieval Europe, especially among the hardworking peasants and serfs).

reject all earthly desires and aspirations. These basic answers would be frankly suicidal if they were not linked up with peculiar mental and moral ideas and practices that constitute the bulk of both religions and that, to a certain extent, modify their radical denial of the world.

I stress this point because, in our time, there are millions of people who have lost faith in any kind of religion. Such people do not understand their religion any longer. While life runs smoothly without religion, the loss remains as good as unnoticed. But when suffering comes, it is another matter. That is when people begin to seek a way out and to reflect about the meaning of life and its bewildering and painful experiences.

It is significant that the psychological doctor (within my experience) is consulted more by Jews and Protestants than by Catholics. This might be expected, for the Catholic Church still feels responsible for the *cura animarum* (the care and welfare of souls). But in this scientific age, the psychiatrist is apt to be asked the questions that once belonged in the domain of the theologian. People feel that it makes, or would make, a great difference if only they had a positive belief in a meaningful way of life or in God and immortality. The specter of approaching death often gives a powerful incentive to such thoughts. From time immemorial, men have had ideas about a Supreme Being (one or several) and about the Land of the

Hereafter. Only today do they think they can do without such ideas.

Because we cannot discover God's throne in the sky with a radio telescope or establish (for certain) that a beloved father or mother is still about in a more or less corporeal form, people assume that such ideas are "not true." I would rather say that they are not "true" *enough*, for these are conceptions of a kind that have accompanied human life from prehistoric times, and that still break through into consciousness at any provocation.

Modern man may assert that he can dispense with them, and he may bolster his opinion by insisting that there is no scientific evidence of their truth. Or he may even regret the loss of his convictions. But since we are dealing with invisible and unknowable things (for God is beyond human understanding, and there is no means of proving immortality), why should we bother about evidence? Even if we did not know by reason our need for salt in our food, we should nonetheless profit from its use. We might argue that the use of salt is a mere illusion of taste or a superstition; but it would still contribute to our well-being. Why, then, should we deprive ourselves of views that would prove helpful in crises and would give a meaning to our existence?

And how do we know that such ideas are not true? Many people would agree with me

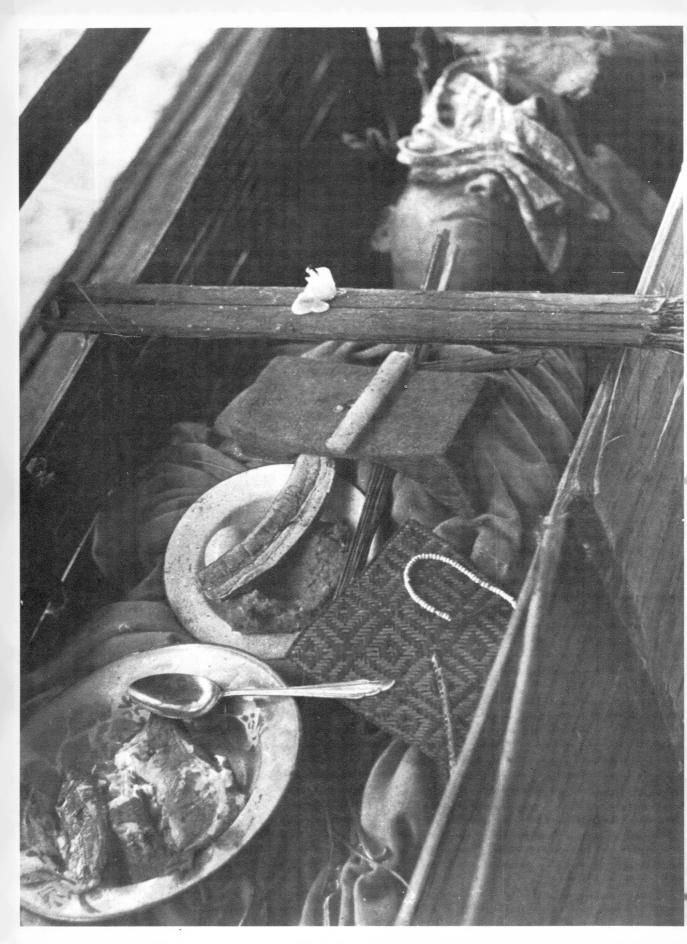

if I stated flatly that such ideas are probably illusions. What they fail to realize is that the denial is as impossible to "prove" as the assertion of religious belief. We are entirely free to choose which point of view we take; it will in any case be an arbitrary decision.

There is, however, a strong empirical reason why we should cultivate thoughts that can never be proved. It is that they are known to be useful. Man positively needs general ideas and convictions that will give a meaning to his life and enable him to find a place for himself in the universe. He can stand the most incredible hardships when he is convinced that they make sense; he is crushed when, on top of all his misfortunes, he has to admit that he is taking part in a "tale told by an idiot."

It is the role of religious symbols to give a meaning to the life of man. The Pueblo Indians believe that they are the sons of Father Sun, and this belief endows their life with a perspective (and a goal) that goes far beyond their limited existence. It gives them ample space for the unfolding of personality and permits them a full life as complete persons. Their plight is infinitely more satisfactory than that of a man in our own civilization who knows that he is (and will remain) nothing more than an underdog with no inner meaning to his life.

A sense of a wider meaning to one's existence is what raises a man beyond mere getting and spending. If he lacks this sense, he is lost and miserable. Had St. Paul been convinced that he was nothing more than a wandering tent-maker he certainly would not have been the man he was. His real and meaningful life lay in the inner certainty that he was the messenger of the Lord. One may accuse him of suffering from megalomania, but this opinion pales before the testimony of history and the judgment of subsequent generations. The myth that took possession of him made him something greater than a mere craftsman.

Such a myth, however, consists of symbols that have not been invented consciously. They have happened. It was not the man Jesus who created the myth of the god-man. It existed for many centuries before his birth. He himself was seized by this symbolic idea, which, as St. Mark tells us, lifted him out of the narrow life of the Nazarene carpenter.

Left, the burial coffin of a South American Cayapas Indian. The dead man is provided with food and clothing for his life after death. Religious symbols and beliefs of every kind give meaning to men's lives: ancient peoples grieved over death (right, an Egyptian figurine representing mourning, which was found in a tomb); yet their beliefs made them also think of death as a positive transformation.

Myths go back to the primitive storyteller and his dreams, to men moved by the stirring of their fantasies. These people were not very different from those whom later generations have called poets or philosophers. Primitive storytellers did not concern themselves with the origin of their fantasies; it was very much later that people began to wonder where a story originated. Yet, centuries ago, in what we now call "ancient" Greece, men's minds were advanced enough to surmise that the tales of the gods were nothing but archaic and exaggerated traditions of long-buried kings or chieftains. Men already took the view that the myth was too improbable to mean what it said. They therefore tried to reduce it to a generally understandable form.

In more recent times, we have seen the same thing happen with dream symbolism. We became aware, in the years when psychology was in its infancy, that dreams had some importance. But just as the Greeks persuaded themselves that their myths were merely elaborations of rational or "normal" history, so some of the pioneers of psychology came to the conclusion that dreams did not mean what they appeared to mean. The images or symbols that they presented were dismissed as bizarre forms in which repressed contents of the psyche appeared to the conscious mind. It thus came to be taken for granted that a dream meant something other than its obvious statement.

I have already described my disagreement with this idea—a disagreement that led me to study the form as well as the content of dreams. Why should they mean something different from their contents? Is there anything in nature that is other than it is? The dream is a normal and natural phenomenon, and it does not mean something it is not. The Talmud even says: "The dream is its own interpretation." The confusion arises because the dream's contents are symbolic and thus have more than one meaning. The symbols point in different directions from those we apprehend with the conscious mind; and therefore they relate to something either unconscious or at least not entirely conscious.

Above, a child's drawing of a tree (with the sun above it). A tree is one of the best examples of a motif that often appears in dreams (and elsewhere) and that can have an incredible variety of meanings. It might symbolize evolution, physical growth, or psychological maturation; it might symbolize sacrifice or death (Christ's crucifixion on the tree); it might be a phallic symbol; it might be a great deal more. And such other common dream motifs as the cross (right) or the *lingam* (far right) can also have a vast array of symbolic meanings.

To the scientific mind, such phenomena as symbolic ideas are a nuisance because they cannot be formulated in a way that is satisfactory to intellect and logic. They are by no means the only case of this kind in psychology. The trouble begins with the phenomenon of "affect" or emotion, which evades all the attempts of the psychologist to pin it down with a final definition. The cause of the difficulty is the same in both cases—the intervention of the unconscious.

I know enough of the scientific point of view to understand that it is most annoying to have to deal with facts that cannot be completely or adequately grasped. The trouble with these phenomena is that the facts are undeniable and yet cannot be formulated in intellectual terms. For this one would have to be able to comprehend life itself, for it is life that produces emotions and symbolic ideas.

The academic psychologist is perfectly free to dismiss the phenomenon of emotion or the concept of the unconscious (or both) from his consideration. Yet they remain facts to which the medical psychologist at least has to pay due attention; for emotional conflicts and the intervention of the unconscious are the classical features of his science. If he treats a patient at all, he comes up against these irrationalities as hard facts, irrespective of his ability to formulate them in intellectual terms. It is, therefore, quite natural that people who have not had the medical psychologist's experience find it difficult to follow what happens when psychology ceases to be a tranquil pursuit for the scientist in his laboratory and becomes an active part of the adventure of real life. Target practice on a shooting range is far from the battlefield; the doctor has to deal with casualties in a genuine war. He must concern himself with psychic realities, even if he cannot embody them in scientific definitions. That is why no textbook can teach psychology; one learns only by actual experience.

We can see this point clearly when we examine certain well-known symbols:

The cross in the Christian religion, for instance, is a meaningful symbol that expresses a multitude of aspects, ideas, and emotions; but a cross after a name on a list simply indicates that the individual is dead. The phallus functions as an all-embracing symbol in the Hindu religion, but if a street urchin draws one on a wall, it just reflects an interest in his penis. Because infantile and adolescent fantasies often continue far into adult life, many dreams occur in which there are unmistakable sexual allusions. It would be absurd to under-

stand them as anything else. But when a mason speaks of monks and nuns to be laid upon each other, or an electrician of male plugs and female sockets, it would be ludicrous to suppose that he is indulging in glowing adolescent fantasies. He is simply using colorful descriptive names for his materials. When an educated Hindu talks to you about the lingam (the phallus that represents the god Siva in Hindu mythology), you will hear things we Westerners would never connect with the penis. The lingam is certainly not an obscene allusion; nor is the cross merely a sign of death. Much depends upon the maturity of the dreamer who produces such an image.

The interpretation of dreams and symbols demands intelligence. It cannot be turned into a mechanical system and then crammed into unimaginative brains. It demands both an increasing knowledge of the dreamer's individuality and an increasing self-awareness on the part of the interpreter. No experienced worker in this field will deny that there are rules of thumb that can prove helpful, but they must be applied with prudence and intelligence. One may follow all the right rules and yet get bogged down in the most appalling nonsense, simply by overlooking a seemingly unimportant detail that a better intelligence would not have missed. Even a man of high intellect can go badly astray for lack of intuition or feeling.

When we attempt to understand symbols, we are not only confronted with the symbol itself, but we are brought up against the wholeness of the symbol-producing individual. This includes a study of his cultural background, and in the process one fills in many gaps in one's own education. I have made it a rule myself to consider every case as an entirely new proposition about which I do not even know the ABC. Routine responses may be practical and useful while one is dealing with the surface, but as soon as one gets in touch with the vital problems, life itself takes over and even the most brilliant theoretical premises become ineffectual words.

Imagination and intuition are vital to our understanding. And though the usual popular opinion is that they are chiefly valuable to poets and artists (that in "sensible" matters one should mistrust them), they are in fact equally vital in all the higher grades of science. Here they play an increasingly important role, which supplements that of the "rational" intellect and its application to a specific problem. Even physics, the strictest of all applied sciences, depends to an astonishing degree upon intuition, which works by way of the unconscious (although it is possible to demonstrate afterward the logical procedures that could have led one to the same result as intuition).

Intuition is almost indispensable in the interpretation of symbols, and it can often ensure that they are immediately understood by the dreamer. But while such a lucky hunch may be subjectively convincing, it can also be rather dangerous. It can so easily lead to a false feeling of security. It may, for instance, seduce both the interpreter and the dreamer into continuing a cosy and relatively easy relation, which may end in a sort of shared dream. The safe basis of real intellectual knowledge and moral understanding gets lost if one is content with the vague satisfaction of having understood by "hunch." One can explain and know only if one has reduced intuitions to an exact knowledge of facts and their logical connections.

An honest investigator will have to admit that he cannot always do this, but it would be dishonest not to keep it always in mind. Even a scientist is a human being. So it is natural for him, like others, to hate the things he cannot explain. It is a common illusion to believe that what we know today is all we ever can know. Nothing is more vulnerable than scientific theory, which is an ephemeral attempt to explain facts and not an everlasting truth in itself.

Ancient mythological beings are now curiosities in museums (right). But the archetypes they expressed have not lost their power to affect men's minds. Perhaps the monsters of modern "horror" films (far right) are distorted versions of archetypes that will no longer be repressed.

The role of symbols

When the medical psychologist takes an interest in symbols, he is primarily concerned with "natural" symbols, as distinct from "cultural" symbols. The former are derived from the unconscious contents of the psyche, and they therefore represent an enormous number of variations on the essential archetypal images. In many cases they can still be traced back to their archaic roots—i.e. to ideas and images that we meet in the most ancient records and in primitive societies. The cultural symbols, on the other hand, are those that have been used to express "eternal truths," and that are still used in many religions. They have gone through many transformations and even a long process of more or less conscious development, and have thus become collective images accepted by civilized societies.

Such cultural symbols nevertheless retain much of their original numinosity or "spell." One is aware that they can evoke a deep emotional response in some individuals, and this psychic change makes them function in much the same way as prejudices. They are a factor with which the psychologist must reckon; it is folly to dismiss them because, in rational terms, they seem to be absurd or irrelevant. They are important constituents of our mental make-up and vital forces in the building up of human society; and they cannot be eradicated without serious loss. Where they are repressed or neglected, their specific energy disappears into the unconscious with unaccountable consequences. The psychic energy that appears to have been lost in this way in fact serves to revive and intensify whatever is uppermost in the unconscious—tendencies, perhaps, that have hitherto had no chance to express themselves or at least have not been allowed an uninhibited existence in our consciousness.

Such tendencies form an ever-present and potentially destructive "shadow" to our conscious mind. Even tendencies that might in some circumstances be able to exert a beneficial influence are transformed into demons when they are repressed. This is why many well-meaning people are understandably afraid of the unconscious, and incidentally of psychology.

Our times have demonstrated what it means for the gates of the underworld to be opened. Things whose enormity nobody could have imagined in the idyllic harmlessness of the first decade of our century have happened and have turned our world upside down. Ever since, the world has remained in a state of schizophrenia. Not only has civilized Germany disgorged its

terrible primitivity, but Russia is also ruled by it, and Africa has been set on fire. No wonder that the Western world feels uneasy.

Modern man does not understand how much his "rationalism" (which has destroyed his capacity to respond to numinous symbols and ideas) has put him at the mercy of the psychic "underworld." He has freed himself from "superstition" (or so he believes), but in the process he has lost his spiritual values to a positively dangerous degree. His moral and spiritual tradition has disintegrated, and he is now paying the price for this break-up in world-wide disorientation and dissociation.

Anthropologists have often described what happens to a primitive society when its spiritual values are exposed to the impact of modern civilization. Its people lose the meaning of their lives, their social organization disintegrates, and they themselves morally decay. We are now in the same condition. But we have never really understood what we have lost, for our spiritual leaders unfortunately were more interested in protecting their institutions than in understanding the mystery that symbols present. In my opinion, faith does not exclude thought (which

is man's strongest weapon), but unfortunately many believers seem to be so afraid of science (and incidentally of psychology) that they turn a blind eye to the numinous psychic powers that forever control man's fate. We have stripped all things of their mystery and numinosity; nothing is holy any longer.

In earlier ages, as instinctive concepts welled up in the mind of man, his conscious mind could no doubt integrate them into a coherent psychic pattern. But the "civilized" man is no longer able to do this. His "advanced" consciousness has deprived itself of the means by which the auxiliary contributions of the instincts and the unconscious can be assimilated. These organs of assimilation and integration were numinous symbols, held holy by common consent.

Today, for instance, we talk of "matter." We describe its physical properties. We conduct laboratory experiments to demonstrate some of its aspects. But the word "matter" remains a dry, inhuman, and purely intellectual concept, without any psychic significance for us. How different was the former image of matter—the Great Mother—that could encompass and ex-

press the profound emotional meaning of Mother Earth. In the same way, what was the spirit is now identified with intellect and thus ceases to be the Father of All. It has degenerated to the limited ego-thoughts of man; the immense emotional energy expressed in the image of "our Father" vanishes into the sand of an intellectual desert.

These two archetypal principles lie at the foundation of the contrasting systems of East and West. The masses and their leaders do not realize, however, that there is no substantial difference between calling the world principle male and a father (spirit), as the West does, or female and a mother (matter), as the Communists do. Essentially, we know as little of the one as of the other. In earlier times, these principles were worshiped in all sorts of rituals, which at least showed the psychic significance they held for man. But now they have become mere abstract concepts.

As scientific understanding has grown, so our world has become dehumanized. Man feels himself isolated in the cosmos, because he is no longer involved in nature and has lost his emotional "unconscious identity" with natural phenomena. These have slowly lost their symbolic implications. Thunder is no longer the voice of an angry god, nor is lightning his avenging missile. No river contains a spirit, no tree is the life principle of a man, no snake the embodiment of wisdom, no mountain cave the home of a great demon. No voices now speak to man from stones, plants, and animals, nor does he speak to them believing they can hear. His contact with nature has gone, and with it has gone the profound emotional energy that this symbolic connection supplied.

Repressed unconscious contents can erupt destructively in the form of negative emotions—as in World War II. Far left, Jewish prisoners in Warsaw after the 1943 uprising; left, footwear of the dead stacked at Auschwitz.

Right, Australian aborigines who have disintegrated since they lost their religious beliefs through contact with civilization. This tribe now numbers only a few hundred.

This enormous loss is compensated for by the symbols of our dreams. They bring up our original nature—its instincts and peculiar thinking. Unfortunately, however, they express their contents in the language of nature, which is strange and incomprehensible to us. It therefore confronts us with the task of translating it into the rational words and concepts of modern speech, which has liberated itself from its primitive encumbrances—notably from its mystical participation with the things it describes. Nowadays, when we talk of ghosts and other numinous figures, we are no longer conjuring them up. The power as well as the glory is drained out of such once-potent words. We have ceased to believe in magic formulas; not many taboos and similar restrictions are left; and our world seems to be disinfected of all such "superstitious" numina as "witches, warlocks, and worricows," to say nothing of werewolves, vampires, bush souls, and all the other bizarre beings that populated the primeval forest.

To be more accurate, the surface of our world seems to be cleansed of all superstitious and irrational elements. Whether, however, the real inner human world (not our wish-fulfilling

95

fiction about it) is also freed from primitivity is another question. Is the number 13 not still taboo for many people? Are there not still many individuals possessed by irrational prejudices, projections, and childish illusions? A realistic picture of the human mind reveals many such primitive traits and survivals, which are still playing their roles just as if nothing had happened during the last 500 years.

It is essential to appreciate this point. Modern man is in fact a curious mixture of characteristics acquired over the long ages of his mental development. This mixed-up being is the man and his symbols that we have to deal with, and we must scrutinize his mental products very carefully indeed. Skepticism and scientific conviction exist in him side by side with old-fashioned prejudices, outdated habits of thought and feeling, obstinate misinterpretations, and blind ignorance.

Such are the contemporary human beings who produce the symbols we psychologists investigate. In order to explain these symbols and their meaning, it is vital to learn whether their representations are related to purely personal experience, or whether they have been chosen by a dream for its particular purpose from a store of general conscious knowledge.

Take, for instance, a dream in which the number 13 occurs. The question is whether the dreamer himself habitually believes in the unlucky quality of the number, or whether the dream merely alludes to people who still indulge in such superstitions. The answer makes a great difference to the interpretation. In the former case, you have to reckon with the fact that the individual is still under the spell of the unlucky 13, and therefore will feel most uncomfortable in Room 13 in a hotel or sitting at a table with 13 people. In the latter case, 13 may not mean any more than a discourteous or abusive remark. The "superstitious" dreamer still feels the "spell" of 13; the more "rational" dreamer has stripped 13 of its original emotional overtones.

This argument illustrates the way in which archetypes appear in practical experience: They are, at the same time, both images and emotions. One can speak of an archetype only when these two aspects are simultaneous. When there is merely the image, then there is simply a word-picture of little consequence. But by being charged with emotion, the image gains numinosity (or psychic energy); it becomes dynamic, and consequences of some kind must flow from it.

I am aware that it is difficult to grasp this concept, because I am trying to use words to describe something whose very nature makes it incapable of precise definition. But since so many people have chosen to treat archetypes as if they were part of a mechanical system that can be learned by rote, it is essential to insist that they are not mere names, or even philosophical concepts. They are pieces of life itself—images that are integrally connected to the living individual by the bridge of the emotions. That is why it is impossible to give an arbitrary (or universal) interpretation of any archetype. It must be explained in the manner indicated by the whole life-situation of the particular individual to whom it relates.

Thus, in the case of a devout Christian, the symbol of the cross can be interpreted only in its Christian context—unless the dream produces a very strong reason to look beyond it. Even then, the specific Christian meaning should be kept in mind. But one cannot say that, at all times and in all circumstances, the symbol of the cross has the same meaning. If that were so, it would be stripped of its numinosity, lose its vitality, and become a mere word.

Those who do not realize the special feeling tone of the archetype end with nothing more than a jumble of mythological concepts, which can be strung together to show that everything means anything—or nothing at all. All the corpses in the world are chemically identical, but living individuals are not. Archetypes come to life only when one patiently tries to discover why and in what fashion they are meaningful to a living individual.

The mere use of words is futile when you do not know what they stand for. This is particularly true in psychology, where we speak of archetypes such as the anima and animus, the wise

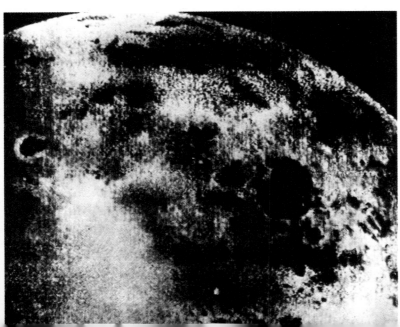

The ancient Chinese connected the moon with the goddess Kwan-Yin (pictured above). Other societies have personified the moon as a divinity. And though modern space flight has proved that the moon is only a cratered ball of dirt (left), we have retained something of the archetypal attitude in our familiar association of the moon with love and romance.

In a child's unconscious we can see the power (and universality) of archetypal symbols. A seven-year-old's painting (left)—a huge sun driving away black birds, demons of the night—has the flavor of a true myth. Children at play (right) spontaneously dance in as natural a form of self-expression as the ceremonial dances of primitives. Ancient folklore still exists in children's "ritual" beliefs: For instance, children all over Britain (and elsewhere) believe it is lucky to see a white horse—which is a well-known symbol of life. A Celtic goddess of creativity, Epona, shown (far right) riding a horse, was often personified as a white mare.

man, the Great Mother, and so on. You can know all about the saints, sages, prophets, and other godly men, and all the great mothers of the world. But if they are mere images whose numinosity you have never experienced, it will be as if you were talking in a dream, for you will not know what you are talking about. The mere words you use will be empty and valueless. They gain life and meaning only when you try to take into account their numinosity—i.e. their relationship to the living individual. Only then do you begin to understand that their names mean very little, whereas the way they are *related* to you is all-important.

The symbol-producing function of our dreams is thus an attempt to bring the original mind of man into "advanced" or differentiated consciousness, where it has never been before and where, therefore, it has never been subjected to critical self-reflection. For, in ages long past, that original mind was the whole of man's personality. As he developed consciousness, so his conscious mind lost contact with some of that primitive psychic energy. And the conscious mind has never known that original mind; for it was discarded in the process of evolving the very differentiated consciousness that alone could be aware of it.

Yet it seems that what we call the unconscious has preserved primitive characteristics that formed part of the original mind. It is to these characteristics that the symbols of dreams constantly refer, as if the unconscious sought to bring back all the old things from which the mind freed itself as it evolved—illusions, fantasies, archaic thought forms, fundamental instincts, and so on.

This is what explains the resistance, even fear, that people often experience in approaching unconscious matters. These relict contents are not merely neutral or indifferent. On the contrary, they are so highly charged that they are often more than merely uncomfortable. They can cause real fear. The more they are repressed, the more they spread through the whole personality in the form of a neurosis.

It is this psychic energy that gives them such vital importance. It is just as if a man who has lived through a period of unconsciousness should suddenly realize that there is a gap in his memory—that important events seem to have taken place that he cannot remember. In so far as he assumes that the psyche is an exclusively personal affair (and this is the usual assumption), he will try to retrieve the apparently lost infantile memories. But the gaps in his childhood memory are merely the symptoms of a much greater loss—the loss of the primitive psyche.

As the evolution of the embryonic body repeats its prehistory, so the mind also develops through a series of prehistoric stages. The main

task of dreams is to bring back a sort of "recollection" of the prehistoric, as well as the infantile world, right down to the level of the most primitive instincts. Such recollections can have a remarkably healing effect in certain cases, as Freud saw long ago. This observation confirms the view that an infantile memory gap (a so-called amnesia) represents a positive loss and its recovery can bring a positive increase in life and well-being.

Because a child is physically small and its conscious thoughts are scarce and simple, we do not realize the far-reaching complications of the infantile mind that are based on its original identity with the prehistoric psyche. That "original mind" is just as much present and still functioning in the child as the evolutionary stages of mankind are in its embryonic body. If the reader remembers what I said earlier about the remarkable dreams of the child who made a present of her dreams to her father, he will get a good idea of what I mean.

In infantile amnesia, one finds strange mythological fragments that also often appear in later psychoses. Images of this kind are highly numinous and therefore very important. If such recollections reappear in adult life, they may in some cases cause profound psychological disturbance, while in other people they can produce miracles of healing or religious conversions. Often they bring back a piece of life,

missing for a long time, that gives purpose to and thus enriches human life.

The recollection of infantile memories and the reproduction of archetypal ways of psychic behavior can create a wider horizon and a greater extension of consciousness—on condition that one succeeds in assimilating and integrating in the conscious mind the lost and regained contents. Since they are not neutral, their assimilation will modify the personality, just as they themselves will have to undergo certain alterations. In this part of what is called "the individuation process" (which Dr. M.-L. von Franz describes in a later section of this book), the interpretation of symbols plays an important practical role. For the symbols are natural attempts to reconcile and unite opposites within the psyche.

Naturally, just seeing and then brushing aside the symbols would have no such effect and would merely re-establish the old neurotic condition and destroy the attempt at a synthesis. But, unfortunately, those rare people who do not deny the very existence of the archetypes almost invariably treat them as mere words and forget their living reality. When their numinosity has thus (illegitimately) been banished, the process of limitless substitution begins—in other words, one glides easily from archetype to archetype, with everything meaning everything. It is true enough that the forms of archetypes are to a considerable extent exchangeable. But their numinosity is and remains a fact, and represents the *value* of an archetypal event.

This emotional value must be kept in mind and allowed for throughout the whole intellectual process of dream interpretation. It is only too easy to lose this value, because thinking and feeling are so diametrically opposed that thinking almost automatically throws out feeling values and vice versa. Psychology is the only science that has to take the factor of value (i.e. feeling) into account, because it is the link between physical events and life. Psychology is often accused of not being scientific on this account; but its critics fail to understand the scientific and practical necessity of giving due consideration to feeling.

Healing the split

Our intellect has created a new world that dominates nature, and has populated it with monstrous machines. The latter are so indubitably useful that we cannot see even a possibility of getting rid of them or our subservience to them. Man is bound to follow the adventurous promptings of his scientific and inventive mind and to admire himself for his splendid achievements. At the same time, his genius shows the uncanny tendency to invent things that become more and more dangerous, because they represent better and better means for wholesale suicide.

In view of the rapidly increasing avalanche of world population, man has already begun to seek ways and means of keeping the rising flood at bay. But nature may anticipate all our attempts by turning against man his own creative mind. The H-bomb, for instance, would put an effective stop to overpopulation. In spite of our proud domination of nature, we are still her victims, for we have not even learned to control our own nature. Slowly but, it appears, inevitably, we are courting disaster.

There are no longer any gods whom we can invoke to help us. The great religions of the world suffer from increasing anemia, because the helpful numina have fled from the woods, rivers, and mountains, and from animals, and the god-men have disappeared underground into the unconscious. There we fool ourselves that they lead an ignominious existence among the relics of our past. Our present lives are dominated by the goddess Reason, who is our greatest and most tragic illusion. By the aid of reason, so we assure ourselves, we have "conquered nature."

But this is a mere slogan, for the so-called conquest of nature overwhelms us with the natural fact of overpopulation and adds to our troubles by our psychological incapacity to make the necessary political arrangements. It remains quite natural for men to quarrel and to struggle for superiority over one another. How then have we "conquered nature"?

As any change must begin somewhere, it is the single individual who will experience it and carry it through. The change must indeed begin with an individual; it might be any one of us. Nobody can afford to look around and to wait for somebody else to do what he is loath to do himself. But since nobody seems to know what to do, it might be worth while for each of us to ask himself whether by any chance his or her unconscious may know something that will help us. Certainly the conscious mind seems unable to do anything useful in this respect. Man today is painfully aware of the fact that neither his great religions nor his various philosophies seem to provide him with those powerful animating ideas that would give him the security he needs in face of the present condition of the world.

I know what the Buddhists would say: Things would go right if people would only follow the "noble eightfold path" of the *Dharma* (doctrine, law) and had true insight into the Self. The Christian tells us that if only people had faith in God, we should have a better world. The rationalist insists that if people were intelligent and reasonable, all our problems would be manageable. The trouble is that none of them manages to solve these problems himself.

Above left, the 20th century's greatest city — New York. Below, the end of another city — Hiroshima, 1945. Though man may seem to have gained ascendance over nature, Jung always pointed out that man has not yet gained control over his *own* nature.

Christians often ask why God does not speak to them, as he is believed to have done in former days. When I hear such questions, it always makes me think of the rabbi who was asked how it could be that God often showed himself to people in the olden days whereas nowadays nobody ever sees him. The rabbi replied: "Nowadays there is no longer anybody who can bow low enough."

This answer hits the nail on the head. We are so captivated by and entangled in our subjective consciousness that we have forgotten the age-old fact that God speaks chiefly through dreams and visions. The Buddhist discards the world of unconscious fantasies as useless illusions; the Christian puts his Church and his Bible between himself and his unconscious; and the rational intellectual does not yet know that his consciousness is not his total psyche. This ignorance persists today in spite of the fact that for more than 70 years the unconscious has been a basic scientific concept that is indispensable to any serious psychological investigation.

We can no longer afford to be so God-Almighty-like as to set ourselves up as judges of the merits or demerits of natural phenomena. We do not base our botany upon the old-fashioned division into useful and useless plants, or our zoology upon the naïve distinction between harmless and dangerous animals. But we still complacently assume that consciousness is sense and the unconscious is nonsense. In science such an assumption would be laughed out of court. Do microbes, for instance, make sense or nonsense?

Whatever the unconscious may be, it is a natural phenomenon producing symbols that prove to be meaningful. We cannot expect someone who has never looked through a microscope to be an authority on microbes; in the same way, no one who has not made a serious study of natural symbols can be considered a competent judge in this matter. But the general undervaluation of the human soul is so great that neither the great religions nor the philosophies nor scientific rationalism have been willing to look at it twice.

In spite of the fact that the Catholic Church admits the occurrence of *somnia a Deo missa* (dreams sent by God), most of its thinkers make no serious attempt to understand dreams. I doubt whether there is a Protestant treatise or doctrine that would stoop so low as to admit the possibility that the *vox Dei* might be perceived in a dream. But if a theologian really believes in God, by what authority does he suggest that God is unable to speak through dreams?

I have spent more than half a century in investigating natural symbols, and I have come to the conclusion that dreams and their symbols are not stupid and meaningless. On the contrary, dreams provide the most interesting information for those who take the trouble to understand their symbols. The results, it is true, have little to do with such worldly concerns as buying and selling. But the meaning of life is not exhaustively explained by one's business life, nor is the deep desire of the human heart answered by a bank account.

In a period of human history when all available energy is spent in the investigation of nature, very little attention is paid to the essence of man, which is his psyche, although many researches are made into its conscious functions. But the really complex and unfamiliar part of the mind, from which symbols are produced, is still virtually unexplored. It seems almost incredible that though we receive signals from it every night, deciphering these communications seems too tedious for any but a very few people to be bothered with it. Man's greatest instrument, his psyche, is little thought of, and it is often directly mistrusted and despised. "It's only psychological" too often means: It is nothing.

Where, exactly, does this immense prejudice come from? We have obviously been so busy with the question of what we think that we entirely forget to ask what the unconscious psyche thinks about us. The ideas of Sigmund Freud confirmed for most people the existing contempt for the psyche. Before him it had been merely overlooked and neglected; it has now become a dump for moral refuse.

This modern standpoint is surely one-sided and unjust. It does not even accord with the known facts. Our actual knowledge of the unconscious shows that it is a natural phenomenon and that, like Nature herself, it is at least *neutral*. It contains all aspects of human nature —light and dark, beautiful and ugly, good and evil, profound and silly. The study of individual, as well as of collective, symbolism is an enormous task, and one that has not yet been mastered. But a beginning has been made at last. The early results are encouraging, and they seem to indicate an answer to many so far unanswered questions of present-day mankind.

Above, Rembrandt's *Philosopher with an Open Book* (1633). The inward-looking old man provides an image of Jung's belief that each of us must explore his own unconscious. The unconscious must not be ignored; it is as natural, as limitless, and as powerful as the stars.

2 Ancient myths and modern man

Joseph L. Henderson

A ceremonial mask from the island of New Ireland (New Guinea)

The eternal symbols

The ancient history of man is being meaningfully rediscovered today in the symbolic images and myths that have survived ancient man. As archaeologists dig deep into the past, it is less the events of historical time that we learn to treasure than the statues, designs, temples, and languages that tell of old beliefs. Other symbols are revealed to us by the philologists and religious historians, who can translate these beliefs into intelligible modern concepts. These in turn are brought to life by the cultural anthropologists. They can show that the same symbolic patterns can be found in the rituals or myths of small tribal societies still existing, unchanged for centuries, on the outskirts of civilization.

All such researches have done much to correct the one-sided attitude of those modern men who maintain that such symbols belong to the peoples of antiquity or to "backward" modern tribes and are therefore irrelevant to the complexities of modern life. In London or New York we may dismiss the fertility rites of neolithic man as archaic superstition. If anyone claims to have seen a vision or heard voices, he is not treated as a saint or as an oracle. It is said he is mentally disturbed. We read the myths of the ancient Greeks or the folk stories of American Indians, but we fail to see any connection between them and our attitudes to the "heroes" or dramatic events of today.

Yet the connections are there. And the symbols that represent them have not lost their relevance for mankind.

One of the main contributions of our time to the understanding and revaluing of such eternal symbols has been made by Dr. Jung's School of Analytical Psychology. It has helped to break down the arbitrary distinction between primitive man, to whom symbols seem a natural part of everyday life, and modern man, for whom symbols are apparently meaningless and irrelevant.

As Dr. Jung has pointed out earlier in this book, the human mind has its own history and the psyche retains traces left from previous stages of its development. More than this, the contents of the unconscious exert a formative influence on the psyche. Consciously we

may ignore them, but unconsciously we respond to them, and to the symbolic forms—including dreams—in which they express themselves.

The individual may feel that his dreams are spontaneous and disconnected. But over a long period of time the analyst can observe a series of dream images and note that they have a meaningful pattern; and by understanding this his patient may eventually acquire a new attitude to life. Some of the symbols in such dreams derive from what Dr. Jung has called "the collective unconscious"—that is, the part of the psyche that retains and transmits the common psychological inheritance of mankind. These symbols are so ancient and unfamiliar to modern man that he cannot directly understand or assimilate them.

It is here that the analyst can help. Possibly the patient must be freed from the encumbrance of symbols that have grown stale and inappropriate. Or possibly he must be assisted to discover the abiding value of an old symbol that, far from being dead, is seeking to be reborn in modern form.

Before the analyst can effectively explore the meaning of symbols with a patient, he must himself acquire a wider knowledge of their origins and significance. For the analogies between ancient myths and the stories that appear in the dreams of modern patients are neither trivial nor accidental. They exist because the unconscious mind of modern man preserves the symbol-making capacity that once found expression in the beliefs and rituals of the primitive. And that capacity still plays a role of vital psychic importance. In more ways than we realize, we are dependent on the messages that are carried by such symbols, and both our attitudes and our behavior are profoundly influenced by them.

In wartime, for instance, one finds increased interest in the works of Homer, Shakespeare, and Tolstoi, and we read with a new understanding those passages that give war its enduring (or "archetypal") meaning. They evoke a response from us that is much more profound than it could be from someone who has never known the intense emotional experience of war. The battles on the plains of Troy were utterly unlike the fighting at Agincourt or Borodino, yet the great writers are able to transcend the differences of time and place and to express themes that are universal. We respond because these themes are fundamentally symbolic.

A more striking example should be familiar to anyone who has grown up in a Christian society. At Christmas we may express our inner feeling for the mythological birth of a semi-

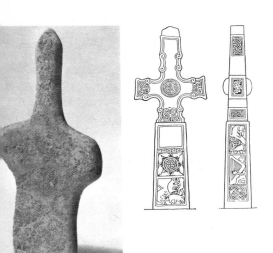

Far left, a symbolic ceremony of antiquity in 20th-century form: The American astronaut John Glenn in a Washington parade after his orbit of the earth in 1962—like a hero of old, after a victory, returning home in a triumphal procession.

Center left, a cross-like sculpture of a Greek fertility goddess (c. 2500 B.C.). Left, two views of a 12th-century Scots stone cross that retains some pagan femaleness: the "breasts" at the crossbar. Right, another age-old archetype reborn in a new guise: a Russian poster for an "atheistic" festival at Easter, to replace the Christian festival—just as the Christian Easter was superimposed on earlier pagan solstice rites.

divine child, even though we may not believe in the doctrine of the virgin birth of Christ or have any kind of conscious religious faith. Unknowingly, we have fallen in with the symbolism of rebirth. This is a relic of an immensely older solstice festival, which carries the hope that the fading winter landscape of the northern hemisphere will be renewed. For all our sophistication we find satisfaction in this symbolic festival, just as we join with our children at Easter in the pleasant ritual of Easter eggs and Easter rabbits.

But do we understand what we do, or see the connection between the story of Christ's birth, death, and resurrection and the folk symbolism of Easter? Usually we do not even care to consider such things intellectually.

Yet they complement each other. Christ's crucifixion on Good Friday seems at first sight to belong to the same pattern of fertility symbolism that one finds in the rituals of such other "saviors" as Osiris, Tammuz, and Orpheus. They, too, were of divine or semi-divine birth, they flourished, were killed, and were reborn. They belonged, in fact, to cyclic religions in which the death and rebirth of the god-king was an eternally recurring myth.

But the resurrection of Christ on Easter Sunday is much less satisfying from a ritual point of view than is the symbolism of the cyclic religions. For Christ ascends to sit at the right hand of God the Father: His resurrection occurs once and for all.

It is this finality of the Christian concept of the resurrection (the Christian idea of the Last Judgment has a similar "closed" theme) that distinguishes Christianity from other god-king myths. It happened once, and the ritual merely commemorates it. But this sense of finality is probably one reason why early Christians, still influenced by pre-Christian traditions, felt that Christianity needed to be supplemented by some elements of an older fertility ritual. They needed the recurring promise of rebirth; and that is what is symbolized by the egg and the rabbit of Easter.

I have taken two quite different examples to show how modern man continues to respond to profound psychic influences of a kind that, consciously, he dismisses as little more than the folk tales of superstitious and uneducated peoples. But it is necessary to go much further than this. The more closely one looks at the history of symbolism, and at the role that sym-

Left, a 13th-century Japanese scroll painting of the destruction of a city; below, similarly dominated by flame and smoke, St. Paul's Cathedral, London, during an air raid in World War II. Methods of warfare have changed over the ages, but the emotional impact of war is timeless and archetypal.

bols have played in the life of many different cultures, the more one understands that there is also a re-creative meaning in these symbols.

Some symbols relate to childhood and the transition to adolescence, others to maturity, and others again to the experience of old age, when man is preparing for his inevitable death. Dr. Jung has described how the dreams of a girl of eight contained the symbols one normally associates with old age. Her dreams presented aspects of initiation into life as belonging to the same archetypal pattern as initiation into death. This progression of symbolic ideas may take place, therefore, within the unconscious mind of modern man just as it took place in the rituals of ancient societies.

This crucial link between archaic or primitive myths and the symbols produced by the unconscious is of immense practical importance to the analyst. It enables him to identify and to interpret these symbols in a context that gives them historical perspective as well as psychological meaning. I shall now take some of the more important myths of antiquity and show how—and to what purpose—they are analogous to the symbolic material that we encounter in our dreams.

Top left, Christ's nativity; center, his crucifixion; bottom, his ascension. His birth, death, and rebirth follows the pattern of many ancient hero myths—a pattern originally based on seasonal fertility rites like those probably held 3000 years ago at England's Stonehenge (seen below at dawn at the summer solstice).

Heroes and hero makers

The myth of the hero is the most common and the best-known myth in the world. We find it in the classical mythology of Greece and Rome, in the Middle Ages, in the Far East, and among contemporary primitive tribes. It also appears in our dreams. It has an obvious dramatic appeal, and a less obvious, but nonetheless profound, psychological importance.

These hero myths vary enormously in detail, but the more closely one examines them the more one sees that structurally they are very similar. They have, that is to say, a universal pattern, even though they were developed by groups or individuals without any direct cultural contact with each other—by, for instance, tribes of Africans or North American Indians, or the Greeks, or the Incas of Peru. Over and over again one hears a tale describing a hero's miraculous but humble birth, his early proof of superhuman strength, his rapid rise to prominence or power, his triumphant struggle with the forces of evil, his fallibility to the sin of pride (*hybris*), and his fall through betrayal or a "heroic" sacrifice that ends in his death.

I shall later explain in more detail why I believe that this pattern has psychological meaning both for the individual, who is endeavoring to discover and assert his personality, and for a whole society, which has an equal need to establish its collective identity. But another important characteristic of the hero myth provides a clue. In many of these stories the early weakness of the hero is balanced by the appearance of strong "tutelary" figures—or guardians—who enable him to perform the superhuman tasks that he cannot accomplish unaided. Among the Greek heroes, Theseus had Poseidon, god of the sea, as his deity; Perseus had Athena; Achilles had Cheiron, the wise centaur, as his tutor.

These godlike figures are in fact symbolic representatives of the whole psyche, the larger

The hero's early proof of strength occurs in most hero myths. Below, the infant Hercules killing two serpents. Top right, the young King Arthur, alone able to draw a magic sword from a stone. Bottom right, America's Davy Crockett, who killed a bear when he was three.

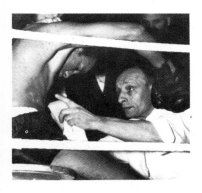

Above, two examples of the hero's betrayal: the biblical hero Samson (top), betrayed by Delilah; and the Persian hero Rustam, led into a trap by a man he trusted. Below, a modern result of *hybris* (over-confidence): German prisoners in Stalingrad, 1941, after Hitler invaded Russia in winter.

Above, three examples of the tutelary or guardian figure that accompanies the archetypal hero. Top, from Greek myth, the centaur Cheiron giving instruction to the youthful Achilles. Center, King Arthur's guardian, the magician Merlin (holding a scroll). Bottom, an instance from modern life: the trainer on whose knowledge and experience a professional boxer often depends.

Most heroes must face and overcome various monsters and forces of evil. Top, the Scandinavian hero Sigurd (lower right of picture) slays the serpent Fafnir. Center, the ancient Babylonian epic hero Gilgamesh battling with a lion. Bottom, the modern American comic-strip hero Superman, whose one-man war against crime often requires him to rescue pretty girls.

and more comprehensive identity that supplies the strength that the personal ego lacks. Their special role suggests that the essential function of the heroic myth is the development of the individual's ego-consciousness—his awareness of his own strengths and weaknesses—in a manner that will equip him for the arduous tasks with which life confronts him. Once the individual has passed his initial test and can enter the mature phase of life, the hero myth loses its relevance. The hero's symbolic death becomes, as it were, the achievement of that maturity.

I have so far been referring to the complete hero myth, in which the whole cycle from birth to death is elaborately described. But it is essential to recognize that at each of the stages in this cycle there are special forms of the hero story that apply to the particular point reached by the individual in the development of his ego-consciousness, and to the specific problem confronting him at a given moment. That is to say, the image of the hero evolves in a manner that reflects each stage of the evolution of the human personality.

This concept can be more easily understood if I present it in what amounts to a diagram. I take this example from the obscure North American tribe of Winnebago Indians, because it sets out quite clearly four distinct stages in the evolution of the hero. In these stories (which Dr. Paul Radin published in 1948 under the title *Hero Cycles of the Winnebago*) we can see the definite progression from the most primitive to the most sophisticated concept of the hero. This progression is characteristic of other hero cycles. Though the symbolic figures in them naturally have different names, their roles are similar, and we shall understand them better once we have grasped the point made by this example.

Dr. Radin noted four distinct cycles in the evolution of the hero myth. He named them the *Trickster* cycle, the *Hare* cycle, the *Red Horn* cycle, and the *Twin* cycle. He correctly perceived the psychology of this evolution when he said: "It represents our efforts to deal with the problem of growing up, aided by the illusion of an eternal fiction."

The Trickster cycle corresponds to the earliest and least developed period of life. Trickster is a figure whose physical appetites dominate his behavior; he has the mentality of an infant. Lacking any purpose beyond the gratification of his primary needs, he is cruel, cynical, and unfeeling. (Our stories of Brer Rabbit or Reynard the Fox preserve the essentials of the Trickster myth.) This figure, which at the outset assumes the form of an animal, passes from one mischievous exploit to another. But, as he does so, a change comes over him. At the end of his rogue's progress he is beginning to take on the physical likeness of a grown man.

The next figure is Hare. He also, like Trickster (whose animal traits are represented among some American Indians by a coyote), first appears in animal form. He has not yet attained mature human stature, but all the same he appears as the founder of human culture—the Transformer. The Winnebago believe that, in giving them their famous Medicine Rite, he became their savior as well as their culture-hero. This myth was so powerful, Dr. Radin tells us, that the members of the Peyote Rite were reluctant to give up Hare when Christianity began to penetrate the tribe. He became merged with the figure of Christ, and some of them argued that they had no need of Christ since they already had Hare. This archetypal figure represents a distinct advance on Trickster: One can see that he is becoming a socialized being, correcting the instinctual and infantile urges found in the Trickster cycle.

Red Horn, the third of this series of hero figures, is an ambiguous person, said to be the youngest of 10 brothers. He meets the requirements of an archetypal hero by passing such tests as winning a race and by proving himself in battle. His superhuman power is shown by his ability to defeat giants by guile (in a game of dice) or by strength (in a wrestling match). He has a powerful companion in the form of a thunderbird called "Storms-as-he-walks," whose strength compensates for whatever weakness

Red Horn may display. With Red Horn we have reached the world of man, though an archaic world, in which the aid of superhuman powers or tutelary gods is needed to ensure man's victory over the evil forces that beset him. Toward the end of the story the hero-god departs, leaving Red Horn and his sons on earth. The danger to man's happiness and security now comes from man himself.

This basic theme (which is repeated in the last cycle, that of the Twins) raises, in effect, the vital question: How long can human beings be successful without falling victims to their own pride or, in mythological terms, to the jealousy of the gods?

Though the Twins are said to be the sons of the Sun, they are essentially human and together constitute a single person. Originally united in the mother's womb, they were forced apart at birth. Yet they belong together, and it is necessary—though exceedingly difficult—to reunite them. In these two children we see the two sides of man's nature. One of them, Flesh, is acquiescent, mild, and without initiative; the other, Stump, is dynamic and rebellious. In some of the stories of the Twin Heroes these attitudes are refined to the point where one figure represents the introvert, whose main strength lies in his powers of reflection, and the other is an extravert, a man of action who can accomplish great deeds.

"Trickster": the first, rudimentary stage in the development of the hero myth, in which the hero is instinctual, uninhibited, and often childish. Far left, the 16th-century Chinese epic hero Monkey, shown (in a modern Peking opera) tricking a river king into giving up a magic staff. Left, on a sixth-century B.C. jar, the infant Hermes in his cradle after having stolen Apollo's cattle. Right, the trouble-making Norse god Loki (a 19th-century sculpture). Far right, Charlie Chaplin creating a disturbance in the 1936 film *Modern Times*—a 20th-century trickster.

For a long time these two heroes are invincible: Whether they are presented as two separate figures or as two-in-one, they carry all before them. Yet, like the warrior gods of Navaho Indian mythology, they eventually sicken from the abuse of their own power. There are no monsters left in heaven or on earth for them to overcome, and their consequent wild behavior brings retribution in its train. The Winnebago say that nothing, in the end, was safe from them—not even the supports on which the world rests. When the Twins killed one of the four animals that upheld the earth, they had overstepped all limits, and the time had come to put a stop to their career. The punishment they deserved was death.

Thus, in both the Red Horn cycle and that of the Twins, we see the theme of sacrifice or death of the hero as a necessary cure for *hybris*, the pride that has over-reached itself. In the primitive societies whose levels of culture correspond to the Red Horn cycle, it appears that this danger may have been forestalled by the institution of propitiatory human sacrifice—a theme that has immense symbolic importance and recurs continually in human history. The Winnebago, like the Iroquois and a few Algonquin tribes, probably ate human flesh as a totemic ritual that could tame their individualistic and destructive impulses.

In the examples of the hero's betrayal or defeat that occur in European mythology, the theme of ritual sacrifice is more specifically employed as a punishment for *hybris*. But the Winnebago, like the Navaho, do not go so far. Though the Twins erred, and though the punishment should have been death, they themselves became so frightened by their irresponsible power that they consented to live in a state of permanent rest: The conflicting sides of human nature were again in equilibrium.

I have given this description of the four types of hero at some length because it provides a clear demonstration of the pattern that occurs both in the historic myths and in the hero dreams of contemporary man. With this in mind we can examine the following dream of a middle-aged patient. The interpretation of this dream shows how the analytical psychologist can, from his knowledge of mythology, help his patient find an answer to what might otherwise seem an insoluble riddle. This man dreamed he was at a theatre, in the role of "an important spectator whose opinion is respected." There was an act in which a white monkey was standing on a pedestal with men around him. In recounting his dream the man said:

My guide explains the theme to me. It is the ordeal of a young sailor who is exposed both to

The second stage in the evolution of the hero is the founder of human culture. Left, a Navaho sand painting of the myth of Coyote, who stole fire from the gods and gave it to man. In Greek myth Prometheus also stole fire from the gods for man— for which he was chained to a rock and tortured by an eagle (below, on a sixth-century B.C. cup).

The hero in the third stage is a powerful man-god—like Buddha. In the first-century sculpture above, Siddhartha begins the journey on which he will receive enlightenment and become Buddha.

Below left, a medieval Italian sculpture of Romulus and Remus, the twins (raised by a wolf) who founded Rome—and who are the best-known instance of the fourth stage of the hero myth.

In the fourth stage, the Twins often misuse their power—as did the Roman heroes Castor and Pollux when they abducted the daughters of Leucippus (below, in a painting by the Flemish artist Rubens).

the wind and to being beaten up. I begin to object that this white monkey is not a sailor at all; but just at that moment a young man in black stands up and I think that he must be the true hero. But another handsome young man strides toward an altar and stretches himself out on it. They are making marks on his bare chest as a preparation to offering him as a human sacrifice.

Then I find myself on a platform with several other people. We could get down by a small ladder, but I hesitate to do so because there are two young toughs standing by and I think that they will stop us. But when a woman in the group uses the ladder unmolested, I see that it is safe and all of us follow the woman down.

Now a dream of this kind cannot be quickly or simply interpreted. We have to unravel it carefully in order to show both its relation to the dreamer's own life and its wider symbolic implications. The patient who produced it was a man who had achieved maturity in a physical sense. He was successful in his career, and he had apparently done pretty well as a husband and father. Yet psychologically he was still immature, and had not completed his youthful phase of development. It was this psychic immaturity that expressed itself in his dreams as different aspects of the hero myth. These images still exerted a strong attraction for his imagination even though they had long since exhausted any

of their meaning in terms of the reality of his everyday life.

Thus, in a dream, we see a series of figures theatrically presented as various aspects of a figure that the dreamer keeps expecting will turn out to be the true hero. The first is a white monkey, the second a sailor, the third a young man in black, and the last a "handsome young man." In the early part of the performance, which is supposed to represent the sailor's ordeal, the dreamer sees only the white monkey. The man in black suddenly appears and as suddenly disappears; he is a new figure who first contrasts with the white monkey and is then for a moment confused with the hero proper. (Such confusion in dreams is not unusual. The dreamer is not usually presented with clear images by the unconscious. He has to puzzle out a meaning from a succession of contrasts and paradoxes.)

Significantly, these figures appear in the course of a theatrical performance, and this context seems to be a direct reference by the dreamer to his own treatment by analysis: The "guide" he mentions is presumably his analyst. Yet he does not see himself as a patient who is being treated by a doctor but as "an important spectator whose opinion is respected." This is the vantage point from which he sees certain figures whom he associates with the experience

An individual psyche develops (as does the hero myth) from a primitive, childish stage—and often images of the early stages can appear in the dreams of psychologically immature adults. The first stage might be represented by the carefree play of children—like the pillow fight (far left) from the 1933 French film *Zéro de Conduite*. The second stage might be the reckless thrill-seeking of early adolescence: Right, American youths test their nerves in a speeding car. A later stage can produce idealism, and self-sacrifice in late adolescence, exemplified in the picture (opposite, far right) taken during the East Berlin rising (June 1953) when young men fought Russian tanks with stones.

of growing up. The white monkey, for instance, reminds him of the playful and somewhat lawless behavior of boys between the ages of seven and 12. The sailor suggests the adventurousness of early adolescence, together with the consequent punishment by "beating" for irresponsible pranks. The dreamer could offer no association to the young man in black, but in the handsome young man about to be sacrificed he saw a reminder of the self-sacrificing idealism of late adolescence.

At this stage it is possible to put together the historical material (or archetypal hero images) and the data from the dreamer's personal experience in order to see how they corroborate, contradict, or qualify each other.

The first conclusion is that the white monkey seems to represent Trickster—or at least those traits of personality that the Winnebago attribute to Trickster. But, to me, the monkey also stands for something that the dreamer has not personally and adequately experienced for himself—he in fact says that in the dream he was a spectator. I found out that as a boy he had been excessively attached to his parents, and that he was naturally introspective. For these reasons he had never fully developed the boisterous qualities natural to late childhood; nor had he joined in the games of his schoolfellows. He had not, as the saying goes, "got up to monkey tricks" or practiced "monkeyshines." The saying provides the clue here. The monkey in the dream is in fact a symbolic form of the Trickster figure.

But why should Trickster appear as a monkey? And why should it be white? As I have already pointed out, the Winnebago myth tells us that, toward the end of the cycle, Trickster begins to emerge in the physical likeness of a man. And here, in the dream, is a monkey—so close to a human being that it is a laughable and not too dangerous caricature of a man. The dreamer himself could offer no personal association that could explain why the monkey was white. But from our knowledge of primitive symbolism we can conjecture that whiteness lends a special quality of "god-likeness" to this otherwise banal figure. (The albino is regarded as sacred in many primitive communities.) This fits in quite well with Trickster's semi-divine or semi-magical powers.

Thus, it seems, the white monkey symbolizes for the dreamer the positive quality of childhood playfulness, which he had insufficiently accepted at the time, and which he now feels called upon to exalt. As the dream tells us, he places it "on a pedestal," where it becomes something more than a lost childhood experience. It is, for the adult man, a symbol of creative experimentalism.

Next we come to the conclusion about the monkey. Is it a monkey, or is it a sailor who has to put up with beatings? The dreamer's own associations pointed to the meaning of this transformation. But in any case the next stage in human development is one in which the irresponsibility of childhood gives way to a period of socialization, and that involves submission to painful discipline. One could say, therefore, that the sailor is an advanced form of Trickster, who is being changed into a socially responsible person by means of an initiation ordeal. Drawing on the history of symbolism, we can assume that the wind represents the natural elements in this process, and the beatings are those that are humanly induced.

At this point, then, we have a reference to the process that the Winnebago describe in the Hare cycle, where the culture-hero is a weak yet struggling figure, ready to sacrifice childishness for the sake of further development. Once again, in this phase of the dream, the patient is acknowledging his failure to experience to the full an important aspect of childhood and early adolescence. He missed out on the playfulness of the child, and also on the rather more ad-vanced pranks of the young teenager, and he is seeking ways in which those lost experiences and personal qualities can be rehabilitated.

Next comes a curious change in the dream. The young man in black appears, and for a moment the dreamer feels that this is the "true hero." That is all we are told about the man in black; yet this fleeting glimpse introduces a theme of profound importance—a theme that occurs frequently in dreams.

This is the concept of the "shadow," which plays such a vital role in analytical psychology. Dr. Jung has pointed out that the shadow cast by the conscious mind of the individual contains the hidden, repressed, and unfavorable (or nefarious) aspects of the personality. But this darkness is not just the simple converse of the conscious ego. Just as the ego contains unfavorable and destructive attitudes, so the shadow has good qualities—normal instincts and creative impulses. Ego and shadow, indeed, although separate, are inextricably linked together in much the same way that thought and feeling are related to each other.

The ego, nevertheless, is in conflict with the shadow, in what Dr. Jung once called "the battle for deliverance." In the struggle of primitive man to achieve consciousness, this conflict is expressed by the contest between the archetypal hero and the cosmic powers of evil, personified by dragons and other monsters. In the developing consciousness of the individual the hero figure is the symbolic means by which the emerging ego overcomes the inertia of the unconscious mind, and liberates the mature

The young, undifferentiated ego-personality is protected by the mother—a protection imaged by the sheltering Madonna, left (in a painting by the 15th-century Italian artist Piero della Francesca), or by the Egyptian sky goddess Nut, right, bending over the earth (in a fifth-century B.C. relief). But the ego must eventually free itself from unconsciousness and immaturity; and its "battle for deliverance" is often symbolized by a hero's battle with a monster—like the Japanese god Susanoo's battle with a serpent, top right (in a 19th-century print). The hero doesn't always win at once: For instance, Jonah was swallowed by the whale (far right, from a 14th-century manuscript).

man from a regressive longing to return to the blissful state of infancy in a world dominated by his mother.

Usually, in mythology, the hero wins his battle against the monster. (I shall say more about this in a moment.) But there are other hero myths in which the hero gives in to the monster. A familiar type is that of Jonah and the whale, in which the hero is swallowed by a sea monster that carries him on a night sea journey from west to east, thus symbolizing the supposed transit of the sun from sunset to dawn. The hero goes into darkness, which represents a kind of death. I have encountered this theme in dreams presented in my own clinical experience.

The battle between the hero and the dragon is the more active form of this myth, and it shows more clearly the archetypal theme of the ego's triumph over regressive trends. For most people the dark or negative side of the personality remains unconscious. The hero, on the contrary, must realize that the shadow exists

The ego's emergence can be symbolized not by a battle but by a sacrifice: death leading to rebirth. Revolution is sacrificial in this way: Delacroix's painting (below), *Greece expiring on the Ruins of Missolonghi*, personifies the country killed by civil war to be liberated and reborn. As individual sacrifices: the British poet Byron (above) died in Greece during the revolution (1824). Below left, the Christian martyr St. Lucia sacrificed her eyes and her life for her religion.

and that he can draw strength from it. He must come to terms with its destructive powers if he is to become sufficiently terrible to overcome the dragon—i.e. before the ego can triumph, it must master and assimilate the shadow.

One can see this theme, incidentally, in a well-known literary hero figure—Goethe's character of Faust. In accepting the wager of Mephistopheles, Faust put himself in the power of a "shadow" figure that Goethe describes as "part of that power which, willing evil, finds the good." Like the man whose dream I have been discussing, Faust had failed to live out to the full an important part of his early life. He was, accordingly, an unreal or incomplete person who lost himself in a fruitless quest for metaphysical goals that failed to materialize. He was still unwilling to accept life's challenge to live both the good and the bad.

It is to this aspect of the unconscious that the young man in black in my patient's dream seems to refer. Such a reminder of the shadow side of his personality, of its powerful potential

and its role in preparing the hero for the struggles of life, is an essential transition from the earlier parts of the dream to the theme of the sacrificial hero: the handsome young man who places himself on an altar. This figure represents the form of heroism that is commonly associated to the ego-building process of late adolescence. A man expresses the ideal principles of his life at this time, sensing their power both to transform himself and to change his relations with others. He is, so to speak, in the bloom of youth, attractive, full of energy and idealism. Why, then, does he willingly offer himself as a human sacrifice?

The reason, presumably, is the same as that which made the Twins of the Winnebago myth give up their power on pain of destruction. The idealism of youth, which drives one so hard, is bound to lead to over-confidence: The human ego can be exalted to experience godlike attributes, but only at the cost of over-reaching itself and falling to disaster. (This is the meaning of the story of Icarus, the youth who is carried

Below, a montage of World War I: a call-to-arms poster, infantry, a military cemetery. Memorials and religious services for soldiers who gave their lives for their country often reflect the cyclic "death and rebirth" theme of the archetypal heroic sacrifice. An inscription on one British memorial to the dead of World War I reads: "At the going down of the sun and in the morning we will remember them."

In mythology, a hero's death is often due to his own *hybris*, which causes the gods to humble him. As a modern example: In 1912 the ship *Titanic* struck an iceberg and sank. (Right, a montage of scenes of the sinking, from the 1943 film *Titanic*.) Yet the *Titanic* had been called "unsinkable": according to the American author Walter Lord, one sailor was heard to say, "God himself couldn't sink this ship!"

up to heaven on his fragile, humanly contrived wings, but who flies too close to the sun and plunges to his doom.) All the same, the youthful ego must always run this risk, for if a young man does not strive for a higher goal than he can safely reach, he cannot surmount the obstacles between adolescence and maturity.

So far, I have been talking about the conclusions that, at the level of his personal associations, my patient could draw from his own dream. Yet there is an archetypal level of the dream—the mystery of the proffered human sacrifice. It is precisely because it is a mystery that it is expressed in a ritual act that, in its symbolism, carries us a long way back into

man's history. Here, as the man lies stretched out on an altar, we see a reference to an act even more primitive than those performed on the altar stone in the temple at Stonehenge. There, as on so many primitive altars, we can imagine a yearly solstice rite combined with the death and rebirth of a mythological hero.

The ritual has a sorrow about it that is also a kind of joy, an inward acknowledgment that death also leads to a new life. Whether it is expressed in the prose epic of the Winnebago Indians, in a lament for the death of Balder in the Norse eddas, in Walt Whitman's poems of mourning for Abraham Lincoln, or in the dream ritual whereby a man returns to his

Heroes often fight monsters to rescue "damsels in distress" (who symbolize the anima). Left, St. George slays a dragon to free a maiden (in a 15th-century Italian painting). Right, in the 1916 film *The Great Secret*, the dragon has become a locomotive but the heroic rescue remains the same.

youthful hopes and fears, it is the same theme —the drama of new birth through death.

The end of the dream brings out a curious epilogue in which the dreamer at last becomes involved in the action of the dream. He and others are on a platform from which they have to descend. He does not trust the ladder because of the possible interference of hoodlums, but a woman encourages him to believe he can go down safely and this is accomplished. Since I found out from his associations that the whole performance he witnessed was part of his analysis—a process of inner change that he was experiencing—he was presumably thinking of the difficulty of getting back to everyday reality again. His fear of the "toughs," as he calls them, suggests his fear that the Trickster archetype may appear in a collective form.

The saving elements in the dream are the man-made ladder, which here is probably a symbol of the rational mind, and the presence of the woman who encourages the dreamer to use it. Her appearance in the final sequence of the dream points to a psychic need to include a feminine principle as a complement to all this excessively masculine activity.

It should not be assumed from what I have said, or from the fact that I have chosen to use the Winnebago myth to illuminate this particular dream, that one must seek for complete and wholly mechanical parallels between a dream and the materials one can find in the history of mythology. Each dream is individual to the dreamer, and the precise form it takes is determined by his own situation. What I have sought to show is the manner in which the unconscious draws on this archetypal material and modifies its patterns to the dreamer's needs. Thus, in this particular dream, one must not look for a direct reference to what the Winnebago describe in the Red Horn or Twin cycles; the reference is rather to the essence of those two themes—to the sacrificial element in them.

As a general rule it can be said that the need for hero symbols arises when the ego needs strengthening—when, that is to say, the conscious mind needs assistance in some task that it cannot accomplish unaided or without drawing on the sources of strength that lie in the unconscious mind. In the dream I have been discussing, for instance, there was no reference to one of the more important aspects of the myth of the typical hero—his capacity to save or protect beautiful women from terrible danger. (The damsel in distress was a favorite myth of medieval Europe.) This is one way in which myths or dreams refer to the "anima"—the feminine element of the male psyche that Goethe called "the Eternal Feminine."

The nature and function of this female element will be discussed later in this book by Dr. von Franz. But its relation to the hero figure can be illustrated here by a dream produced by another patient, also a man of mature years. He began by saying:

"I had returned from a long hike through India. A woman had equipped myself and a friend for the journey, and on my return I reproached her for failing to give us black rain-hats, telling her that through this oversight we had been soaked by the rain."

This introduction to the dream, it later emerged, referred to a period in this man's youth when he was given to taking "heroic" walks through dangerous mountain country in company with a college friend. (As he had never been to India, and in view of his own associations to this dream, I concluded that the dream journey signified his exploration of a new region—not, that is to say, a real place but the realm of the unconscious.)

In his dream the patient seems to feel that a woman—presumably a personification of his anima—has failed to prepare him properly for this expedition. The lack of a suitable rainhat suggests that he feels in an unprotected state of mind, in which he is uncomfortably affected by exposure to new and not altogether pleasant experiences. He believes that the woman should have provided a rainhat for him, just as his mother provided clothes for him to wear as a boy. This episode is reminiscent of his early picaresque wanderings, when he was sustained by the assumption that his mother (the original feminine image) would protect him against all dangers. As he grew older, he saw that this was a childish illusion, and he now blames his misfortune on his own anima, not his mother.

In the next stage of the dream the patient speaks of participating in a hike with a group of people. He grows tired and returns to an outdoor restaurant where he finds his raincoat, together with the rainhat that he had missed earlier. He sits down to rest; and, as he does so, he notices a poster stating that a local high-school boy is taking the part of Perseus in a play. Then the boy in question appears—who turns out to be not a boy at all but a husky

young man. He is dressed in gray with a black hat, and he sits down to talk with another young man dressed in a black suit. Immediately after this scene the dreamer feels a new vigor, and finds that he is capable of rejoining his party. They all then climb over the next hill. There, below them, he sees their destination; it is a lovely harbor town. He feels both heartened and rejuvenated by the discovery.

Here, in contrast to the restless, uncomfortable, and lonely journey of the first episode, the dreamer is with a group. The contrast marks a change from an earlier pattern of isolation and youthful protest to the socializing influence of a relation to others. Since this implies a new capacity for relatedness, it suggests that his anima must now be functioning better than it was before—symbolized by his discovery of the missing hat that the anima figure had previously failed to provide for him.

But the dreamer is tired, and the scene at the restaurant reflects his need to look at his earlier attitudes in a new light, with the hope of renewing his strength by this regression. And so it turns out. What he first sees is a poster suggesting the enactment of a youthful hero role—a high-school boy playing the part of Perseus. Then he sees the boy, now a man, with a friend who makes a sharp contrast to him. The one dressed in light gray, the other in black, can be recognized, from what I have previously said, as a version of the Twins. They

are hero-figures expressing the opposites of ego and alter-ego, which, however, appear here in a harmonious and unified relation.

The patient's associations confirmed this and emphasized that the figure in gray represents a well-adapted, worldly attitude to life, whereas the figure in black represents the spiritual life, in the sense that a clergyman wears black. That they wore hats (and he now had found his own) points to their having achieved a relatively mature identity of a kind that he had felt to be severely lacking in his own earlier adolescent years, when the quality of "Tricksterism" still clung to him, in spite of his idealistic self-image as a seeker of wisdom.

His association to the Greek hero Perseus was a curious one, which proved especially significant because it revealed a glaring inaccuracy. It turned out that he thought Perseus was the hero who slew the Minotaur and rescued Ariadne from the Cretan labyrinth. As he wrote the name down for me, he discovered his mistake—that it was Theseus, not Perseus, who slew the Minotaur—and this mistake became suddenly meaningful, as such slips often do, by making him notice what these two heroes had in common. They both had to overcome their fear of unconscious demonic maternal powers and had to liberate from these powers a single youthful feminine figure.

Perseus had to cut off the head of the gorgon Medusa, whose horrifying visage and snaky locks turned all who gazed upon them to stone. He later had to overcome the dragon that guarded Andromeda. Theseus represented the young patriarchal spirit of Athens who had to brave the terrors of the Cretan labyrinth with its monstrous inmate, the Minotaur, which perhaps symbolized the unhealthy decadence of matriarchal Crete. (In all cultures, the labyrinth has the meaning of an entangling and confusing representation of the world of matriarchal consciousness; it can be traversed only by those who are ready for a special initiation into the mysterious world of the collective unconscious.) Having overcome this danger, Theseus rescued Ariadne, a maiden in distress.

This rescue symbolizes the liberation of the anima figure from the devouring aspect of the mother image. Not until this is accomplished can a man achieve his first true capacity for relatedness to women. The fact that this man had failed adequately to separate the anima from the mother was emphasized in another dream, in which he encountered a dragon—a symbolic image for the "devouring" aspect of his attachment to his mother. This dragon pursued him, and because he had no weapon he began to get the worst of the struggle.

Significantly, however, his wife appeared in the dream, and her appearance somehow made the dragon smaller and less threatening. This change in the dream showed that in his marriage the dreamer was belatedly overcoming

Some heroic battles and rescues from Greek myth: Far left, Perseus slays Medusa (on a sixth-century B.C. vase); left, Perseus with Andromeda (from a first-century B.C. mural) whom he saved from a monster. Right, Theseus kills the Minotaur (on a first-century B.C. jar) watched by Ariadne; below, on a Cretan coin (67 B.C.), the Minotaur's labyrinth.

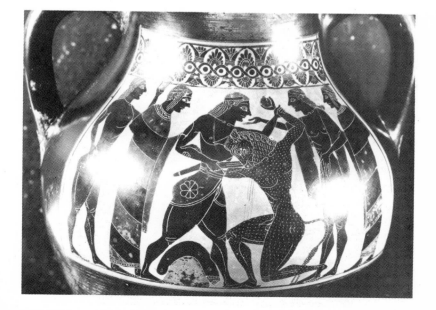

the attachment to his mother. In other words, he had to find a means of freeing the psychic energy attached to the mother-son relationship, in order to achieve a more adult relation to women—and, indeed, to adult society as a whole. The hero-dragon battle was the symbolic expression of this process of "growing up."

But the hero's task has an aim that goes beyond biological and marital adjustment. It is to liberate the anima as that inner component of the psyche that is necessary for any true creative achievement. In this man's case we have to guess the probability of this outcome because it is not directly stated in the dream of the Indian journey. But I am sure he would confirm my hypothesis that his journey over the hill and the sight of his goal as a peaceful harbor town contained the rich promise that he would discover his authentic anima function. He would thus be cured of his early resentment at not being given protection (the rainhat) by the woman for his journey through India. (In dreams, significantly placed towns can often be anima symbols.)

The man had won this promise of security for himself by his contact with the authentic hero archetype, and had found a new co-operative and related attitude to the group. His sense of rejuvenation naturally followed. He had drawn on the inner source of strength that the hero archetype represents; he had clarified and developed that part of him which was symbolized by the woman; and he had, by his ego's heroic act, liberated himself from his mother.

These and many other examples of the hero myth in modern dreams show that the ego as hero is always essentially a bearer of culture rather than a purely egocentric exhibitionist. Even Trickster, in his misguided or unpurposive way, is a contributor to the cosmos as primitive man sees it. In Navaho mythology, as Coyote, he hurled the stars into the sky as an act of creation, he invented the necessary contingency of death, and in the myth of emergence he helped lead the people through the hollow reed whereby they escaped from one world to another above it where they were safe from the threat of flood.

We have here a reference to that form of creative evolution which evidently begins on a childlike, preconscious, or animal level of existence. The ego's rise to effective conscious action becomes plain in the true culture-hero. In the same fashion the childish or adolescent ego frees itself from the oppression of parental expectations and becomes individual. As part of this rise to consciousness the hero-dragon battle may have to be fought and refought to liberate energy for the multitude of human tasks that can form a culture pattern out of chaos.

The hero's rescue of a maiden can symbolize the freeing of the anima from the "devouring" aspect of the mother. This aspect is represented, far left, by Balinese dancers wearing the mask of Rangda (left), a malign female spirit; or by the serpent that swallowed and then regurgitated the Greek hero Jason (above).

As in the dream discussed on p. 124, a common anima symbol is a harbor town. Below, a poster by Marc Chagall personifies Nice as a mermaid.

NICE Soleil Fleurs   Marc Chagall

When this is successful, we see the full hero image emerging as a kind of ego strength (or, if we are speaking in collective terms, a tribal identity) that has no further need to overcome the monsters and the giants. It has reached the point where these deep forces can be personalized. The "feminine element" no longer appears in dreams as a dragon, but as a woman; similarly, the "shadow" side of the personality takes on a less menacing form.

This important point is illustrated in the dream of a man nearing 50. All his life he had suffered from periodic attacks of anxiety associated with fear of failure (originally engendered by a doubting mother). Yet his actual achievements, both in his profession and in his personal relations, were well above average. In his dream his nine-year-old son appeared as a young man of about 18 or 19, dressed in the shining armor of a medieval knight. The young man is called upon to fight a host of men in black, which he prepares at first to do. Then he suddenly removes his helmet, and smiles at the leader of the menacing host; it is clear that they will not engage in the battle but will become friends.

The son in the dream is the man's own youthful ego, which had frequently felt threatened by the shadow in the form of self-doubt. He had, in a sense, waged a successful crusade against this adversary all his mature life. Now, partly through the actual encouragement of seeing his son grow up without such doubts, but mainly by forming a suitable image of the hero in the form closest to his own environmental pattern, he finds it no longer necessary to fight the shadow; he can accept it. That is what is symbolized in the act of friendship. He is no longer driven to a competitive struggle for individual supremacy, but is assimilated to the cultural task of forming a democratic sort of community. Such a conclusion, reached in the fullness of life, goes beyond the heroic task and leads one to a truly mature attitude.

This change, however, does not take place automatically. It requires a period of transition, which is expressed in the various forms of the archetype of initiation.

The archetype of initiation

In a psychological sense the hero image is not to be regarded as identical with the ego proper. It is better described as the symbolic means by which the ego separates itself from the archetypes evoked by the parental images in early childhood. Dr. Jung has suggested that each human being has originally a feeling of wholeness, a powerful and complete sense of the Self. And from the Self—the totality of the psyche—the individualized ego-consciousness emerges as the individual grows up.

Within the past few years, the works of certain followers of Jung have begun to document the series of events by which the individual ego emerges during the transition from infancy through childhood. This separation can never become final without severe injury to the original sense of wholeness. And the ego must continually return to re-establish its relation to

the Self in order to maintain a condition of psychic health.

It would appear from my studies that the hero myth is the first stage in the differentiation of the psyche. I have suggested that it seems to go through a fourfold cycle by which the ego seeks to achieve its relative autonomy from the original condition of wholeness. Unless some degree of autonomy is achieved, the individual is unable to relate himself to his adult environment. But the hero myth does not ensure that this liberation will occur. It only shows how it is possible for it to occur, so that the ego may achieve consciousness. There remains the problem of maintaining and developing that consciousness in a meaningful way, so that the individual can live a useful life and can achieve the necessary sense of self-distinction in society.

Ancient history and the rituals of contemporary primitive societies have provided us with a wealth of material about myths and rites of initiation, whereby young men and women are weaned away from their parents and forcibly made members of their clan or tribe. But in making this break with the childhood world, the original parent archetype will be injured, and the damage must be made good by a healing process of assimilation into the life of the group. (The identity of the group and the individual is often symbolized by a totem animal.) Thus the group fulfills the claims of the injured archetype and becomes a kind of second parent to which the young are first symbolically sacrificed, only to re-emerge into a new life.

In this "drastic ceremony, which looks very like a sacrifice to the powers that might hold the young man back," as Dr. Jung has put it,

A primitive tribe's *totem* (often an animal) symbolizes each tribesman's identity with the tribal unit. Left, an Australian aborigine imitating (in a ritual dance) his tribe's totem —an emu. Many modern groups use totem-like animals as emblems: Below, a heraldic lion (from the Belgian coat of arms) on a 17th-century allegorical map of Belgium. Right, the falcon is the mascot of the American Air Force Academy's football team. Far right, modern totemistic emblems that aren't animals: a shop window display of ties, badges, etc. of British schools and clubs.

we see how the power of the original archetype can never be permanently overcome, in the manner envisaged by the hero-dragon battle, without a crippling sense of alienation from the fruitful powers of the unconscious. We saw in the myth of the Twins how their *hybris*, expressing excessive ego-Self separation, was corrected by their own fear of the consequences, which forced them back into a harmonious ego-Self relation.

In tribal societies it is the initiation rite that most effectively solves this problem. The ritual takes the novice back to the deepest level of original mother-child identity or ego-Self identity, thus forcing him to experience a symbolic death. In other words, his identity is temporarily dismembered or dissolved in the collective unconscious. From this state he is then ceremonially rescued by the rite of the new birth. This is the first act of true consolidation of the ego with the larger group, expressed as totem, clan, or tribe, or all three combined.

The ritual, whether it is found in tribal groups or in more complex societies, invariably insists upon this rite of death and rebirth, which provides the novice with a "rite of passage" from one stage of life to the next, whether it is from early childhood to later childhood or from early to late adolescence and from then to maturity.

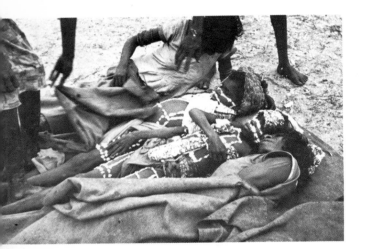

Initiatory events are not, of course, confined to the psychology of youth. Every new phase of development throughout an individual's life is accompanied by a repetition of the original conflict between the claims of the Self and the claims of the ego. In fact, this conflict may be expressed more powerfully at the period of transition from early maturity to middle age (between 35 and 40 in our society) than at any other time in life. And the transition from middle age to old age creates again the need for affirmation of the difference between the ego and the total psyche; the hero receives his last call to action in defense of ego-consciousness against the approaching dissolution of life in death.

At these crucial periods, the archetype of initiation is strongly activated to provide a meaningful transition that offers something more spiritually satisfying than the adolescent rites with their strong secular flavor. The archetypal patterns of initiation in this religious sense —known since ancient times as "the mysteries" —are woven into the texture of all ecclesiastical rituals requiring a special manner of worship at the time of birth, marriage, or death.

As in our study of the hero myth, so in the study of initiation we must look for examples in the subjective experiences of modern people and especially of those who have undergone analysis. It is not surprising that there should appear, in the unconscious of someone who is seeking help from a doctor specializing in psychic disorders, images that duplicate the major patterns of initiation as we know them from history.

Perhaps the commonest of these themes to be found in young people is the ordeal, or trial of strength. This might seem to be identical with what we have already noticed in modern dreams illustrating the hero myth, such as the sailor who had to submit to the weather and to beatings, or that proof of fitness represented in the hike through India of the man without a rainhat. We can also see this theme of physical suffering carried to its logical end in the first dream I discussed, when the handsome young man became a human sacrifice on an altar. This sacrifice resembled the approach to initiation, but its end was obscured. It seemed to round off the hero cycle, to make way for a new theme.

There is one striking difference between the hero myth and the initiation rite. The typical hero figures exhaust their efforts in achieving the goal of their ambitions; in short, they become successful even if immediately afterward they are punished or killed for their *hybris*. In contrast to this, the novice for initiation is called upon to give up willful ambition

Primitive initiation rituals bring the youth into adulthood and into the tribe's collective identity. In many primitive societies, initiation is accomplished by circumcision (a symbolic sacrifice). Here are four stages in a circumcision rite of Australian aborigines. Far left, top and center: The boys are placed under blankets (a symbolic death from which they will be reborn). Bottom, they are removed and held by the men for the actual operation. Left, the circumcised boys are given men's conical caps, a mark of their new status. Right, they are finally isolated from the tribe to be purified and given instruction.

and all desire and to submit to the ordeal. He must be willing to experience this trial without hope of success. In fact, he must be prepared to die; and though the token of his ordeal may be mild (a period of fasting, the knocking out of a tooth, or tattooing) or agonizing (the infliction of the wounds of circumcision, subincision, or other mutilations), the purpose remains always the same: To create the symbolic mood of death from which may spring the symbolic mood of rebirth.

A young man of 25 dreams of climbing a mountain on top of which there is a kind of altar. Near the altar he sees a sarcophagus with a statue of himself upon it. Then a veiled priest approaches carrying a staff on which there glows a living sun-disk. (Discussing the dream later, the young man said that climbing a mountain reminded him of the effort he was making in his analysis to achieve self-mastery.) To his surprise, he finds himself, as it were, dead, and instead of a sense of achievement he feels deprivation and fear. Then comes a feeling of strength and rejuvenation as he is bathed in the warm rays of the sun-disk.

This dream shows quite succinctly the distinction we must make between initiation and the hero myth. The act of climbing the mountain seems to suggest a trial of strength: It is the will to achieve ego-consciousness in the heroic phase of adolescent development. The patient had evidently thought that his approach to therapy would be like his approach to other tests of manhood, which he had approached in the competitive manner characteristic of young men in our society. But the scene by the altar corrected this mistaken assumption, showing him that his task is rather to submit to a power greater than himself. He must see himself as if he were dead and entombed in a symbolic form (the sarcophagus) that recalls the archetypal mother as the original container of all life. Only by such an act of submission can he experience rebirth. An invigorating ritual brings him to life again as the symbolic son of a Sun Father.

Here again we might confuse this with a hero cycle—that of the Twins, the "children of the Sun." But in this case we have no indication that the initiate will over-reach himself. Instead, he has learned a lesson in humility by experiencing a rite of death and rebirth that marks his passage from youth to maturity.

According to his chronological age he should already have made this transition, but a prolonged period of arrested development has held him back. This delay had plunged him into a neurosis for which he had come for treatment, and the dream offers him the same wise counsel that he could have been given by any good tribal medicine man—that he should give up scaling mountains to prove his strength and submit to the meaningful ritual of an initiatory change that could fit him for the new moral responsibilities of manhood.

The theme of submission as an essential attitude toward promotion of the successful initiation rite can be clearly seen in the case of girls or women. Their rite of passage initially emphasizes their essential passivity, and this is reinforced by the psychological limitation on their autonomy imposed by the menstrual cycle. It has been suggested that the menstrual cycle may actually be the major part of initiation from a woman's point of view, since it has the power to awaken the deepest sense of obedience to life's creative power over her. Thus she willingly gives herself to her womanly function, much as a man gives himself to his assigned role in the community life of his group.

On the other hand, the woman, no less than the man, has her initial trials of strength that

A sarcophagus from second-century A.D. Thebes that reveals a symbolic connection with the archetypal Great Mother (the container of all life). The inside of the cover bears a portrait of the Egyptian goddess Nut; thus the goddess would "embrace" the body of the deceased (whose portrait is on the base, far right).

lead to a final sacrifice for the sake of experiencing the new birth. This sacrifice enables a woman to free herself from the entanglement of personal relations and fits her for a more conscious role as an individual in her own right. In contrast, a man's sacrifice is a surrender of his sacred independence: He becomes more consciously related to woman.

Here we come to that aspect of initiation which acquaints man with woman and woman with man in such a way as to correct some sort of original male-female opposition. Man's knowledge (Logos) then encounters woman's relatedness (Eros) and their union is represented as that symbolic ritual of a sacred marriage which has been at the heart of initiation since its origins in the mystery-religions of antiquity. But this is exceedingly difficult for modern people to grasp, and it frequently takes a special crisis in their lives to make them understand it.

Several patients have told me dreams in which the motif of sacrifice is combined with the motif of the sacred marriage. One of these was produced by a young man who had fallen in love but was unwilling to marry for fear that marriage would become a kind of prison presided over by a powerful mother figure. His own mother had been a strong influence in his childhood, and his future mother-in-law presented a similar threat. Would not his wife-to-

Four varied initiation ceremonies: Top left, novices in a convent perform such humble duties as scrubbing a floor (from the 1958 film *The Nun's Story*), and have their hair cut off (from a medieval painting). Center, ship's passengers crossing the equator must undergo a "rite of passage." Bottom, American college freshmen in a traditional battle with their seniors.

Marriage can be seen as an initiation rite in which the man and the woman must submit to one another. But in some societies the man offsets his submission by ritually "abducting" his bride—as do the Dyaks of Malaysia and Borneo (right, from the 1955 film *The Lost Continent*). A remnant of this practice exists in today's custom of carrying the bride across the threshold (far right).

be dominate him in the same way these mothers had dominated their children?

In his dream he was engaged in a ritual dance along with another man and two other women, one of whom was his fiancée. The others were an older man and wife, who impressed the dreamer because, despite their closeness to each other, they seemed to have room for their individual differences, and did not appear to be possessive. These two therefore represented to this young man a married state that did not impose undue constraint on the development of the individual nature of the two partners. If it were possible for him to achieve this condition, marriage would then become acceptable to him.

In the ritual dance each man faced his woman partner, and all four took their places at the corners of a square dancing ground. As they danced, it became apparent that this was also a kind of sword dance. Each dancer had in his hand a short sword with which to perform a difficult arabesque, moving arms and legs in a series of movements that suggested alternate impulses of aggression and submission to each other. In the final scene of the dance all four dancers had to plunge the swords into their own breasts and die. Only the dreamer refused to accomplish the final suicide, and was left standing alone after the others had fallen.

He felt deeply ashamed of his cowardly failure to sacrifice himself with the others.

This dream brought home to my patient the fact that he was more than ready to change his attitude to life. He had been self-centered, seeking the illusory safety of personal independence but inwardly dominated by the fears caused by childhood subjection to his mother. He needed a challenge to his manhood in order to see that unless he sacrificed his childish state of mind he would be left isolated and ashamed. The dream, and his subsequent insight into its meaning, dispelled his doubts. He had passed through the symbolic rite by which a young man gives up his exclusive autonomy and accepts his shared life in a related, not just heroic, form.

And so he married and found appropriate fulfillment in his relationship with his wife. Far from impairing his effectiveness in the world, his marriage actually enhanced it.

Quite apart from the neurotic fear that invisible mothers or fathers may be lurking behind the marriage veil, even the normal young man has good reason to feel apprehensive about the wedding ritual. It is essentially a woman's initiation rite, in which a man is bound to feel like anything but a conquering hero. No wonder we find, in tribal societies, such counterphobic rituals as the abduction or

rape of the bride. These enable the man to cling to the remnants of his heroic role at the very moment that he must submit to his bride and assume the responsibilities of marriage.

But the theme of marriage is an image of such universality that it also has a deeper meaning. It is an acceptable, even necessary, symbolic discovery of the feminine component of a man's own psyche, just as much as it is the acquisition of a real wife. So one may encounter this archetype in a man of any age in response to a suitable stimulus.

Not all women, however, react trustingly to the married state. A woman patient who had unfulfilled longings for a career, which she had had to give up for a very difficult and short-lived marriage, dreamed that she was kneeling opposite a man who was also kneeling. He had a ring that he prepared to put on her finger, but she stretched out her right-hand ring finger in a tense manner—evidently resisting this ritual of marital union.

It was easy to point out her significant error. Instead of offering the left-hand ring finger (by which she could accept a balanced and natural relation to the masculine principle) she had wrongly assumed that she had to put her entire conscious (i.e. right-sided) identity in the service of the man. In fact, marriage required her to share with him only that subliminal, natural (i.e. left-sided) part of herself in which the principle of union would have a symbolic, not a literal or absolute, meaning. Her fear was the fear of the woman who dreads to lose her identity in a strongly patriarchal marriage, which this woman had good reason to resist.

Nevertheless, the sacred marriage as an archetypal form has a particularly important meaning for the psychology of women, and one for which they are prepared during their adolescence by many preliminary events of an initiatory character.

The archetypal sacred marriage (the union of opposites, of the male and female principles) represented here by a 19th-century Indian sculpture of the deities Siva and Parvati.

Beauty and the Beast

Girls in our society share in the masculine hero myths because, like boys, they must also develop a reliable ego-identity and acquire an education. But there is an older layer of the mind that seems to come to the surface in their feelings, with the aim of making them into women, not into imitation men. When this ancient content of the psyche begins to make its appearance, the modern young woman may repress it because it threatens to cut her off from the emancipated equality of friendship and opportunity to compete with men that have become her modern privileges.

This repression may be so successful that for a time she will maintain an identification with the masculine intellectual goals she learned at school or college. Even when she marries, she will preserve some illusion of freedom, despite her ostensible act of submission to the archetype of marriage—with its implicit injunction to become a mother. And so there may occur, as we very frequently see today, that conflict which in the end forces the woman to rediscover her buried womanhood in a painful (but ultimately rewarding) manner.

I saw an example of this in a young married woman who did not yet have any children but who intended to have one or two eventually, because it would be expected of her. Meanwhile her sexual response was unsatisfactory. This worried her and her husband, though they were unable to offer any explanation for it. She had graduated with honors from a good women's college and enjoyed a life of intellectual companionship with her husband and other men. Although this side of her life went well enough much of the time, she had occasional outbursts of temper and talked in an aggressive fashion that alienated men and gave her an intolerable feeling of dissatisfaction with herself.

She had a dream at this time that seemed so important she sought professional advice to understand it. She dreamed she was in a line of young women like herself, and as she looked ahead to where they were going she saw that as each came to the head of the line she was decapitated by a guillotine. Without any fear the dreamer remained in the line, presumably quite willing to submit to the same treatment when her turn came.

I explained to her that this meant she was ready to give up the habit of "living in her head"; she must learn to free her body to discover its natural sexual response and the fulfillment of its biological role in motherhood. The dream expressed this as the need to make a drastic change; she had to sacrifice the "masculine" hero role.

As one might expect, this educated woman had no difficulty in accepting this interpretation at an intellectual level, and she set about trying to change herself into a more submissive kind of woman. She did then improve her love-life and became the mother of two very satisfactory children. As she grew to know herself better, she began to see that for a man (or the masculine-trained mind in women) life is something that has to be taken by storm, as an act of the heroic will; but for a woman to feel right about herself, life is best realized by a process of awakening.

A universal myth expressing this kind of awakening is found in the fairy tale of Beauty and the Beast. The best-known version of this story relates how Beauty, the youngest of four daughters, becomes her father's favorite because of her unselfish goodness. When she asks her father only for a white rose, instead of the more costly presents demanded by the others, she is aware only of her inner sincerity of feeling. She does not know that she is about to endanger her father's life and her ideal relation with him. For he steals the white rose from the enchanted garden of Beast, who is stirred to anger by the theft and requires him to return in three months for his punishment, presumably death.

(In allowing the father this reprieve to go home with his gift, Beast behaves out of character, especially when he also offers to send him a trunk full of gold when he gets home. As Beauty's father comments, the Beast seems cruel and kind at the same time.)

Beauty insists upon taking her father's punishment and returns after three months to the enchanted castle. There she is given a beautiful room where she has no worries and nothing to fear except the occasional visits of Beast, who repeatedly comes to ask her if she will someday marry him. She always refuses. Then, seeing in a magic mirror a picture of her father lying ill, she begs Beast to allow her to return to comfort him, promising to return in a week. Beast tells her that he will die if she deserts him, but she may go for a week.

At home, her radiant presence brings joy to her father and envy to her sisters, who plot to detain her longer than her promised stay. At length she dreams that Beast is dying of despair. So, realizing she has overstayed her time, she returns to resuscitate him.

Quite forgetting the dying Beast's ugliness, Beauty ministers to him. He tells her that he was unable to live without her, and that he will die happy now that she has returned. But Beauty realizes that she cannot live without Beast, that she has fallen in love with him. She tells him so, and promises to be his wife if only he will not die.

At this the castle is filled with a blaze of light and the sound of music, and Beast disappears. In his place stands a handsome prince, who tells Beauty that he had been enchanted by a witch and turned into the Beast. The spell was ordained to last until a beautiful girl should love Beast for his goodness alone.

In this story, if we unravel the symbolism, we are likely to see that Beauty is any young girl or woman who has entered into an emotional bond with her father, no less binding because of its spiritual nature. Her goodness is symbolized by her request for a white rose, but in a significant twist of meaning her unconscious intention puts her father and then herself in the power of a principle that expresses not goodness alone, but cruelty and kindness combined. It is as if she wished to be rescued from a love holding her to an exclusively virtuous and unreal attitude.

By learning to love Beast she awakens to the power of human love concealed in its animal (and therefore imperfect) but genuinely erotic form. Presumably this represents an awakening of her true function of relatedness, enabling her to accept the erotic component of her original wish, which had to be repressed because of a fear of incest. To leave her father she had, as it were, to accept the incest-fear, to allow herself to live in its presence in fantasy until she could get to know the animal man and discover her own true response to it as a woman.

Three scenes from the 1946 film of *Beauty and the Beast* (directed by France's Jean Cocteau): Left, Beauty's father caught stealing the white rose from the Beast's garden; right, the Beast dying; far right, the Beast transformed into a Prince, walking with Beauty. The story can be said to symbolize a young girl's initiation—i.e. her release from her bond with the father, in order to come to terms with the erotic animal side of her nature. Until this is done, she cannot achieve a true relationship with a man.

In this way she redeems herself and her image of the masculine from the forces of repression, bringing to consciousness her capacity to trust her love as something that combines spirit and nature in the best sense of the words.

A dream of an emancipated woman patient of mine represented this need to remove the incest-fear, a very real fear in this patient's thoughts, because of her father's over-close attachment to her following his wife's death. The dream showed her being chased by a furious bull. She fled at first, but realized it was no use. She fell and the bull was upon her. She knew her only hope was to sing to the bull, and when she did, though in a quavering voice, the bull calmed down and began licking her hand with its tongue. The interpretation showed that she could now learn to relate to men in a more confidently feminine way—not only sexually, but erotically in the wider sense of relatedness on the level of her conscious identity.

But in the cases of older women, the Beast theme may not indicate the need to find the answer to a personal fixation or to release a sexual inhibition, or any of the things that the psychoanalytically minded rationalist may see in the myth. It can be, in fact, the expression of a certain kind of woman's initiation, which may be just as meaningful at the onset of the menopause as at the height of adolescence; and it may appear at any age, when the union of spirit and nature has been disturbed.

A woman of menopausal age reported the following dream:

I am with several anonymous women whom I don't seem to know. We go downstairs in a strange house, and are confronted suddenly by some grotesque "ape-men" with evil faces dressed in fur with gray and black rings, with tails, horrible and leering. We are completely in their power, but suddenly I feel the only way we can save ourselves is not to panic and run or fight, but to treat these creatures with humanity as if to make them aware of their better side. So one of the ape-men comes up to me and I greet him like a dancing partner and begin to dance with him.

Later, I have been given supernatural healing powers and there is a man who is at death's door. I have a kind of quill or perhaps a bird's beak through which I blow air into his nostrils and he begins to breathe again.

During the years of her marriage and the raising of her children, this woman had been obliged to neglect her creative gift, with which she had once made a small but genuine reputation as a writer. At the time of her dream she had been trying to force herself back to work again, at the same time criticizing herself unmercifully for not being a better wife, friend, and mother. The dream showed her problem in the light of other women who might be going through a similar transition, descending, as the dream puts it, into the lower regions of a strange house from a too highly conscious level.

This we can guess to be the entrance to some meaningful aspect of the collective unconscious, with its challenge to accept the masculine principle as animal-man, that same heroic, clown-like Trickster figure we met at the beginning of the primitive hero cycles.

For her to relate to this ape-man, and humanize him by bringing out what is good in him, meant that she would first have to accept some unpredictable element of her natural creative spirit. With this she could cut across the conventional bonds of her life and learn to write in a new way, more appropriate for her in the second part of life.

That this impulse is related to the creative masculine principle is shown in the second scene where she resuscitates a man by blowing air through a kind of bird's beak into his nose. This pneumatic procedure suggests the need for a revival of the spirit rather than the principle of erotic warmth. It is a symbolism known all over the world: The ritual act brings the creative breath of life to any new achievement.

The dream of another woman emphasizes the "nature" aspect of Beauty and the Beast:

Something flies or is thrown in through the window, like a large insect with whirling spiral legs, yellow and black. It then becomes a queer animal, striped yellow and black, like a tiger, with bear-like, almost human paws and a pointed wolf-like face. It may run loose and harm children. It is Sunday afternoon, and I see a little girl all dressed in white on her way to Sunday school. I must get the police to help.

But then I see the creature has become part woman, part animal. It fawns upon me, wants to be loved. I feel it's a fairy-tale situation, or a dream, and only kindness can transform it. I try to embrace it warmly, but I can't go through with it. I push it away. But I have the feeling I must keep it near and get used to it and maybe someday I'll be able to kiss it.

Here we have a different situation from the previous one. This woman had been too intensively carried away by the masculine creative function within herself, which had become a compulsive, mental (that is, "air-borne") preoccupation. Thus she has been prevented from discharging her feminine, wifely function in a natural way. (In association to this dream she said: "When my husband comes home, my creative side goes underground and I become the over-organized housewife.") Her dream takes this unexpected turn of transforming her spirit gone bad into the woman she must accept and cultivate in herself; in this way she can harmonize her creative intellectual interests with the instincts that enable her to relate warmly to others.

This involves a new acceptance of the dual principle of life in nature, of that which is cruel but kind, or, as we might say in her case, ruthlessly adventurous but at the same time humbly and creatively domestic. These opposites obviously cannot be reconciled except on a highly sophisticated psychological level of awareness, and would of course be harmful to that innocent child in her Sunday-school dress.

The interpretation one could place on this woman's dream is that she needed to overcome some excessively naïve image of herself. She had to be willing to embrace the full polarity of her feelings—just as Beauty had to give up the innocence of trusting in a father who could not give her the pure white rose of his feeling without awakening the beneficent fury of the Beast.

Above, the Greek god Dionysus ecstatically playing the lute (in a vase painting). The frenzied and orgiastic rites of the Dionysiac cults symbolized initiation into nature's mysteries. Right, Maenads worshiping Dionysus; far right, satyrs in the same wild worship.

Orpheus and the Son of Man

"Beauty and the Beast" is a fairy tale with the quality of a wild flower, appearing so unexpectedly and creating in us such a natural sense of wonder that we do not notice for the moment that it belongs to a definite class, genus, and species of plant. The kind of mystery inherent in such a story is given a universal application not only in a larger historical myth, but also in the rituals whereby the myth is expressed or from which it may be derived.

The type of ritual and myth appropriately expressing this type of psychological experience is exemplified in the Greco-Roman religion of Dionysus, and in its successor, the religion of Orpheus. Both of these religions provided a significant initiation of the type known as "mysteries." They brought forth symbols associated with a god-man of androgynous character who was supposed to have an intimate understanding of the animal or plant world and to be the master of initiation into their secrets.

The Dionysiac religion contained orgiastic rites that implied the need for an initiate to abandon himself to his animal nature and thereby experience the full fertilizing power of the Earth Mother. The initiating agent for this rite of passage in the Dionysiac ritual was wine. It was supposed to produce the symbolic lowering of consciousness necessary to introduce the novice into the closely guarded secrets of nature, whose essence was expressed by a symbol of erotic fulfillment: the god Dionysus joined with Ariadne, his consort, in a sacred marriage ceremony.

In time the rites of Dionysus lost their emotive religious power. There emerged an almost oriental longing for liberation from their exclusive preoccupation with the purely natural symbols of life and love. The Dionysiac religion, shifting constantly from spiritual to physical and back again, perhaps proved too wild and turbulent for some more ascetic souls. These came to experience their religious ecstasies inwardly, in the worship of Orpheus.

Orpheus was probably a real man, a singer, prophet, and teacher, who was martyred and

whose tomb became a shrine. No wonder the early Christian church saw in Orpheus the prototype of Christ. Both religions brought to the late Hellenistic world the promise of a future divine life. Because they were men, yet also mediators of the divine, for the multitudes of the dying Grecian culture in the days of the Roman Empire they held the longed-for hope of a future life.

There was, however, one important difference between the religion of Orpheus and the religion of Christ. Though sublimated into a mystical form, the Orphic mysteries kept alive the old Dionysiac religion. The spiritual impetus came from a demi-god, in whom was preserved the most significant quality of a religion rooted in the art of agriculture. That quality was the old pattern of the fertility gods who came only for the season—in other words, the eternally recurrent cycle of birth, growth, fullness, and decay.

Christianity, on the other hand, dispelled the mysteries. Christ was the product and reformer of a patriarchal, nomadic, pastoral religion, whose prophets represented their Messiah as a being of absolutely divine origin. The Son of Man, though born of a human virgin, had his beginning in heaven, whence he came in an act of God's incarnation in man. After his death, he returned to heaven—but returned once and for all, to reign on the right hand of God until the Second Coming "when the dead shall arise."

Of course the asceticism of early Christianity did not last. The memory of the cyclic mysteries haunted its followers to the extent that the Church eventually had to incorporate many practices from the pagan past into its rituals. The most meaningful of these may be found in the old records of what was done on Holy Saturday and Easter Sunday in celebration of the resurrection of Christ—the baptismal service that the medieval church made into a suitable and deeply meaningful initiation rite. But that ritual has scarcely survived into modern times, and it is completely absent in Protestantism.

The ritual that has survived much better, and that still contains the meaning of a central initiation mystery for the devout, is the Catholic practice of the elevation of the chalice. It has been described by Dr. Jung in his "Transformation Symbolism in the Mass":

"The lifting up of the chalice in the air prepares the spiritualization . . . of the wine. This is confirmed by the invocation to the Holy

Ghost that immediately follows. . . . The invocation serves to infuse the wine with holy spirit, for it is the Holy Ghost who begets, fulfills, and transforms. . . . After the elevation, the chalice was, in former times, set down to the right of the Host, to correspond with the blood that flowed from the right side of Christ."

The ritual of communion is everywhere the same, whether it is expressed by drinking of the cup of Dionysus or of the holy Christian chalice; but the level of awareness each brings to the individual participant is different. The Dionysiac participant looks back to the origin of things, to the "storm-birth" of the god who is blasted from the resistant womb of Mother Earth. In the frescoes of the Villa de Misteri in Pompeii, the enacted rite evoked the god as a mask of terror reflected in the cup of Dionysus offered by the priest to the initiate. Later we find the winnowing basket, with its precious fruits of the earth, and the phallus as creative symbols of the god's manifestation as the principle of breeding and growth.

In contrast to this backward look, with its central focus on nature's eternal cycle of birth and death, the Christian mystery points forward to the initiate's ultimate hope of union with a transcendent god. Mother Nature, with

Above, a Dionysiac ritual depicted on the great fresco in the Villa of the Mysteries at Pompeii. In the center an initiate is offered the ceremonial cup of Dionysus, in which he sees a reflection of the god-mask held behind. This is a symbolic infusion of the drink with the god's spirit—which can be said to parallel the Roman Catholic ceremony of elevating the chalice during Mass (below).

Left, Orpheus charming the beasts with his song (in a Roman mosaic); above, the murder of Orpheus by Thracian women (on a Greek vase). Below left, Christ as the Good Shepherd (a sixth-century mosaic). Both Orpheus and Christ parallel the archetype of the man of nature —also reflected in the painting by Cranach (below) of "natural man's" innocence. Facing page, left, the 18th-century French philosopher Rousseau, who put forward the idea of the "noble savage"—the simple child of nature free of sin and evil. Far right, the title page of *Walden*, by the 19th-century American writer Thoreau, who believed in and followed a natural way of life almost wholly independent of civilization.

all her beautiful seasonal changes, has been left behind, and the central figure of Christianity offers spiritual certainty, for he is the Son of God in heaven.

Yet the two somehow fuse in the figure of Orpheus, the god who remembers Dionysus but looks forward to Christ. The psychological sense of this intermediate figure has been described by the Swiss author Linda Fierz-David, in her interpretation of the Orphic rite pictured in the Villa de Misteri:

"Orpheus taught while he sang and played the lyre, and his singing was so powerful that it mastered all nature; when he sang to his lyre the birds flew about him, the fish left the water and sprang to him. The wind and the sea became still, the rivers flowed upward toward him. It did not snow and there was no hail. Trees and the very stones followed after Orpheus; tiger and lion lay down near him next to the sheep, and the wolves next to the stag and the roe. Now what does this mean? It surely means that through a divine insight into the meaning of natural events . . . nature's happenings become harmoniously ordered from within. Everything becomes light and all creatures appeased when the mediator, in the act of worshiping, represents the light of nature. Orpheus is an embodiment of devotion and piety; he symbolizes the religious attitude that solves all conflicts, since thereby the whole soul is turned toward that which lies on the other side of all conflict. . . . And as he does this, he is truly Orpheus; that is, a good shepherd, his primitive embodiment. . . ."

Both as good shepherd and as mediator, Orpheus strikes the balance between the Dionysiac religion and the Christian religion, since we find both Dionysus and Christ in similar roles, though, as I have said, differently oriented as to time and direction in space—one a cyclic religion of the nether world, the other heavenly and eschatological, or final. This series of initiatory events, drawn from the context of religious history, is repeated endlessly and with practically every conceivable individual twist of meaning in the dreams and fantasies of modern people.

In a state of heavy fatigue and depression, a woman undergoing analysis had this fantasy:

I sit on the side of a long narrow table in a high vaulted room with no window. My body is hunched over and shrunken. There is nothing over me but a long white linen cloth that hangs from my shoulders to the floor. Something crucial has happened to me. There is not much life left in me. Red crosses on gold disks appear before my eyes. I recall that I have made some sort of commitment a long time ago and wherever I am now must be part of this. I sit there a long time.

Now I slowly open my eyes and I see a man who sits beside me who is to heal me. He appears natural and kind and he is talking to me though I don't hear him. He seems to know all about where I have been. I am aware that I am very ugly and that there must be an odor of death around me. I wonder if he will be repelled. I look at him for a very long time. He does not turn away. I breathe more easily.

Then I feel a cool breeze, or cool water, pour over my body. I wrap the white linen cloth across me now and prepare for a natural sleep. The man's healing hands are on my shoulders. I recall vaguely that there was a time when there were wounds there but the pressure of his hands seems to give me strength and healing.

This woman had previously felt threatened by doubts about her original religious affiliation. She had been brought up as a devout

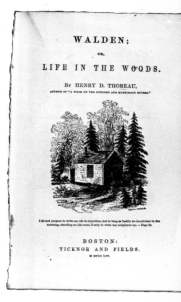

Catholic of the old school, but since her youth she had struggled to free herself from the formal religious conventions followed by her family. Yet the symbolic events of the church year and the richness of her insight into their meaning remained with her throughout the process of her psychological change; and in her analysis I found this working knowledge of religious symbolism most helpful.

The significant elements she singled out of her fantasy were the white cloth, which she understood as a sacrificial cloth; the vaulted room, which she considered to be a tomb; and her commitment, which she associated with the experience of submission. This commitment, as she called it, suggested a ritual of initiation with a perilous descent into the vault of death, which symbolized the way she had left church and family to experience God in her own fashion. She had undergone an "imitation of Christ" in the true symbolic sense, and like him she had suffered the wounds that preceded this death.

The sacrificial cloth suggests the winding sheet or shroud in which the crucified Christ was wrapped and then placed in the tomb. The end of the fantasy introduces the healing figure of a man, loosely associated with me as her analyst but appearing also in his natural role as a friend fully aware of her experience. He speaks to her in words she cannot yet hear, but his hands are reassuring and give a sense of healing. One senses in this figure the touch and the word of the good shepherd, Orpheus or Christ, as mediator and also, of course, as healer. He is on the side of life and has to convince her that she may now come back from the vault of death.

Shall we call this rebirth or resurrection? Both, perhaps, or neither. The essential rite proclaims itself at the end: The cool breeze or water flowing over her body is the primordial act of purification or cleansing of the sin of death, the essence of true baptism.

The same woman had another fantasy in which she felt that her birthday fell upon the day of Christ's resurrection. (This was much more meaningful for her than the memory of her mother, who had never given her the feel-

ing of reassurance and renewal she so much wished for on her childhood birthdays.) But this did not mean she identified herself with the figure of Christ. For all his power and glory, something was lacking; and as she tried to reach him through prayer, he and his cross were lifted up to heaven out of her human reach.

In this second fantasy she fell back upon the symbol of rebirth as a rising sun, and a new feminine symbol began to make its appearance. First of all it appeared as an "embryo in a watery sack." Then she was carrying an eight-year-old boy through the water "passing a danger point." Then a new movement occurred in which she no longer felt threatened or under the influence of death. She was "in a forest by a little spring waterfall . . . green vines grow all around. In my hands I have a stone bowl in which there is spring water, some green moss, and violets. I bathe myself under the waterfall. It is golden and 'silky' and I feel like a child."

The sense of these events is clear, though it is possible to miss the inner meaning in the cryptic description of so many changing images. Here we have, it seems, a process of rebirth in which a larger spiritual self is reborn and baptized in nature as a child. Meanwhile she has rescued an older child who was, in some way, her own ego at the most traumatic period of her childhood. She then carried it through water past the danger point, thus indicating her fear of a paralyzing sense of guilt if she should

depart too far from her family's conventional religion. But religious symbolism is significant by its absence. All is in the hands of nature; we are clearly in the realm of the shepherd Orpheus rather than the risen Christ.

A dream followed this sequence, which brought her to a church resembling the church in Assisi with Giotto's frescoes of St. Francis. She felt more at home here than she would in other churches because St. Francis, like Orpheus, was a religious man of nature. This revived her feelings about the change in her religious affiliation that had been so painful to undergo, but now she believed she could joyfully face the experience, inspired by the light of nature.

The series of dreams ended with a distant echo of the religion of Dionysus. (One could say that this was a reminder that even Orpheus can at times be a little too far removed from the fecundating power of the animal-god in man.) She dreamed that she was leading a fair-haired child by the hand. "We are happily participating in a festival that includes the sun and the forests and flowers all around. The child has a little white flower in her hand, and she places it on the head of a black bull. The bull is part of the festival and is covered with festive decorations." This reference recalls the ancient rites that celebrated Dionysus in the guise of a bull.

But the dream did not end there. The woman added: "Some time later the bull is

Above left, the Persian god Mithras sacrificing the bull. The sacrifice (also part of Dionysiac rites) can be seen as a symbol of the victory of man's spiritual nature over his animality—of which the bull is a common symbol. (This may explain the popularity in some countries of bullfighting, left.) Right, an etching by Picasso (1935) depicts a girl threatened by a Minotaur—here, as in the myth of Theseus, a symbol of man's uncontrollable instinctive forces.

pierced by a golden arrow." Now, besides Dionysus, there is another pre-Christian rite in which the bull plays a symbolic role. The Persian sun-god Mithras sacrifices a bull. He, like Orpheus, represents the longing for a life of the spirit that might triumph over the primitive animal passions of man and, after a ceremony of initiation, give him peace.

This series of images confirms a suggestion that is found in many fantasy or dream sequences of this type—that there is no final peace, no resting point. In their religious quest men and women—especially those who live in modern Western Christianized societies—are still in the power of those early traditions that strive within them for supremacy. It is a conflict of pagan or Christian beliefs, or, one might say, of rebirth or resurrection.

A more direct clue to the solution of this dilemma is to be found, in this woman's first fantasy, in a curious piece of symbolism that could easily be overlooked. The woman says that in her death vault she saw before her eyes a vision of red crosses on gold disks. As became clear later in her analysis, she was about to experience a profound psychic change and to emerge out of this "death" into a new kind of life. We might imagine, therefore, that this image, which came to her in the depth of her despair of life, should in some way herald her future religious attitude. In her subsequent work she did in fact produce evidence for thinking that the red crosses represented her devotion to the Christian attitude, while the gold disks represented her devotion to the pre-Christian mystery religions. Her vision had told her that she must reconcile these Christian and pagan elements in the new life that lay ahead.

One last, but important, observation concerns the ancient initiation rites and their relation to Christianity. The initiation rite celebrated in the Eleusinian mysteries (the rites of worship of the fertility goddesses Demeter and Persephone) was not considered appropriate merely for those who sought to live life more abundantly; it was also used as a preparation for death, as if death also required an initiatory rite of passage of the same kind.

On a funeral urn found in a Roman grave near the Columbarium on the Esquiline Hill we find a clear bas-relief representing scenes of the final stage of initiation where the novice is admitted to the presence and converse of the goddesses. The rest of the design is devoted to two preliminary ceremonies of purification—the sacrifice of the "mystic pig," and a mysticized version of the sacred marriage. This all points to an initiation into death, but in a form that lacks the finality of mourning. It hints at that element of the later mysteries—especially of Orphism—which makes death carry a promise of immortality. Christianity went even further. It promised something more than immortality (which in the old sense of the cyclic mysteries might merely mean reincarnation), for it offered the faithful an everlasting life in heaven.

So we see again, in modern life, the tendency to repeat old patterns. Those who have to learn to face death may have to relearn the old message that tells us that death is a mystery for which we must prepare ourselves in the same spirit of submission and humility as we once learned to prepare ourselves for life.

Symbols of transcendence

The symbols that influence man vary in their purpose. Some men need to be aroused, and experience their initiation in the violence of a Dionysiac "thunder rite." Others need to be subdued, and they are brought to submission in the ordered design of temple precinct or sacred cave, suggestive of the Apollonian religion of later Greece. A full initiation embraces both themes, as we can see when we look either at the material drawn from ancient texts or at living subjects. But it is quite certain that the fundamental goal of initiation lies in taming the original Trickster-like wildness of the juvenile nature. It therefore has a civilizing or spiritualizing purpose, in spite of the violence of the rites that are required to set this process in motion.

There is, however, another kind of symbolism, belonging to the earliest known sacred traditions, that is also connected with the periods of transition in a person's life. But these symbols do not seek to integrate the initiate with any religious doctrine or secular group-consciousness. On the contrary, they point to man's need for liberation from any state of being that is too immature, too fixed or final. In other words, they concern man's release from—or transcendence of—any confining pattern of existence, as he moves toward a superior or more mature stage in his development.

A child, as I have said, possesses a sense of completeness, but only before the initial emergence of his ego-consciousness. In the case of an adult, a sense of completeness is achieved through a union of the consciousness with the unconscious contents of the mind. Out of this union arises what Jung called "the transcendent function of the psyche," by which a man can achieve his highest goal: the full realization of the potential of his individual Self.

Both a bird and a shaman (i.e. a primitive medicine man) are common symbols of transcendence, and often are combined: Left, a prehistoric cave painting at Lascaux shows a shaman in a bird mask. Below, a shaman priestess of a Siberian people, in a bird costume. Right, a shaman's coffin (also Siberian) with bird figures on the posts.

Thus, what we call "symbols of transcendence" are the symbols that represent man's striving to attain this goal. They provide the means by which the contents of the unconscious can enter the conscious mind, and they also are themselves an active expression of those contents.

These symbols are manifold in form. Whether we encounter them in history or in the dreams of contemporary men and women who are at a critical stage in their lives, we can see their importance. At the most archaic level of this symbolism we again meet the Trickster theme. But this time he no longer appears as a lawless would-be hero. He has become the shaman—the medicine man—whose magical practices and flights of intuition stamp him as a primitive master of initiation. His power resides in his supposed ability to leave his body and fly about the universe as a bird.

In this case the bird is the most fitting symbol of transcendence. It represents the peculiar nature of intuition working through a "medium," that is, an individual who is capable of obtaining knowledge of distant events—or facts of which he consciously knows nothing—by going into a trancelike state.

Evidence of such powers can be found as far back as the paleolithic period of prehistory, as the American scholar Joseph Campbell has pointed out in commenting upon one of the famous cave paintings recently discovered in France. At Lascaux, he writes, "there is a shaman depicted, lying in a trance, wearing a bird mask with a figure of a bird perched on a staff beside him. The shamans of Siberia wear such bird costumes to this day, and many are believed to have been conceived by their mothers from the descent of a bird . . . . The shaman, then, is not only a familiar denizen, but even the favored scion of those realms of power that are invisible to our normal waking consciousness, which all may visit briefly in vision, but through which he roams, a master."

At the highest level of this type of initiatory activity, far from those tricks-of-the-trade by which magic so frequently replaces true spiritual insight, we find the Hindu master yogis. In their trance states they go far beyond the normal categories of thought.

One of the commonest dream symbols for this type of release through transcendence is the theme of the lonely journey or pilgrimage, which somehow seems to be a spiritual pilgrim-

In myths or dreams, a lonely journey often symbolizes the liberation of transcendence. Above left, a 15th-century painting of the poet Dante holding his book (the *Divine Comedy*) which relates his dream of a journey to hell (lower left of picture), purgatory, and heaven. Far left, an engraving of the journey made by the pilgrim in the British author John Bunyan's *Pilgrim's Progress* (1678). (Note that the journey is a circular movement toward an inner center.) This book, too, is told as a dream; left, the pilgrim dreaming.

Many people want some change from a containing pattern of life; but the freedom gained by travel (urged by the "run away to sea" poster, right) is no substitute for a true inner liberation.

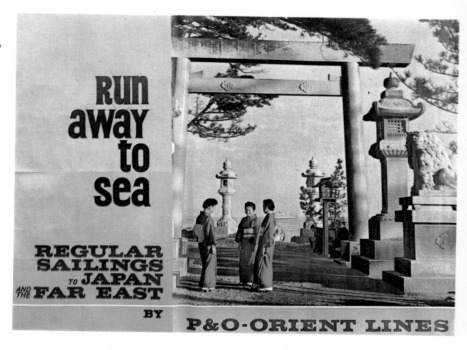

run away to sea

REGULAR SAILINGS TO JAPAN AND THE FAR EAST BY P&O-ORIENT LINES

age on which the initiate becomes acquainted with the nature of death. But this is not death as a last judgment or other initiatory trial of strength; it is a journey of release, renunciation, and atonement, presided over and fostered by some spirit of compassion. This spirit is more often represented by a "mistress" rather than a "master" of initiation, a supreme feminine (i.e. anima) figure such as Kwan-Yin in Chinese Buddhism, Sophia in the Christian-Gnostic doctrine, or the ancient Greek goddess of wisdom Pallas Athena.

Not only the flight of birds or the journey into the wilderness represents this symbolism, but any strong movement exemplifying release. In the first part of life, when one is still attached to the original family and social group, this may be experienced as that moment of initiation at which one must learn to take the decisive steps into life alone. It is the moment that T. S. Eliot describes in "The Waste Land," when one faces

The awful daring of a moment's surrender,
which an age of prudence can never retract.

At a later period of life one may not need to break all ties with the symbols of meaningful containment. But nonetheless one can be filled with that spirit of divine discontent which forces all free men to face some new discovery or to live their lives in a new way. This change may become especially important in the period between middle age and old age, which is the time in life when so many people are considering what to do in their retirement—whether to work or to play, whether to stay at home or to travel.

If their lives have been adventurous, insecure, or full of change, they may long for a settled life and the consolations of religious certainty. But if they have lived chiefly within the social pattern in which they were born, they may desperately need a liberating change. This need may be filled, temporarily, by a trip around the world, or by nothing more than a move to a smaller house. But none of these external changes will serve unless there has been some inner transcendence of old values in creating, not just inventing, a new pattern of life.

A case of this latter sort is a woman who had lived in a style of life that she, her family, and friends had long enjoyed because it was so well rooted, culturally nourishing, and secure from transitory fashions. She had this dream:

I found some strange pieces of wood, not carved but with natural beautiful shapes. Some-

Left, the British explorer R. F. Scott and his companions, photographed in the Antarctic in 1911. Explorers, venturing into the unknown, provide an apt image of the liberation, the breaking out of containment, that characterizes transcendence.

The symbol of the snake is commonly linked with transcendence, because it was traditionally a creature of the underworld—and thus was a "mediator" between one way of life and another. Right, the snake and staff symbol of the Greco-Roman god of medicine Asklepios on a card used to identify a doctor's car in modern France.

152

one said: "Neanderthal man brought them."
Then I saw at a distance these Neanderthal men
looking like a dark mass, but I could not see one
of them distinctly. I thought I would take back
from this place a piece of their wood.

Then I went on, as if on a journey by myself,
and I looked down into an enormous abyss like
an extinct volcano. There was water in part of it
and there I expected to see more Neanderthal
men. But instead I saw black water pigs that had
come out of the water and were running in and
out of the black volcanic rocks.

In contrast to this woman's family attach-
ments and her highly cultivated style of life,
the dream takes her to a prehistoric period
more primitive than anything we can visualize.
She can find no social group among these
ancient men: She sees them as an embodiment
of a truly unconscious, collective "dark mass"
in the distance. Yet they are alive, and she may
carry away a piece of their wood. The dream
emphasizes that the wood is natural, not carved;
therefore it comes from a primordial, not a culturally conditioned, level of the unconscious.
The piece of wood, remarkable for its great age,
links this woman's contemporary experience to
the distant origins of human life.

We know from many examples that an
ancient tree or plant represents symbolically the

growth and development of psychic life (as
distinct from instinctual life, commonly symbolized by animals). Hence, in this piece of wood,
this woman acquired a symbol of her link with
the deepest layers of the collective unconscious.

Next she speaks of continuing her journey
alone. This theme, as I have already pointed
out, symbolizes the need for release as an initiatory experience. So here we have another symbol of transcendence.

Then, in the dream, she sees a huge crater of
an extinct volcano, which has been the channel
for a violent eruption of fire from the deepest
layers of the earth. We can surmise that this
refers to a significant memory trace, which leads
back to a traumatic experience. This she associated to a personal experience early in her life
when she had felt the destructive, yet creative,
force of her passions to such an extent that she
feared she would go out of her mind. She had
found, in late adolescence, a quite unexpected
need to break away from her family's excessively conventional social pattern. She had
achieved this break without serious distress, and
had been able to return eventually to make her
peace with the family. But there lingered a
profound wish to make a still greater differentiation from her family background and to find
freedom from her own pattern of existence.

This dream recalls another. It came from a
young man who had a totally different problem
but who seemed to need a similar type of insight. He too had the urge to achieve differentiation. He dreamed of a volcano, and from its
crater he saw two birds taking flight as if in
fear that the volcano was about to erupt. This
was in a strange, lonely place with a body of
water between him and the volcano. In this
case, the dream represented an individual
initiation journey.

It is similar to cases reported among the
simple food-gathering tribes, which are the least
family-conscious groups we know. In these
societies the young initiate must take a lonely
journey to a sacred place (in Indian cultures of
the North Pacific coast, it may actually be a
crater lake) where, in a visionary or trancelike
state, he encounters his "guardian spirit" in the

form of an animal, a bird, or natural object. He closely identifies himself with this "bush soul" and thereby becomes a man. Without such an experience he is regarded, as an Achumaui medicine man put it, as "an ordinary Indian, nobody."

The young man's dream came at the beginning of his life, and it pointed to his future independence and identity as a man. The woman I have described was approaching the end of her life, and she experienced a similar journey and seemed to need to acquire a similar independence. She could live out the remainder of her days in harmony with an eternal human law that, by its antiquity, transcended the known symbols of culture.

But such independence does not end in a state of yogi-like detachment that would mean a renunciation of the world with all its impurities. In the otherwise dead and blasted landscape of her dream the woman saw signs of animal life. These are "water pigs," unknown to her as a species. They therefore would carry the meaning of a special type of animal, one that can live in two environments, in water or on the earth.

This is the universal quality of the animal as a symbol of transcendence. These creatures, figuratively coming from the depths of the ancient Earth Mother, are symbolic denizens of the collective unconscious. They bring into the field of consciousness a special chthonic (underworld) message that is somewhat different from the spiritual aspirations symbolized by the birds in the young man's dream.

Other transcendent symbols of the depths are rodents, lizards, snakes, and sometimes fish. These are intermediate creatures that combine underwater activity and the bird-flight with an intermediate terrestrial life. The wild duck or the swan are cases in point. Perhaps the commonest dream symbol of transcendence is the snake, as represented by the therapeutic symbol of the Roman god of medicine Aesculapius, which has survived to modern times as a sign of the medical profession. This was originally a nonpoisonous tree snake; as we see it, coiled around the staff of the healing god, it seems to embody a kind of mediation between earth and heaven.

A still more important and widespread symbol of chthonic transcendence is the motif of the two entwined serpents. These are the famous Naga serpents of ancient India; and we also find them in Greece as the entwined serpents on the end of the staff belonging to the god Hermes. An early Grecian herm is a stone pillar with a bust of the god above. On one side are the entwined serpents and on the other an erect phallus. As the serpents are represented

Left, a 17th-century French painting reveals the snake's role as mediator between this world and the next. Orpheus is playing his lyre; he and his audience fail to notice that Eurydice (center of picture) has been bitten by a snake—a fatal wound that symbolizes her descent into the underworld.

Above, the Egyptian god Thoth with the head of a bird (an ibis), in a relief from *c.* 350 B.C. Thoth is an "underworld" figure associated with transcendence; it was he who judged the souls of the dead. The Greek god Hermes, who was called "psycho-pomp" (soul-guide), had the function of guiding the dead to the underworld. Left, a stone *herm*, which was placed at crossroads (symbolizing the god's role as a mediator between two worlds). On the side of the herm is a snake twined around a staff; this symbol (the *caduceus*) was carried over to the Roman god Mercury (right, a 16th-century Italian bronze), who also acquired wings, recalling the bird as a symbol of spiritual transcendence.

in the act of sexual union and the erect phallus is unequivocally sexual, we can draw certain conclusions about the function of the herm as a symbol of fertility.

But we are mistaken if we think this only refers to biological fertility. Hermes is Trickster in a different role as a messenger, a god of the cross-roads, and finally the leader of souls to and from the underworld. His phallus therefore penetrates from the known into the unknown world, seeking a spiritual message of deliverance and healing.

Originally in Egypt Hermes was known as the ibis-headed god Thoth, and therefore was conceived as the bird form of the transcendent principle. Again, in the Olympian period of Greek mythology, Hermes recovered attributes of the bird life to add to his chthonic nature as serpent. His staff acquired wings above the serpents, becoming the *caduceus* or winged staff of Mercury, and the god himself became the "flying man" with his winged hat and sandals.

Here we see his full power of transcendence, whereby the lower transcendence from underworld snake-consciousness, passing through the medium of earthly reality, finally attains transcendence to superhuman or transpersonal reality in its winged flight.

Such a composite symbol is found in other representations as the winged horse or winged dragon or other creatures that abound in the artistic expressions of alchemy, so fully illustrated in Dr. Jung's classic work on this subject. We follow the innumerable vicissitudes of these symbols in our work with patients. They show what our therapy can expect to achieve when it liberates the deeper psychic contents so that they can become part of our conscious equipment for understanding life more effectively.

It is not easy for modern man to grasp the significance of the symbols that come down to us from the past or that appear in our dreams. Nor is it easy to see how the ancient conflict between symbols of containment and liberation

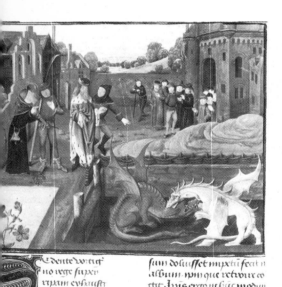

Winged dragons (above, from a 15th-century manuscript) combine the transcendent symbolism of the snake and the bird. Right, an image of spiritual transcendence: Mohammed on the winged mare Buraq flies through the celestial spheres.

relates to our own predicament. Yet it becomes easier when we realize it is only the specific forms of these archaic patterns that change, not their psychic meaning.

We have been talking of wild birds as symbols of release or liberation. But today we could as well speak of jet planes and space rockets, for they are the physical embodiment of the same transcendent principle, freeing us at least temporarily from gravity. In the same way the ancient symbols of containment, which once gave stability and protection, now appear in modern man's search for economic security and social welfare.

Any of us can see, of course, that there is a conflict in our lives between adventure and discipline, or evil and virtue, or freedom and security. But these are only phrases we use to describe an ambivalence that troubles us, and to which we never seem able to find an answer.

There is an answer. There is a meeting point between containment and liberation, and we can find it in the rites of initiation that I have been discussing. They can make it possible for individuals, or whole groups of people, to unite the opposing forces within themselves and achieve an equilibrium in their lives.

But the rites do not offer this opportunity invariably, or automatically. They relate to particular phases in the life of an individual, or of a group, and unless they are properly understood and translated into a new way of life, the moment can pass. Initiation is, essentially, a process that begins with a rite of submission, followed by a period of containment, and then by a further rite of liberation. In this way every individual can reconcile the conflicting elements of his personality: He can strike a balance that makes him truly human, and truly the master of himself.

In the dreams and fantasies of many modern people, the flights of the great rockets of space research have often appeared as symbolic 20th-century embodiments of the urge toward liberation and release that is called transcendence.

3 The process of individuation

M.-L. von Franz

The pattern of psychic growth

At the beginning of this book Dr. C. G. Jung introduced the reader to the concept of the unconscious, its personal and collective structures, and its symbolic mode of expression. Once one has seen the vital importance (that is, the healing or destructive impact) of the symbols produced by the unconscious, there remains the difficult problem of interpretation. Dr. Jung has shown that everything depends on whether any particular interpretation "clicks" and is meaningful to the individual concerned. In this way he has indicated the possible meaning and function of dream symbolism.

But, in the development of Jung's theory, this possibility raised another question: What is the purpose of the *total* dream life of the individual? What role do dreams play, not only in the immediate psychic economy of the human being, but in his life as a whole?

By observing a great many people and studying their dreams (he estimated that he interpreted at least 80,000 dreams), Jung discovered not only that all dreams are relevant in varying degrees to the life of the dreamer, but that they are all parts of one great web of psychological factors. He also found that, on the whole, they seem to follow an arrangement or pattern. This pattern Jung called "the process of individuation." Since dreams produce different scenes and images every night, people who are not careful observers will probably be unaware of any pattern. But if one watches one's own dreams over a period of years and studies the entire sequence, one will see that certain contents emerge, disappear, and then turn up again. Many people even dream repeatedly of the same figures, landscapes, or situations; and if one follows these through a whole series, one will see that they change slowly but perceptibly. These changes can be accelerated if the dreamer's conscious attitude is influenced by appropriate interpretation of the dreams and their symbolic contents.

Below, a "meander" (a decoration in a seventh-century manuscript). Individual dreams seem as strange and fragmented as the detail, above, from the decoration; but over a lifetime's dreaming, a meandering pattern appears—revealing the process of psychic growth.

Thus our dream life creates a meandering pattern in which individual strands or tendencies become visible, then vanish, then return again. If one watches this meandering design over a long period of time, one can observe a sort of hidden regulating or directing tendency at work, creating a slow, imperceptible process of psychic growth—the process of individuation.

Gradually a wider and more mature personality emerges, and by degrees becomes effective and even visible to others. The fact that we often speak of "arrested development" shows that we assume that such a process of growth and maturation is possible with every individual. Since this psychic growth cannot be brought about by a conscious effort of will power, but happens involuntarily and naturally, it is in dreams frequently symbolized by the tree, whose slow, powerful, involuntary growth fulfills a definite pattern.

The organizing center from which the regulatory effect stems seems to be a sort of "nuclear atom" in our psychic system. One could also call it the inventor, organizer, and source of dream images. Jung called this center the "Self" and described it as the totality of the whole psyche, in order to distinguish it from the "ego," which constitutes only a small part of the total psyche.

Throughout the ages men have been intuitively aware of the existence of such an inner center. The Greeks called it man's inner *daimon*; in Egypt it was expressed by the concept of the *Ba-soul*; and the Romans worshiped it as the "genius" native to each individual. In more primitive societies it was often thought of as a protective spirit embodied within an animal or a fetish.

This inner center is realized in exceptionally pure, unspoiled form by the Naskapi Indians, who still exist in the forests of the Labrador peninsula. These simple people are hunters who live in isolated family groups, so far from one

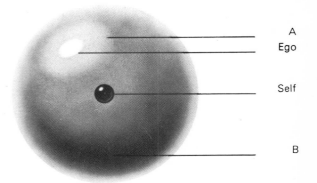

The psyche can be compared to a sphere with a bright field (A) on its surface, representing consciousness. The *ego* is the field's center (only if "I" know a thing is it conscious). The *Self* is at once the nucleus and the whole sphere (B); its internal regulating processes produce dreams.

another that they have not been able to evolve tribal customs or collective religious beliefs and ceremonies. In his lifelong solitude the Naskapi hunter has to rely on his own inner voices and unconscious revelations; he has no religious teachers who tell him what he should believe, no rituals, festivals, or customs to help him along. In his basic view of life, the soul of man is simply an "inner companion," whom he calls "my friend" or *Mista'peo*, meaning "Great Man." Mista'peo dwells in the heart and is immortal; in the moment of death, or shortly before, he leaves the individual, and later reincarnates himself in another being.

Those Naskapi who pay attention to their dreams and who try to find their meaning and test their truth can enter into a deeper connection with the Great Man. He favors such people and sends them more and better dreams. Thus the major obligation of an individual Naskapi is to follow the instructions given by his dreams, and then to give permanent form to their contents in art. Lies and dishonesty drive the Great Man away from one's inner realm, whereas generosity and love of one's neighbors and of animals attract him and give him life. Dreams give the Naskapi complete ability to find his way in life, not only in the inner world but also in the outer world of nature. They help him to foretell the weather and give him invaluable guidance in his hunting, upon which his life depends. I mention these very primitive people because they are uncontaminated by our civilized ideas and still have natural insight into the essence of what Jung calls the Self.

The Self can be defined as an inner guiding factor that is different from the conscious personality and that can be grasped only through the investigation of one's own dreams. These show it to be the regulating center that brings about a constant extension and maturing of the personality. But this larger, more nearly total aspect of the psyche appears first as merely an inborn possibility. It may emerge very slightly, or it may develop relatively completely during one's lifetime. How far it develops depends on whether or not the ego is willing to listen to the messages of the Self./Just as the Naskapi have noticed that a person who is receptive to the hints of the Great Man gets better and more helpful dreams, we could add that the inborn Great Man becomes more real within the receptive person than in those who neglect him. Such a person also becomes a more complete human being./

It even seems as if the ego has not been produced by nature to follow its own arbitrary impulses to an unlimited extent, but to help to make real the totality—the whole psyche. It is the ego that serves to light up the entire system, allowing it to become conscious and thus to be realized. If, for example, I have an artistic talent of which my ego is not conscious, nothing will happen to it. The gift may as well be nonexistent. Only if my ego notices it can I bring it into reality. The inborn but hidden totality of the psyche is not the same thing as a wholeness that is fully realized and lived.

One could picture this in the following way: The seed of a mountain pine contains the whole future tree in a latent form; but each seed falls at a certain time onto a particular place, in which there are a number of special factors, such as the quality of the soil and the stones, the slope of the land, and its exposure to sun and wind. The latent totality of the pine in the seed reacts to these circumstances by avoiding the stones and inclining toward the sun, with the result that the tree's growth is shaped. Thus an individual pine slowly comes into existence, constituting the fulfillment of its totality, its emergence into the realm of reality. Without the living tree, the image of the pine is only a possibility or an abstract idea. Again, the realization of this uniqueness in the individual man is the goal of the process of individuation.

From one point of view this process takes place in man (as well as in every other living being) by itself and in the unconscious; it is a process by which man lives out his innate human nature. Strictly speaking, however, the process of individuation is real only if the individual is aware of it and consequently makes a living connection with it. We do not know whether the pine tree is aware of its own growth, whether it enjoys and suffers the different vicissitudes that shape it. But man certainly is able to participate consciously in his development. He even feels that from time to time, by making free decisions, he can co-operate actively with it. This co-operation belongs to the process of individuation in the narrower sense of the word.

Man, however, experiences something that is not contained in our metaphor of the pine tree. The individuation process is more than a coming to terms between the inborn germ of wholeness and the outer acts of fate. Its subjective experience conveys the feeling that some supra-personal force is actively interfering in a creative way. One sometimes feels that the unconscious is leading the way in accordance with a secret design. It is as if something is looking at me, something that I do not see but that sees me—perhaps that Great Man in the heart, who tells me his opinions about me by means of dreams.

But this creatively active aspect of the psychic nucleus can come into play only when the ego gets rid of all purposive and wishful aims and tries to get to a deeper, more basic form of existence. The ego must be able to listen attentively and to give itself, without any further design or purpose, to that inner urge toward growth. Many existentialist philosophers try to describe this state, but they go only as far as stripping off the illusions of consciousness: They go right up to the door of the unconscious and then fail to open it.

People living in cultures more securely rooted than our own have less trouble in understanding that it is necessary to give up the utilitarian attitude of conscious planning in order to make way for the inner growth of the personality. I once met an elderly lady who had not achieved much in her life, in terms of outward achievement. But she had in fact made a good marriage with a difficult husband, and had somehow developed into a mature personality. When she complained to me that she had not "done" anything in her life, I told her a story related by a Chinese sage, Chuang-Tzu. She understood immediately and felt great relief. This is the story:

A wandering carpenter, called Stone, saw on his travels a gigantic old oak tree standing in a field near an earth-altar. The carpenter said to his apprentice, who was admiring the oak: "This is

An earth altar beneath a tree (in a 19th-century Chinese painting). Such round or square structures usually symbolize the Self, to which the ego must submit to fulfill the process of individuation.

a useless tree. If you wanted to make a ship, it would soon rot; if you wanted to make tools, they would break. You can't do anything useful with this tree, and that's why it has become so old."

But in an inn, that same evening, when the carpenter went to sleep, the old oak tree appeared to him in his dream and said: "Why do you compare me to your cultivated trees such as whitethorn, pear, orange, and apple trees, and all the others that bear fruit? Even before they can ripen their fruit, people attack and violate them. Their branches are broken, their twigs are torn. Their own gifts bring harm to them, and they cannot live out their natural span. That is what happens everywhere, and that is why I have long since tried to become completely useless. You poor mortal! Imagine if I had been useful in any way, would I have reached this size? Furthermore, you and I are both creatures, and how can one creature set himself so high as to judge another creature? You useless mortal man, what do you know about useless trees?"

The carpenter woke up and meditated upon his dream, and later, when his apprentice asked him why just this one tree served to protect the earth-altar, he answered, "Keep your mouth shut! Let's hear no more about it! The tree grew here on purpose because anywhere else people would have ill-treated it. If it were not the tree of the earth-altar, it might have been chopped down."

The carpenter obviously understood his dream. He saw that simply to fulfill one's destiny is the greatest human achievement, and that our utilitarian notions have to give way in the face of the demands of our unconscious psyche. If we translate this metaphor into psychological language, the tree symbolizes the process of individuation, giving a lesson to our shortsighted ego.

Under the tree that fulfilled its destiny, there was—in Chuang-Tzu's story—an earth-altar. This was a crude, unwrought stone upon which people made sacrifices to the local god who "owned" this piece of land. The symbol of the earth-altar points to the fact that in order to bring the individuation process into reality, one must surrender consciously to the power of the unconscious, instead of thinking in terms of what one should do, or of what is generally thought right, or of what usually happens. One must simply listen, in order to learn what the inner totality—the Self—wants one to do here and now in a particular situation.

Our attitude must be like that of the mountain pine mentioned above: It does not get annoyed when its growth is obstructed by a stone, nor does it make plans about how to overcome the obstacles. It merely tries to feel whether it should grow more toward the left or the right, toward the slope or away from it. Like the tree, we should give in to this almost imperceptible, yet powerfully dominating, impulse—an impulse that comes from the urge toward unique, creative self-realization. And this is a process in which one must repeatedly seek out and find something that is not yet known to anyone. The guiding hints or impulses come, not from the ego, but from the totality of the psyche: the Self.

It is, moreover, useless to cast furtive glances at the way someone else is developing, because each of us has a unique task of self-realization. Although many human problems are similar, they are never identical. All pine trees are very much alike (otherwise we should not recognize them as pines), yet none is exactly the same as another. Because of these factors of sameness and difference, it is difficult to summarize the infinite variations of the process of individua-

tion. The fact is that each person has to do something different, something that is uniquely his own.

Many people have criticized the Jungian approach for not presenting psychic material systematically. But these critics forget that the material itself is a living experience charged with emotion, by nature irrational and ever-changing, which does not lend itself to systematization except in the most superficial fashion. Modern depth psychology has here reached the same limits that confront microphysics. That is, when we are dealing with statistical averages, a rational and systematic description of the facts is possible. But when we are attempting to describe a single psychic event, we can do no more than present an honest picture of it from as many angles as possible. In the same way, scientists have to admit that they do not know what light is. They can say only that in certain experimental conditions it seems to consist of particles, while in other experimental conditions it seems to consist of waves. But what it is "in itself" is not known. The psychology of the unconscious and any description of the process of individuation encounter comparable difficulties of definition. But I will try here to give a sketch of some of their most typical features.

The first approach of the unconscious

For most people the years of youth are characterized by a state of gradual awakening in which the individual slowly becomes aware of the world and of himself. Childhood is a period of great emotional intensity, and a child's earliest dreams often manifest in symbolic form the basic structure of the psyche, indicating how it will later shape the destiny of the individual concerned. For example, Jung once told a group of students about a young woman who was so haunted by anxiety that she committed suicide at the age of 26. As a small child, she had dreamed that "Jack Frost" had entered her room while she was lying in bed and pinched her on the stomach. She woke and discovered that she had pinched herself with her own hand. The dream did not frighten her; she merely remembered that she had had such a dream. But the fact that she did not react emotionally to her strange encounter with the demon of the cold—of congealed life—did not augur well for the future and was itself abnormal. It was with a cold, unfeeling hand that she later put an end to her life. From this single dream it is possible to deduce the tragic fate of the dreamer, which was anticipated by her psyche in childhood.

Sometimes it is not a dream but some very impressive and unforgettable real event that, like a prophecy, anticipates the future in symbolic form. It is well known that children often forget events that seem impressive to adults but keep a vivid recollection of some incident or story that no one else has noticed. When we look into one of these childhood memories, we usually find that it depicts (if interpreted as if it were a symbol) a basic problem of the child's psychic makeup.

When a child reaches school age, the phase of building up the ego and of adapting to the outer world begins. This phase generally brings a number of painful shocks. At the same time, some children begin to feel very different from others, and this feeling of being unique brings a certain sadness that is part of the loneliness of many youngsters. The imperfections of the world, and the evil within oneself as well as out-

A child, adapting to the outside world, receives many psychological shocks: far left, the fearful first day at school; center, the surprise and pain resulting from an attack by another child; left, the grief and bewilderment of the first experience of death. As in effect a protection from such shocks, the child may dream or draw a circular, quadrangular, nuclear motif (above) that symbolizes the all-important center of the psyche.

side, become conscious problems; the child must try to cope with urgent (but not yet understood) inner impulses as well as the demands of the outer world.

If the development of consciousness is disturbed in its normal unfolding, children frequently retire from outer or inner difficulties into an inner "fortress"; and when that happens, their dreams and symbolic drawings of unconscious material often reveal to an unusual degree a type of circular, quadrangular, and "nuclear" motif (which I will explain later). This refers to the previously mentioned psychic nucleus, the vital center of the personality from which the whole structural development of consciousness stems. It is natural that the image of the center should appear in an especially striking way when the psychic life of the individual is threatened. From this central nucleus (as far as we know today), the whole building up of ego consciousness is directed, the ego apparently being a duplicate or structural counterpart of the original center.

In this early phase there are many children who earnestly seek for some meaning in life that could help them to deal with the chaos both within and outside themselves. There are others, however, who are still unconsciously carried

along by the dynamism of inherited and instinctive archetypal patterns. These young people are not concerned about the deeper meaning of life, because their experiences with love, nature, sport, and work contain an immediate and satisfying meaning for them. They are not necessarily more superficial; usually they are carried by the stream of life with less friction and disturbance than their more introspective fellows. If I travel in a car or train without looking out, it is only the stops, starts, and sudden turns that make me realise I am moving at all.

The actual process of individuation—the conscious coming-to-terms with one's own inner center (psychic nucleus) or Self—generally begins with a wounding of the personality and the suffering that accompanies it. This initial shock amounts to a sort of "call," although it is not often recognized as such. On the contrary, the ego feels hampered in its will or its desire and usually projects the obstruction onto something external. That is, the ego accuses God or the economic situation or the boss or the marriage partner of being responsible for whatever is obstructing it.

Or perhaps everything seems outwardly all right, but beneath the surface a person is suffering from a deadly boredom that makes every-

thing seem meaningless and empty. Many myths and fairy tales symbolically describe this initial stage in the process of individuation by telling of a king who has fallen ill or grown old. Other familiar story patterns are that a royal couple is barren; or that a monster steals all the women, children, horses, and wealth of the kingdom; or that a demon keeps the king's army or his ship from proceeding on its course; or that darkness hangs over the lands, wells dry up, and flood, drought, and frost afflict the country. Thus it seems as if the initial encounter with the Self casts a dark shadow ahead of time, or as if the "inner friend" comes at first like a trapper to catch the helplessly struggling ego in his snare.

In myths one finds that the magic or talisman that can cure the misfortune of the king or his country always proves to be something very special. In one tale "a white blackbird" or "a fish that carries a golden ring in its gills" is needed to restore the king's health. In another, the king wants "the water of life" or "three golden hairs from the head of the devil" or "a woman's golden plait" (and afterward, naturally, the owner of the plait). Whatever it is, the thing that can drive away the evil is always unique and hard to find.

It is exactly the same in the initial crisis in the life of an individual. One is seeking something that is impossible to find or about which nothing is known. In such moments all well-meant, sensible advice is completely useless—advice that urges one to try to be responsible, to take a holiday, not to work so hard (or to work harder), to have more (or less) human contact, or to take up a hobby. None of that helps, or at best only rarely. There is only one thing that seems to work; and that is to turn directly toward the approaching darkness without prejudice and totally naïvely, and to try to find out what its secret aim is and what it wants from you.

The hidden purpose of the oncoming darkness is generally something so unusual, so unique and unexpected, that as a rule one can find out what it is only by means of dreams and fantasies welling up from the unconscious. If one focuses attention on the unconscious without rash assumptions or emotional rejection, it often breaks through in a flow of helpful symbolic images. But not always. Sometimes it first offers a series of painful realizations of what is wrong with oneself and one's conscious attitudes. Then one must begin the process by swallowing all sorts of bitter truths.

Far left, a woodcut from a 17th-century alchemical manuscript depicts a king who has fallen ill—a common symbolic image of the emptiness and boredom (in the consciousness) that can mark the initial stage of the individuation process. Left, from the 1960 Italian film *La Dolce Vita,* another image of this psychological state: Guests explore the run-down interior of a decayed aristocrat's castle.

Right, a painting by the modern Swiss artist Paul Klee entitled *Fairy Tale.* It illustrates a tale of a young man who sought and found the "bluebird of happiness," and so could marry a princess. In many fairy tales such a talisman is necessary to cure illness or misfortune, symbols of our feelings of emptiness and futility.

The realization of the shadow

Whether the unconscious comes up at first in a helpful or a negative form, after a time the need usually arises to readapt the conscious attitude in a better way to the unconscious factors—therefore to accept what seems to be "criticism" from the unconscious. Through dreams one becomes acquainted with aspects of one's own personality that for various reasons one has preferred not to look at too closely. This is what Jung called "the realization of the shadow." (He used the term "shadow" for this unconscious part of the personality because it actually often appears in dreams in a personified form.)

The shadow is not the whole of the unconscious personality. It represents unknown or little-known attributes and qualities of the ego —aspects that mostly belong to the personal sphere and that could just as well be conscious. In some aspects, the shadow can also consist of collective factors that stem from a source outside the individual's personal life.

When an individual makes an attempt to see his shadow, he becomes aware of (and often ashamed of) those qualities and impulses he denies in himself but can plainly see in other people—such things as egotism, mental laziness, and sloppiness; unreal fantasies, schemes, and plots; carelessness and cowardice; inordinate love of money and possessions—in short, all the little sins about which he might previously have told himself: "That doesn't matter; nobody will notice it, and in any case other people do it too."

If you feel an overwhelming rage coming up in you when a friend reproaches you about a fault, you can be fairly sure that at this point you will find a part of your shadow, of which you are unconscious. It is, of course, natural to become annoyed when others who are "no better" criticize you because of shadow faults. But what can you say if your own dreams—an inner judge in your own being—reproach you? That is the moment when the ego gets caught, and the result is usually embarrassed silence. Afterward the painful and lengthy work of self-education begins—a work, we might say, that is the psychological equivalent of the labors of Hercules. This unfortunate hero's first task, you will remember, was to clean up in one day the Augean Stables, in which hundreds of cattle had dropped their dung for many decades—a task

Three examples of a "collective infection" that can weld people into an irrational mob—and to which the *shadow* (the dark side of the ego-personality) is vulnerable. Left, a scene from a 1961 Polish film concerning 17th-century French nuns who were "possessed by the devil." Right, a drawing by Brueghel depicts the affliction (largely psychosomatic) called "St. Vitus' Dance," which was widespread in the Middle Ages. Far right, the fiery-cross emblem of the Ku Klux Klan, the white supremacy "secret society" of America's South whose racial intolerance has often led to acts of mob violence.

so enormous that the ordinary mortal would be overcome by discouragement at the mere thought of it.

The shadow does not consist only of omissions. It shows up just as often in an impulsive or inadvertent act. Before one has time to think, the evil remark pops out, the plot is hatched, the wrong decision is made, and one is confronted with results that were never intended or consciously wanted. Furthermore, the shadow is exposed to collective infections to a much greater extent than is the conscious personality. When a man is alone, for instance, he feels relatively all right; but as soon as "the others" do dark, primitive things, he begins to fear that if he doesn't join in, he will be considered a fool. Thus he gives way to impulses that do not really belong to him at all. It is particularly in contacts with people of the same sex that one stumbles over both one's own shadow and those of other people. Although we do see the shadow in a person of the opposite sex, we are usually much less annoyed by it and can more easily pardon it.

In dreams and myths, therefore, the shadow appears as a person of the same sex as that of the dreamer. The following dream may serve as an example. The dreamer was a man of 48 who tried to live very much for and by himself, working hard and disciplining himself, repressing pleasure and spontaneity to a far greater extent than suited his real nature.

I owned and inhabited a very big house in town, and I didn't yet know all its different parts. So I took a walk through it and discovered, mainly in the cellar, several rooms about which I knew nothing and even exits leading into other cellars or into subterranean streets. I felt uneasy when I found that several of these exits were not locked and some had no locks at all. Moreover, there were some laborers at work in the neighborhood who could have sneaked in. . . .

When I came up again to the ground floor, I passed a back yard where again I discovered different exits into the street or into other houses. When I tried to investigate them more closely, a man came up to me laughing loudly and calling out that we were old pals from the elementary school. I remembered him too, and while he was telling me about his life, I walked along with him toward the exit and strolled with him through the streets.

There was a strange chiaroscuro in the air as we walked through an enormous circular street

and arrived at a green lawn where three galloping horses suddenly passed us. They were beautiful, strong animals, wild but well-groomed, and they had no rider with them. (Had they run away from military service?)

The maze of strange passages, chambers, and unlocked exits in the cellar recalls the old Egyptian representation of the underworld, which is a well-known symbol of the unconscious with its unknown possibilities. It also shows how one is "open" to other influences in one's unconscious shadow side, and how uncanny and alien elements can break in. The cellar, one can say, is the basement of the dreamer's psyche. In the back yard of the strange building (which represents the still unperceived psychic scope of the dreamer's personality) an old school friend suddenly turns up. This person obviously personifies another aspect of the dreamer himself—an aspect that had been part of his life as a child but that he had forgotten and lost. It often happens that a person's childhood qualities (for instance, gaiety, irascibility, or perhaps trustfulness) suddenly

disappear, and one does not know where or how they have gone. It is such a lost characteristic of the dreamer that now returns (from the back yard) and tries to make friends again. This figure probably stands for the dreamer's neglected capacity for enjoying life and for his extraverted shadow side.

But we soon learn why the dreamer feels "uneasy" just before meeting this seemingly harmless old friend. When he strolls with him in the street, the horses break loose. The dreamer thinks they may have escaped from military service (that is to say, from the conscious discipline that has hitherto characterized his life). The fact that the horses have no rider shows that instinctive drives can get away from conscious control. In this old friend, and in the horses, all the positive force reappears that was lacking before and that was badly needed by the dreamer.

This is a problem that often comes up when one meets one's "other side." The shadow usually contains values that are needed by consciousness, but that exist in a form that makes it

difficult to integrate them into one's life. The
passages and the large house in this dream also
show that the dreamer does not yet know his
own psychic dimensions and is not yet able to
fill them out.

The shadow in this dream is typical for an
introvert (a man who tends to retire too much
from outer life). In the case of an extravert, who
is turned more toward outer objects and outer
life, the shadow would look quite different.

A young man who had a very lively temperament
embarked again and again on successful
enterprises, while at the same time his dreams
insisted that he should finish off a piece of private
creative work he had begun. The following
was one of those dreams:

A man is lying on a couch and has pulled the
cover over his face. He is a Frenchman, a desperado
who would take on any criminal job. An
official is accompanying me downstairs, and I
know that a plot has been made against me:
namely, that the Frenchman should kill me as if
by chance. (That is how it would look from the
outside.) He actually sneaks up behind me when

we approach the exit, but I am on my guard. A
tall, portly man (rather rich and influential) suddenly
leans against the wall beside me, feeling ill.
I quickly grab the opportunity to kill the official
by stabbing his heart. "One only notices a bit of
moisture"—this is said like a comment. Now I
am safe, for the Frenchman won't attack me since
the man who gave him his orders is dead. (Probably
the official and the successful portly man
are the same person, the latter somehow replacing
the former.)

The desperado represents the other side of
the dreamer—his introversion—which has
reached a completely destitute state. He lies on
a couch (i.e. he is passive) and pulls the cover
over his face because he wants to be left alone.
The official, on the other hand, and the prosperous
portly man (who are secretly the same person)
personify the dreamer's successful outer responsibilities
and activities. The sudden illness
of the portly man is connected with the fact that
this dreamer had in fact become ill several times
when he had allowed his dynamic energy to explode
too forcibly in his external life. But this

171

successful man has no blood in his veins—only a sort of moisture—which means that these external ambitious activities of the dreamer contain no genuine life and no passion, but are bloodless mechanisms. Thus it would be no real loss if the portly man were killed. At the end of the dream, the Frenchman is satisfied; he obviously represents a positive shadow figure who had turned negative and dangerous only because the conscious attitude of the dreamer did not agree with him.

This dream shows us that the shadow can consist of many different elements—for instance, of unconscious ambition (the successful portly man) and of introversion (the Frenchman). This particular dreamer's association to the French, moreover, was that they know how to handle love affairs very well. Therefore the two shadow figures also represent two well-known drives: power and sex. The power drive appears momentarily in a double form, both as an official and as a successful man. The official, or civil servant, personifies collective adaptation, whereas the successful man denotes ambition; but naturally both serve the power drive. When the dreamer succeeds in stopping this dangerous inner force, the Frenchman is suddenly no longer hostile. In other words, the equally dangerous aspect of the sex drive has also surrendered.

Obviously, the problem of the shadow plays a great role in all political conflicts. If the man who had this dream had not been sensible about his shadow problem, he could easily have identified the desperate Frenchman with the "dangerous Communists" of outer life, or the official plus the prosperous man with the "grasping capitalists." In this way he would have avoided seeing that he had within him such warring elements. If people observe their own unconscious tendencies in other people, this is called a "projection." Political agitation in all countries is full of such projections, just as much as the back-yard gossip of little groups and individuals. Projections of all kinds obscure our view of our fellow men, spoiling its objectivity, and thus spoiling all possibility of genuine human relationships.

"For over five years this man has been chasing around Europe like a madman in search of something he could set on fire. Unfortunately he again and again finds hirelings who open the gates of their country to this international incendiary."

172

And there is an additional disadvantage in projecting our shadow. If we identify our own shadow with, say, the Communists or the capitalists, a part of our own personality remains on the opposing side. The result is that we shall constantly (though involuntarily) do things behind our own backs that support this other side, and thus we shall unwittingly help our enemy. If, on the contrary, we realize the projection and can discuss matters without fear or hostility, dealing with the other person sensibly, then there is a chance of mutual understanding—or at least of a truce.

Whether the shadow becomes our friend or enemy depends largely upon ourselves. As the dreams of the unexplored house and the French desperado both show, the shadow is not necessarily always an opponent. In fact, he is exactly like any human being with whom one has to get along, sometimes by giving in, sometimes by resisting, sometimes by giving love—whatever the situation requires. The shadow becomes hostile only when he is ignored or misunderstood.

Sometimes, though not often, an individual feels impelled to live out the worse side of his nature and to repress his better side. In such cases the shadow appears as a positive figure in his dreams. But to a person who lives out his natural emotions and feelings, the shadow may appear as a cold and negative intellectual; it then personifies poisonous judgments and negative thoughts that have been held back. So, whatever form it takes, the function of the shadow is to represent the opposite side of the ego and to embody just those qualities that one dislikes most in other people.

It would be relatively easy if one could integrate the shadow into the conscious personality just by attempting to be honest and to use one's insight. But, unfortunately, such an attempt does not always work. There is such a passionate drive within the shadowy part of oneself that reason may not prevail against it. A bitter experience coming from the outside may occasionally help; a brick, so to speak, has to drop on one's head to put a stop to shadow drives and impulses. At times a heroic decision may serve to halt them, but such a superhuman effort is usually possible only if the Great Man within (the Self) helps the individual to carry it through.

The fact that the shadow contains the overwhelming power of irresistible impulse does not mean, however, that the drive should always be heroically repressed. Sometimes the shadow is powerful because the urge of the Self is pointing in the same direction, and so one does not know whether it is the Self or the shadow that is behind the inner pressure. In the unconscious, one is unfortunately in the same situation as in a moonlit landscape: All the contents are blurred and merge into one another, and one never knows exactly what or where anything is, or where one thing begins and ends. (This is known as the "contamination" of unconscious contents.)

When Jung called one aspect of the unconscious personality the shadow, he was referring to a relatively well-defined factor. But sometimes everything that is unknown to the ego is mixed up with the shadow, including even the most valuable and highest forces. Who, for in-

Rather than face our defects as revealed by the shadow, we *project* them on to others—for instance, on to our political enemies. Above left, a poster made for a parade in Communist China shows America as an evil serpent (bearing Nazi swastikas) killed by a Chinese hand. Left, Hitler during a speech; the quotation is *his* description of Churchill. Projections also flourish in malicious gossip (right, from the British television series *Coronation Street*).

Above, the wild white stallion from
the 1953 French film *Crin Blanc*.
Wild horses often symbolize the
uncontrollable instinctive drives
that can erupt from the unconscious
—and that many people try to repress.
In the film, the horse and a boy
form a strong attachment (though
the horse still runs wild with his
herd). But local horsemen set out
to capture the wild horses. The
stallion and his boy rider are
pursued for miles; finally they
are cornered on the seashore.
Rather than submit to capture, the
boy and the horse plunge into the
sea to be swept away. Symbolically,
the story's end seems to represent
an escape into the unconscious
(the sea) as a way to avoid facing
reality in the outside world.

stance, could be quite sure whether the French desperado in the dream I quoted was a useless tramp or a most valuable introvert? And the bolting horses of the preceding dream—should they be allowed to run free or not? In a case when the dream itself does not make things clear, the conscious personality will have to make the decision.

If the shadow figure contains valuable, vital forces, they ought to be assimilated into actual experience and not repressed. It is up to the ego to give up its pride and priggishness and to live out something that seems to be dark, but actually may not be. This can require a sacrifice just as heroic as the conquest of passion, but in an opposite sense.

The ethical difficulties that arise when one meets one's shadow are well described in the 18th Book of the Koran. In this tale Moses meets Khidr ("the Green One" or "first angel of God") in the desert. They wander along together, and Khidr expresses his fear that Moses will not be able to witness his deeds without indignation. If Moses cannot bear with him and trust him, Khidr will have to leave.

Presently Khidr scuttles the fishing boat of some poor villagers. Then, before Moses's eyes, he kills a handsome young man, and finally he restores the fallen wall of a city of unbelievers. Moses cannot help expressing his indignation, and so Khidr has to leave him. Before his departure, however, he explains the reasons for his actions: By scuttling the boat he actu-

ally saved it for its owners because pirates were on their way to steal it. As it is, the fishermen can salvage it. The handsome young man was on his way to commit a crime, and by killing him Khidr saved his pious parents from infamy. By restoring the wall, two pious young men were saved from ruin because their treasure was buried under it. Moses, who had been so morally indignant, saw now (too late) that his judgment had been too hasty. Khidr's doings had seemed to be totally evil, but in fact they were not.

Looking at this story naïvely, one might assume that Khidr is the lawless, capricious, evil shadow of pious, law-abiding Moses. But this is not the case. Khidr is much more the personification of some secret creative actions of the Godhead. (One can find a similar meaning in the famous Indian story of "The King and the Corpse" as interpreted by Henry Zimmer.) It is no accident that I have not quoted a dream to illustrate this subtle problem. I have chosen this well-known story from the Koran because it sums up the experience of a lifetime, which would very rarely be expressed with such clarity in an individual dream.

When dark figures turn up in our dreams and seem to want something, we cannot be sure whether they personify merely a shadowy part of ourselves, or the Self, or both at the same time. Divining in advance whether our dark partner symbolizes a shortcoming that we should overcome or a meaningful bit of life that we

The shadow can be said to have two aspects, one dangerous, the other valuable. The painting of the Hindu god Vishnu, far left, images such a duality: Usually considered a benevolent god, Vishnu here appears in a demonic aspect, tearing a man apart. Left, from a Japanese temple (A.D. 759), a sculpture of Buddha also expresses duality: The god's many arms hold symbols of both good and evil. Right, the doubt-stricken Martin Luther (portrayed by Albert Finney in the 1961 play *Luther* by Britain's John Osborne): Luther was never sure whether his break from the Church was inspired by God or arose from his own pride and obstinacy (in symbolic terms, the "evil" side of his shadow).

should accept—this is one of the most difficult problems that we encounter on the way to individuation. Moreover, the dream symbols are often so subtle and complicated that one cannot be sure of their interpretation. In such a situation all one can do is accept the discomfort of ethical doubt—making no final decisions or commitments and continuing to watch the dreams. This resembles the situation of Cinderella when her stepmother threw a heap of good and bad peas in front of her and asked her to sort them out. Although it seemed quite hopeless, Cinderella began patiently to sort the peas, and suddenly doves (or ants, in some versions) came to help her. These creatures symbolize helpful, deeply unconscious impulses that can only be felt in one's body, as it were, and that point to a way out.

Somewhere, right at the bottom of one's own being, one generally does know where one should go and what one should do. But there are times when the clown we call "I" behaves in such a distracting fashion that the inner voice cannot make its presence felt.

Sometimes all attempts to understand the hints of the unconscious fail, and in such a difficulty one can only have the courage to do what seems to be right, while being ready to change course if the suggestions of the unconscious should suddenly point in another direction. It may also happen (although this is unusual) that a person will find it better to resist the urge of the unconscious, even at the price of feeling warped by doing so, rather than depart too far from the state of being human. (This would be the situation of people who had to live out a criminal disposition in order to be completely themselves.)

The strength and inner clarity needed by the ego in order to make such a decision stem secretly from the Great Man, who apparently does not want to reveal himself too clearly. It may be that the Self wants the ego to make a free choice, or it may be that the Self depends on human consciousness and its decisions to help him to become manifest. When it comes to such difficult ethical problems, no one can truly judge the deeds of others. Each man has

to look to his own problem and try to determine what is right for himself. As an old Zen Buddhist Master said, we must follow the example of the cowherd who watches his ox "with a stick so that it will not graze on other people's meadows."

These new discoveries of depth psychology are bound to make some change in our collective ethical views, for they will compel us to judge all human actions in a much more individual and subtle way. The discovery of the unconscious is one of the most far-reaching discoveries of recent times. But the fact that recognition of its unconscious reality involves honest self-examination and reorganization of one's life causes many people to continue to behave as if nothing at all has happened. It takes a lot of courage to take the unconscious seriously and to tackle the problems it raises. Most people are too indolent to think deeply about even those moral aspects of their behavior of which they are conscious; they are certainly too lazy to consider how the unconscious affects them.

The anima: the woman within

Difficult and subtle ethical problems are not invariably brought up by the appearance of the shadow itself. Often another "inner figure" emerges. If the dreamer is a man, he will discover a female personification of his unconscious; and it will be a male figure in the case of a woman. Often this second symbolic figure turns up behind the shadow, bringing up new and different problems. Jung called its male and female forms "animus" and "anima."

The anima is a personification of all feminine psychological tendencies in a man's psyche, such as vague feelings and moods, prophetic hunches, receptiveness to the irrational, capacity for personal love, feeling for nature, and—last but not least—his relation to the unconscious. It is no mere chance that in olden times priestesses (like the Greek Sibyl) were used to fathom the divine will and to make connection with the gods.

A particularly good example of how the anima is experienced as an inner figure in a man's psyche is found in the medicine men and prophets (shamans) among the Eskimo and other arctic tribes. Some of these even wear women's clothes, or have breasts depicted on their garments, in order to manifest their inner feminine side—the side that enables them to connect with the "ghost land" (i.e. what we call the unconscious).

One reported case tells of a young man who was being initiated by an older shaman and who was buried by him in a snow hole. He fell into a state of dreaminess and exhaustion. In this coma he suddenly saw a woman who emitted light. She instructed him in all he needed to know and later, as his protective spirit, helped him to practice his difficult profession by relating him to the powers of the be-

The anima (the female element in a male psyche) is often personified as a witch or a priestess—women who have links with "forces of darkness" and "the spirit world" (i.e. the unconscious). Left, a sorceress with imps and demons (in a 17th-century engraving). Below, a shaman of a Siberian tribe, who is a man dressed as a woman—because women are thought to be more able to contact spirits.

Above, a woman spiritualist or medium (from the 1951 film *The Medium*, based on an opera by Gian Carlo Menotti). The majority of modern mediums are probably women; the belief is still widespread that women are more receptive than men to the irrational.

yond. Such an experience shows the anima as the personification of a man's unconscious.

In its individual manifestation the character of a man's anima is as a rule shaped by his mother. If he feels that his mother had a negative influence on him, his anima will often express itself in irritable, depressed moods, uncertainty, insecurity, and touchiness. (If, however, he is able to overcome the negative assaults on himself, they can even serve to reinforce his masculinity.) Within the soul of such a man the negative mother-anima figure will endlessly repeat this theme: "I am nothing. Nothing makes any sense. With others it's different, but for me . . . I enjoy nothing." These "anima moods" cause a sort of dullness, a fear of disease, of impotence, or of accidents. The whole of life takes on a sad and oppressive aspect. Such dark moods can even lure a man to suicide, in which case the anima becomes a death demon. She appears in this role in Cocteau's film *Orphée*.

The French call such an anima figure a *femme fatale*. (A milder version of this dark anima is personified by the Queen of the Night in Mozart's *Magic Flute*.) The Greek Sirens or the German Lorelei also personify this dangerous aspect of the anima, which in this form symbolizes destructive illusion. The following Siberian tale illustrates the behavior of such a destructive anima:

One day a lonely hunter sees a beautiful woman emerging from the deep forest on the other side of the river. She waves at him and sings:
Oh, come, lonely hunter in the stillness of dusk.
Come, come! I miss you, I miss you!
Now I will embrace you, embrace you!
Come, come! My nest is near, my nest is near.
Come, come, lonely hunter, now in the stillness of dusk.
He throws off his clothes and swims across the river, but suddenly she flies away in the form of an owl, laughing mockingly at him. When he tries to swim back to find his clothes, he drowns in the cold river.

In this tale the anima symbolizes an unreal dream of love, happiness, and maternal warmth (her nest) — a dream that lures men away from

The anima (like the shadow) has two aspects, benevolent and malefic (or negative). Left, a scene from *Orphée* (a film version by Cocteau of the Orpheus myth): The woman can be seen as a lethal anima, for she has led Orpheus (being carried by dark "underworld" figures) to his doom. Also malevolent are the Lorelei of Teutonic myth (below, in a 19th-century drawing), water spirits whose singing lures men to their death. Below right, a parallel from Slavonic myth: the Rusalka. These beings were thought to be spirits of drowned girls who bewitch and drown passing men.

reality. The hunter is drowned because he ran after a wishful fantasy that could not be fulfilled.

Another way in which the negative anima in a man's personality can be revealed is in waspish, poisonous, effeminate remarks by which he devalues everything. Remarks of this sort always contain a cheap twisting of the truth and are in a subtle way destructive. There are legends throughout the world in which "a poison damsel" (as they call her in the Orient) appears. She is a beautiful creature who has weapons hidden in her body or a secret poison with which she kills her lovers during their first night together. In this guise the anima is as cold and reckless as certain uncanny aspects of nature itself, and in Europe is often expressed to this day by the belief in witches.

If, on the other hand, a man's experience of his mother has been positive, this can also affect his anima in typical but different ways, with the result that he either becomes effeminate or is preyed upon by women and thus is unable to cope with the hardships of life. An anima of this sort can turn men into sentimentalists, or they may become as touchy as old maids or as sensitive as the fairy-tale princess who could feel a pea under 30 mattresses. A still more subtle manifestation of a negative anima appears in some fairy tales in the form of a princess who asks her suitors to answer a series of riddles or, perhaps, to hide themselves under her nose. If they cannot give the answers, or if she can find them, they must die—and she invariably wins. The anima in this guise involves men in a destructive intellectual game. We can notice the effect of this anima trick in all those neurotic pseudo-intellectual dialogues that inhibit a man from getting into direct touch with life and its real decisions. He reflects about life so much that he cannot live it and loses all his spontaneity and outgoing feeling.

The most frequent manifestation of the anima takes the form of erotic fantasy. Men may be driven to nurse their fantasies by looking at films and strip-tease shows, or by daydreaming over pornographic material. This is a crude, primitive aspect of the anima, which

Above, four scenes from the 1930 German film *The Blue Angel,* which concerns a strait-laced professor's infatuation with a cabaret singer, clearly a negative anima figure. The girl uses her charm to degrade the professor, even making him a buffoon in her cabaret act. Right, a drawing of Salome with the head of John the Baptist, whom she had killed to prove her power over King Herod.

Above, a painting by the 15th-century Italian artist Stefano di Giovanni depicting St. Anthony confronted by an attractive young girl. But her bat-like wings reveal that she is actually a demon, one of the many temptations offered to St. Anthony —and another embodiment of the deadly anima figure.

Above right, a British cinema poster advertising the French film *Eve* (1962). The film is concerned with the exploits of a *femme fatale* (played by the French actress Jeanne Moreau)—a widely known term for the "dangerous" women whose relationships with men clearly image the nature of the negative anima.

The following is a description (taken from the poster above) of the central character of the film (a melodramatic description, but one that might fit many personifications of the negative anima): "Mysterious —tantalizing—alluring—wanton— but deep within her burning the violent fires that destroy a man."

becomes compulsive only when a man does not sufficiently cultivate his feeling relationships— when his feeling attitude toward life has remained infantile.

All these aspects of the anima have the same tendency that we have observed in the shadow: That is, they can be projected so that they appear to the man to be the qualities of some particular woman. It is the presence of the anima that causes a man to fall suddenly in love when he sees a woman for the first time and knows at once that this is "she." In this situation, the man feels as if he has known this woman intimately for all time; he falls for her so helplessly that it looks to outsiders like complete madness. Women who are of "fairy-like" character especially attract such anima projections, because men can attribute almost anything to a creature who is so fascinatingly vague, and can thus proceed to weave fantasies around her.

The projection of the anima in such a sudden and passionate form as a love affair can greatly disturb a man's marriage and can lead to the so-called "human triangle," with its accompanying difficulties. A bearable solution to such a drama can be found only if the anima is recognized as an inner power. The secret aim of the unconscious in bringing about such an entanglement is to force a man to develop and to bring his *own* being to maturity by integrating more of his unconscious personality and bringing it into his real life.

But I have said enough about the negative side of the anima. There are just as many important positive aspects. The anima is, for instance, responsible for the fact that a man is able to find the right marriage partner. Another function is at least equally important: Whenever a man's logical mind is incapable of discerning facts that are hidden in his unconscious, the anima helps him to dig them out. Even more vital is the role that the anima plays in putting a man's mind in tune with the right inner values and thereby opening the way into more profound inner depths. It is as if an inner "radio" becomes tuned to a certain wavelength that excludes irrelevancies but allows the voice of the Great Man to be heard. In establishing this inner "radio" reception, the anima takes

A man's stress on intellectualism
can be due to a negative anima—
often represented in legends and
myths by the female figure who
asks riddles that men must answer
or die. Above, a 19th-century
French painting depicts Oedipus
answering the Sphinx's riddle.

Left, a traditional view of the
demonic anima as an ugly witch—
in a 16th-century German woodcut,
"The Bewitched Groom."

The anima appears in crude, childish
form in men's erotic fantasies—
which many men indulge through
forms of pornography. Below, part
of a show in a modern British
strip-tease night club.

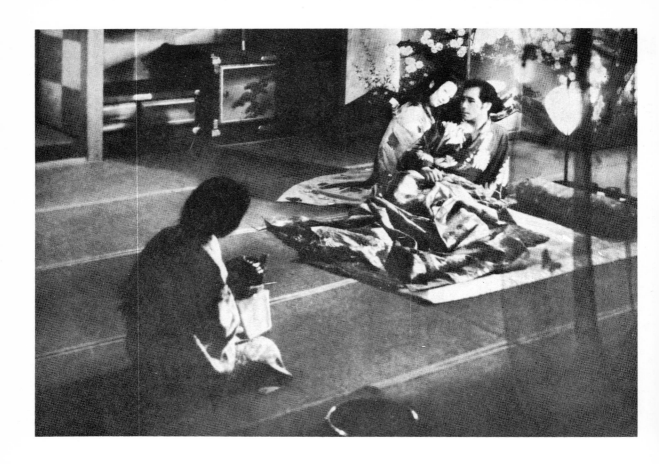

In the 1953 Japanese film *Ugetsu Monogatari,* a man comes under the spell of a ghost princess (center, above) —an image of a projection of the anima on to a "fairy-like" woman, producing a destructive fantasy relationship.

In *Madame Bovary* the 19th-century French novelist Flaubert describes a "love madness" caused by an anima projection: "By her constantly changing moods, sometimes mystical, sometimes gay, now talkative, now silent, sometimes passionate, sometimes superior—she knew how to evoke a thousand desires in him, a thousand instincts and memories. She was the beloved one of all novels, the heroine of all plays, the 'she' of all poems he had ever read. On her shoulders he found the 'amber glow' of the bathing Odalisque; she had the long waist of ladies in the chivalric age; she also looked like 'the pale lady of Barcelona'; but she was always an angel." Left, Emma Bovary (in the 1949 film of the novel) with her husband (left) and lover.

on the role of guide, or mediator, to the world within and to the Self. That is how she appears in the example of the initiations of shamans that I described earlier; this is the role of Beatrice in Dante's *Paradiso*, and also of the goddess Isis when she appeared in a dream to Apuleius, the famous author of *The Golden Ass*, in order to initiate him into a higher, more spiritual form of life.

The dream of a 45-year-old psychotherapist may help to make clear how the anima can be an inner guide. As he was going to bed on the evening before he had this dream, he thought to himself that it was hard to stand alone in life, lacking the support of a church. He found himself envying people who are protected by the maternal embrace of an organization. (He had been born a Protestant but no longer had any religious affiliation.) This was his dream:

I am in the aisle of an old church filled with people. Together with my mother and my wife, I sit at the end of the aisle in what seem to be extra seats.

I am to celebrate the Mass as a priest, and I have a big Mass book in my hands, or, rather, a prayer book or an anthology of poems. This book is not familiar to me, and I cannot find the right text. I am very excited because I have to begin soon, and, to add to my troubles, my mother and wife disturb me by chattering about unimportant trifles. Now the organ stops, and everybody is waiting for me, so I get up in a determined way and ask one of the nuns who is kneeling behind me to hand me her Mass book and point out the right place—which she does in an obliging manner. Now, like a sort of sexton, this same nun precedes me to the altar, which is somewhere behind me and to the left, as if we are approaching it from a side aisle. The Mass book is like a sheet of pictures, a sort of board, three feet long and a foot wide, and on it is the text with ancient pictures in columns, one beside the other.

First the nun has to read a part of the liturgy before I begin, and I have still not found the right place in the text. She has told me that it is Number 15, but the numbers are not clear, and I cannot find it. With determination, however, I turn toward the congregation, and now I have found Number 15 (the next to the last on the board), although I do not yet know if I shall be able to decipher it. I want to try all the same. I wake up.

Men project the anima on to things as well as women. For instance, ships are always known as "she": above, the female figurehead on the old British clipper ship *Cutty Sark*. The captain of a ship is symbolically "her" husband, which may be why he must (according to tradition) go down with the ship if "she" sinks.

A car is another kind of possession that is usually feminized—i.e. that can become the focus of many men's anima projections. Like ships, cars are called "she," and their owners caress and pamper them (below) like favorite mistresses.

This dream expressed in a symbolic way an answer from the unconscious to the thoughts that the dreamer had had the evening before. It said to him, in effect: "You yourself must become a priest in your own inner church—in the church of your soul." Thus the dream shows that the dreamer does have the helpful support of an organization; he is contained in a church—not an external church but one that exists inside his own soul.

The people (all his own psychic qualities) want him to function as the priest and celebrate the Mass himself. Now the dream cannot mean the actual Mass, for its Mass book is very different from the real one. It seems that the idea of the Mass is used as a symbol, and therefore it means a sacrificial act in which the Divinity is present so that man can communicate with it. This symbolic solution is, of course, not generally valid but relates to this particular dreamer. It is a typical solution for a Protestant, because a man who through real faith is

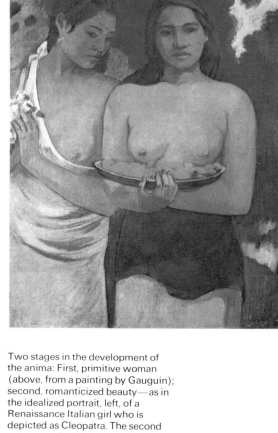

Two stages in the development of the anima: First, primitive woman (above, from a painting by Gauguin); second, romanticized beauty—as in the idealized portrait, left, of a Renaissance Italian girl who is depicted as Cleopatra. The second stage was classically embodied in Helen of Troy (below, with Paris).

still contained in the Catholic Church usually experiences his anima in the image of the Church herself, and her sacred images are for him the symbols of the unconscious.

Our dreamer did not have this ecclesiastical experience, and this is why he had to follow an inner way. Furthermore, the dream told him what he should do. It said: "Your mother-boundness and your extraversion (represented by the wife who is an extravert) distract you and make you feel insecure, and by meaning-less talk keep you from celebrating the inner Mass. But if you follow the nun (the introverted anima), she will lead you as both a servant and a priest. She owns a strange Mass book which is composed of 16 (four times four) ancient pic-tures. Your Mass consists of your contemplation of these psychic images that your religious anima reveals to you." In other words, if the dreamer overcomes his inner uncertainty, caused by his mother complex, he will find that his life task has the nature and quality of a religious service and that if he meditates about the symbolic meaning of the images in his soul, they will lead him to this realization.

In this dream the anima appears in her pro-per positive role—that is, as a mediator between the ego and the Self. The four-times-four con-figuration of the pictures points to the fact that the celebration of this inner Mass is performed in the service of totality. As Jung has demon-strated, the nucleus of the psyche (the Self) normally expresses itself in some kind of four-fold structure. The number four is also con-nected with the anima because, as Jung noted, there are four stages in its development. The first stage is best symbolized by the figure of Eve, which represents purely instinctual and biological relations. The second can be seen in Faust's Helen: She personifies a romantic and aesthetic level that is, however, still character-ized by sexual elements. The third is represen-ted, for instance, by the Virgin Mary—a figure who raises love (*eros*) to the heights of spiritual devotion. The fourth type is symbolized by Sapientia, wisdom transcending even the most holy and the most pure. Of this another symbol is the Shulamite in the Song of Solomon. (In the

Above, the anima's third stage is personified as the Virgin Mary (in a painting by van Eyck). The red of her robe is the symbolic color of feeling (or *eros*); but in this stage the *eros* has become spiritualized. Below, two examples of the fourth stage: the Greek goddess of wisdom Athena (left), and the *Mona Lisa*.

psychic development of modern man this stage is rarely reached. The Mona Lisa comes nearest to such a wisdom anima.)

At this stage I am only pointing out that the concept of fourfoldness frequently occurs in certain types of symbolic material. The essential aspects of this will be discussed later.

But what does the role of the anima as guide to the inner world mean in practical terms? This positive function occurs when a man takes seriously the feelings, moods, expectations, and fantasies sent by his anima and when he fixes them in some form—for example, in writing, painting, sculpture, musical composition, or dancing. When he works at this patiently and slowly, other more deeply unconscious material wells up from the depths and connects with the earlier material. After a fantasy has been fixed in some specific form, it must be examined both intellectually and ethically, with an evaluating feeling reaction. And it is essential to regard it as being absolutely real; there must be no lurking doubt that this is "only a fantasy." If this is practiced with devotion over a long period,

the process of individuation gradually becomes the single reality and can unfold in its true form.

Many examples from literature show the anima as a guide and mediator to the inner world: Francesco Colonna's *Hypnerotomachia*, Rider Haggard's *She*, or "the eternal feminine" in Goethe's *Faust*. In a medieval mystical text, an anima figure explains her own nature as follows:

I am the flower of the field and the lily of the valleys. I am the mother of fair love and of fear and of knowledge and of holy hope. . . . I am the mediator of the elements, making one to agree with another; that which is warm I make cold and the reverse, and that which is dry I make moist and the reverse, and that which is hard I soften. . . . I am the law in the priest and the word in the prophet and the counsel in the wise. I will kill and I will make to live and there is none that can deliver out of my hand.

In the Middle Ages there took place a perceptible spiritual differentiation in religious, poetical, and other cultural matters; and the fantasy world of the unconscious was recog-

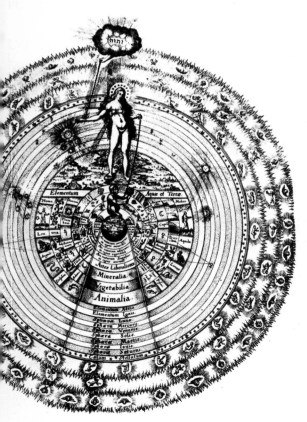

Left, a 17th-century engraving dominated by the symbolic figure of the anima as mediator between this world (the monkey, probably representing man's instinctual nature) and the next (the hand of God, reaching from the clouds). The anima figure seems to parallel the woman of the Apocalypse, who also wore a crown of 12 stars; antiquity's moon goddesses; the Old Testament's Sapientia (the fourth stage of the anima, p. 185); and the Egyptian goddess Isis (who also had flowing hair, a half-moon at her womb, and stood with one foot on land and one on water).

Right, the anima as mediator (or guide) in a drawing by William Blake: It illustrates a scene from the "Purgatorio" of Dante's *Divine Comedy*, and shows Beatrice leading Dante along a symbolically tortuous mountain path. Far right, from an early film of Rider Haggard's novel *She*, a mysterious woman leads explorers through mountains.

nized more clearly than before. During this period, the knightly cult of the lady signified an attempt to differentiate the feminine side of man's nature in regard to the outer woman as well as in relation to the inner world.

The lady to whose service the knight pledged himself, and for whom he performed his heroic deeds, was naturally a personification of the anima. The name of the carrier of the Grail, in Wolfram von Eschenbach's version of the legend, is especially significant: *Conduir-amour* ("guide in love matters"). She taught the hero to differentiate both his feelings and his behavior toward women. Later, however, this individual and personal effort of developing the relationship with the anima was abandoned when her sublime aspect fused with the figure of the Virgin, who then became the object of boundless devotion and praise. When the anima, as Virgin, was conceived as being all-positive, her negative aspects found expression in the belief in witches.

In China the figure parallel to that of Mary is the goddess Kwan-Yin. A more popular

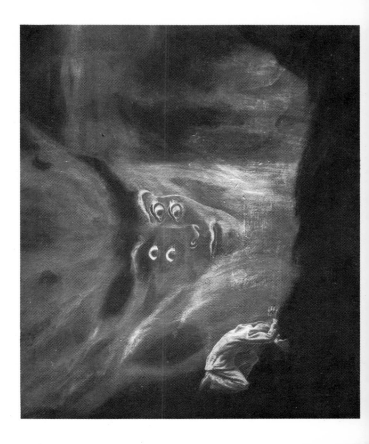

A connection between the motif of four and the anima appears above in a painting by the Swiss artist Peter Birkhäuser. A four-eyed anima appears as an overwhelming, terrifying vision. The four eyes have a symbolic significance similar to that of the 16 pictures in the dream quoted on p. 183: They allude to the fact that the anima contains the possibility of achieving wholeness.

In the painting, right, by the modern artist Slavko, the Self is separate from the anima but still merged with nature. The painting can be called a "soul landscape": On the left sits a dark-skinned, naked woman—the anima. On the right is a bear, the animal soul or instinct. Near the anima is a double tree— symbolizing the individuation process in which the inner opposites unite. In the background one at first sees a glacier, but on looking closely one sees that it is also a face. This face (from which the life-stream flows) is the Self. It has four eyes, and looks something like an animal, because it comes from instinctive nature. (The painting thus provides a good example of the way an unconscious symbol can inadvertently find its way into a fantasy landscape.)

Chinese anima-figure is the "Lady of the Moon," who bestows the gift of poetry or music on her favorites and can even give them immortality. In India the same archetype is represented by Shakti, Parvati, Rati, and many others; among the Moslems she is chiefly Fatima, the daughter of Mohammed.

Worship of the anima as an officially recognized religious figure brings the serious disadvantage that she loses her individual aspects. On the other hand, if she is regarded as an exclusively personal being, there is the danger that, if she is projected into the outer world, it is only there that she can be found. This latter state of affairs can create endless trouble, because man becomes either the victim of his erotic fantasies or compulsively dependent on one actual woman.

Only the painful (but essentially simple) decision to take one's fantasies and feelings seriously can at this stage prevent a complete stagnation of the inner process of individuation, because only in this way can a man discover what this figure means as an inner reality. Thus the anima becomes again what she originally was—the "woman within," who conveys the vital messages of the Self.

Medieval Europe's idea of "courtly love" was influenced by the worship of the Virgin Mary: Ladies to whom knights pledged love were believed to be as pure as the Virgin (of whom a typical medieval image was the doll-like carving, top of page, c. 1400). On a 15th-century shield, far left, a knight kneels to his lady, with death behind him. This idealized view of woman produced an opposing view: the belief in witches. Left, a 19th-century painting of a witches' sabbath.

When the anima is projected on to an "official" personification, she tends to fall apart into a double aspect, such as Mary and witch. Left, another opposing duality (from a 15th-century manuscript): personifications of the Church (on the right, identified with Mary) and of the Synagogue (here identified with the sinful Eve).

The animus: the man within

The male personification of the unconscious in woman—the animus—exhibits both good and bad aspects, as does the anima in man. But the animus does not so often appear in the form of an erotic fantasy or mood; it is more apt to take the form of a hidden "sacred" conviction. When such a conviction is preached with a loud, insistent, masculine voice or imposed on others by means of brutal emotional scenes, the underlying masculinity in a woman is easily recognized. However, even in a woman who is outwardly very feminine the animus can be an equally hard, inexorable power. One may suddenly find oneself up against something in a woman that is obstinate, cold, and completely inaccessible.

One of the favorite themes that the animus repeats endlessly in the ruminations of this kind of woman goes like this: "The only thing in the world that I want is love—and he doesn't love me"; or "In this situation there are only two possibilities—and both are equally bàd."

(The animus never believes in exceptions.) One can rarely contradict an animus opinion because it is usually right in a general way; yet it seldom seems to fit the individual situation. It is apt to be an opinion that seems reasonable but beside the point.

Just as the character of a man's anima is shaped by his mother, so the animus is basically influenced by a woman's father. The father endows his daughter's animus with the special coloring of unarguable, incontestably "true" convictions—convictions that never include the personal reality of the woman herself as she actually is.

This is why the animus is sometimes, like the anima, a demon of death. For example, in a gypsy fairy tale a handsome stranger is received by a lonely woman in spite of the fact that she has had a dream warning her that he is the king of the dead. After he has been with her for a time, she presses him to tell her who he really is. At first he refuses, saying that she will

Above, Joan of Arc (played by Ingrid Bergman in the 1948 film), whose *animus*—the male side of the female psyche—took the form of a "sacred conviction." Right, two images of the negative animus: a 16th-century painting of a woman dancing with death; and (from a manuscript *c.* 1500) Hades with Persephone, whom he abducted to the underworld.

189

Heathcliff, the sinister protagonist of the British author Emily Brontë's novel, *Wuthering Heights* (1847), is partly a negative, demonic animus figure—probably a manifestation of Emily Brontë's own animus. In the montage above, Heathcliff (played by Laurence Olivier in the 1939 film) confronts Emily (a portrait by her brother); in the background, Wuthering Heights as it is today.

Two examples of dangerous animus figures: Left, an illustration (by the 19th-century French artist Gustave Doré) to the folk tale of Bluebeard. Here Bluebeard warns his wife against opening a certain door. (Of course, she does so—and finds the corpses of Bluebeard's former wives. She is caught, and joins her predecessors.) Right, a 19th-century painting of the highwayman Claude Duval, who once robbed a lady traveler but gave his booty back on the condition that she dance with him by the roadside.

die if he tells her. She insists, however, and suddenly he reveals to her that he is death himself. The woman immediately dies of fright.

Viewed mythologically, the beautiful stranger is probably a pagan father-image or god-image, who appears here as king of the dead (like Hades' abduction of Persephone). But psychologically he represents a particular form of the animus that lures women away from all human relationships and especially from all contacts with real men. He personifies a cocoon of dreamy thoughts, filled with desire and judgments about how things "ought to be," which cut a woman off from the reality of life.

The negative animus does not appear only as a death-demon. In myths and fairy tales he plays the role of robber and murderer. One example is Bluebeard, who secretly kills all his wives in a hidden chamber. In this form the animus personifies all those semiconscious, cold, destructive reflections that invade a woman in the small hours, especially when she has failed to realize some obligation of feeling. It is then that she begins to think about the family heritage and matters of that kind—a sort of web of calculating thoughts, filled with malice and intrigue, which get her into a state where she even wishes death to others. ("When one of us dies, I'll move to the Riviera," said a woman to her husband when she saw the beautiful Mediterranean coast—a thought that was rendered relatively harmless by reason of the fact that she said it!)

By nursing secret destructive attitudes, a wife can drive her husband, and a mother her children, into illness, accident, or even death. Or she may decide to keep the children from marrying—a deeply hidden form of evil that rarely comes to the surface of the mother's conscious mind. (A naïve old woman once said to me, while showing me a picture of her son, who was drowned when he was 27: "I prefer it this way; it's better than giving him away to another woman.")

A strange passivity and paralysis of all feeling, or a deep insecurity that can lead almost to a sense of nullity, may sometimes be the result of an unconscious animus opinion. In the depths of the woman's being, the animus whispers: "You are hopeless. What's the use of trying? There is no point in doing anything. Life will never change for the better."

The animus is often personified as a group of men. A negative group animus might appear as a dangerous band of criminals like the wreckers (above, in an 18th-century Italian painting) who once lured ships onto rocks with lights, killed survivors, and looted the wrecks.

A frequent personification of the
negative group animus in women's
dreams has been the band of romantic
but dangerous outlaws. Above, an
ominous group of bandits from the
1953 Brazilian film *The Bandit*,
concerning an adventurous woman
schoolteacher who falls in love
with a bandit leader.

Below, an illustration by Fuseli of
Shakespeare's *Midsummer Night's
Dream*. The fairy queen has been
caused (by magic) to fall in love
with a peasant who has been given
an ass's head, also by magic. This
is a comic twist on the tales in
which a girl's love releases a man
from a magic spell.

Peignez-vous de Psyché l'extase et le délire,
Vous, qui savez tout ce qu'amour inspire.

Unfortunately, whenever one of these personifications of the unconscious takes possession of our mind, it seems as if we ourselves are having such thoughts and feelings. The ego identifies with them to the point where it is unable to detach them and see them for what they are. One is really "possessed" by the figure from the unconscious. Only after the possession has fallen away does one realize with horror that one has said and done things diametrically opposed to one's real thoughts and feelings—that one has been the prey of an alien psychic factor.

Like the anima, the animus does not merely consist of negative qualities such as brutality, recklessness, empty talk, and silent, obstinate, evil ideas. He too has a very positive and valuable side; he too can build a bridge to the Self through his creative activity. The following dream of a woman of 45 may help to illustrate this point:

Two veiled figures climb onto the balcony and into the house. They are swathed in black hooded coats, and they seem to want to torment me and my sister. She hides under the bed, but they pull her out with a broom and torture her. Then it is my turn. The leader of the two pushes me against the wall, making magical gestures before my face. In the meantime his helper makes a sketch on the wall, and when I see it, I say (in order to seem friendly), "Oh! But this is well drawn!" Now suddenly my tormentor has the noble head of an artist, and he says proudly, "Yes, indeed," and begins to clean his spectacles.

Above left, the singer Franz Grass in the title role of Wagner's opera *The Flying Dutchman,* based on the tale of the sea captain doomed to sail a ghost ship until a woman's love breaks the curse on him.

In many myths a woman's lover is a figure of mystery whom she must never try to see. Left, a late 18th-century engraving of an example from Greek myth: The maiden Psyche, loved by Eros but forbidden to try to look at him. Eventually she did so and he left her; she was able to regain his love only after a long search and much suffering.

The sadistic aspect of these two figures was well known to the dreamer, for in reality she frequently suffered bad attacks of anxiety during which she was haunted by the thought that people she loved were in great danger—or even that they were dead. But the fact that the animus figure in the dream is double suggests that the burglars personify a psychic factor that is dual in its effect, and that could be something quite different from these tormenting thoughts. The sister of the dreamer, who runs away from the men, is caught and tortured. In reality this sister died when fairly young. She had been artistically gifted, but had made very little use of her talent. Next the dream reveals that the veiled burglars are actually disguised artists, and that if the dreamer recognizes their gifts (which are her own), they will give up their evil intentions.

What is the deeper meaning of the dream? It is that behind the spasms of anxiety there is indeed a genuine and mortal danger; but there is also a creative possibility for the dreamer. She, like the sister, had some talent as a painter, but she doubted whether painting could be a meaningful activity for her. Now her dream tells her in the most earnest way that she must live out this talent. If she obeys, the destructive, tormenting animus will be transformed into a creative and meaningful activity.

As in this dream, the animus often appears as a group of men. In this way the unconscious symbolizes the fact that the animus represents a collective rather than a personal element. Because of this collective-mindedness women habitually refer (when their animus is speaking through them) to "one" or "they" or "everybody," and in such circumstances their speech frequently contains the words "always" and "should" and "ought."

A vast number of myths and fairy tales tell of a prince, turned by witchcraft into a wild animal or monster, who is redeemed by the love of a girl—a process symbolizing the manner in which the animus becomes conscious. (Dr. Henderson has commented on the significance of this "Beauty and the Beast" motif in the preceding chapter.) Very often the heroine is not

allowed to ask questions about her mysterious, unknown lover and husband; or she meets him only in the dark and may never look at him. The implication is that, by blindly trusting and loving him, she will be able to redeem her bridegroom. But this never succeeds. She always breaks her promise and finally finds her lover again only after a long, difficult quest and much suffering.

The parallel in life is that the conscious attention a woman has to give to her animus problem takes much time and involves a lot of suffering. But if she realizes who and what her animus is and what he does to her, and if she faces these realities instead of allowing herself to be possessed, her animus can turn into an invaluable inner companion who endows her with the masculine qualities of initiative, courage, objectivity, and spiritual wisdom.

The animus, just like the anima, exhibits four stages of development. He first appears as a personification of mere physical power—for instance, as an athletic champion or "muscle man." In the next stage he possesses initiative and the capacity for planned action. In the third phase, the animus becomes the "word," often appearing as a professor or clergyman. Finally, in his fourth manifestation, the animus is the incarnation of *meaning*. On this highest level he becomes (like the anima) a mediator of the religious experience whereby life acquires new meaning. He gives the woman spiritual firmness, an invisible inner support that compensates for her outer softness. The animus in his most developed form sometimes connects the woman's mind with the spiritual evolution

Embodiments of the four stages of the animus: First, the wholly physical man—the fictional jungle hero Tarzan (top, played by Johnny Weismuller). Second, the "romantic" man—the 19th-century British poet Shelley (center left); or the "man of action"—America's Ernest Hemingway, war hero, hunter, etc. Third, the bearer of the "word" —Lloyd George, the great political orator. Fourth, the wise guide to spiritual truth—often projected on to Gandhi (left).

Above right, an Indian miniature of a girl gazing with love at a man's portrait. A woman falling in love with a picture (or a film star) is clearly projecting her animus onto the man. The actor Rudolph Valentino (right, in a film made in 1922) became the focus of animus projection for thousands of women while he lived—and even after he died. Far right, part of the immense floral tribute sent by women all over the world to Valentino's funeral in 1926.

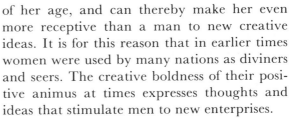

of her age, and can thereby make her even more receptive than a man to new creative ideas. It is for this reason that in earlier times women were used by many nations as diviners and seers. The creative boldness of their positive animus at times expresses thoughts and ideas that stimulate men to new enterprises.

The "inner man" within a woman's psyche can lead to marital troubles similar to those mentioned in the section on the anima. What makes things especially complicated is the fact that the possession of one partner by the animus (or anima) may automatically exert such an irritating effect upon the other that he (or she) becomes possessed too. Animus and anima always tend to drag conversation down to a very low level and to produce a disagreeable, irascible, emotional atmosphere.

As I mentioned before, the positive side of the animus can personify an enterprising spirit, courage, truthfulness, and in the highest form, spiritual profundity. Through him a woman can experience the underlying processes of her cultural and personal objective situation, and can find her way to an intensified spiritual attitude to life. This naturally presupposes that her animus ceases to represent opinions that are above criticism. The woman must find the courage and inner broadmindedness to question the sacredness of her own convictions. Only then will she be able to take in the suggestions of the unconscious, especially when they contradict her animus opinions. Only then will the manifestations of the Self get through to her, and will she be able consciously to understand their meaning.

The Self: symbols of totality

If an individual has wrestled seriously enough and long enough with the anima (or animus) problem so that he, or she, is no longer partially identified with it, the unconscious again changes its dominant character and appears in a new symbolic form, representing the Self, the inner-most nucleus of the psyche. In the dreams of a woman this center is usually personified as a superior female figure—a priestess, sorceress, earth mother, or goddess of nature or love. In the case of a man, it manifests itself as a masculine initiator and guardian (an Indian *guru*), a wise old man, a spirit of nature, and so forth. Two folk tales illustrate the role that such a figure can play. The first is an Austrian tale:

A king has ordered soldiers to keep the night watch beside the corpse of a black princess, who has been bewitched. Every midnight she rises and kills the guard. At last one soldier, whose turn it is to stand guard, despairs and runs away into the woods. There he meets an "old guitarist who is our Lord Himself." This old musician tells him where to hide in the church and instructs him on how to behave so that the black princess cannot get him. With this divine help the soldier actually manages to redeem the princess and marry her.

Clearly, "the old guitarist who is our Lord Himself" is, in psychological terms, a symbolic personification of the Self. With his help the ego avoids destruction and is able to overcome —and even redeem—a highly dangerous aspect of his anima.

In a woman's psyche, as I have said, the Self assumes feminine personifications. This is illustrated in the second story, an Eskimo tale:

A lonely girl who has been disappointed in love meets a wizard traveling in a copper boat. He is the "Spirit of the Moon," who has given all the animals to mankind and who also bestows luck in hunting. He abducts the girl to the heavenly realm. Once, when the Spirit of the Moon has left her, she visits a little house near the Moon Ghost's mansion. There she finds a tiny woman clothed in the "intestinal membrane of the bearded seal," who warns the heroine against the Spirit of the Moon, saying that he plans to kill her. (It appears that he is a killer of women, a sort of Bluebeard.) The tiny woman fashions a long rope by means of which the girl can descend to earth at the time of the new moon, which is the moment when the little woman can weaken the Moon Spirit. The girl climbs down, but when she arrives on earth, she does not open her eyes as quickly as the little woman told her to. Because of this, she is turned into a spider and can never become human again.

As we have noted, the divine musician in the first tale is a representation of the "wise old man," a typical personification of the Self. He is akin to the sorcerer Merlin of medieval legend or to the Greek god Hermes. The little woman in her strange membrane-clothing is a parallel figure, symbolizing the Self as it appears in the feminine psyche. The old musician saves the hero from the destructive anima, and the little woman protects the girl against the Eskimo "Bluebeard" (who is, in the form of the Moon Spirit, her animus). In this case, however, things go wrong—a point that I shall take up later.

The Self, however, does not always take the form of a wise old man or wise old woman. These paradoxical personifications are attempts to express something that is not entirely contained in time—something simultaneously young and old. The dream of a middle-aged man shows the Self appearing as a young man:

Coming from the street, a youth rode down into our garden. (There were no bushes and no fence as there are in real life, and the garden lay open.) I did not quite know if he came on purpose, or if the horse carried him here against his will.

I stood on the path that leads to my studio and watched the arrival with great pleasure. The sight

The Self—the inner center of the total psyche—is often personified in dreams as a superior human figure. To women, the Self might appear as a wise and powerful goddess—like the ancient Greek mother goddess Demeter (right, shown with her son Triptolemus and daughter Kore, in a fifth-century-B.C. relief). The "fairy godmother" of many tales is also a symbolic personification of the female Self: above, Cinderella's godmother (from an illustration by Gustave Doré). Below, a helpful old woman (also a fairy godmother) rescues a girl in an illustration of a Hans Christian Andersen tale.

Personifications of the Self in men's dreams often take the form of "wise old men." Far left, the magician Merlin of the Arthurian legends (in a 14th-century English manuscript). Center, a *guru* (wise man) from an 18th-century Indian painting. Left, a winged old man like this appeared in one of Dr. Jung's own dreams carrying keys: according to Dr. Jung he represented "superior insight."

Thomas Sully. Washington at the Passage of the Delaware. *Courtesy Museum of Fine Arts, Boston*

The Self usually appears in dreams at crucial times in the dreamer's life—turning points when his basic attitudes and whole way of life are changing. The change itself is often symbolized by the action of crossing water. Above, an actual river crossing that accompanied an important upheaval: George Washington's crossing of the Delaware River during the American Revolution (in a 19th-century American painting). Left, another major event that involved crossing water: the first attack launched against the Normandy beaches on D-day, June 1944.

The Self is not always personified as a superior *old* person. Left, a painting (of a dream) by Peter Birkhäuser, in which the Self appears as a marvelous youth. While the artist was working on the painting, other associations and ideas came up from his unconscious. The round object like a sun behind the youth is a symbol of totality, and the boy's four arms recall other "fourfold" symbols that characterize psychological wholeness. Before the boy's hands hovers a flower—as if he need only raise his hands and a magical flower will appear. He is black because of his nocturnal (i.e. unconscious) origin.

of the boy on his beautiful horse impressed me deeply.

The horse was a small, wild, powerful animal, a symbol of energy (it resembled a boar), and it had a thick, bristly, silvery-gray coat. The boy rode past me between the studio and house, jumped off his horse, and led him carefully away so that he would not trample on the flower bed with its beautiful red and orange tulips. The flower bed had been newly made and planted by my wife (a dream occurrence).

This youth signifies the Self, and with it renewal of life, a creative *élan vital*, and a new spiritual orientation by means of which everything becomes full of life and enterprise.

If a man devotes himself to the instructions of his own unconscious, it can bestow this gift, so that suddenly life, which has been stale and dull, turns into a rich, unending inner adventure, full of creative possibilities. In a woman's psychology, this same youthful personification of the Self can appear as a supernaturally gifted girl. The dreamer in this instance is a woman in her late forties:

I stood in front of a church and was washing the pavement with water. Then I ran down the street just at the moment when the students from the high school were let out. I came to a stagnant river across which a board or tree trunk had been laid; but when I was attempting to walk across, a mischievous student bounced on the board so that it cracked and I nearly fell into the water.

"Idiot!" I yelled out. On the other side of the river three little girls were playing, and one of them stretched out her hand as if to help me. I thought that her small hand was not strong enough to help me, but when I took it, she succeeded, without the slightest effort, in pulling me across and up the bank on the other side.

The dreamer is a religious person, but according to her dream she cannot remain in the Church (Protestant) any longer; in fact, she seems to have lost the possibility of entering it, although she tries to keep the access to it as clean as she can. According to the dream, she must now cross a stagnant river, and this indicates that the flow of life is slowed down because of the unresolved religious problem. (Crossing a river is a frequent symbolic image for a fundamental change of attitude.) The student was interpreted by the dreamer herself as the personification of a thought that she had previously had—namely, that she might satisfy her spiritual yearning by attending high school. Obviously the dream does not think much of this plan. When she dares to cross the river alone, a personification of the Self (the girl), small but supernaturally powerful, helps her.

But the form of a human being, whether youthful or old, is only one of the many ways in which the Self can appear in dreams or visions. The various ages it assumes show not only that it is with us throughout the whole of life, but also that it exists beyond the con-

Many people today personify the Self in their dreams as prominent public figures. Jungian psychologists find that, in men's dreams, Dr. Albert Schweitzer (far left) and Sir Winston Churchill (left) often appear; in women's dreams, Eleanor Roosevelt (right) and Queen Elizabeth II (far right, a portrait on an African house).

sciously realized flow of life—which is what creates our experience of time.

Just as the Self is not entirely contained in our conscious experience of time (in our space-time dimension), it is also simultaneously omnipresent. Moreover, it appears frequently in a form that hints at a special omnipresence; that is, it manifests itself as a gigantic, symbolic human being who embraces and contains the whole cosmos. When this image turns up in the dreams of an individual, we may hope for a creative solution to his conflict, because now the vital psychic center is activated (i.e. the whole being is condensed into oneness) in order to overcome the difficulty.

It is no wonder that this figure of the Cosmic Man appears in many myths and religious teachings. Generally he is described as something helpful and positive. He appears as Adam, as the Persian Gayomart, or as the Hindu Purusha. This figure may even be described as the basic principle of the whole world. The ancient Chinese, for instance, thought that before anything whatever was created, there was a colossal divine man called P'an Ku who gave heaven and earth their form. When he cried, his tears made the Yellow River and the Yangtze River; when he breathed, the wind rose; when he spoke, thunder was loosed; and when he looked around, lightning flashed. If he was in a good mood, the weather was fine; if he was sad, it clouded over. When he died, he fell apart, and from his body the five holy mountains of China sprang into existence. His head became the T'ai mountain in the East, his trunk became the Sung mountain in the center, his right arm the Heng mountain in the North, his left arm the Heng mountain in the South, and his feet the Hua mountain in the West. His eyes became the sun and moon.

We have already seen that symbolic structures that seem to refer to the process of individuation tend to be based on the motif of the number four—such as the four functions of consciousness, or the four stages of the anima or animus. It reappears here in the cosmic shape of P'an Ku. Only under specific circumstances do other combinations of numbers appear in the psychic material. The natural unhampered manifestations of the center are characterized by fourfoldness—that is to say, by having four divisions, or some other structure deriving from the numerical series of 4, 8, 16, and so on. Number 16 plays a particularly important role, since it is composed of four fours.

In our Western civilization, similar ideas of a Cosmic Man have attached themselves to the symbol of Adam, the First Man. There is a Jewish legend that when God created Adam, he first gathered red, black, white, and yellow dust from the four corners of the world, and thus Adam "reached from one end of the world to the other." When he bent down, his head was in the East and his feet in the West. According to another Jewish tradition, the whole of mankind was contained in Adam from the beginning, which meant the soul of everybody who would ever be born. The soul of Adam, therefore, was "like the wick of a lamp composed of innumerable strands." In this symbol the idea of a total oneness of all human existence, beyond all individual units, is clearly expressed.

In ancient Persia, the same original First Man—called Gayomart—was depicted as a huge figure emitting light. When he died, every kind of metal sprang from his body, and from his soul came gold. His semen fell upon the earth, and from it came the first human couple in the form of two rhubarb shrubs. It is striking

（會圖才三）氏古盤

ふ。〔三五

〔歷記〕未

有三天地

之時、混沌

如二雞子一、

盤古生二其

中一萬八

千歲、天地

開闢、清陽爲レ天、濁陰爲レ地、盤古在二其中一、云

Non est potestas super Terram quae Comparetur ei Iob. 41. 24.

LEVIATHAN
Or
THE MATTER, FORME
and POWER of A COMMON-
WEALTH ECCLESIASTICALL
and CIVIL
By THOMAS HOBBES
of MALMESBURY

London
Printed for Andrew Crooke
1651

Cosmic Man—the gigantic, all-embracing figure that personifies and contains the entire universe—is a common representation of the Self in myths and dreams. Left, the title page of *Leviathan,* by the 17th-century English philosopher Thomas Hobbes. The gigantic figure of Leviathan is made up of all the people of the "commonwealth"—Hobbes's ideal society, in which the people choose their own central authority (or "sovereign," hence Leviathan's crown, sword, and scepter). Above, the cosmic figure of ancient China's P'an Ku—shown covered in leaves to indicate that Cosmic Man (or First Man) simply existed, like a plant, grown in nature. Below, on a leaf from an 18th-century Indian illuminated manuscript, the Cosmic Lion Goddess holding the sun (the lion is made up of many people and animals).

that the Chinese P'an Ku was also depicted covered by leaves like a plant. Perhaps this is because the First Man was thought of as a self-grown, living unit that just existed without any animal impulse or self-will. Among a group of people who live on the banks of the Tigris, Adam is still, at the present time, worshiped as the hidden "super-soul" or mystical "protective spirit" of the entire human race. These people say that he came from a date palm—another repetition of the plant motif.

In the East, and in some gnostic circles in the West, people soon recognized that the Cosmic Man was more an inner psychic image than a concrete outer reality. According to Hindu tradition, for instance, he is something that lives within the individual human being and is the only part that is immortal. This inner Great Man redeems the individual by leading him out of creation and its sufferings, back into his original eternal sphere. But he can do this only if man recognizes him and rises from his sleep in order to be led. In the symbolic myths of

old India, this figure is known as the Purusha, a name that simply means "man" or "person." The Purusha lives within the heart of every individual, and yet at the same time he fills the entire cosmos.

According to the testimony of many myths, the Cosmic Man is not only the beginning but also the final goal of all life—of the whole of creation. "All cereal nature means wheat, all treasure nature means gold, all generation means man," says the medieval sage Meister Eckhart. And if one looks at this from a psychological standpoint, it is certainly so. The whole inner psychic reality of each individual is ultimately oriented toward this archetypal symbol of the Self.

In practical terms this means that the existence of human beings will never be satisfactorily explained in terms of isolated instincts or purposive mechanism such as hunger, power, sex, survival, perpetuation of the species, and so on. That is, man's main purpose is not to eat, drink, etc., but *to be human*. Above and beyond these drives, our inner psychic reality serves to manifest a living mystery that can be expressed only by a symbol, and for its expression the unconscious often chooses the powerful image of the Cosmic Man.

In our Western civilization the Cosmic Man has been identified to a great extent with Christ, and in the East with Krishna or with Buddha. In the Old Testament this same symbolic figure turns up as the "Son of Man" and in later Jewish mysticism is called Adam Kadmon. Certain religious movements of late antiquity simply called him Anthropos (the Greek word for man). Like all symbols this image points to

Top left, a Rhodesian rock painting of a creation myth, in which the First Man (the moon) mates with the morning star and evening star to produce the creatures of earth. Cosmic Man often appears as an Adam-like original man—and Christ, too, has become identified with this personification of the Self: Top right, a painting by the 15th-century German artist Grünewald shows the figure of Christ with all the majesty of Cosmic Man.

an unknowable secret—to the ultimate unknown meaning of human existence.

As we have noted, certain traditions assert that the Cosmic Man is the goal of creation, but the achievement of this should not be understood as a possible external happening. From the point of view of the Hindu, for example, it is not so much that the external world will one day dissolve into the original Great Man, but that the ego's extraverted orientation toward the external world will disappear in order to make way for the Cosmic Man. This happens when the ego merges into the Self. The ego's discursive flow of representations (which goes from one thought to another) and its desires (which run from one object to another) calm down when the Great Man within is encountered. Indeed, we must never forget that for us outer reality exists only in so far as we perceive it consciously, and that we cannot prove that it exists "in and by itself."

The many examples coming from various civilizations and different periods show the uni-

Examples of the "royal couple" (a symbolic image of psychic totality and the Self): left, a third-century A.D. Indian sculpture of Siva and Parvati, hermaphroditically joined; below, the Hindu deities Krishna and Radha in a grove.

The Greek head, below left, was shown by Dr. Jung to be subtly two-sided (i.e. hermaphroditic). In a letter to the owner Júng added that the head "has, like his analogs Adonis, Tammuz, and . . . Baldur, all the grace and charm of either sex."

Right, a pre-Roman sculpture of the Celtic bear-goddess Artio, found at Berne (which means "bear"). She was probably a mother goddess, resembling the she-bear in the dream quoted on this page. Further correspondences to symbolic images in this dream: Center, Australian aborigines with their "sacred stones," which they believe contain the spirits of the dead. Bottom, from a 17th-century alchemical manuscript, the symbolic royal couple as a pair of lions.

versality of the symbol of the Great Man. His image is present in the minds of men as a sort of goal or expression of the basic mystery of our life. Because this symbol represents that which is whole and complete, it is often conceived of as a bisexual being. In this form the symbol reconciles one of the most important pairs of psychological opposites—male and female. This union also appears frequently in dreams as a divine, royal, or otherwise distinguished couple. The following dream of a man of 47 shows this aspect of the Self in a dramatic way:

I am on a platform, and below me I see a huge, black, beautiful she-bear with a rough but well-groomed coat. She is standing on her hind legs, and on a stone slab she is polishing a flat oval black stone, which becomes increasingly shiny. Not far away a lioness and her cub do the same thing, but the stones they are polishing are bigger and round in shape. After a while the she-bear turns into a fat, naked woman with black hair and dark, fiery eyes. I behave in an erotically provocative way toward her, and suddenly she moves nearer in order to catch me. I get frightened and take refuge up on the building of scaffolding where I was before. Later I am in the midst of many women, half of whom are primitive and have rich black hair (as if they are transformed from animals); the other half are our women [of the same nationality as the dreamer] and have blonde or brown hair. The primitive women sing a very sentimental song in melancholy, high-pitched voices. Now, in a high elegant carriage, there comes a young man who wears on his head a royal golden crown, set with shining rubies—

Spiritus & Anima funt conjungendi & redigendi ad corpus fuum.

a very beautiful sight. Beside him sits a blonde young woman, probably his wife, but without a crown. It seems that the lioness and her cub have been transformed into this couple. They belong to the group of primitives. Now all the women (the primitives and the others) intone a solemn song, and the royal carriage slowly travels toward the horizon.

Here the inner nucleus of the dreamer's psyche shows itself at first in a temporary vision of the royal couple, which emerges from the depths of his animal nature and the primitive layer of his unconscious. The she-bear in the beginning is a sort of mother goddess. (Artemis, for instance, was worshiped in Greece as a she-bear.) The dark oval stone that she rubs and polishes probably symbolizes the dreamer's innermost being, his true personality. Rubbing and polishing stones is a well-known, exceedingly ancient activity of man. In Europe "holy" stones, wrapped in bark and hidden in caves, have been found in many places; as containers of divine powers they were probably kept there by men of the Stone Age. At the present time some of the Australian aborigines believe that their dead ancestors continue to exist in stones as virtuous and divine powers, and that if they rub these stones, the power increases (like charging them with electricity) for the benefit of both the living and the dead.

The man who had the dream we are discussing had hitherto refused to accept a marital bond with a woman. His fear of being caught by this aspect of life caused him, in the dream, to flee from the bear-woman to the spectator's platform where he could passively watch things without becoming entangled. Through the motif of the stone being rubbed by the bear, the unconscious is trying to show him that he should let himself come into contact with this side of life; it is through the frictions of married life that his inner being can be shaped and polished.

When the stone is polished, it will begin to shine like a mirror so that the bear can see herself in it; this means that only by accepting earthly contact and suffering can the human soul be transformed into a mirror in which the divine powers can perceive themselves. But the

In dreams a mirror can symbolize the power of the unconscious to "mirror" the individual objectively —giving him a view of himself that he may never have had before. Only through the unconscious can such a view (which often shocks and upsets the conscious mind) be obtained— just as in Greek myth the Gorgon Medusa, whose look turned men to stone, could be gazed upon only in a mirror. Below, Medusa reflected in a shield (a painting by the 17th-century artist Caravaggio).

dreamer runs away to a higher place—i.e. into all sorts of reflections by which he can escape the demands of life. The dream then shows him that if he runs away from the demands of life, one part of his soul (his anima) will remain undifferentiated, a fact symbolized by the group of nondescript women that splits apart into a primitive half and a more civilized one.

The lioness and her son, which then appear on the scene, personify the mysterious urge toward individuation, indicated by their work at shaping the round stones. (A round stone is a symbol of the Self.) The lions, a royal couple, are in themselves a symbol of totality. In medieval symbolism, the "philosopher's stone" (a

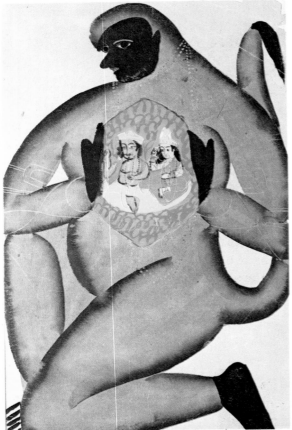

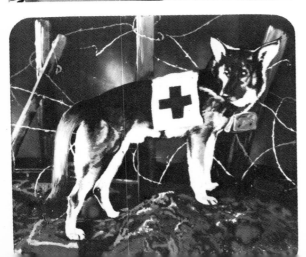

pre-eminent symbol of man's wholeness) is represented as a pair of lions or as a human couple riding on lions. Symbolically, this points to the fact that often the urge toward individuation appears in a veiled form, hidden in the overwhelming passion one may feel for another person. (In fact, passion that goes beyond the natural measure of love ultimately aims at the mystery of becoming whole, and this is why one feels, when one has fallen passionately in love, that becoming one with the other person is the only worthwhile goal of one's life.)

As long as the image of totality in this dream expresses itself in the form of a pair of lions, it is still contained in some such overwhelming passion. But when lion and lioness have turned into a king and queen, the urge to individuate has reached the level of conscious realization, and can now be understood by the ego as being the real goal of life.

Before the lions had transformed themselves into human beings, it was only the primitive women who sang, and they did so in a sentimental manner; that is to say, the feelings of the dreamer remained on a primitive and sentimental level. But in honor of the humanized lions, both the primitive and the civilized women chant a common hymn of praise. Their expression of their feelings in a united form shows that the inner split in the animal has now changed into inner harmony.

Still another personification of the Self appears in a report of a woman's so-called "active imagination." (Active imagination is a certain way of meditating imaginatively, by

Often the Self is represented as a helpful animal (a symbol of the psyche's instinctual basis). Top left, the magic fox of Grimm's fairy tale "The Golden Bird." Center, the Hindu monkey god Hanuman carrying two gods in his heart. Bottom, Rin Tin Tin the heroic dog once popular in American films and television.

Stones are frequent images of the Self (because they are complete—i.e. unchanging—and lasting). Many people today look for stones of special beauty—perhaps on beaches, top right. Some Hindus pass from father to son stones (center) believed to have magical powers. "Precious" stones, like the jewels of Queen Elizabeth I (1558-1603), bottom, are an outward sign of wealth and position.

which one may deliberately enter into contact with the unconscious and make a conscious connection with psychic phenomena. Active imagination is among the most important of Jung's discoveries. While it is in a sense comparable to Eastern forms of meditation, such as the technique of Zen Buddhism or of Tantric Yoga, or to Western techniques like those of the Jesuit Exercitia, it is fundamentally different in that the meditator remains completely devoid of any conscious goal or program. Thus the meditation becomes the solitary experiment of a free individual, which is the reverse of a guided attempt to master the unconscious. This, however, is not the place to enter into a detailed analysis of active imagination; the reader will find one of Jung's descriptions of it in his paper on "The Transcendent Function.")

In the woman's meditation the Self appeared as a deer, which said to the ego: "I am your child and your mother. They call me the 'connecting animal' because I connect people, animals, and even stones with one another if I enter them. I am your fate or the 'objective I.' When I appear, I redeem you from the meaningless hazards of life. The fire burning inside me burns in the whole of nature. If a man loses it, he becomes egocentric, lonely, disoriented, and weak."

The Self is often symbolized as an animal, representing our instinctive nature and its connectedness with one's surroundings. (That is why there are so many helpful animals in myths and fairy tales.) This relation of the Self to all surrounding nature and even the cosmos probably comes from the fact that the "nuclear atom" of our psyche is somehow woven into the whole world, both outer and inner. All the higher manifestations of life are somehow tuned to the surrounding space-time continuum. Animals, for example, have their own special foods, their particular home-building materials, and their definite territories, to all of which their instinctive patterns are exactly tuned and adapted. Time rhythms also play their part: We have only to think of the fact that most grass-eating animals have their young at precisely the time of year when the grass is richest and most abundant. With such considerations in mind, a well-known zoologist has said that the "inwardness" of each animal reaches far out into the world around it and "psychifies" time and space.

In ways that are still completely beyond our comprehension, our unconscious is similarly attuned to our surroundings—to our group, to society in general, and, beyond these, to the space-time continuum and the whole of nature. Thus the Great Man of the Naskapi Indians does not merely reveal inner truths; he also gives hints about where and when to hunt. And so from dreams the Naskapi hunter evolves the words and melodies of the magical songs with which he attracts the animals.

But this specific help from the unconscious is not given to primitive man alone. Jung discovered that dreams can also give civilized man the guidance he needs in finding his way through the problems of both his inner and his outer life. Indeed, many of our dreams are concerned with details of our outer life and our surroundings. Such things as the tree in front of the window, one's bicycle or car, or a stone picked up during a walk may be raised to the

level of symbolism through our dream life and become meaningful. If we pay attention to our dreams, instead of living in a cold, impersonal world of meaningless chance, we may begin to emerge into a world of our own, full of important and secretly ordered events.

Our dreams, however, are not as a rule primarily concerned with our adaptation to outer life. In our civilized world, most dreams have to do with the development (by the ego) of the "right" inner attitude toward the Self, for this relationship is far more disturbed in us by modern ways of thinking and behaving than is the case with primitive people. They generally live directly from the inner center, but we, with our uprooted consciousness, are so entangled with external, completely foreign matters that it is very difficult for the messages of the Self to get through to us. Our conscious mind continually creates the illusion of a clearly shaped, "real" outer world that blocks off many other perceptions. Yet through our unconscious nature we are inexplicably connected to our psychic and physical environment.

I have already mentioned the fact that the Self is symbolized with special frequency in the

The "eternal" quality of stones can be seen in pebbles or mountains. Left, rocks beneath Mt. Williamson, California. Thus stone has always been used for memorials—like the heads of four U.S. presidents (above) carved in the cliff face of Mt. Rushmore, South Dakota. Stones were also often used to mark places of worship—as was the sacred stone in the Temple of Jerusalem (far right). It was the center of the city; and (as the medieval map, right, shows) the city was seen as the center of the world.

form of a stone, precious or otherwise. We saw an example of this in the stone that was being polished by the she-bear and the lions. In many dreams the nuclear center, the Self, also appears as a crystal. The mathematically precise arrangement of a crystal evokes in us the intuitive feeling that even in so-called "dead" matter there is a spiritual ordering principle at work. Thus the crystal often symbolically stands for the union of extreme opposites—of matter and spirit.

Perhaps crystals and stones are especially apt symbols of the Self because of the "just-so-ness" of their nature. Many people cannot refrain from picking up stones of a slightly unusual color or shape and keeping them, without knowing why they do this. It is as if the stones held a living mystery that fascinates them. Men have collected stones since the beginning of time and have apparently assumed that certain ones were the containers of the life-force with all its mystery. The ancient Germans, for instance, believed that the spirits of the dead continued to live in their tombstones. The custom of placing stones on graves may spring partly from the symbolic idea that something eternal of the dead person remains, which can be most fittingly represented by a stone. For while the human being is as different as possible from a stone, yet man's innermost center is in a strange and special way akin to it (perhaps because the stone symbolizes mere existence at the farthest remove from the emotions, feelings, fantasies, and discursive thinking of ego-consciousness). In this sense the stone symbolizes what is perhaps the simplest and deepest experience—the experience of something eternal that man can have in those moments when he feels immortal and unalterable.

The urge that we find in practically all civilizations to erect stone monuments to famous men or on the site of important events probably also stems from this symbolic meaning of the stone. The stone that Jacob placed on the spot where he had his famous dream, or certain stones left by simple people on the tombs of local saints or heroes, show the original nature of the human urge to express an otherwise inexpressible experience by the stone-symbol. It is no wonder that many religious cults use a stone to signify God or to mark a place of worship. The holiest sanctuary of the Islamic world is the

Ka'aba, the black stone in Mecca to which all pious Moslems hope to make their pilgrimage.

According to Christian ecclesiastical symbolism, Christ is "the stone which the builders rejected," which became "the head of the corner" (Luke xx: 17). Alternatively he is called the "spiritual rock" from which the water of life springs (1 Cor. x: 4). Medieval alchemists, who searched for the secret of matter in a pre-scientific way, hoping to find God in it, or at least the working of divine activity, believed that this secret was embodied in their famous "philosopher's stone." But some of the alchemists dimly perceived that their much-sought-after stone was a symbol of something that can be found only within the psyche of man. An old Arabian alchemist, Morienus, said: "This thing [the philosopher's stone] is extracted from *you*: *you* are its mineral, and one can find it in you; or, to put it more clearly, they [the alchemists] take it from you. If you recognize this, the love and approbation of the stone will grow within you. Know that this is true without doubt."

The alchemical stone (the *lapis*) symbolizes something that can never be lost or dissolved, something eternal that some alchemists compared to the mystical experience of God within one's own soul. It usually takes prolonged suffering to burn away all the superfluous psychic elements concealing the stone. But some profound inner experience of the Self does occur to most people at least once in a lifetime. From the psychological standpoint, a genuinely religious attitude consists of an effort to discover this unique experience, and gradually to keep in tune with it (it is relevant that a stone is itself something permanent), so that the Self becomes an inner partner toward whom one's attention is continually turned.

The fact that this highest and most frequent symbol of the Self is an object of lifeless matter points to yet another field of inquiry and speculation: that is, the still unknown relationship between what we call the unconscious psyche and what we call "matter"—a mystery with which psychosomatic medicine endeavors to grapple. In studying this still undefined and

Left, the Black Stone of Mecca, blessed by Mohammed (in an Arabic manuscript illustration) to integrate it into the Islamic religion. It is carried by four tribal chieftains (at the four corners of a carpet) into the Ka'aba, the holy sanctuary to which thousands of Moslems make an annual pilgrimage (below left).

Right, another symbolic stone: the Stone of Scone (or Stone of Destiny) on which Scottish kings were formerly crowned. It was taken to England's Westminster Abbey in the 13th century, but it never lost its importance for Scotland. On Christmas Day, 1950, a group of Scottish Nationalists stole the Stone from the Abbey and took it back to Scotland. (It was returned to the Abbey in April 1951.)

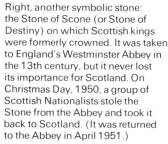

Right, a tourist kisses the famous "Blarney Stone" of Irish legend. It is supposed to confer the gift of eloquence on those who kiss it.

unexplained connection (it may prove to be that "psyche" and "matter" are actually the same phenomenon, one observed from "within" and the other from "without"), Dr. Jung put forward a new concept that he called *synchronicity*. This term means a "meaningful coincidence" of outer and inner events that are not themselves causally connected. The emphasis lies on the word "meaningful."

If an aircraft crashes before my eyes as I am blowing my nose, this is a coincidence of events that has no meaning. It is simply a chance occurrence of a kind that happens all the time. But if I bought a blue frock and, by mistake, the shop delivered a black one on the day one of my near relatives died, this would be a meaningful coincidence. The two events are not causally related, but they are connected by the symbolic meaning that our society gives to the color black.

Wherever Dr. Jung observed such meaningful coincidences in an individual's life, it seemed (as the individual's dreams revealed) that there was an archetype activated in the unconscious of the individual concerned. To illustrate this by my example of the black frock: In such a case the person who receives the black frock might also have had a dream on the theme of death. It seems as if the underlying archetype is manifesting itself simultaneously in inner and external events. The common denominator is a symbolically expressed message—in this case a message about death.

As soon as we notice that certain types of event "like" to cluster together at certain times, we begin to understand the attitude of the Chinese, whose theories of medicine, philosophy, and even building are based on a "science" of meaningful coincidences. The classical Chinese texts did not ask what *causes* what, but rather what "likes" to *occur with* what. One can

see much the same underlying theme in astrology, and in the way various civilizations have depended on consulting oracles and paying attention to omens. All of these are attempts to provide an explanation of coincidence that is different from one that depends on straightforward cause and effect.

In creating the concept of synchronicity, Dr. Jung sketched a way in which we might penetrate deeper into the inter-relation of psyche and matter. And it is precisely toward such a relation that the symbol of the stone seems to point. But this is still a completely open and insufficiently explored matter, with which future generations of psychologists and physicists must deal.

It may seem that my discussion of synchronicity has led me away from my main theme, but I feel it is necessary to make at least a brief introductory reference to it because it is a Jungian hypothesis that seems to be pregnant with future possibilities of investigation and application. Synchronistic events, moreover, almost invariably accompany the crucial phases of the process of individuation. But too often they pass unnoticed, because the individual has not learned to watch for such coincidences and to make them meaningful in relation to the symbolism of his dreams.

A painting by the modern artist Hans Haffenrichter resembles the pattern of a crystal—like ordinary stone, a symbol of wholeness.

The relation to the Self

Nowadays more and more people, especially those who live in large cities, suffer from a terrible emptiness and boredom, as if they were waiting for something that never arrives. Movies and television, spectator sports and political excitements may divert them for a while, but again and again, exhausted and disenchanted, they have to return to the wasteland of their own lives.

The only adventure that is still worthwhile for modern man lies in the inner realm of the unconscious psyche. With this idea vaguely in mind, many now turn to Yoga and other Eastern practices. But these offer no genuine new adventure, for in them one only takes over what is already known to the Hindus or the Chinese without directly meeting one's own inner life center. While it is true that Eastern methods serve to concentrate the mind and direct it inward (and that this procedure is in a sense similar to the introversion of an analytical treatment), there is a very important difference. Jung evolved a way of getting to one's inner center and making contact with the living mystery of the unconscious, alone and unaided. That is utterly different from following a well-worn path.

Trying to give the living reality of the Self a constant amount of daily attention is like trying to live simultaneously on two levels or in two different worlds. One gives one's mind, as before, to outer duties, but at the same time one remains alert for hints and signs, both in dreams and in external events, that the Self uses to symbolize its intentions—the direction in which the life-stream is moving.

Old Chinese texts that are concerned with this kind of experience often use the simile of the cat watching the mousehole. One text says that one should allow no other thoughts to intrude, but one's attention should not be too sharp—nor should it be too dull. There is exactly the right level of perception. "If the training is undergone in this manner . . . it will be effective as time goes on, and when the cause comes to fruition, like a ripe melon that automatically falls, anything it may happen to touch or make contact with will suddenly cause the individual's supreme awakening. This is the moment when the practitioner will be like one who drinks water and alone knows whether it is cold or warm. He becomes free of all doubts about himself and experiences a great happiness similar to that one feels in meeting one's own father at the crossroads."

Thus, in the midst of ordinary outer life, one is suddenly caught up in an exciting inner adventure; and because it is unique for each individual, it cannot be copied or stolen.

There are two main reasons why man loses contact with the regulating center of his soul. One of them is that some single instinctive drive

or emotional image can carry him into a one-sidedness that makes him lose his balance. This also happens to animals; for example, a sexually excited stag will completely forget hunger and security. This one-sidedness and consequent loss of balance are much dreaded by primitives, who call it "loss of soul." Another threat to the inner balance comes from excessive daydreaming, which in a secret way usually circles around particular complexes. In fact, daydreams arise just because they connect a man with his complexes; at the same time they threaten the concentration and continuity of his consciousness.

The second obstacle is exactly the opposite, and is due to an over-consolidation of ego-consciousness. Although a disciplined consciousness is necessary for the performance of civilized activities (we know what happens if a railway signalman lapses into daydreaming), it has the serious disadvantage that it is apt to block the reception of impulses and messages coming from the center. This is why so many dreams of civilized people are concerned with restoring this receptivity by attempting to correct the attitude of consciousness toward the unconscious center or Self.

Among the mythological representations of the Self one finds much emphasis on the four corners of the world, and in many pictures the Great Man is represented in the center of a circle divided into four. Jung used the Hindu word *mandala* (magic circle) to designate a structure of this order, which is a symbolic representation of the "nuclear atom" of the human psyche—whose essence we do not know. In this connection it is interesting that a Naskapi hunter pictorially represented his Great Man not as a human being but as a mandala.

Whereas the Naskapi experience the inner center directly and naïvely, without the help of religious rites or doctrines, other communities use the mandala motif in order to restore a lost inner balance. For instance, the Navaho Indians try, by means of mandala-structured sand paintings, to bring a sick person back into harmony with himself and with the cosmos—and thereby to restore his health.

In Eastern civilizations similar pictures are used to consolidate the inner being, or to enable one to plunge into deep meditation. The contemplation of a mandala is meant to bring an inner peace, a feeling that life has again found its meaning and order. The mandala also conveys this feeling when it appears spontaneously in the dreams of modern men who are not influenced by any religious tradition of this sort and know nothing about it. Perhaps the positive effect is even greater in such cases because knowledge and tradition sometimes blur or even block the spontaneous experience.

An example of a spontaneously produced mandala occurs in the following dream of a 62-

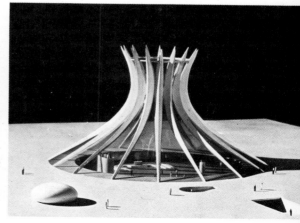

The feelings of boredom and apathy from which city dwellers today often suffer is only temporarily offset by such artificial excitements as adventure films (far left) and time-killing "amusements" (left). Jung stressed that the only real adventure remaining for each individual is the exploration of his own unconscious. The ultimate goal of such a search is the forming of a harmonious and balanced relationship with the Self. The circular mandala images this perfect balance—embodied in the structure of the modern cathedral (right) of the city of Brasilia.

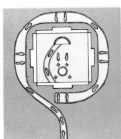

Top, a Navaho makes a sand painting (a mandala) in a healing ritual; the patient sits in the painting. Above, a plan of a sand painting; it must be circled by a patient before entering.

Left, a winter landscape by the German artist Kaspar Friedrich. Landscape paintings usually express indefinable "moods"—as do symbolic landscapes in dreams.

year-old woman. It emerged as a prelude to a new phase of life in which she became very creative:

I see a landscape in a dim light. In the background I see the rising and then evenly continuing crest of a hill. Along the line where it rises moves a quadrangular disk that shines like gold. In the foreground I see dark plowed earth that is beginning to sprout. Now I suddenly perceive a round table with a gray stone slab as its top, and at the same moment the quadrangular disk suddenly stands upon the table. It has left the hill, but how and why it has changed its place I do not know.

Landscapes in dreams (as well as in art) frequently symbolize an inexpressible mood. In this dream, the dim light of the landscape indicates that the clarity of daytime consciousness is dimmed. "Inner nature" may now begin to reveal itself in its own light, so we are told that the quadrangular disk becomes visible on the horizon. Hitherto the symbol of the Self, the disk, had been largely an intuitive idea on the dreamer's mental horizon, but now in the dream it shifts its position and becomes the center of the landscape of her soul. A seed, sown long ago, begins to sprout: for a long time previously the dreamer had paid careful attention to her dreams, and now this work bears fruit. (One is reminded of the relation between the symbol of the Great Man and plant life, which

I mentioned before.) Now the golden disk suddenly moves to the "right" side—the side where things become conscious. Among other things "right" often means, psychologically, the side of consciousness, of adaptation, of being "right," while "left" signifies the sphere of unadapted, unconscious reactions or sometimes even of something "sinister." Then, finally, the golden disk stops its movement and comes to rest on—significantly—a round stone table. It has found a permanent base.

As Aniela Jaffé observes later in this book, roundness (the mandala motif) generally symbolizes a natural wholeness, whereas a quadrangular formation represents the realization of this in consciousness. In the dream the square disk and the round table meet, and thus a conscious realization of the center is at hand. The round table, incidentally, is a well-known symbol of wholeness and plays a role in mythology —for instance, King Arthur's round table, which itself is an image derived from the table of the Last Supper.

In fact, whenever a human being genuinely turns to the inner world and tries to know himself—not by ruminating about his subjective thoughts and feelings, but by following the expressions of his own objective nature such as dreams and genuine fantasies—then sooner or later the Self emerges. The ego will then find an inner power that contains all the possibilities of renewal.

In the paintings, left, of the dream quoted on this page (painted by the dreamer), the mandala motif appears as a quadrangle rather than a circle. Usually quadrangular forms symbolize conscious realization of inner wholeness; the wholeness itself is most often represented in circular forms, such as the round table that also appears in the dream. Right, the legendary Round Table of King Arthur (from a 15th-century manuscript), at which the Holy Grail appeared in a vision and started the knights on the famous quest. The Grail itself symbolizes the inner wholeness for which men have always been searching.

But there is a great difficulty that I have mentioned only indirectly up till now. This is that every personification of the unconscious—the shadow, the anima, the animus, and the Self—has both a light and a dark aspect. We saw before that the shadow may be base or evil, an instinctive drive that one ought to overcome. It may, however, be an impulse toward growth that one should cultivate and follow. In the same way the anima and animus have dual aspects: They can bring life-giving development and creativeness to the personality, or they can cause petrification and physical death. And even the Self, the all-embracing symbol of the unconscious, has an ambivalent effect, as for instance in the Eskimo tale (page 196), when the "little woman" offered to save the heroine from the Moon Spirit but actually turned her into a spider.

The dark side of the Self is the most dangerous thing of all, precisely because the Self is the greatest power in the psyche. It can cause people to "spin" megalomaniac or other delusory fantasies that catch them up and "possess" them. A person in this state thinks with mounting excitement that he has grasped and solved the great cosmic riddles; he therefore loses all touch with human reality. A reliable symptom of this condition is the loss of one's sense of humor and of human contacts.

Thus the emerging of the Self may bring great danger to a man's conscious ego. The double aspect of the Self is beautifully illustrated by this old Iranian fairy tale, called "The Secret of the Bath Bâdgerd":

The great and noble Prince Hâtim Tâi receives orders from his king to investigate the mysterious Bath Bâdgerd [castle of nonexistence]. When he approaches it, having gone through many dangerous adventures, he hears that nobody ever returned from it, but he insists on going on. He is received at a round building by a barber with a mirror who leads him into the bath, but as soon as the prince enters the water, a thunderous noise breaks out, it gets completely dark, the barber disappears, and slowly the water begins to rise.

Hâtim swims desperately round until the water finally reaches the top of the round cupola, which forms the roof of the bath. Now he fears he is lost, but he says a prayer and grabs the centerstone of the cupola. Again a thunderous noise, everything changes, and Hâtim stands alone in a desert.

After long and painful wandering, he comes to a beautiful garden in the middle of which is a circle of stone statues. In the center of the statues, he sees a parrot in its cage, and a voice from above says to him: "Oh, hero, you probably will not escape alive from this bath. Once Gayomart [the First Man] found an enormous diamond that shone more brightly than sun and moon. He decided to hide it where no one can find it, and therefore he built this magical bath in order to

protect it. The parrot that you see here forms part of the magic. At its feet lie a golden bow and arrow on a golden chain, and with them you may try three times to shoot the parrot. If you hit him the curse will be lifted; if not, you will be petrified, as were all these other people."

Hâtim tries once, and fails. His legs turn to stone. He fails once more and is petrified up to his chest. The third time he just shuts his eyes, exclaiming "God is great," shoots blindly, and this time hits the parrot. An outbreak of thunder, clouds of dust. When all this has subsided, in place of the parrot is an enormous, beautiful diamond, and all the statues have come to life again. The people thank him for their redemption.

The reader will recognize the symbols of the Self in this story—the First Man Gayomart, the round mandala-shaped building, the centerstone, and the diamond. But this diamond is surrounded by danger. The demonic parrot signifies the evil spirit of imitation that makes one miss the target and petrify psychologically. As I pointed out earlier, the process of individuation excludes any parrot-like imitation of others. Time and again in all countries people have tried to copy in "outer" or ritualistic behavior the original religious experience of their great religious teachers—Christ or Buddha or some other master—and have therefore become "petrified." To follow in the steps of a great spiritual leader does not mean that one should copy and act out the pattern of the individuation process made by his life. It means that we should try with a sincerity and devotion equal to his to live our own lives.

The barber with the mirror, who vanishes, symbolizes the gift of reflection that Hâtim loses when he wants it most; the rising waters represent the risk that one may drown in the unconscious and get lost in one's own emotions. In order to understand the symbolic indications of the unconscious, one must be careful not to get outside oneself or "beside oneself," but to stay emotionally within oneself. Indeed, it is vitally important that the ego should continue to function in normal ways. Only if I remain an ordinary human being, conscious of my incompleteness, can I become receptive to the significant contents and processes of the unconscious. But how can a human being stand the tension of feeling himself at one with the whole universe, while at the same time he is only a miserable earthly human creature? If, on the one hand, I despise myself as merely a statistical cipher, my life has no meaning and is not worth living. But if, on the other hand, I feel myself to be part of something much greater, how am I to keep my feet on the ground? It is very difficult indeed to keep these inner opposites united within oneself without toppling over into one or the other extreme.

Far left, the torrential waters of the river Heraclitos overwhelm a Greek temple, in a painting by the modern French artist André Masson. The painting can be seen as an allegory of the results of imbalance: Greek overemphasis on logic and reason (the temple) leading to a destructive eruption of instinctual forces. Left, a more direct allegory, from a 15th-century illustration to the French allegorical poem *Le Roman de la Rose*: the figure of Logic (on the right) is thrown into confusion when confronted by Nature.

Right, the repentant St. Mary Magdalen gazes into a mirror (in a painting by the 17th-century French artist Georges de la Tour). Here, as in the tale of the Bath Bâdgerd, the mirror symbolizes the much-needed faculty of true, inward-looking "reflection."

The social aspect of the Self

Today the enormous growth of population, especially obvious in large cities, inevitably has a depressing effect on us. We think, "Oh, well, I am only so-and-so living at such-and-such an address, like thousands of other people. If a few of them get killed, what difference can it make? There are far too many people in any case." And when we read in the paper about the deaths of innumerable unknown people who personally mean nothing to us, the feeling that our lives count for nothing is further increased. This is the moment when attention to the unconscious brings the greatest help, for dreams show the dreamer how each detail of his life is interwoven with the most significant realities.

What we all know theoretically—that every thing depends on the individual—becomes through dreams a palpable fact that everyone can experience for himself. Sometimes we have a strong feeling that the Great Man wants something from us and has set us very special tasks. Our response to this experience can help us to acquire the strength to swim against the stream of collective prejudice by taking our own soul seriously into account.

Naturally this is not always an agreeable task. For instance, you want to make a trip with friends next Sunday; then a dream forbids it and demands that you do some creative work instead. If you listen to your unconscious and obey it, you must expect constant interference with your conscious plans. Your will is crossed by other intentions—intentions that you must submit to, or at any rate must seriously consider. This is partly why the obligation attached to the process of individuation is often felt to be a burden rather than an immediate blessing.

St. Christopher, the patron of all travelers, is a fitting symbol for this experience. According to the legend, he felt an arrogant pride in his tremendous physical strength, and was willing to serve only the strongest. First he served a king; but when he saw that the king feared the devil, he left him and became the devil's servant. Then one day he discovered that the devil feared the crucifix, and so he decided to serve Christ if he could find him. He followed the advice of a priest who told him to wait for Christ at a ford. In the years that passed he carried many people across the river. But once, on a dark, stormy night, a small child called out that he wanted to be carried over the river. With the greatest ease, St. Christopher lifted the child on to his shoulders, but he walked

The achievement of psychological maturity is an individual task—and so is increasingly difficult today when man's individuality is threatened by widespread conformity. Far left, a British housing development with its stereotyped dwellings; left, a Swiss athletics display provides an image of mass regimentation.

more slowly with every step, for his burden became heavier and heavier. When he arrived in midstream, he felt "as if he carried the whole universe." He realized then that he had taken Christ upon his shoulders—and Christ gave him remission of his sins and eternal life.

This miraculous child is a symbol of the Self that literally "depresses" the ordinary human being, even though it is the only thing that can redeem him. In many works of art the Christ child is depicted as, or with, the sphere of the world, a motif that clearly denotes the Self, for a child and a sphere are both universal symbols of totality.

When a person tries to obey the unconscious, he will often, as we have seen, be unable to do just as he pleases. But equally he will often be unable to do what other people want him to do. It often happens, for instance, that he must separate from his group—from his family, his partner, or other personal connections—in order to find himself. That is why it is sometimes said that attending to the unconscious makes people antisocial and egocentric. As a rule this is not true, for there is a little-known factor that enters into this attitude: the collective (or, we could even say, social) aspect of the Self.

Above, a page from William Blake's *Songs of Innocence and Experience,* in which the poems reveal Blake's concept of the "divine child"—a well-known symbol of the Self. Right, a 16th-century painting of St. Christopher carrying Christ as a divine child (who is encircled by a world sphere—a mandala and a symbol of the Self). This burden symbolizes the "weight" of the task of individuation—just as St. Christopher's role as the patron of travelers (far right, a St. Christopher medallion on a car's ignition key) reflects his link with man's need to travel the path to psychological wholeness.

From a practical angle this factor reveals itself in that an individual who follows his dreams for a considerable time will find that they are often concerned with his relationships with other people. His dreams may warn him against trusting a certain person too much, or he may dream about a favorable and agreeable meeting with someone whom he may previously have never consciously noticed. If a dream does pick up the image of another person for us in some such fashion, there are two possible interpretations. First, the figure may be a projection, which means that the dream-image of this person is a symbol for an inner aspect of the dreamer himself. One dreams, for instance, of a dishonest neighbor, but the neighbor is used by the dream as a picture of one's own dishonesty. It is the task of dream interpretation to find out in which special areas one's own dishonesty comes into play. (This is called dream interpretation on the subjective level.)

But it also happens at times that dreams genuinely tell us something about other people. In this way, the unconscious plays a role that is far from being fully understood. Like all the higher forms of life, man is in tune with the living beings around him to a remarkable degree. He perceives their sufferings and problems, their positive and negative attributes and values, instinctively—quite independently of his conscious thoughts about other people.

Our dream life allows us to have a look at these subliminal perceptions and shows us that they have an effect upon us. After having an agreeable dream about somebody, even without interpreting the dream, I shall involuntarily look at that person with more interest. The dream image may have deluded me, because of my projections; or it may have given me objective information. To find out which is the

The conscious realization of the Self can create a bond among people that ignores more obvious, natural groups like the family (above left). A mental kinship on a conscious level can often be the nucleus of cultural development: above, the 18th-century French encyclopedists (including Voltaire, with raised hand); below, a painting by Max Ernst of the early 20th-century "Dadaist" artists; and research physicists at Britain's Wills Laboratory.

The psychological balance and unity that man needs today have been symbolized in many modern dreams by the union of the French girl and the Japanese man in the widely popular French film *Hiroshima Mon Amour* (1959), above. And in the same dreams, the opposite extreme from wholeness (i.e. complete psychological dissociation, or madness) has been symbolized by a related 20th-century image— a nuclear explosion (right).

correct interpretation requires an honest, attentive attitude and careful thought. But, as is the case with all inner processes, it is ultimately the Self that orders and regulates one's human relationships, so long as the conscious ego takes the trouble to detect the delusive projections and deals with these inside himself instead of outside. It is in this way that spiritually attuned and similarly oriented people find their way to one another, to create a group that cuts across all the usual social and organizational affiliations of people. Such a group is not in conflict with others; it is merely different and independent. The consciously realized process of individuation thus changes a person's relationships. The familiar bonds such as kinship or common interests are replaced by a different type of unity—a bond through the Self.

All activities and obligations that belong exclusively to the outer world do definite harm to the secret activities of the unconscious. Through these unconscious ties those who belong together come together. That is one reason why attempts to influence people by advertisements and political propaganda are destructive, even when inspired by idealistic motives.

This raises the important question of whether the unconscious part of the human psyche can be influenced at all. Practical experience and accurate observation show that one cannot influence one's own dreams. There are people, it is true, who assert that they can influence them. But if you look into their dream material, you find that they do only what I do with my disobedient dog; I order him to do those things I notice he wants to do anyhow, so that I can preserve my illusion of authority. Only a long process of interpreting one's dreams and confronting oneself with what they have to say can gradually transform the unconscious. And conscious attitudes also must change in this process.

If a man who wants to influence public opinion misuses symbols for this purpose, they will naturally impress the masses in so far as they are true symbols, but whether or not the mass unconscious will be emotionally gripped by them is something that cannot be calculated in advance, something that remains completely irrational. No music publisher, for instance, can tell in advance whether a song will become a hit or not, even though it may draw on popular images and melodies. No deliberate attempts to influence the unconscious have yet produced any significant results, and it seems that the mass unconscious preserves its autonomy just as much as the individual unconscious.

At times, in order to express its purposes, the unconscious may use a motif from our external world and thus may seem to have been influenced by it. For instance, I have come across many dreams of modern people that have to do with Berlin. In these dreams Berlin stands as a symbol of the psychic weak spot—the place of danger—and for this reason is the place where the Self is apt to appear. It is the point where the dreamer is torn by conflict and where he might, therefore, be able to unite the inner opposites. I have also encountered an extraordinary number of dream reactions to the film *Hiroshima Mon Amour*. In most of these dreams the idea was expressed that either the two lovers in the film must unite (which symbolizes the union of inner opposites) or there would be an atomic explosion (a symbol of complete dissociation, equivalent to madness).

Only when the manipulators of public opinion add commercial pressure or acts of violence to their activities do they seem to achieve a temporary success. But in fact this merely causes a repression of the genuine unconscious reactions. And mass repression leads to the same result as individual repression; that is, to neurotic dissociation and psychological illness. All such attempts to repress the reactions of the unconscious must fail in the long run, for they are basically opposed to our instincts.

We know from studying the social behavior of the higher animals that small groups (from approximately 10 to 50 individuals) create the

As in the dream quoted on p. 223, positive anima figures often assist and guide men. Top of page, from a 10th-century psalter, David inspired by the muse. Above, a goddess saves a shipwrecked sailor (in a 16th-century painting). Right, on an early 20th-century postcard from Monte Carlo, gamblers' "Lady Luck"—also a helpful anima.

Right, Liberty leading the French revolutionaries (in a painting by Delacroix) images the anima's function of assisting individuation by liberating unconscious contents. Far right, in a scene from the 1925 fantasy film *Metropolis,* a woman urges robot-like workers to find spiritual "liberation."

best possible living conditions for the single animal as well as for the group, and man seems to be no exception in this respect. His physical well-being, his spiritual psychic health, and, beyond the animal realm, his cultural efficiency seem to flourish best in such a social function. As far as we at present understand the process of individuation, the Self apparently tends to produce such small groups by creating at the same time sharply defined ties of feeling between certain individuals and feelings of relatedness to all people. Only if these connections are created by the Self can one feel any assurance that envy, jealousy, fighting, and all manner of negative projections will not break up the group. Thus an unconditional devotion to one's own process of individuation also brings about the best possible adaptation.

This does not mean, of course, that there will not be collisions of opinion and conflicting obligations, or disagreement about the "right" way, in the face of which one must constantly withdraw and listen to one's inner voice in order to find the individual standpoint that the Self intends one to have.

Fanatical political activity (but not the performance of essential duties) seems somehow incompatible with individuation. A man who devoted himself entirely to freeing his country from foreign occupation had this dream:

With some of my compatriots I go up a stairway to the attic of a museum, where there is a hall painted black and looking like a cabin on a ship. A distinguished-looking middle-aged lady opens the door; her name is X, daughter of X. [X was a famous national hero of the dreamer's country who attempted some centuries ago to free it. He might be compared to Joan of Arc or William Tell. In reality X had no children.] In the hall we see the portraits of two aristocratic ladies dressed in flowery brocaded garments. While Miss X is explaining these pictures to us, they suddenly come to life; first the eyes begin to live, and then the chest seems to breathe. People are surprised and go to a lecture room where Miss X will speak to them about the phenomenon. She says that through her intuition and feeling these portraits came alive; but some of the people are indignant and say that Miss X is mad; some even leave the lecture room.

The important feature of this dream is that the anima figure, Miss X, is purely a creation of the dream. She has, however, the name of a famous national hero-liberator (as if she were, for instance, Wilhelmina Tell, the daughter of William Tell). By the implications contained in the name, the unconscious is pointing to the fact that today the dreamer should not try, as X did long ago, to free his country in an outer way. Now, the dream says, liberation is accomplished by the anima (by the dreamer's soul), who accomplishes it by bringing the images of the unconscious to life.

That the hall in the attic of the museum looks partly like a ship's cabin painted black is very meaningful. The black color hints at darkness, night, a turning inward, and if the hall is

a cabin, then the museum is somehow also a ship. This suggests that when the mainland of collective consciousness becomes flooded by unconsciousness and barbarism, this museum-ship, filled with living images, may turn into a saving ark that will carry those who enter it to another spiritual shore. Portraits hanging in a museum are usually the dead remains of the past, and often the images of the unconscious are regarded in the same way until we discover that they are alive and meaningful. When the anima (who appears here in her rightful role of soul-guide) contemplates the images with intuition and feeling, they begin to live.

The indignant people in the dream represent the side of the dreamer that is influenced by collective opinion—something in him that distrusts and rejects the bringing to life of psychic images. They personify a resistance to the unconscious that might express itself something like this: "But what if they begin dropping atom bombs on us? Psychological insight won't be much help then!"

This resistant side is unable to free itself from statistical thinking and from extraverted rational prejudices. The dream, however, points out that in our time genuine liberation can start only with a psychological transformation. To what end does one liberate one's country if afterward there is no meaningful goal of life—no goal for which it is worthwhile to be free? If man no longer finds any meaning in his life, it makes no difference whether he wastes away under a Communist or a capitalist regime. Only if he can use his freedom to create something meaningful is it relevant that he should be free. That is why finding the inner meaning of life is more important to the individual than anything else, and why the process of individuation must be given priority.

Attempts to influence public opinion by means of newspapers, radio, television, and advertising are based on two factors. On the one hand, they rely on sampling techniques that reveal the trend of "opinion" or "wants"—that is, of collective attitudes. On the other, they express prejudices, projections, and unconscious complexes (mainly the power complex)

of those who manipulate public opinion. But statistics do no justice to the individual. Although the average size of stones in a heap may be five centimeters, one will find very few stones of exactly this size in the heap.

That the second factor cannot create anything positive is clear from the start. But if a single individual devotes himself to individuation, he frequently has a positive contagious effect on the people around him. It is as if a spark leaps from one to another. And this usually occurs when one has no intention of influencing others and often when one uses no words. It is onto this inner path that Miss X tried to lead the dreamer.

Nearly all religious systems on our planet contain images that symbolize the process of individuation, or at least some stages of it. In Christian countries the Self is projected, as I said before, onto the second Adam: Christ. In the East the relevant figures are those of Krishna and Buddha.

For people who are contained in a religion (that is, who still really believe in its content and teachings), the psychological regulation of their lives is effected by religious symbols, and even their dreams often revolve around them. When the late Pope Pius XII issued the declaration of the Assumption of Mary, a Catholic woman dreamed, for instance, that she was a Catholic priestess. Her unconscious seemed to extend the dogma in this way: "If Mary is now almost a goddess, she should have priestesses." Another Catholic woman, who had resistances to some of the minor and outer aspects of her creed, dreamed that the church of her home city had been pulled down and rebuilt, but that the tabernacle with the consecrated host and the statue of the Virgin Mary were to be transferred from the old to the new church. The dream showed her that some of the man-made aspects of her religion needed renewal, but that its basic symbols—God's having become Man, and the Great Mother, the Virgin Mary—would survive the change.

Such dreams demonstrate the living interest that the unconscious takes in the conscious religious representations of an individual. This raises the question whether it is possible to detect a general trend in all the religious dreams of contemporary people. In the manifestations of the unconscious found in our modern Christian culture, whether Protestant or Catholic, Dr. Jung often observed that there is an unconscious tendency at work to round off our trinitarian formula of the Godhead with a fourth element, which tends to be feminine, dark, and even evil. Actually this fourth element has always existed in the realm of our religious representations, but it was separated from the image of God and became his counterpart, in the form of matter itself (or the lord of matter—i.e. the devil). Now the unconscious seems to want to reunite these extremes, the light having become too bright and the darkness too somber. Naturally it is the central symbol of religion, the image of the Godhead, that is most exposed to unconscious tendencies toward transformation.

A Tibetan abbot once told Dr. Jung that the most impressive mandalas in Tibet are built up by imagination, or directed fantasy, when the psychological balance of the group is disturbed or when a particular thought cannot be rendered because it is not yet contained in the sacred doctrine and must therefore be searched for. In these remarks, two equally important basic aspects of mandala symbolism emerge. The mandala serves a conservative purpose—namely, to restore a previously existing order.

But it also serves the creative purpose of giving expression and form to something that does not yet exist, something new and unique. The second aspect is perhaps even more important than the first, but does not contradict it. For, in most cases, what restores the old order simultaneously involves some element of new creation. In the new order the older pattern returns on a higher level. The process is that of the ascending spiral, which grows upward while simultaneously returning again and again to the same point.

A painting by a simple woman who was brought up in Protestant surroundings shows a mandala in the form of a spiral. In a dream this woman received an order to paint the Godhead. Later (also in a dream) she saw it in a book. Of God himself she saw only his wafting cloak, the drapery of which made a beautiful display of light and shadow. This contrasted impressively with the stability of the spiral in the deep blue sky. Fascinated by the cloak and the spiral, the dreamer did not look closely at the other figure on the rocks. When she awoke and thought about who these divine figures were, she suddenly realized that it was "God himself." This gave her a frightful shock, which she felt for a long time.

Usually the Holy Ghost is represented in Christian art by a fiery wheel or a dove, but here it has appeared as a spiral. This is a new thought, "not yet contained in the doctrine,"

This 15th-century statue of Mary contains within it images of both God and Christ—a clear expression of the fact that the Virgin Mary can be said to be a representation of the "Great Mother" archetype.

A miniature from the 15th-century French *Book of Hours*, showing Mary with the Holy Trinity. The Catholic Church's dogma of the Assumption of the Virgin—in which Mary, as *domina rerum*, Queen of Nature, was declared to have entered heaven with soul and body reunited—can be said to have made the Trinity fourfold, corresponding with the basic archetype of completeness.

which has spontaneously arisen from the unconscious. That the Holy Ghost is the power that works for the further development of our religious understanding is not a new idea, of course, but its symbolic representation in the form of a spiral is new.

The same woman then painted a second picture, also inspired by a dream, showing the dreamer with her positive animus standing above Jerusalem when the wing of Satan descends to darken the city. The satanic wing strongly reminded her of the wafting cloak of God in the first painting, but in the former dream the spectator is high up, somewhere in heaven, and sees in front of her a terrific split between the rocks. The movement in the cloak of God is an attempt to reach Christ, the figure on the right, but it does not quite succeed. In the second painting, the same thing is seen from below—from a human angle. Looking at it from a higher angle, what is moving and spreading is a part of God; above that rises the spiral as a symbol of possible further development. But seen from the basis of our human reality, this same thing in the air is the dark, uncanny wing of the devil.

In the dreamer's life these two pictures became real in a way that does not concern us here, but it is obvious that they also contain a collective meaning that reaches beyond the personal. They may prophesy the descent of a divine darkness upon the Christian hemisphere, a darkness that points, however, toward the possibility of further evolution. Since the axis of the spiral does not move upward but into the background of the picture, the further evolution will lead neither to greater spiritual height nor down into the realm of matter, but to another dimension, probably into the background of these divine figures. And that means into the unconscious.

When religious symbols that are partly different from those we know emerge from the unconscious of an individual, it is often feared that these will wrongfully alter or diminish the officially recognized religious symbols. This fear even causes many people to reject analytical psychology and the entire unconscious.

If I look at such a resistance from a psychological point of view, I should have to comment that as far as religion is concerned, human beings can be divided into three types. First, there are those who still genuinely believe their religious doctrines, whatever they may be. For these people, the symbols and doctrines "click" so satisfyingly with what they feel deep inside themselves that serious doubts have no chance to sneak in. This happens when the views of consciousness and the unconscious background are in relative harmony. People of this sort can afford to look at new psychological discoveries and facts without prejudice and need not fear that they may be caused to lose their faith. Even if their dreams should bring up some relatively unorthodox details, these can be integrated into their general view.

The second type consists of those people who have completely lost their faith and have replaced it with purely conscious, rational opinions. For these people, depth psychology simply means an introduction into newly discovered areas of the psyche, and it should cause no trouble when they embark on the new adventure and investigate their dreams to test the truth of them.

Then there is a third group of people who in one part of themselves (probably the head) no longer believe in their religious traditions, whereas in some other part they still do believe. The French philosopher Voltaire is an illustration of this. He violently attacked the Catholic Church with rational argument (*écrasez l'infâme*), but on his deathbed, according to some reports, he begged for extreme unction. Whether this is true or not, his head was certainly unreligious, whereas his feelings and emotions seem still to have been orthodox. Such people remind one of a person getting stuck in the automatic doors of a bus; he can neither get out into free space nor re-enter the bus. Of course the dreams of such persons could probably help them out of their dilemma, but such people frequently have trouble turning toward the unconscious because they themselves do not know what they think and want. To take the unconscious seriously is ultimately a matter of personal courage and integrity.

The complicated situation of those who are caught in a no-man's-land between the two states of mind is partly created by the fact that all official religious doctrines actually belong to the collective consciousness (what Freud called the super-ego); but once, long ago, they sprang from the unconscious. This is a point that many historians of religion and theologians challenge. They choose to assume that there was once some sort of "revelation." I have searched for many years for concrete evidence for the Jun-

Paintings of the dreams discussed on pp. 225-6: Left, the spiral (a form of mandala) represents the Holy Ghost; right, the dark wing of Satan, from the second dream. Neither motif would be a familiar religious symbol to most people (nor were they to the dreamer): Each emerged spontaneously from the unconscious.

gian hypothesis about this problem; but it has been difficult to find because most rituals are so old that one cannot trace their origin. The following example, however, seems to me to offer a most important clue:

Black Elk, a medicine man of the Oglala Sioux, who died not long ago, tells us in his autobiography *Black Elk Speaks* that, when he was nine years old, he became seriously ill and during a sort of coma had a tremendous vision. He saw four groups of beautiful horses coming from the four corners of the world, and then, seated within a cloud, he saw the Six Grandfathers, the ancestral spirits of his tribe, "the grandfathers of the whole world." They gave him six healing symbols for his people and showed him new ways of life. But when he was 16 years old, he suddenly developed a terrible phobia whenever a thunder storm was approaching, because he heard "thunder beings" calling to him "to make haste." It reminded him of the thundering noise made by the approaching horses in his vision. An old medicine man explained to him that his fear came from the fact that he was keeping his vision to himself, and said that he must tell it to his tribe. He did so, and later he and his people acted out the vision in a ritual, using real horses. Not merely Black Elk himself, but many other members of his tribe felt infinitely better after this play. Some were even cured of their diseases. Black Elk said: "Even the horses seemed to be healthier and happier after the dance."

The ritual was not repeated because the tribe was destroyed soon afterward. But here is a different case in which a ritual still survives. Several Eskimo tribes living near the Colville River in Alaska explain the origin of their eagle festival in the following way:

A young hunter shot dead a very unusual eagle and was so impressed by the beauty of the dead bird that he stuffed and made a fetish of him, honoring him by sacrifices. One day, when the hunter had traveled far inland during his hunting, two animal-men suddenly appeared in the role of messengers and led him to the land of the eagles. There he heard a dark drumming noise, and the messengers explained that this was the heartbeat of the dead eagle's mother. Then the eagle spirit appeared to the hunter as a woman clothed in black. She asked him to initiate an eagle festival among his people to honor her dead son. After the eagle people had shown him how to do this, he suddenly found himself, exhausted, back in the place where he had met the messengers. Returning home, he taught his people how to perform the great eagle festival—as they have done faithfully ever since.

From such examples we see how a ritual or religious custom can spring directly from an unconscious revelation experienced by a single individual. Out of such beginnings, people living in cultural groups develop their various religious activities with their enormous influence on the entire life of the society. During a long process of evolution the original material is shaped and reshaped by words and actions, is beautified, and acquires increasingly definite forms. This crystallizing process, however, has a great disadvantage. More and more people have no personal knowledge of the original experience and can only believe what their elders and teachers tell them about it. They no longer know that such happenings are real, and they are of course ignorant about how one feels during the experience.

In their present forms, worked over and exceedingly aged, such religious traditions often resist further creative alterations by the unconscious. Theologians sometimes even defend these "true" religious symbols and symbolic doctrines against the discovery of a religious function in the unconscious psyche, forgetting that the values they fight for owe their existence to that very same function. Without a human psyche to receive divine inspirations and utter them in words or shape them in art, no religious symbol has ever come into the reality of our human life. (We need only think of the prophets and the evangelists.)

If someone objects that there is a religious reality in itself, independent of the human psyche, I can only answer such a person with this question: "Who says this, if not a human psyche?" No matter what we assert, we can never get away from the existence of the psyche —for we are contained within it, and it is the only means by which we can grasp reality.

Thus the modern discovery of the unconscious shuts one door forever. It definitely excludes the illusory idea, so favored by some individuals, that a man can know spiritual reality in itself. In modern physics, too, a door has been closed by Heisenberg's "principle of indeterminacy," shutting out the delusion that we can comprehend an absolute physical reality. The discovery of the unconscious, however, compensates for the loss of these beloved illusions by opening before us an immense and unexplored new field of realizations, within which objective scientific investigation combines in a strange new way with personal ethical adventure.

But, as I said at the outset, it is practically impossible to impart the whole reality of one's experience in the new field. Much is unique and can be only partially communicated by language. Here, too, a door is shut against the illusion that one can completely understand another person and tell him what is right for him. Once again, however, one can find a compensation for this in the new realm of experience by the discovery of the social function of the Self, which works in a hidden way to unite separate individuals who belong together.

Intellectual chit-chat is thus replaced by meaningful events that occur in the reality of the psyche. Hence, for the individual to enter seriously into the process of individuation in the way that has been outlined means a completely new and different orientation toward life. For scientists it also means a new and different scientific approach to outer facts. How this will work out in the field of human knowledge and in the social life of human beings cannot be predicted. But to me it seems certain that Jung's discovery of the process of individuation is a fact that future generations will have to take into account if they want to avoid drifting into a stagnant or even regressive outlook.

This painting (by Erhard Jacoby) illustrates the fact that each of us, perceiving the world through an individual psyche, perceives it in a slightly different way from others. The man, woman, and child are looking at the same scene; but, for each, different details become clear or obscured. Only by means of our conscious perception does the world exist "outside": We are surrounded by something completely unknown and unknowable (here represented by the painting's gray background).

4   Symbolism in the visual arts

Aniela Jaffé

Sacred symbols—the stone and the animal

The history of symbolism shows that everything can assume symbolic significance: natural objects (like stones, plants, animals, men, mountains and valleys, sun and moon, wind, water, and fire), or man-made things (like houses, boats, or cars), or even abstract forms (like numbers, or the triangle, the square, and the circle). In fact, the whole cosmos is a potential symbol.

Man, with his symbol-making propensity, unconsciously transforms objects or forms into symbols (thereby endowing them with great psychological importance) and expresses them in both his religion and his visual art. The intertwined history of religion and art, reaching back to prehistoric times, is the record that our ancestors have left of the symbols that were meaningful and moving to them. Even today, as modern painting and sculpture show, the interplay of religion and art is still alive.

For the first part of my discussion of symbolism in the visual arts, I intend to examine some of the specific motifs that have been universally sacred or mysterious to man. Then, for the remainder of the chapter, I wish to discuss the phenomenon of 20th-century art, not in terms of its use of symbols, but in terms of its significance as a *symbol itself*—a symbolic expression of the psychological condition of the modern world.

In the following pages, I have chosen three recurring motifs with which to illustrate the presence and nature of symbolism in the art of many different periods. These are the symbols of the stone, the animal, and the circle—each of which has had enduring psychological significance from the earliest expressions of human consciousness to the most sophisticated forms of 20th-century art.

We know that even unhewn stones had a highly symbolic meaning for ancient and primitive societies. Rough, natural stones were often believed to be the dwelling places of spirits or gods, and were used in primitive cultures as

tombstones, boundary stones, or objects of religious veneration. Their use may be regarded as a primeval form of sculpture—a first attempt to invest the stone with more expressive power than chance and nature could give it.

The Old Testament story of Jacob's dream is a typical example of how, thousands of years ago, man felt that a living god or a divine spirit was embodied in the stone and how the stone became a symbol:

And Jacob . . . went toward Haran. And he lighted upon a certain place, and tarried there all night, because the sun was set; and he took of the stones of the place, and put them for his pillows and lay down in that place to sleep. And he dreamed, and behold a ladder set up on the earth, and the top of it reached to heaven, and behold the angels of God ascending and descending on it. And, behold, the Lord stood above it, and said, I am the Lord God of Abraham thy father, and the God of Isaac: the land whereon thou liest, to thee will I give it, and to thy seed.

And Jacob awaked out of his sleep, and he said, Surely the Lord is in this place; and I knew it not. And he was afraid, and said, How dreadful is this place! this is none other but the house of God, and this is the gate of heaven. And Jacob rose up early in the morning and took the stone that he had put for his pillows, and set it up for a pillar, and poured oil upon the top of it. And he called the name of that place Beth-el.

For Jacob, the stone was an integral part of the revelation. It was the mediator between himself and God.

In many primitive stone-sanctuaries, the deity is represented not by a single stone but by a great many unhewn stones, arranged in distinct patterns. (The geometrical stone alignments in Brittany and the stone circle at Stonehenge are famous examples.) Arrangements of rough natural stones also play a considerable part in the highly civilized rock gardens of Zen Buddhism. Their arrangement is not geometrical but seems to have come about by pure chance. In fact, however, it is the expression of a most refined spirituality.

Very early in history, men began trying to express what they felt to be the soul or spirit of a rock by working it into a recognizable form. In many cases, the form was a more or less definite approximation to the human figure—for instance, the ancient menhirs with their crude outlines of faces, or the herms that developed out of boundary stones in ancient Greece, or the

Above left, the stone alignments at Carnac in Brittany, dating from *c*. 2000 B.C.—crude stones set upright in rows that are thought to have been used in sacred rituals and religious processions. Left, rough stones resting on raked sand in a Zen Buddhist rock garden (in the Ryoanji temple, Japan). Though apparently haphazard, the stones' arrangement in fact expresses a highly refined spirituality.

Right, a prehistoric *menhir*—a rock that has been slightly carved into a female form (probably a mother goddess). Far right, a sculpture by Max Ernst (born 1891) has also hardly altered the natural shape of the stone.

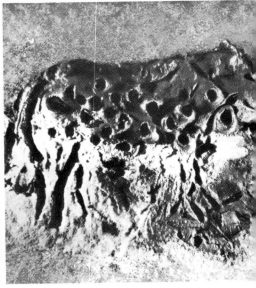

many primitive stone idols with human features. The animation of the stone must be explained as the projection of a more or less distinct content of the unconscious into the stone.

The primitive tendency to give merely a hint of a human figure, and to retain much of the stone's natural form, can also be seen in modern sculpture. Many examples show the artists' concern with the "self-expression" of the stone; to use the language of myth, the stone is allowed to "speak for itself." This can be seen, for instance, in the work of the Swiss sculptor Hans Aeschbacher, the American sculptor James Rosati, and the German-born artist Max Ernst. In a letter from Maloja in 1935, Ernst wrote: "Alberto [the Swiss artist Giacometti] and I are afflicted with sculpturitis. We work on granite boulders, large and small, from the moraine of the Forno glacier. Wonderfully polished by time, frost, and weather, they are in themselves fantastically beautiful. No human hand can do that. So why not leave the spadework to the elements, and confine ourselves to scratching on them the runes of our own mystery?"

What Ernst meant by "mystery" is not explained. But later in this chapter I shall try to show that the "mysteries" of the modern artist are not very different from those of the old masters who knew the "spirit of the stone."

The emphasis on this "spirit" in much sculpture is one indication of the shifting, indefinable borderline between religion and art. Sometimes one cannot be separated from the other. The same ambivalence can also be seen in another symbolic motif, as it appears in age-old works of art: the symbol of the animal.

Animal pictures go back to the last Ice Age (between 60,000 and 10,000 B.C.). They were discovered on the walls of caves in France and Spain at the end of the last century, but it was not until early in the present century that archaeologists began to realize their extreme importance and to inquire into their meaning. These inquiries revealed an infinitely remote prehistoric culture whose existence had never even been suspected.

Even today, a strange music seems to haunt the caves that contain the rock engravings and paintings. According to the German art historian Herbert Kühn, inhabitants of the areas in Africa, Spain, France, and Scandinavia where such paintings are found could not be induced to go near the caves. A kind of religious awe, or perhaps a fear of spirits hovering among the rocks and the paintings, held them back. Passing nomads still lay their votive offerings before the old rock paintings in North Africa. In the 15th century, Pope Calixtus II prohibited religious ceremonies in the "cave with the horse-pictures." Which cave the pope meant is not known, but there can be no doubt that it was a cave of the Ice Age containing animal pictures. All this goes to prove that the caves and rocks

Far left, animal paintings on cave walls at Lascaux. The paintings were not simply decorative; they had a magical function. Left, a drawing of a bison covered with arrow and spear marks: The cave dwellers believed that by ritually "killing" the image, they would be more likely to kill the animal.

Even today the destruction of an effigy or statue is a symbolic killing of the person depicted. Right, a statue of Stalin destroyed by Hungarian rebels in 1956; far right, rebels hang a bust of the former Stalinist Hungarian premier Matyas Rakosi.

with the animal paintings have always been instinctively felt to be what they originally were—religious places. The *numen* of the place has outlived the centuries.

In a number of caves the modern visitor must travel through low, dark, and damp passages till he reaches the point where the great painted "chambers" suddenly open out. This arduous approach may express the desire of the primitive men to safeguard from common sight all that was contained and went on in the caves, and to protect their mystery. The sudden and unexpected sight of the paintings in the chambers, coming after the difficult and awe-inspiring approach, must have made an overwhelming impression on primitive man.

The paleolithic cave paintings consist almost entirely of figures of animals, whose movements and postures have been observed in nature and rendered with great artistic skill. There are, however, many details that show that the figures were intended to be something more than naturalistic reproductions. Kühn writes: "The strange thing is that a good many primitive paintings have been used as targets. At Montespan there is an engraving of a horse that is being driven into a trap; it is pitted with the marks of missiles. A clay model of a bear in the same cave has 42 holes."

These pictures suggest a hunting-magic like that still practiced today by hunting tribes in Africa. The painted animal has the function of a "double"; by its symbolic slaughter, the hunters attempt to anticipate and ensure the death of the real animal. This is a form of sympathetic magic, which is based on the "reality" of a double represented in a picture: What happens to the picture will happen to the original. The underlying psychological fact is a strong identification between a living being and its image, which is considered to be the being's soul. (This is one reason why a great many primitive people today will shrink from being photographed.)

Other cave pictures must have served magic fertility rites. They show animals at the moment of mating; an example can be seen in the figures of a male and female bison in the Tuc d'Audubert cave in France. Thus the realistic picture of the animals was enriched by overtones of magic and took on a symbolic significance. It became the image of the living essence of the animal.

The most interesting figures in the cave paintings are those of semihuman beings in animal disguise, which are sometimes to be found besides the animals. In the Trois Frères cave in France, a man wrapped in an animal hide is playing a primitive flute as if he meant to put a spell on the animals. In the same cave, there is a dancing human being, with antlers, a horse's head, and bear's paws. This figure, dominating a medley of several hundred animals, is unquestionably the "Lord of the Animals."

The customs and usages of some primitive African tribes today can throw some light on the meaning of these mysterious and doubtless symbolic figures. In initiations, secret societies, and even the institution of monarchy in these tribes, animals and animal disguises often play an important part. The king and chief are animals too—generally lions or leopards. Vestiges of this custom may be discerned in the title of the last emperor of Ethiopia, Haile Selassie (Lion of Judah), or the honorific name of Dr. Hastings Banda (The Lion of Malawi).

The further back we go in time, or the more primitive and close to nature the society is, the more literally such titles must be taken. A primitive chief is not only disguised as the animal; when he appears at initiation rites in full animal disguise, he *is* the animal. Still more, he is an animal spirit, a terrifying demon who performs circumcision. At such moments he incorporates or represents the ancestor of the tribe and the clan, and therefore the primal god himself. He represents, and is, the "totem" animal. Thus we probably should not go far wrong in seeing in the figure of the dancing animal-man in the Trois Frères cave a kind of chief who has been transformed by his disguise into an animal demon.

In the course of time, the complete animal disguise was superseded in many places by animal and demon masks. Primitive men lavished all their artistic skill on these masks, and many of them are still unsurpassed in the power and intensity of their expression. They are often the objects of the same veneration as the god or demon himself. Animal masks play a part in the folk arts of many modern countries, like Switzerland, or in the magnificently expressive masks of the ancient Japanese *No* drama, which is still performed in modern Japan. The symbolic function of the mask is the same as that of the original animal disguise. Individual human expression is submerged, but in its place the wearer assumes the dignity and the beauty (and also the horrifying expression) of an animal demon. In psychological terms, the mask transforms its wearer into an archetypal image.

Dancing, which was originally nothing more than a completion of the animal disguise by appropriate movements and gestures, was probably supplementary to the initiation or other rites. It was, so to speak, performed by demons in honor of a demon. In the soft clay of the Tuc d'Audubert cave, Herbert Kühn found footprints that led around animal figures. They show that dancing was part of even the Ice Age rites. "Only heel prints can be seen," Kühn writes. "The dancers had moved like bisons. They had danced a bison dance for the fertility and increase of the animals and for their slaughter."

In his introductory chapter, Dr. Jung has pointed out the close relation, or even identifi-

Far left, a prehistoric painting from Trois Frères cave includes (lower right corner) a human figure, perhaps a shaman, with horns and hoofs. As examples of "animal" dances: left, a Burmese buffalo dance in which masked dancers are possessed by the buffalo spirit; right, a Bolivian devil dance in which the dancers wear demonic animal masks; far right, an old southwest German folk dance in which the dancers are disguised as witches and as animal-like "wild men."

cation, between the native and his totem animal (or "bush-soul"). There are special ceremonies for the establishment of this relationship, especially the initiation rites for boys. The boy enters into possession of his "animal soul," and at the same time sacrifices his own "animal being" by circumcision. This dual process admits him to the totem clan and establishes his relationship to his totem animal. Above all, he becomes a man, and (in a still wider sense) a human being.

East Coast Africans described the uncircumcised as "animals." They had neither received an animal soul nor sacrificed their "animality." In other words, since neither the human nor the animal aspect of an uncircumcised boy's soul had become conscious, his animal aspect was regarded as dominant.

The animal motif is usually symbolic of man's primitive and instinctual nature. Even civilized men must realize the violence of their instinctual drives and their powerlessness in face of the autonomous emotions erupting from the unconscious. This is still more the case with primitive men, whose consciousness is not highly developed and who are still less well equipped to weather the emotional storm. In the first chapter of this book, when Dr. Jung is discussing the ways in which man developed the power of reflection, he takes an example of an African who fell into a rage and killed his beloved little son. When the man recovered himself, he was overwhelmed with grief and remorse for what he had done. In this case a negative impulse broke loose and did its deadly work regardless of the conscious will. The animal demon is a highly expressive symbol for such an impulse. The vividness and concreteness of the image enables man to establish a relationship with it as a representative of the overwhelming power in himself. He fears it and seeks to propitiate it by sacrifice and ritual.

A large number of myths are concerned with a primal animal, which must be sacrificed in the cause of fertility or even creation. One example of this is the sacrifice of a bull by the Persian sun-god Mithras, from which sprang the earth with all wealth and fruitfulness. In the Christian legend of St. George slaying the dragon, the primeval rite of sacrificial slaughter again appears.

In the religions and religious art of practically every race, animal attributes are ascribed to the supreme gods, or the gods are represented as animals. The ancient Babylonians translated their gods into the heavens in the shape of the Ram, the Bull, the Crab, the Lion, the Scorpion, the Fish, and so on—the signs of the Zodiac. The Egyptians represented the goddess Hathor as cow-headed, the god Amon as ram-headed, and Thoth as ibis-headed or in the shape of a baboon. Ganesha, the Hindu god of good fortune, has a human body but the head

of an elephant, Vishnu is a boar, Hanuman is an ape-god, etc. (The Hindus, incidentally, do not assign the first place in the hierarchy of being to man: The elephant and lion stand higher.)

Greek mythology is full of animal symbolism. Zeus, the father of the gods, often approaches a girl whom he desires in the shape of a swan, a bull, or an eagle. In Germanic mythology, the cat is sacred to the goddess Freya, while the boar, the raven, and the horse are sacred to Wotan.

Even in Christianity, animal symbolism plays a surprisingly great part. Three of the Evangelists have animal emblems: St. Luke has the ox, St. Mark the lion, and St. John the eagle. Only one, St. Matthew, is represented as a man or as an angel. Christ himself symbolically appears as the Lamb of God or the Fish, but he is also the serpent exalted on the cross, the lion, and in rarer cases the unicorn. These animal attributes of Christ indicate that even the Son of God (the supreme personification of man) can no more dispense with his animal nature than with his higher, spiritual nature. The sub-human as well as the superhuman is felt to belong to the realm of the divine; the relationship of these two aspects of man is beautifully symbolized in the Christmas picture of the birth of Christ, in a stable among animals.

The boundless profusion of animal symbolism in the religion and art of all times does not

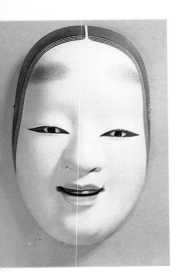

Left, a mask used in the ancient *No* drama of Japan, in which the players often portray gods, spirits, or demons. Above right, masked performers in Japanese dance theater. Below right, an actor in Japan's Kabuki drama, dressed as a medieval hero, with mask-like make-up.

merely emphasize the importance of the symbol; it shows how vital it is for men to integrate into their lives the symbol's psychic content—instinct. In itself, an animal is neither good nor evil; it is a piece of nature. It cannot desire anything that is not in its nature. To put this another way, it obeys its instincts. These instincts often seem mysterious to us, but they have their parallel in human life: The foundation of human nature is instinct.

But in man, the "animal being" (which lives in him as his instinctual psyche) may become dangerous if it is not recognized and integrated in life. Man is the only creature with the power to control instinct by his own will, but he is also able to suppress, distort, and wound it—and an animal, to speak metaphorically, is never so wild and dangerous as when it is wounded. Suppressed instincts can gain control of a man; they can even destroy him.

The familiar dream in which the dreamer is pursued by an animal nearly always indicates that an instinct has been split off from consciousness and ought to be (or is trying to be) readmitted and integrated into life. The more dangerous the behavior of the animal in the dream, the more unconscious is the primitive and instinctual soul of the dreamer, and the more imperative is its integration into his life if some irreparable evil is to be forestalled.

Suppressed and wounded instincts are the dangers threatening civilized man; uninhibited drives are the dangers threatening primitive man. In both cases the "animal" is alienated from its true nature; and for both, the acceptance of the animal soul is the condition for wholeness and a fully lived life. Primitive man must tame the animal in himself and make it his helpful companion: civilized man must heal the animal in himself and make it his friend.

Other contributors to this book have discussed the importance of the stone and animal motifs in terms of dream and myth; I have used them here only as general examples of the appearance of such living symbols throughout the history of art (and especially religious art). Let us now examine in the same way a most powerful and universal symbol: the circle.

Examples of animal symbols of divinities from three religions: Top of page, the Hindu god Ganesha (a painted sculpture from the Royal Palace of Nepal), god of prudence and wisdom; above, the Greek god Zeus in the form of a swan (with Leda); right, on opposite sides of a medieval coin, the crucified Christ shown as a man and as a serpent.

The symbol of the circle

Dr. M.-L. von Franz has explained the circle (or sphere) as a symbol of the Self. It expresses the totality of the psyche in all its aspects, including the relationship between man and the whole of nature. Whether the symbol of the circle appears in primitive sun worship or modern religion, in myths or dreams, in the mandalas drawn by Tibetan monks, in the ground plans of cities, or in the spherical concepts of early astronomers, it always points to the single most vital aspect of life—its ultimate wholeness.

An Indian creation myth relates that the god Brahma, standing on a huge, thousand-petaled lotus, turned his eyes to the four points of the compass. This fourfold survey from the circle of the lotus was a kind of preliminary orientation, an indispensable taking of bearings, before he began his work of creation.

A similar story is told of Buddha. At the moment of his birth, a lotus flower rose from the earth and he stepped into it to gaze into the 10 directions of space. (The lotus in this case was eight-rayed; and Buddha also gazed upward and downward, making 10 directions.) This symbolic gesture of survey was the most concise method of showing that from the moment of his birth, the Buddha was a unique personality, predestined to receive illumination. His personality and his further existence were given the imprint of wholeness.

The spatial orientation performed by Brahma and Buddha may be regarded as symbolic of the human need for psychic orientation. The four functions of consciousness described by Dr. Jung in his chapter, p. 61—thought, feeling, intuition, and sensation—equip man to deal with the impressions of the world he receives from within and without. It is by means of these functions that he comprehends and assimilates his experience; it is by means of them that he can respond. Brahma's four-fold survey of the universe symbolizes the necessary integration of these four functions that man must achieve. (In art, the circle is often eight-rayed. This expresses a reciprocal overlapping of the four functions of consciousness, so that four further intermediate functions come about—for instance, thought colored by feeling or intuition, or feeling tending toward sensation.)

In the visual art of India and the Far East, the four- or eight-rayed circle is the usual pattern of the religious images that serve as instruments of meditation. In Tibetan Lamaism especially, richly figured mandalas play an important part. As a rule, these mandalas represent the cosmos in its relation to divine powers.

But a great many of the eastern meditation figures are purely geometrical in design; these are called *yantras*. Aside from the circle, a very common yantra motif is formed by two interpenetrating triangles, one point-upward, the other point-downward. Traditionally, this shape symbolizes the union of Shiva and Shakti, the male and female divinities, a subject that also appears in sculpture in countless variations. In terms of psychological symbolism, it expresses the union of opposites—the union of the personal, temporal world of the ego with the non-personal, timeless world of the non-ego. Ultimately, this union is the fulfillment and goal of all religions: It is the union of the soul with God. The two interpenetrating triangles have a symbolic meaning similar to that of the more

Right, a *yantra* (a form of mandala), composed of nine linked triangles. The mandala, symbolizing wholeness, is often connected with exceptional beings of myth or legend. Far right, a Tibetan painting of the birth of Buddha; in the lower left corner, Buddha takes his first steps on a cross formed of circular blossoms. Above right, the birth of Alexander the Great (a 16th-century manuscript illustration) heralded by comets—in circular or mandala form.

common circular mandala. They represent the wholeness of the psyche or Self, of which consciousness is just as much a part as the unconscious.

In both the triangle yantras and the sculptural representations of the union of Shiva and Shakti, the emphasis lies on a tension between the opposites. Hence the marked erotic and emotional character of many of them. This dynamic quality implies a process—the creation, or coming into being, of wholeness—while the four- or eight-rayed circle represents wholeness as such, as an existing entity.

The abstract circle also figures in Zen painting. Speaking of a picture entitled *The Circle*, by the famous Zen priest Sangai, another Zen master writes: "In the Zen sect, the circle represents enlightenment. It symbolizes human perfection."

Abstract mandalas also appear in European Christian art. Some of the most splendid examples are the rose windows of the cathedrals. These are representations of the Self of man transposed onto the cosmic plane. (A cosmic mandala in the shape of a shining white rose was revealed to Dante in a vision.) We may regard as mandalas the haloes of Christ and the Christian saints in religious paintings. In many cases, the halo of Christ is alone divided into four, a significant allusion to his sufferings as the Son of Man and his death on the Cross, and at the same time a symbol of his differentiated wholeness. On the walls of early Romanesque churches, abstract circular figures can sometimes be seen; they may go back to pagan originals.

In non-Christian art, such circles are called "sun wheels." They appear in rock engravings that date back to the neolithic epoch before the wheel was invented. As Jung has pointed out, the term "sun wheel" denotes only the external aspect of the figure. What really mattered at all times was the experience of an archetypal,

Left, an example of the mandala in religious architecture: the Angkor Wat Buddhist temple in Cambodia, a square building with entrances at the four corners. Right, the ruins of a fortified camp in Denmark (c. A.D. 1000), which was laid out in a circle—as is the fortress town (center right) of Palmanova, Italy (built in 1593), with its star-shaped fortifications. Far right, the streets that meet at L'Étoile, Paris, to form a mandala.

inner image, which Stone Age man rendered in his art as faithfully as he depicted bulls, gazelles, or wild horses.

Many pictorial mandalas are to be found in Christian art: for example, the rather rare picture of the Virgin in the center of a circular tree, which is the God-symbol of the burning bush. The most widely current mandalas in Christian art are those of Christ surrounded by the four Evangelists. These go back to the ancient Egyptian representations of the god Horus and his four sons.

In architecture the mandala also plays an important part—but one that often passes unnoticed. It forms the ground plan of both secular and sacred buildings in nearly all civilizations; it enters into classical, medieval, and even modern town planning. A classical example appears in Plutarch's account of the foundation of Rome. According to Plutarch, Romulus sent for builders from Etruria who instructed him by sacred usages and written rules about all the ceremonies to be observed—in the same way "as in the mysteries." First they dug a round pit where the Comitium, or Court of Assembly, now stands, and into this pit they threw symbolic offerings of the fruits of the earth. Then each man took a small piece of earth of the land from which he came, and these were all thrown into the pit together. The pit was given the name of *mundus* (which also meant the cosmos). Around it Romulus drew the boundary of the city in a circle with a plow drawn by a bull and a cow. Wherever a gate was planned, the plowshare was taken out and the plow carried over.

The city founded in this solemn ceremony was circular in shape. Yet the old and famous description of Rome is *urbs quadrata*, the square city. According to one theory that attempts to reconcile this contradiction, the word *quadrata* must be understood to mean "quadripartite"; that is, the circular city was divided into four parts by two main arteries running from north to south and west to east. The point of intersection coincided with the *mundus* mentioned by Plutarch.

According to another theory, the contradiction can be understood only as a symbol, namely as a visual representation of the mathematically insoluble problem of the squaring of the circle, which had greatly preoccupied the Greeks and was to play so great a part in alchemy. Strangely enough, before describing the circle ceremony of the foundation of the city by Romulus, Plutarch also speaks of Rome as *Roma quadrata*, a square city. For him, Rome was both a circle and a square.

In each theory a true mandala is involved, and that links up with Plutarch's statement that the foundation of the city was taught by the Etruscans "as in the mysteries," as a secret rite. It was more than a mere outward form. By its mandala ground plan, the city, with its inhabitants, is exalted above the purely secular realm. This is further emphasized by the fact that the city has a center, the *mundus*, which established the city's relationship to the "other" realm, the abode of the ancestral spirits. (The *mundus* was covered by a great stone, called the "soul stone." On certain days the stone was removed, and then, it was said, the spirits of the dead rose from the shaft.)

A number of medieval cities were founded on the ground plan of a mandala and were

242

surrounded by an approximately circular wall. In such a city, as in Rome, two main arteries divided it into "quarters" and led to the four gates. The church or cathedral stood at the point of intersection of these arteries. The inspiration of the medieval city with its quarters was the Heavenly Jerusalem (in the Book of Revelation), which had a square ground plan and walls with three times four gates. But Jerusalem had no temple at its center, for God's immediate presence was the center of it. (The mandala ground plan for a city is by no means outmoded. A modern example is the city of Washington, D.C.)

Whether in classical or in primitive foundations, the mandala ground plan was never dictated by considerations of aesthetics or economics. It was a transformation of the city into an ordered cosmos, a sacred place bound by its center to the other world. And this transformation accorded with the vital feelings and needs of religious man.

Every building, sacred or secular, that has a mandala ground plan is the projection of an archetypal image from within the human unconscious onto the outer world. The city, the fortress, and the temple become symbols of psychic wholeness, and in this way exercise a specific influence on the human being who enters or lives in the place. (It need hardly be emphasized that even in architecture the projection of the psychic content was a purely unconscious process. "Such things cannot be thought up," Dr. Jung has written, "but must grow again from the forgotten depths if they are to express the deepest insights of consciousness and the loftiest intuitions of the spirit, thus amalgamating the uniqueness of present-day consciousness with the age-old past of humanity.")

The central symbol of Christian art is not the mandala, but the cross or crucifix. Up to Carolingian times, the equilateral or Greek cross was the usual form, and therefore the mandala was indirectly implied. But in the course of time the

Medieval religious architecture was usually based on the shape of the cross. Left, a 13th-century church (in Ethiopia) cut from the rock.

Renaissance religious art shows a reorientation to the earth and the body: Right, a plan for a circular church or basilica based on the body's proportions, drawn by the 15th-century Italian artist and architect Francesco di Giorgio.

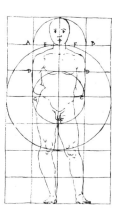

243

center moved upward until the cross took on the Latin form, with the stake and the crossbeam, that is customary today. This development is important because it corresponds to the inward development of Christianity up to the high Middle Ages. In simple terms, it symbolized the tendency to remove the center of man and his faith from the earth and to "elevate" it into the spiritual sphere. This tendency sprang from the desire to put into action Christ's saying: "My kingdom is not of this world." Earthly life, the world, and the body were therefore forces that had to be overcome. Medieval man's hopes were thus directed to the beyond, for it was only from paradise that the promise of fulfillment beckoned.

This endeavor reached its climax in the Middle Ages and in medieval mysticism. The hopes of the beyond found expression not only in the raising of the center of the cross; it can also be seen in the increasing height of the Gothic cathedrals, which seem to set the laws of gravity at defiance. Their cruciform ground plan is that of the elongated Latin cross (though the baptisteries, with the font in the center, have a true mandala ground plan).

With the dawning of the Renaissance, a revolutionary change began to occur in man's conception of the world. The "upward" movement (which reached its climax in the late Middle Ages) went into reverse; man turned back to the earth. He rediscovered the beauties of nature and the body, made the first circumnavigation of the globe, and proved the world to be a sphere. The laws of mechanics and causality became the foundations of science. The world of religious feeling, of the irrational, and of mysticism, which had played so great a part in medieval times, was more and more submerged by the triumphs of logical thought.

Similarly, art became more realistic and sensuous. It broke away from the religious subjects of the Middle Ages and embraced the whole visible world. It was overwhelmed by the manifoldness of the earth, by its splendor and horror, and became what Gothic art had been before it: a true symbol of the spirit of the age. Thus it can hardly be regarded as accidental that

a change also came over ecclesiastical building. In contrast to the soaring Gothic cathedrals, there were more circular ground plans. The circle replaced the Latin cross.

This change in form, however—and this is the important point for the history of symbolism—must be attributed to aesthetic, and not to religious, causes. That is the only possible explanation for the fact that the center of these round churches (the truly "holy" place) is empty, and that the altar stands in a recess in a wall away from the center. For that reason the plan cannot be described as a true mandala. An important exception is St. Peter's in Rome, which was built to the plans of Bramante and Michelangelo. Here the altar stands in the center. One is tempted, however, to attribute this exception to the genius of the architects, for great genius is always both of and beyond its time.

In spite of the far-reaching changes in art, philosophy, and science brought about by the Renaissance, the central symbol of Christianity remained unchanged. Christ was still represented on the Latin cross, as he is today. That meant that the center of religious man remained anchored on a higher, more spiritual plane than that of earthly man, who had turned back to nature. Thus a rift arose between man's traditional Christianity and his rational or intellectual mind. Since that time, these two sides of modern man have never been brought together. In the course of the centuries, with man's growing insight into nature and its laws, this division has gradually grown wider; and it still splits the psyche of the western Christian in the 20th century.

Of course, the brief historical summary given here has been over-simplified. Moreover, it omits the secret religious movements within Christianity that took account, in their beliefs, of what was usually ignored by most Christians: the question of evil, the chthonic (or earthly) spirit. Such movements were always in a minority and seldom had any very visible influence, but in their way they fulfilled the important role of a contrapuntal accompaniment to Christian spirituality.

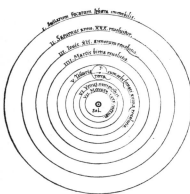

The Renaissance interest in outer reality produced the Copernican sun-centered universe (left) and turned artists away from "imaginative" art to nature: Below left, Leonardo's study of the human heart.

Renaissance art—with its sensuous concern with light, nature, and the body (far left, a Tintoretto, 16th century)—set a pattern that lasted until the Impressionists. Below, a painting by Renoir (1841-1919).

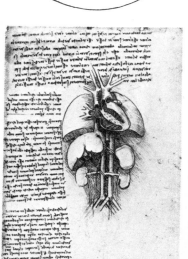

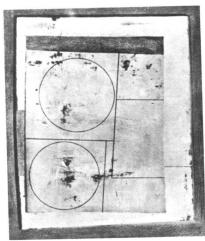

Far left, the symbolic alchemical concept of the squared circle— symbol of wholeness and of the union of opposites (note the male and female figures): Left, a modern squared circle by the British artist Ben Nicholson (born 1894): It is a strictly geometrical, empty form possessing aesthetic harmony and beauty but without symbolic meaning.

Right, a "sun wheel" in a painting by the modern Japanese artist Sofu Teshigahara (born 1900) follows the tendency of many modern painters, when using "circular" shapes, to make them asymmetrical.

Among the many sects and movements that arose about A.D. 1000, the alchemists played a very important part. They exalted the mysteries of matter and set them alongside those of the "heavenly" spirit of Christianity. What they sought was a wholeness of man encompassing mind and body, and they invented a thousand names and symbols for it. One of their central symbols was the *quadratura circuli* (the squaring of the circle), which is no more than the true mandala.

The alchemists not only recorded their work in their writings; they created a wealth of pictures of their dreams and visions—symbolic pictures that are still as profound as they are baffling. They were inspired by the dark side of nature—evil, the dream, the spirit of earth. The mode of expression was always fabulous, dreamlike, and unreal, in both word and picture. The great 15th-century Flemish painter Hieronymus Bosch may be regarded as the most important representative of this kind of imaginative art.

But at the same time, more typical Renaissance painters (working in the full light of day, so to speak) were producing the most splendid works of sensuous art. Their fascination with earth and nature went so deep that it practically determined the development of visual art for the next five centuries. The last great representatives of sensuous art, the art of the passing moment, of light and air, were the 19th-century impressionists.

We may here discriminate between two radically different modes of artistic representation. Many attempts have been made to define their characteristics. Recently Herbert Kühn (whose work on the cave-paintings I have already mentioned) has tried to draw a distinction between what he calls the "imaginative" and the "sensory" style. The "sensory" style generally depicts a direct reproduction of nature or of the picture-subject. The "imaginative," on the other hand, presents a fantasy or experience of the artist in an "unrealistic," even dreamlike, and sometimes "abstract" manner. Kühn's two conceptions seem so simple and so clear that I am glad to make use of them.

The first beginnings of imaginative art go back very far in history. In the Mediterranean basin, its efflorescence dates from the third millennium B.C. It has only recently been realized that these ancient works of art are not the results of incompetence or ignorance; they are modes of expression of a perfectly definite religious and spiritual emotion. And they have a special appeal today, for, during the last half-century, art has been passing once more through a phase that can be described by the term "imaginative."

Today the geometrical, or "abstract," symbol of the circle has again come to play a considerable role in painting. But with few exceptions the traditional mode of representation has undergone a characteristic transformation that corresponds to the dilemma of modern man's ex-

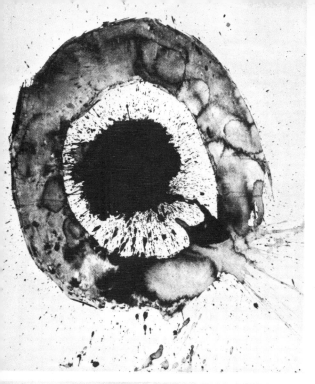

istence. The circle is no longer a single meaningful figure that embraces a whole world and dominates the picture. Sometimes the artist has taken it out of its dominant position, replacing it by a loosely organized group of circles. Sometimes the plane of the circle is asymmetrical.

An example of the asymmetrical circular plane may be seen in the famous sun disks of the French painter Robert Delaunay. A painting by the modern English painter Ceri Richards, now in Dr. Jung's collection, contains an entirely asymmetrical circular plane, while far to the left there appears a very much smaller and empty circle.

In the French painter Henri Matisse's *Still Life with Vase of Nasturtiums*, the focus of vision is a green sphere on a slanting black beam, which seems to gather into itself the manifold circles of the nasturtium leaves. The sphere overlaps a rectangular figure, the top left-hand corner of which is folded over. Given the artistic perfection of the painting it is easy to forget that in the past these two abstract figures (the circle and the square) would have been united, and would have expressed a world of thoughts and feelings. But anyone who does remember, and raises the question of meaning, will find food for thought: The two figures that from the beginning of time have formed a whole are in this painting torn apart or incoherently related. Yet both are there and are touching each other.

In a picture painted by the Russian-born artist Wassily Kandinsky there is a loose assembly of colored balls or circles that seem to be drifting like soap bubbles. They, too, are tenuously connected with a background of one large rectangle with two small, almost square rectangles contained in it. In another picture, which he called *A Few Circles*, a dark cloud (or is it a

Left, *Limits of Understanding* by Paul Klee (1879-1940) — one 20th-century painting in which the symbol of the circle retains a dominant position.

247

swooping bird?) again bears a loosely arranged group of bright balls or circles.

Circles often appear in unexpected connections in the mysterious compositions of the British artist Paul Nash. In the primeval solitude of his landscape *Event on the Downs*, a ball lies in the right foreground. Though it is apparently a tennis ball, the design on its surface forms the *Tai-gi-tu*, the Chinese symbol of eternity; thus it opens up a new dimension in the loneliness of the landscape. Something similar happens in Nash's *Landscape from a Dream*. Balls are rolling out of sight in an infinitely wide mirrored landscape, with a huge sun visible on the horizon. Another ball lies in the foreground, in front of the roughly square mirror.

In his drawing *Limits of Understanding*, the Swiss artist Paul Klee places the simple figure of a sphere or a circle above a complex struc-

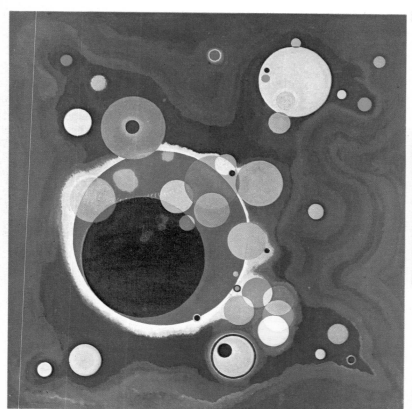

Circles appear broken or loosely scattered in *The Sun and the Moon*, top, by Robert Delaunay (1885-1941); in *A Few Circles*, left, by Kandinsky (1866-1944); and in *Landscape from a Dream*, right, by Paul Nash (1889-1946). Below, *Composition* by Piet Mondrian (1872-1944) is dominated by squares.

ture of ladders and lines. Dr. Jung has pointed out that a true symbol appears only when there is a need to express what thought cannot think or what is only divined or felt; that is the purpose of Klee's simple figure at the "limits of understanding."

It is important to note that the square, or groups of rectangles and squares, or rectangles and rhomboids, have appeared in modern art just as often as the circle. The master of harmonious (indeed, "musical") compositions with squares is the Dutch-born artist Piet Mondrian. As a rule there is no actual center in any of his pictures, yet they form an ordered whole in their own strict, almost ascetic fashion. Still more common are paintings by other artists with irregular quaternary compositions, or numerous rectangles combined in more or less loose groups.

The circle is a symbol of the psyche (even Plato described the psyche as a sphere). The square (and often the rectangle) is a symbol of earthbound matter, of the body and reality. In most modern art, the connection between these two primary forms is either nonexistent, or loose and casual. Their separation is another symbolic expression of the psychic state of 20th-century man: His soul has lost its roots and he is threatened by dissocia-

tion. Even in the world situation of today (as Dr. Jung pointed out in his opening chapter), this split has become evident: The western and eastern halves of the earth are separated by an Iron Curtain.

But the frequency with which the square and the circle appear must not be overlooked. There seems to be an uninterrupted psychic urge to bring into consciousness the basic factors of life that they symbolize. Also, in certain abstract pictures of our time (which merely represent a colored structure or a kind of "primal matter"), these forms occasionally appear as if they were germs of new growth.

The symbol of the circle has played a curious part in a very different phenomenon of the life of our day, and occasionally still does so. In the last years of the Second World War, there arose the "visionary rumor" of round flying bodies that became known as "flying saucers" or UFOs (unidentified flying objects). Jung has explained the UFOs as a projection of a psychic content (of wholeness) that has at all times been symbolized by the circle. In other words, this "visionary rumor," as can also be seen in many dreams of our time, is an attempt by the unconscious collective psyche to heal the split in our apocalyptic age by means of the symbol of the circle.

Above, an illustration from a 16th-century German broadsheet of some strange circular objects seen in the sky—similar to the "flying saucers" that have been seen in recent years. Jung has suggested that such visions are projections of the archetype of wholeness.

Modern painting as a symbol

The terms "modern art" and "modern painting" are used in this chapter as the layman uses them. What I will be dealing with, to use Kühn's term, is modern *imaginative* painting. Pictures of this kind can be "abstract" (or rather "non-figurative") but they need not always be so. There will be no attempt to distinguish among such various forms as fauvism, cubism, expressionism, futurism, suprematism, constructivism, orphism, and so on. Any specific allusion to one or the other of these groups will be quite exceptional.

And I am not concerned with an aesthetic differentiation of modern paintings; nor, above all, with artistic evaluations. Modern imaginative painting is here taken simply as a phenomenon of our time. That is the only way in which the question of its symbolic content can be justified and answered. In this brief chapter it is possible to mention only a few artists, and to select a few of their works more or less at random. I must content myself with discussing modern painting in terms of a small number of its representatives.

My starting point is the psychological fact that the artist has at all times been the instrument and spokesman of the spirit of his age. His work can be only partly understood in terms of his personal psychology. Consciously or unconsciously, the artist gives form to the nature and values of his time, which in their turn form him.

The modern artist himself often recognizes the interrelation of the work of art and its time. Thus the French critic and painter Jean Bazaine writes in his *Notes on Contemporary Painting*: "Nobody paints as he likes. All a painter can do is to will with all his might the painting his age is capable of." The German artist Franz Marc, who died in the First World War, said: "The great artists do not seek their forms in the mist of the past, but take the deepest soundings they can of the genuine, pro-foundest center of gravity of their age." And, as far back as 1911, Kandinsky wrote in his famous essay "Concerning the Spiritual in Art": "Every epoch is given its own measure of artistic freedom, and even the most creative genius may not leap over the boundary of that freedom."

For the last 50 years, "modern art" has been a general bone of contention, and the discussion has lost none of its heat. The "yeas" are as passionate as the "nays"; yet the reiterated prophecy that "modern" art is finished has never come true. The new way of expression has been triumphant to an unimagined degree. If it is threatened at all, it will be because it has degenerated into mannerism and modishness. (In the Soviet Union, where non-figurative art has often been officially discouraged and produced only in private, figurative art is threatened by a similar degeneration.)

The general public, in Europe at any rate, is still in the heat of the battle. The violence of the discussion shows that feeling runs high in both camps. Even those who are hostile to modern art cannot avoid being impressed by the works they reject; they are irritated or repelled, but (as the violence of their feelings shows) they are moved. As a rule, the negative fascination is no less strong than the positive. The stream of visitors to exhibitions of modern art, wherever and whenever they take place, testifies to something more than curiosity. Curiosity would be satisfied sooner. And the fantastic prices that are paid for works of modern art are a measure of the status conferred upon them by society.

Fascination arises when the unconscious has been moved. The effect produced by works of modern art cannot be explained entirely by their visible form. To the eye trained in "classic" or "sensory" art, they are new and alien. Nothing in works of non-figurative art reminds the spectator of his own world—no objects in their own everyday surroundings, no human being or animal that speaks a familiar language. There is no welcome, no visible accord in the cosmos created by the artist. And yet, without any question, there is a human bond. It may be even more intense than in works of sensory art, which make a direct appeal to feeling and empathy.

It is the aim of the modern artist to give expression to his inner vision of man, to the spiritual background of life and the world. The modern work of art has abandoned not only the realm of the concrete, "natural," sensuous world, but also that of the individual. It has become highly collective and therefore (even in the abbreviation of the pictorial hieroglyph) touches not only the few but the many. What remains individual is the manner of representation, the style and quality of the modern work of art. It is often difficult for the layman to recognize whether the artist's intentions are genuine and his expressions spontaneous, neither imitated nor aimed at effect. In many cases he must accustom himself to new kinds of line and color. He must learn them, as he would learn a foreign language, before he can judge their expressiveness and quality.

The pioneers of modern art have apparently understood how much they were asking of the public. Never have artists published so many "manifestoes" and explanations of their aims as in the 20th century. It is, however, not only to others that they are striving to explain and justify what they are doing; it is also to themselves. For the most part, these manifestoes are artistic confessions of faith—poetic and often confused or self-contradictory attempts to give clarity to the strange outcome of today's artistic activities.

What really matters, of course, is (and always has been) the direct encounter with the work of art. Yet, for the psychologist who is concerned with the symbolic content of modern art, the study of these writings is most instructive. For that reason the artists, wherever possible, will be allowed in the following discussion to speak for themselves.

The beginnings of modern art appeared in the early 1900s. One of the most impressive personalities of that initiatory phase was Kandinsky, whose influence is still clearly traceable in the paintings of the second half of the century. Many of his ideas have proved prophetic. In his essay "Concerning Form," he writes: "The art of today embodies the spiritual matured to the point of revelation. The forms of this embodiment may be arranged between two poles: (1) great abstraction; (2) great realism. These two poles open two paths, which both lead to *one* goal in the end. These two elements have always been present in art; the first was expressed in the second. Today it looks as if they were about to carry on separate existences. Art seems to have put an end to the pleasant completion of the abstract by the concrete, and vice versa."

Sensory (or representational) art *versus* imaginative (or "unrealistic") art: Right, a painting by the 19th-century British artist William Frith, part of a sequence depicting a gambler's downfall. This is one extreme of representational art: It has declined into mannerism and sentiment. Left, an extreme of imaginative (and, here, "abstract") art by Kasimir Malevich (1878-1935).

Suprematist Composition. White on White 1918.
Collection, The Museum of Modern Art, New York

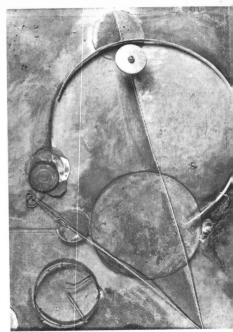

Left and above, two compositions by Kurt Schwitters (1887-1948). His kind of imaginative art uses (and transforms) ordinary *things*— in this case, old tickets, paper, metal, etc. Below left, pieces of wood similarly used by Hans Arp (1887-1966). Below, in a sculpture by Picasso (1881-1973), ordinary objects—leaves—are part of the subject rather than the material.

To illustrate Kandinsky's point that the two elements of art, the abstract and the concrete, have parted company: In 1913, the Russian painter Kasimir Malevich painted a picture that consisted only of a black square on a white ground. It was perhaps the first purely "abstract" picture ever painted. He wrote of it: "In my desperate struggle to liberate art from the ballast of the world of objects, I took refuge in the form of the square."

A year later, the French painter Marcel Duchamp set up an object chosen at random (a bottle rack) on a pedestal and exhibited it. Jean Bazaine wrote of it: "This bottle rack, torn from its utilitarian context and washed up on the beach, has been invested with the lonely dignity of the derelict. Good for nothing, there to be used, ready for anything, it is alive. It lives on the fringe of existence its own disturbing, absurd life. The disturbing object—that is the first step to art."

In its weird dignity and abandonment, the object was immeasurably exalted and given significance that can only be called magical. Hence its "disturbing, absurd life." It became an idol and at the same time an object of mockery. Its intrinsic reality was annihilated.

Both Malevich's square and Duchamp's bottle rack were symbolic gestures that had nothing to do with art in the strict sense of the word. Yet they mark the two extremes ("great abstraction" and "great realism") between which the imaginative art of the succeeding decades may be aligned and understood.

From the psychological standpoint, the two gestures toward the naked object (matter) and the naked non-object (spirit) point to a collective psychic rift that created its symbolic expression in the years before the catastrophe of the First World War. This rift had first appeared in the Renaissance, when it became manifest as a conflict between knowledge and faith. Meanwhile, civilization was removing man further and further from his instinctual foundation, so that a gulf opened between nature and mind, between the unconscious and consciousness. These opposites characterize the psychic situation that is seeking expression in modern art.

The secret soul of things

As we have seen, the starting point of "the concrete" was Duchamp's famous—or notorious—bottle rack. The bottle rack was not intended to be artistic in itself. Duchamp called himself an "anti-artist." But it brought to light an element that was to mean a great deal to artists for a long time to come. The name they gave to it was *objet trouvé* or "ready-made."

The Spanish painter Joan Miró, for instance, goes to the beach every dawn "to collect things washed up by the tide. Things lying there, waiting for someone to discover their personality." He keeps his finds in his studio. Now and then he assembles some of them and the most curious compositions result: "The artist is often surprised himself at the shapes of his own creation."

As far back as 1912, the Spanish-born artist Pablo Picasso and the French artist Georges Braque made what they called "collages" from scraps of rubbish. Max Ernst cut clippings from the illustrated papers of the so-called age of big business, assembled them as the fancy took him, and so transformed the stuffy solidity of the bourgeois age into a demonic, dreamlike unreality. The German painter Kurt Schwitters worked with the contents of his ash can: He used nails, brown paper, ragged scraps of newspaper, railway tickets, and remnants of cloth. He succeeded in assembling this rubbish with such seriousness and freshness that surprising effects of strange beauty came about. In Schwitters' obsession with things, however, this manner of composition occasionally became merely absurd. He made a construction of rubbish that he called "a cathedral built for things." Schwitters worked on it for 10 years, and three stories of his own house had to be demolished to give him the space he needed.

Schwitters' work, and the magical exaltation of the object, give the first hint of the place of modern art in the history of the human mind, and of its symbolic significance. They reveal the tradition that was being unconsciously perpetuated. It is the tradition of the hermetic Christian brotherhoods of the Middle Ages, and of the alchemists, who conferred even on matter, the stuff of the earth, the dignity of their religious contemplation.

Schwitters' exaltation of the grossest material to the rank of art, to a "cathedral" (in which the rubbish would leave no room for a human being), faithfully followed the old alchemical tenet according to which the sought-for precious object is to be found in filth. Kandinsky expressed the same ideas when he wrote: "Everything that is *dead* quivers. Not only the things of poetry, stars, moon, wood, flowers, but even a white trouser button glittering out of a puddle in the street . . . . Everything has a secret soul, which is silent more often than it speaks."

What the artists, like the alchemists, probably did not realize was the psychological fact that they were projecting part of their psyche into matter or inanimate objects. Hence the "mysterious animation" that entered into such things, and the great value attached even to rubbish. They projected their own darkness, their earthly shadow, a psychic content that they and their time had lost and abandoned.

Unlike the alchemists, however, men like Schwitters were not contained in and protected by the Christian order. In one sense, Schwitters' work is opposed to it: A kind of monomania binds him to matter, while Christianity seeks to vanquish matter. And yet, paradoxically, it is Schwitters' monomania that robs the material in his creations of its inherent significance as concrete reality. In his pictures, matter is transformed into an "abstract" composition. Therefore it begins to discard its substantiality, and to dissolve. In that very process, these pictures become a symbolic expression of our time, which has seen the concept of the "absolute" concreteness of matter undermined by modern atomic physics.

Painters began to think about the "magic object" and the "secret soul" of things. The Italian painter Carlo Carrà wrote: "It is common things that reveal those forms of simplicity through which we can realize that higher, more significant condition of being where the whole splendor of art resides." Paul Klee said: "The object expands beyond the bounds of its appearance by our knowledge that the thing is more than its exterior presents to our eyes." And Jean Bazaine wrote: "An object awakens our love just because it seems to be the bearer of powers that are greater than itself."

Sayings of this kind recall the old alchemical concept of a "spirit in matter," believed to be the spirit in and behind inanimate objects like metal or stone. Psychologically interpreted, this spirit is the unconscious. It always manifests itself when conscious or rational knowledge has reached its limits and mystery sets in, for man tends to fill the inexplicable and mysterious with the contents of his unconscious. He projects them, as it were, into a dark, empty vessel.

The feeling that the object was "more than met the eye," which was shared by many artists, found a most remarkable expression in the work of the Italian painter Giorgio de Chirico. He was a mystic by temperament, and a tragic seeker who never found what he sought. On his self-portrait (1908) he wrote: *Et quid amabo nisi quod aenigma est* ("And what am I to love if not the enigma?").

Chirico was the founder of the so-called *pittura metafisica*. "Every object," he wrote, "has two aspects: The common aspect, which is the one we generally see and which is seen by everyone, and the ghostly and metaphysical aspect, which only rare individuals see at moments of clairvoyance and metaphysical meditation. A work of art must relate something that does not appear in its visible form."

Chirico's works reveal this "ghostly aspect" of things. They are dreamlike transpositions of reality, which arise as visions from the unconscious. But his "metaphysical abstraction" is expressed in a panic-stricken rigidity, and the atmosphere of the pictures is one of nightmare and of fathomless melancholy. The city squares of Italy, the towers and objects, are set in an over-acute perspective, as if they were in a vacuum, illuminated by a merciless, cold light

An example of "surrealist" art:
Les Souliers Rouges, by the French
painter René Magritte (1898-1967).
Much of the disturbing effect of
surrealist painting comes from its
association and juxtaposition of
unrelated objects—often absurd,
irrational, and dreamlike.

from an unseen source. Antique heads or
statues of gods conjure up the classical past.

In one of the most terrifying of his pictures,
he has placed beside the marble head of a goddess a pair of red rubber gloves, a "magic
object" in the modern sense. A green ball on the
ground acts as a symbol, uniting the crass
opposites; without it, there would be more than
a hint of psychic disintegration. This picture was
clearly not the result of over-sophisticated deliberation; it must be taken as a dream picture.

Chirico was deeply influenced by the philosophies of Nietzsche and Schopenhauer. He
wrote: "Schopenhauer and Nietzsche were the
first to teach the deep significance of the senselessness of life, and to show how this senselessness could be transformed into art . . . . The
dreadful void they discovered is the very soul-
less and untroubled beauty of matter." It may
be doubted whether Chirico succeeded in trans-
posing the "dreadful void" into "untroubled
beauty." Some of his pictures are extremely
disturbing; many are as terrifying as night-
mares. But in his effort to find artistic expres-

sion for the void, he penetrated to the core of
the existential dilemma of contemporary man.

Nietzsche, whom Chirico quotes as his authority, has given a name to the "dreadful void"
in his saying "God is dead." Without referring
to Nietzsche, Kandinsky wrote in *On the Spiritual in Art*: "Heaven is empty. God is dead."
A phrase of this kind may sound abominable.
But it is not new. The idea of the "death of God"
and its immediate consequence, the "metaphysical void," had troubled the minds of 19th-
century poets, especially in France and Germany. It was a long development that, in the
20th century, reached the stage of open discussion and found expression in art. The cleavage
between modern art and Christianity was finally accomplished.

Dr. Jung also came to realize that this
strange and mysterious phenomenon of the
death of God is a psychic fact of our time. In
1937 he wrote: "I know—and here I am expressing what countless other people know—
that the present time is the time of God's dis-
appearance and death." For years he had observed the Christian God-image fading in his
patients' dreams—that is, in the unconscious of
modern men. The loss of that image is the loss
of the supreme factor that gives life a meaning.

It must be pointed out, however, that neither
Nietzsche's assertion that God is dead, nor
Chirico's "metaphysical void," nor Jung's deductions from unconscious images, have anything final to say about the reality and existence of God or of a transcendental being or
not-being. They are human assertions. In each
case they are based, as Jung has shown in
Psychology and Religion, on contents of the
unconscious psyche that have entered consciousness in tangible form as images, dreams, ideas,
or intuitions. The origin of these contents, and
the cause of such a transformation (from a
living to a dead God), must remain unknown,
on the frontier of mystery.

Chirico never came to a solution of the problem presented to him by the unconscious. His
failure may be seen most clearly in his representation of the human figure. Given the present
religious situation, it is man himself to whom

Both Giorgio de Chirico (born 1888) and Marc Chagall (born 1887) have sought to look behind the outward appearances of things; their work seems to have risen from the depths of the unconscious. But Chirico's vision (below, his *Philosopher and Poet*) was gloomy, melancholy, even nightmarish. Chagall's has always been rich, warm, and alive. Right, one of his great stained-glass windows created in 1962 for a Jerusalem synagogue.

In Chirico's *Song of Love* (left), the marble head of the goddess and the rubber glove are crass opposites. The green ball seems to act as a uniting symbol.

Right, *Metaphysical Muse* by—Carlo Carrà (1881-1966). The faceless manikin was a frequent theme of Chirico's as well.

should be accorded a new, if impersonal, dignity and responsibility. (Jung described it as a responsibility to consciousness.) But in Chirico's work, man is deprived of his soul; he becomes a *manichino*, a puppet without a face (and therefore also without consciousness).

In the various versions of his *Great Metaphysician*, a faceless figure is enthroned on a pedestal made of rubbish. The figure is a consciously or unconsciously ironical representation of the man who strives to discover the "truth" about metaphysics, and at the same time a symbol of ultimate loneliness and senselessness. Or perhaps the *manichini* (which also haunt the works of other contemporary artists) are a premonition of the faceless mass man.

When he was 40, Chirico, abandoned his *pittura metafisica*; he turned back to traditional modes, but his work lost depth. Here is certain proof that there is no "back to where you came from" for the creative mind whose unconscious has been involved in the fundamental dilemma of modern existence.

A counterpart to Chirico might be seen in the Russian-born painter Marc Chagall. His quest in his work is also a "mysterious and lonely poetry" and "the ghostly aspect of things that only rare individuals may see." But Chagall's rich symbolism is rooted in the piety of Eastern Jewish Hassidism and in a warm feeling for life. He was faced with neither the problem of the void nor the death of God. He wrote: "Everything may change in our demoralized world except the heart, man's love, and his striving to know the divine. Painting, like all poetry, has its part in the divine; people feel this today just as much as they used to."

The British author Sir Herbert Read once wrote of Chagall that he never quite crossed the threshold into the unconscious, but "has always kept one foot on the earth that had nourished him." This is exactly the "right" relation to the unconscious. It is all the more important that, as Read emphasizes, "Chagall has remained one of the most influential artists of our time."

With the contrast between Chagall and Chirico, a question arises that is important for the understanding of symbolism in modern art: How does the relationship between consciousness and the unconscious take shape in the work of modern artists? Or, to put it another way, where does man stand?

One answer may be found in the movement called surrealism, of which the French poet André Breton is regarded as the founder. (Chirico too may be described as a surrealist.) As a student of medicine, Breton had been introduced to the work of Freud. Thus dreams came to play an important part in his ideas. "Can dreams not be used to solve the fundamental problems of life?" he wrote. "I believe that the apparent antagonism between dream and reality will be resolved in a kind of absolute reality—in surreality."

Breton grasped the point admirably. What he sought was a reconciliation of the opposites, consciousness and the unconscious. But the way he took to reach his goal could only lead him astray. He began to experiment with Freud's method of free association as well as with automatic writing, in which the words and phrases arising from the unconscious are set down without any conscious control. Breton called it: "thought's dictation, independent of any aesthetic or moral preoccupation."

But that process simply means that the way is opened to the stream of unconscious images, and the important or even decisive part to be played by consciousness is ignored. As Dr. Jung has shown in his chapter, it is consciousness that holds the key to the values of the unconscious, and that therefore plays the decisive part. Consciousness alone is competent to determine the meaning of the images and to recognize their significance for man here and now, in the concrete reality of the present. Only in an *interplay* of consciousness and the unconscious can the unconscious prove its value, and perhaps even show a way to overcome the melancholy of the void. If the unconscious, once in action, is left to itself, there is a risk that its contents will become overpowering or will manifest their negative, destructive side.

If we look at surrealist pictures (like Salvador Dali's *The Burning Giraffe*) with this in mind,

we may feel the wealth of their fantasy and the overwhelming power of their unconscious imagery, but we realize the horror and the symbolism of the end of all things that speaks from many of them. The unconscious is pure nature, and, like nature, pours out its gifts in profusion. But left to itself and without the human response from consciousness, it can (again like nature) destroy its own gifts and sooner or later sweep them into annihilation.

The question of the role of consciousness in modern painting also arises in connection with the use of *chance* as a means of composing paintings. In *Beyond Painting* Max Ernst wrote: "The association of a sewing machine and an umbrella cn a surgical table [he is quoting from the poet Lautréamont] is a familiar example, which has now become classical, of the phenomenon discovered by the surrealists, that the association of two (or more) apparently alien elements on a plane alien to both is the most potent ignition of poetry."

That is probably as difficult for the layman to comprehend as the comment Breton made to the same effect: "The man who cannot visualize a horse galloping on a tomato is an idiot."

One of the best-known of modern "surrealist" painters is Salvador Dali (born 1904). Above, his famous painting *The Burning Giraffe*. Below, one of Max Ernst's *frottages* (usually rubbings taken from scratches on tiles), from his *Natural History*.

Ernst's *Natural History* resembles the interest taken in the past in "accidental" patterns in nature. Below, an engraving of an 18th-century Dutch museum exhibit that is also a kind of surrealist "natural history" with its inclusion of coral, stones, and skeletons.

(We might recall here the "chance" association of a marble head and red rubber gloves in Chirico's picture.) Of course, many of these associations were intended as jokes and nonsense. But most modern artists have been concerned with something radically different from jokes.

Chance plays a significant part in the work of the French sculptor Jean (or Hans) Arp. His woodcuts of leaves and other forms, thrown together at random, were another expression of the quest for, as he put it, "a secret, primal meaning slumbering beneath the world of appearances." He called them *Leaves arranged according to the laws of chance* and *Squares arranged according to the laws of chance*. In these compositions it is chance that gives depth to the work of art; it points to an unknown but active principle of order and meaning that becomes manifest in *things* as their "secret soul."

It was above all the desire to "make chance essential" (in Paul Klee's words) that underlay the surrealists' efforts to take the grain of wood, cloud formations, and so on as a starting point for their visionary painting. Max Ernst, for instance, went back to Leonardo da Vinci, who wrote an essay on Botticelli's remark that if

you throw a paint-soaked sponge at a wall, in the splashes it makes you will see heads, animals, landscapes, and a host of other configurations.

Ernst has described how a vision pursued him in 1925. It forced itself on him as he was staring at a tiled floor marked by thousands of scratches. "In order to give foundation to my powers of meditation and hallucination, I made a series of drawings of the tiles by laying sheets of paper on them at random and then taking graphite rubbings. When I fixed my eyes on the result, I was astounded by a suddenly sharpened sense of a hallucinatory series of contrasting and superposed pictures. I made a collection of the first results obtained from these 'frottages' and called it *Histoire Naturelle*."

It is important to note that Ernst placed over or behind some of these *frottages* a ring or circle, which gives the picture a peculiar atmosphere and depth. Here the psychologist can recognize the unconscious drive to oppose the chaotic hazards of the image's natural language by the symbol of a self-contained psychic whole, thus establishing equilibrium. The ring or circle dominates the picture. Psychic wholeness rules nature, itself meaningful and giving meaning.

Right, Roman coins used in places progressively farther away from Rome. On the last coin (farthest from the controlling center) the face has disintegrated. This strangely corresponds to the psychic disintegration that such drugs as LSD-25 can induce. Below, drawings done by an artist who took this drug in a test held in Germany in 1951. The drawings grow more abstract as conscious control is overcome by the unconscious.

In Max Ernst's efforts to pursue the secret pattern in things, we may detect an affinity with the 19th-century Romantics. They spoke of nature's "handwriting," which can be seen everywhere, on wings, eggshells, in clouds, snow, ice crystals, and other "strange conjunctions of chance" just as much as in dreams or visions. They saw everything as the expression of one and the same "pictorial language of nature." Thus it was a genuinely romantic gesture when Max Ernst called the pictures produced by his experiments "natural history." And he was right, for the unconscious (which had conjured up the pictures in the chance configuration of things) *is* nature.

It is with Ernst's *Natural History* or Arp's compositions of chance that the reflections of the psychologist begin. He is faced with the question of what meaning a chance arrangement—wherever and whenever it comes about—can have for the man who happens on it. With this question, man and consciousness come into the matter, and with them the possibility of meaning.

The chance-created picture may be beautiful or ugly, harmonious or discordant, rich or poor in content, well- or ill-painted. These factors determine its artistic value, but they cannot satisfy the psychologist (often to the distress of the artist or of anyone who finds supreme satisfaction in the contemplation of form). The psychologist seeks further and tries to understand the "secret code" of chance arrangement—in so far as man can decipher it at all. The number and form of the objects thrown together at random by Arp raise as many questions as any

detail of Ernst's fantastic *frottages*. For the psychologist, they are symbols; and therefore they can not only be felt but (up to a certain point) can also be interpreted.

The apparent or actual retreat of man from many modern works of art, the lack of reflection, and the predominance of the unconscious over consciousness offer critics frequent points of attack. They speak of pathological art or compare it with pictures by the insane, for it is characteristic of psychosis that consciousness and the ego-personality are submerged and "drowned" by floods of contents from the unconscious regions of the psyche.

It is true that the comparison is not so odious today as it was even a generation ago. When Dr. Jung first pointed out a connection of this kind in his essay on Picasso (1932), it provoked a storm of indignation. Today, the catalogue of a well-known Zürich art gallery speaks of the "almost schizophrenic obsession" of a famous artist, and the German writer Rudolf Kassner described Georg Trakl as "one of the greatest German poets," continuing: "There was something schizophrenic about him. It can be felt in his work; there is a touch of schizophrenia in it too. Yes, Trakl is a great poet."

It is now realized that a state of schizophrenia and the artistic vision are not mutually exclusive. To my mind, the famous experiments with mescalin and similar drugs have contributed to this change of attitude. These drugs create a condition accompanied by intense visions of colors and forms—not unlike schizophrenia. More than one artist of today has sought inspiration in such a drug.

The retreat from reality

Franz Marc once said: "The art that is coming will give formal expression to our scientific conviction." This was a truly prophetic saying. We have traced the influence on artists of Freud's psychoanalysis and of the discovery (or rediscovery) of the unconscious in the early years of the 20th century. Another important point is the connection between modern art and the results of research in nuclear physics.

To put it in simple, nonscientific terms, nuclear physics has robbed the basic units of matter of their absolute concreteness. It has made matter mysterious. Paradoxically, mass and energy, wave and particle, have proved to be interchangeable. The laws of cause and effect have become valid only up to a certain point. It does not matter at all that these relativities, discontinuities, and paradoxes hold good only on the margins of our world—only for the infinitely small (the atom) and the infinitely great (the cosmos). They have caused a revolutionary change in the concept of reality, for a new, totally different, and irrational reality has dawned behind the reality of our "natural" world, which is ruled by the laws of classical physics.

Corresponding relativities and paradoxes were discovered in the domain of the psyche. Here, too, another world dawned on the margin of the world of consciousness, governed by new and hitherto unknown laws that are strangely akin to the laws of nuclear physics. The parallelism between nuclear physics and the psychology of the collective unconscious was often a subject of discussion between Jung and Wolfgang Pauli, the Nobel prizewinner in physics. The space-time continuum of physics and the collective unconscious can be seen, so to speak, as the outer and inner aspects of one and the same reality behind appearances. (The relationship between physics and psychology will be discussed by Dr. M.-L. von Franz in her concluding essay.)

It is characteristic of this one world behind the worlds of physics and the psyche that its laws, processes, and contents are unimaginable. That is a fact of outstanding importance for the understanding of the art of our time. For the main subject of modern art is, in a certain sense, unimaginable too. Therefore much modern art has become "abstract." The great artists of this century have sought to give visible form to the "life behind things" and so their works are a symbolic expression of a world behind

The paintings on these pages, all by Franz Marc (1880-1916), show his gradual development away from a concern with outward things, toward a more completely "abstract" art. Far left, *Blue Horses* (1911); center, *Roes in a Wood* (1913-14); below, *Play of Forms* (1914).

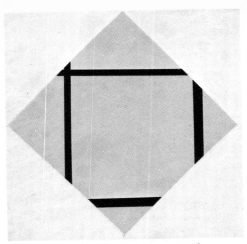

Painting No. 1, 1926. *Collection, The Museum of Modern Art, New York*

consciousness (or, indeed, behind dreams, for dreams are only rarely non-figurative). Thus they point to the "one" reality, the "one" life, which seems to be the common background of the two domains of physical and psychic appearances.

Only a few artists realized the connection between their form of expression and physics and psychology. Kandinsky is one of the masters who expressed the deep emotion he felt at the early discoveries of modern physical research. "In my mind, the collapse of the atom was the collapse of the whole world: Suddenly the stoutest walls fell. Everything turned unstable, insecure, and soft. I would not have been surprised if a stone had melted into thin air before my eyes. Science seemed to have been annihilated." What resulted from this disillusion was the artist's withdrawal from the "realm of nature," from the "populous foreground of things." "It seemed," Kandinsky added, "as if I saw art steadily disengaging itself from nature."

This separation from the world of things happened more or less at the same time to other artists, too. Franz Marc wrote: "Have we not learned from a thousand years of experience that things cease to speak the more we hold up to them the visual mirror of their appearance? Appearance is eternally flat . . . ." For Marc, the goal of art was "to reveal unearthly life dwelling behind everything, to break the mirror of life so that we may look being in the face." Paul Klee wrote: "The artist does not ascribe to the natural form of

appearance the same convincing significance as the realists who are his critics. He does not feel so intimately bound to that reality, because he cannot see in the formal products of nature the essence of the creative process. He is more concerned with formative powers than with formal products." Piet Mondrian accused cubism of not having pursued abstraction to its logical end, "the expression of pure reality." That can only be attained by the "creation of pure form," unconditioned by subjective feelings and ideas. "Behind changing natural forms there lies changeless pure reality."

A great number of artists were seeking to get past appearances into the "reality" of the background or the "spirit in matter" by a transmutation of things—through fantasy, surrealism, dream pictures, the use of chance, etc. The "abstract" artists, however, turned their backs on things. Their paintings contained no identifiable concrete objects; they were, in Mondrian's words, simply "pure form."

But it must be realized that what these artists were concerned with was something far greater than a problem of form and the distinction between "concrete" and "abstract," figurative and non-figurative. Their goal was the center of life and things, their changeless background, and an inward certitude. Art had become mysticism.

The spirit in whose mystery art was submerged was an earthly spirit, which the medieval alchemists had called Mercurius. He is a symbol of the spirit that these artists divined or sought behind nature and things, "behind the

appearance of nature." Their mysticism was alien to Christianity, for that "Mercurial" spirit is alien to a "heavenly" spirit. Indeed, it was Christianity's dark adversary that was forging its way in art. Here we begin to see the real historical and symbolic significance of "modern art." Like the hermetic movements in the Middle Ages, it must be understood as a mysticism of the spirit of earth, and therefore as an expression of our time compensatory to Christianity.

No artist sensed this mystic background of art more clearly or spoke of it with greater passion than Kandinsky. The importance of the great works of art of all time did not lie, in his eyes, "on the surface, in externals, but in the root of all roots—in the mystical content of art." Therefore he says: "The artist's eye should always be turned in upon his inner life, and his ear should be always alert for the voice of inward necessity. This is the only way of giving expression to what the mystic vision commands."

Kandinsky called his pictures a spiritual expression of the cosmos, a music of the spheres, a harmony of colors and forms. "Form, even if it is quite abstract and geometrical, has an inward clang; it is a spiritual being with effects that coincide absolutely with that form." "The impact of the acute angle of a triangle on a circle is actually as overwhelming in effect as the finger of God touching the finger of Adam in Michelangelo."

In 1914, Franz Marc wrote in his *Aphorisms:* "Matter is a thing that man can at best

tolerate; he refuses to recognize it. The contemplation of the world has become the penetration of the world. There is no mystic who, in his moments of sublimest rapture, ever attained the perfect abstraction of modern thought, or took his soundings with a deeper plummet."

Paul Klee, who may be regarded as the poet among modern painters, says: "It is the artist's mission to penetrate as far as may be toward that secret ground where primal law feeds growth. Which artist would not wish to dwell at the central organ of all motion in space-time (be it the brain or the heart of creation) from which all functions derive their life? In the womb of nature, in the primal ground of creation, where the secret key to all things lies hidden? . . . Our beating heart drives us downward, far down to the primal ground." What is encountered on this journey "must be taken most seriously when it is perfectly fused with the appropriate artistic means in visible form," because, as Klee adds, it is not a question of merely reproducing what is seen; "the secretly perceived is made visible." Klee's work is rooted in that primal ground. "My hand is entirely the instrument of a more distant sphere. Nor is it my head that functions in my work; it is something else . . . ." In his work the spirit of nature and the spirit of the unconscious became inseparable. They have drawn him and draw us, the onlookers, into their magic circle.

Klee's work is the most complex expression —now poetic, now demonic—of the chthonic spirit. Humor and bizarre ideas build a bridge from the realm of the dark underworld to the

263

human world; the bond between his fantasy and the earth is the careful observation of the laws of nature and the love for all creatures. "For the artist," he once wrote, "the dialogue with nature is the *conditio sine qua non* of his work."

A different expression of the hidden unconscious spirit can be found in one of the most notable of the younger "abstract" painters, Jackson Pollock, an American who was killed in a car accident when he was 44. His work has had a great influence on the younger artists of our time. In *My Painting,* he revealed that he painted in a kind of trance: "When I am in my painting I am not aware of what I am doing. It is only after a sort of 'get acquainted' period that I see what I have been about. I have no fears about making changes, destroying the image, etc., because the painting has a life of its own. I try to let it come through. It is only when I lose contact with the painting that the result is a mess. Otherwise there is pure harmony, an easy give and take, and the painting comes out well."

Pollock's pictures, which were painted practically unconsciously, are charged with boundless emotional vehemence. In their lack of structure they are almost chaotic, a glowing lava stream of colors, lines, planes, and points. They may be regarded as a parallel to what the alchemists called the *massa confusa,* the *prima materia,* or chaos—all ways of defining the precious prime matter of the alchemical process, the starting point of the quest for the essence of being. Pollock's pictures represent the nothing that is everything—that is, the unconscious itself. They seem to live in a time before the emergence of consciousness and being, or to be fantastic landscapes of a time after the extinction of consciousness and being.

In the middle of our century, the purely abstract picture without any regular order of forms and colors has become the most frequent expression in painting. The deeper the dissolution of "reality," the more the picture loses its symbolic content. The reason for this lies in the nature of the symbol and its function. The symbol is an object of the known world hinting at something unknown; it is the known expressing the life and sense of the inexpressible. But in merely abstract paintings, the world of the known has completely vanished. Nothing is left to form a bridge to the unknown.

On the other hand, these paintings reveal an unexpected background, a hidden sense. They often turn out to be more or less exact images of nature itself, showing an astounding similarity with the molecular structure of organic and inorganic elements of nature. This is a perplexing fact. Pure abstraction has become an image of concrete nature. But Jung may give us the key to understanding:

"The deeper layers of the psyche," he has said, "lose their individual uniqueness as they retreat farther and farther into darkness. 'Lower down,' that is to say, as they approach the autonomous functional systems, they become increasingly collective until they are universalized and extinguished in the body's materiality, i.e. in chemical substances. The body's carbon is simply carbon. Hence 'at bottom' the psyche is simply 'world.'"

A comparison of abstract paintings and microphotographs shows that utter abstraction of imaginative art has in a secret and surprising way become "naturalistic," its subject being elements of matter. The "great abstraction" and the "great realism," which parted at the beginning of our century, have come together again. We remember Kandinsky's words: "The poles open two paths, which both lead to *one* goal at the end." This "goal," the point of union, is reached in modern abstract paintings. But it is attained completely unconsciously. The artist's intention plays no part in the process.

This point leads to a most important fact about modern art: The artist is, as it were, not so free in his creative work as he may think he is. If his work is performed in a more or less unconscious way, it is controlled by laws of nature that, on the deepest level, correspond to the laws of the psyche, and vice versa.

The great pioneers of modern art gave clearest expression to its true aims and to the depths from which the spirit rose that left its imprint on them. This point is important, though later artists, who may have failed to realize it, did not always plumb the same depths. Yet neither Kandinsky, nor Klee, nor any other of the early masters of modern painting, was ever aware of the grave psychological danger he was undergoing with the mystical submersion in the chthonic spirit and the primal ground of nature. That danger must now be explained.

As a starting point we may take another aspect of abstract art. The German writer Wilhelm Worringer interpreted abstract art as the expression of a metaphysical unease and anxiety that seemed to him to be more pronounced among northern peoples. As he explained, they suffer from reality. The naturalness of the southern peoples is denied to them and they long for a super-real and super-sensual world to which they give expression in imaginative or abstract art.

But, as Sir Herbert Read remarks in his *Concise History of Modern Art*, metaphysical anxiety is no longer only Germanic and northern; it now characterizes the whole of the modern world. Read quotes Klee, who wrote in his *Diary* at the beginning of 1915: "The more horrifying this world becomes (as it is in these days) the more art becomes abstract; while a world at peace produces realistic art." To Franz Marc, abstraction offered a refuge from the evil and ugliness in this world. "Very early in life I felt that man was ugly. The animals seemed to be more lovely and pure, yet even among them I discovered so much that was revolting and hideous that my painting became more and more schematic and abstract."

A good deal may be learned from a conversation that took place in 1958 between the Italian sculptor Marino Marini and the writer Edouard Roditi. The dominant subject that Marini treated for years in many variations is the nude figure of a youth on a horse. In the early versions, which he described in the conversation as "symbols of hope and gratitude" (after the end of the Second World War), the rider sits his horse with outstretched arms, his

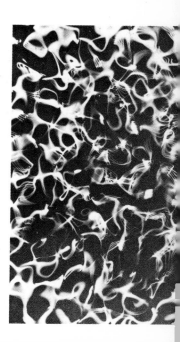

The paintings of Jackson Pollock (left, his *No. 23*) were painted in a trance (unconsciously) as are the works of other modern artists—such as the French "action" painter Georges Mathieu (far left). The chaotic but powerful result may be compared to the *massa confusa* of alchemy, and strangely resembles the hitherto hidden forms of matter as revealed in microphotographs (see p. 22). Right, a similar configuration: a vibration pattern made by sound waves in glycerine.

body bending slightly backward. In the course of years the treatment of the subject became more "abstract." The more or less "classical" form of the rider gradually dissolved.

Speaking of the feeling underlying this change, Marini said: "If you look at my equestrian statues of the last 12 years in order of time, you will notice that the animal's panic steadily increases, but that it is frozen with terror and stands paralyzed rather than rearing or taking flight. That is all because I believe that we are approaching the end of the world. In every figure, I strove to express a deepening fear and despair. In this way I am attempting to symbolize the last stage of a dying myth, the myth of the individual, victorious hero, of the humanist's man of virtue."

In fairy tale and myth, the "victorious hero" is a symbol of consciousness. His defeat, as Marini says himself, means the death of the individual, a phenomenon that appears in a social context as the submergence of the individual in the mass, and in art as the decline of the human element.

When Roditi asked whether Marini's style was abandoning the classical canon on its way to becoming "abstract," Marini replied, "As soon as art has to express fear, it must of itself depart from the classical ideal." He found subjects for his work in the bodies excavated at Pompeii. Roditi called Marini's art a "Hiroshima style," for it conjures up visions of the end of a world. Marini admitted it. He felt, he said, as if he had been expelled from an earthly paradise. "Until recently, the sculptor aimed at full sensual and powerful forms. But for the last 15 years, sculpture prefers forms in disintegration."

The conversation between Marini and Roditi explains the transformation of "sensory" art into abstraction that should be clear to anyone who has ever walked open-eyed through an exhibition of modern art. However much he may appreciate or admire its formal qualities, he can scarcely fail to sense the fear, despair, aggression, and mockery that sounds like a cry from many works. The "metaphysical anxiety" that is expressed by the distress in these pictures

and sculptures may have arisen from the despair of a doomed world, as it did with Marini. In other cases, the emphasis may lie on the religious factor, on the feeling that God is dead. There is a close connection between the two.

At the root of this inner distress lies the defeat (or rather the retreat) of consciousness. In the upsurge of mystical experience, everything that once bound man to the human world, to earth, to time and space, to matter and the natural living of life, has been cast aside or dissolved. But unless the unconscious is balanced by the experience of consciousness, it will implacably reveal its contrary or negative aspect. The wealth of creative sound that made the harmony of the spheres, or the wonderful mysteries of the primal ground, have yielded to destruction and despair. In more than one case the artist has become the passive victim of the unconscious.

In physics, too, the world of the background has revealed its paradoxical nature; the laws of the inmost elements of nature, the newly discovered structures and relations in its basic unit, the atom, have become the scientific foundation for unprecedented weapons of destruction, and opened the way to annihilation. Ultimate knowledge and the destruction of the world are the two aspects of the discovery of the primal ground of nature.

Jung, who was as familiar with the dangerous dual nature of the unconscious as with the

importance of human consciousness, could offer mankind only one weapon against catastrophe: the call for individual consciousness, which seems so simple and yet is so arduous. Consciousness is not only indispensable as a counterpoise to the unconscious, and not only gives the possibility of meaning to life. It has also an eminently practical function. The evil witnessed in the world outside, in neighbors or neighboring peoples, can be made conscious as evil contents of our own psyche as well, and this insight would be the first step to a radical change in our attitude to our neighbors.

Envy, lust, sensuality, lies, and all known vices are the negative, "dark" aspect of the unconscious, which can manifest itself in two ways. In the positive sense, it appears as a "spirit of nature," creatively animating man, things, and the world. It is the "chthonic spirit" that has been mentioned so often in this chapter. In the negative sense, the unconscious (that same spirit) manifests itself as a spirit of evil, as a drive to destroy.

As has already been pointed out, the alchemists personified this spirit as "the spirit Mercurius" and called it, with good reason, *Mercurius duplex* (the two-faced, dual Mercurius). In the religious language of Christianity, it is called the devil. But, however improbable it may seem, the devil too has a dual aspect. In the positive sense, he appears as Lucifer—literally, the light-bringer.

Looked at in the light of these difficult and paradoxical ideas, modern art (which we have recognized as symbolic of the chthonic spirit) also has a dual aspect. In the positive sense it is the expression of a mysteriously profound nature-mysticism; in the negative, it can only be interpreted as the expression of an evil or destructive spirit. The two sides belong together, for the paradox is one of the basic qualities of the unconscious and its contents.

To prevent any misunderstanding, it must once more be emphasized that these considerations have nothing to do with artistic and aesthetic values, but are solely concerned with the interpretation of modern art as a symbol of our time.

Top left and center, two sculptures by Marino Marini (1901-66), from 1945 and 1951 respectively, show how the theme of horse and rider was altered from an expression of tranquility to one of tortured fear and despair, while the sculptures themselves grew correspondingly more and more abstract. Marini's later work was influenced by the equally panic-stricken shapes of bodies found at Pompeii (left).

Union of opposites

There is one more point to be made. The spirit of the age is in constant movement. It is like a river that flows on, invisibly but surely, and given the momentum of life in our century, even 10 years is a long time.

About the middle of this century a change began to come over painting. It was nothing revolutionary, nothing like the change that happened about 1910, which meant the reconstruction of art to its very foundations. But there were groups of artists who formulated their aims in ways not heard before. This transformation is going on within the frontiers of abstract painting.

The representation of concrete reality, which springs from the primal human need of catching the passing moment on the wing, has become a truly concrete sensuous art in the photography of such men as France's Henri Cartier-Bresson, Switzerland's Werner Bischof, and others. We can therefore understand why artists continued on their own way of inwardness and imagination. For a good many of the young artists, however, abstract art as it had been practiced for many years offered no adventure, no field of conquest. Seeking the new, they found it in what lay nearest, yet had been lost —in nature and man. They were not and are not concerned with the reproduction of nature in pictures, but with the expression of their own emotional experience of nature.

The French painter Alfred Manessier defined the aims of his art in these words: "What we have to reconquer is the weight of lost reality. We must make for ourselves a new heart, a new spirit, a new soul, in the measure of man. The painter's true reality lies neither in abstraction nor in realism, but in the reconquest of his weight as a human being. At present non-figurative art seems to me to offer the one opportunity for the painter to approach the inward reality of himself and to grasp the consciousness of his essential self, or even of his being. It is only by the reconquest of his position, I believe, that the painter will be able, in the time to come, to return slowly to himself, to rediscover his own weight and so to strengthen it that it can even reach the outward reality of the world."

Jean Bazaine speaks in similar terms: "It is a great temptation for the painter of today to paint the pure rhythm of his feeling, the most secret pulse of his heart, instead of embodying it in a concrete form. That, however, leads only to a desiccated mathematics or a kind of abstract expressionism, which ends in monotony and a progressive impoverishment of form. . . . But a form that can reconcile man with his world is an 'art of communion' by which man, at any moment, can recognize his own unformed countenance in the world."

What in fact artists now have at heart is a conscious reunion of their own inward reality with the reality of the world or of nature; or, in the last resort, a new union of body and soul, matter and spirit. That is their way to the "reconquest of their weight as human beings." Only now is the great rift that set in with modern art (between "great abstraction" and "great realism") being made conscious and on the way to being healed.

For the onlooker, this first becomes evident in the changed atmosphere in the works of these artists. There radiates from the pictures of such artists as Alfred Manessier or the Belgian-born painter Gustave Singier, in spite of all abstraction, a belief in the world, and, in spite of all intensity of feeling, a harmony of forms and colors that often attains serenity. In the French painter Jean Lurçat's famous tapestries of the

In this century the depiction of actuality—once the province of the painter and sculptor—has been taken over by the photographer, whose camera can not only record but (like any landscape painting of past centuries) can express the photographer's own emotional experience of the subject. Right, a Japanese scene photographed by Werner Bischof (1916-54).

1950s the exuberance of nature pervades the picture. His art could be called sensuous as well as imaginative.

We find a serene harmony of forms and colors also in the work of Paul Klee. This harmony was what he had always been striving for. Above all, he had realized the necessity of not denying evil. "Even evil must not be a triumphant or degrading enemy, but a power collaborating in the whole." But Klee's starting point was not the same. He lived near "the dead and the unborn" at an almost cosmic distance from this world, while the younger generation of painters can be said to be more firmly rooted in earth.

An important point to notice is that modern painting, just when it has advanced far enough to discern the union of the opposites, has taken up religious themes. The "metaphysical void" seems to have been overcome. And the utterly unexpected has happened: The Church has become a patron of modern art. We need only mention here All Saints at Basle, with windows by Alfred Manessier; Assy church, with pictures by a large number of modern artists; the Matisse chapel at Vence; and the church at Audincourt, which has works by Jean Bazaine and the French artist Fernand Léger.

The admission of modern art to the Church means more than an act of broadmindedness on the part of its patrons. It is symbolic of the fact that the part played by modern art in relation to Christianity is changing. The compensatory function of the old hermetic movements has made way for the possibility of collaboration. In discussing the animal symbols of Christ, it was pointed out that the light and the chthonic spirits belonged to each other. It seems as if the moment had come today when a new stage in the solution of this millennial problem might be reached.

What the future will yield we cannot know—whether the bridging of the opposites will give positive results, or whether the way will lead through yet more unimaginable catastrophes. There is too much anxiety and too much dread at work in the world, and this is still the predominant factor in art and society. Above all, there is still too much unwillingness on the part of the individual to apply to himself and his life the conclusions that can be drawn from art, although he might be ready to accept them in art. The artist can often express many things, unconsciously and without awakening hostility, which are resented when they are expressed by a psychologist (a fact that could be demonstrated even more conclusively in literature than in the visual arts). Confronted by the statements of the psychologist, the individual feels directly challenged; but what the artist has to say, particularly in our century, usually remains in an impersonal sphere.

And yet it seems important that the suggestion of a more whole, and therefore more human, form of expression should have become visible in our time. It is a glimmer of hope, symbolized for me (at the time of writing: 1961) by a number of paintings by the French artist Pierre Soulages. Behind a cataract of huge, black rafters there glimmers a clear, pure blue or a radiant yellow. Light is dawning behind darkness.

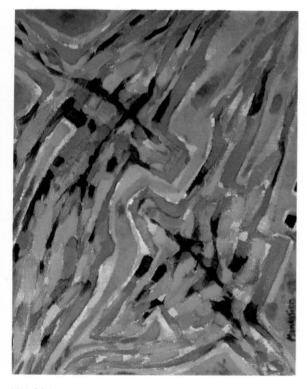

Mid-20th-century art seems to be moving away from a Marini-like despair—as is seen in the gesture of Jean Lurçat, who exhibited his work in a field (top left), a link with nature and the earth. Above, *Dédicace à Sainte Marie Madeleine* by Alfred Manessier (born 1911). Top right, *Pour la Naissance du Surhomme* by France's Pierre-Yves Trémois (born 1921). Both works indicate a tendency toward life and wholeness. The painting, right, by Pierre Soulages (born 1919) might be understood as a symbol of hope: Behind the cataclysmic darkness can be seen a glimmer of light.

5   Symbols in an individual analysis

Jolande Jacobi

A 17th-century engraving of "The Palace of Dreams."

The beginning of the analysis

There is a widespread belief that the methods of Jungian psychology are applicable only to middle-aged people. True, many men and women reach middle age without achieving psychological maturity, and it is therefore necessary to help them through the neglected phases of their development. They have not completed the first part of the process of individuation that Dr. M.-L. von Franz has described. But it is also true that a young person can encounter serious problems as he grows up. If a young person is afraid of life and finds it hard to adjust to reality, he might prefer to dwell in his fantasies or to remain a child. In such a young person (especially if he is introverted) one can sometimes discover unexpected treasures in the unconscious, and by bringing them into consciousness strengthen his ego and give him the psychic energy he needs to grow into a mature person. That is the function of the powerful symbolism of our dreams.

Other contributors to this book have described the nature of these symbols and the role they play in man's psychological nature. I wish to show how analysis can aid the individuation process by taking the example of a young engineer, aged 25, whom I shall call Henry.

Henry came from a rural district in eastern Switzerland. His father, of Protestant peasant stock, was a general practitioner: Henry described him as a man with high moral standards, but a rather withdrawn person who found it difficult to relate to other people. He was more of a father to his patients than to his children. At home, Henry's mother was the dominant personality. "We were raised by the strong hand of our mother," he said on one occasion. She came from a family with an academic background and wide artistic interests. She herself, in spite of her strictness, had a broad spiritual horizon; she was impulsive and romantic (she had a great love for Italy). Though she was by birth a Catholic, her children had been brought up in the Protestantism of their father. Henry had a sister, older than himself, with whom he had a good relationship.

Henry was introverted, shy, finely drawn, and very tall, with light hair, a high pale forehead, and blue eyes with dark shadows. He did not think that neurosis (the most usual reason) had brought him to me, but rather an inner urge to work on his psyche. A strong mother-tie, however, and a fear of committing himself to life were hidden behind this urge; but these were only discovered during the analytical work with me. He had just completed his studies and taken a position in a large factory, and he was facing the many problems of a young man on the threshold of manhood. "It appears to me," he wrote in a letter asking for an interview, "that this phase of my life is particularly important and meaningful. I must decide either to remain unconscious in a well-protected security, or else to venture on a yet unknown way of which I have great hopes." The choice thus confronting him was whether to remain a lonely, vacillating, and unrealistic youth or to become a self-sufficient and responsible adult.

Henry told me that he preferred books to society; he felt inhibited among people, and was often tormented by doubts and self-criticism. He was well read for his age and had a leaning toward aesthetic intellectualism. After an earlier atheistic stage, he became rigorously Protestant, but finally his religious attitude became completely neutral. He had chosen a technical education because he felt his talents lay in mathematics and geometry. He possessed a logical mind, trained in the natural sciences, but he also had a propensity toward the irrational and mystical that he did not want to admit even to himself.

About two years before his analysis began, Henry had become engaged to a Catholic girl from the French part of Switzerland. He described her as charming, efficient, and full of initiative. Nevertheless, he was uncertain whether he should undertake the responsibility of marriage. Since he had so little acquaintance with girls, he thought it might be better to wait, or even to remain a bachelor dedicated to a scholarly life. His doubts were strong enough to prevent his reaching a decision; he needed a further step toward maturity before he could feel sure of himself.

Although qualities of both his parents were combined in Henry, he was markedly mother-bound. In his consciousness, he was identified with his real (or "light") mother, who represented high ideals and intellectual ambitions. But in his unconscious he was deeply in the power of the dark aspects of his mother-bound condition. His unconscious still held his ego in a strangle-hold. All his clear-cut thinking and his efforts to find a firm standpoint in the purely rational remained nothing more than an intellectual exercise.

The need to escape from this "mother-prison" was expressed in hostile reactions to his real mother and a rejection of the "inner mother" as a symbol of the feminine side of the unconscious. But an inner power sought to hold him back in the condition of childhood, resisting everything that attracted him to the outside world. Even the attractions of his fiancée were not enough to free him from his mother-ties, and thus help him find himself. He was not aware that his inner urge for growth (which he felt strongly) included the need to detach himself from his mother.

My analytical work with Henry lasted nine months. Altogether, there were 35 sessions in which he presented 50 dreams. So short an analysis is rare. It is only possible when energy-laden dreams like Henry's speed up the process of development. Of course, from the Jungian point of view, there is no rule for the length of time required for a successful analysis. All depends on the individual's readiness to realize inner facts and on the material presented by his unconscious.

Like most introverts, Henry led a rather monotonous outer life. During the day he was completely involved in his job. In the evenings he sometimes went out with his fiancée or with friends, with whom he liked to have literary discussions. Quite often he sat in his lodgings absorbed in a book or in his own thoughts. Though we regularly discussed the happenings of his daily life, and also his childhood and youth, we usually got fairly quickly to the investigation of his dreams and the problems his inner life presented to him. It was extraordinary to see how strongly his dreams emphasized his "call" to spiritual development.

But I must make it clear that not everything described here was told to Henry. In analysis one must always remain conscious of how ex-

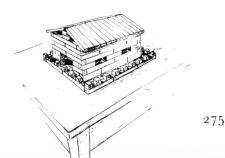

Left, the palace and monastery of Escorial, Spain, built by Philip II about 1563. Its fortress structure images the introvert's withdrawal from the world. Below, a drawing by Henry of a barn he built as a child with fortress-like battlements.

275

plosive the dreamer's dream symbols may be
for him. The analyst can hardly be too careful
and reserved. If too bright a light is thrown on
the dream-language of symbols, the dreamer
can be driven into anxiety, and thus led into
rationalization as a defense mechanism. Or he
can no longer assimilate them, and can fall into
a severe psychic crisis. Also, the dreams reported and commented on here are by no
means all the dreams that Henry had during
his analysis. I can discuss only an important
few that influenced his development.

In the beginning of our work, childhood
memories with important symbolic meanings
came up. The oldest dated back to Henry's
fourth year. He said: "One morning I was
allowed to go with my mother to the baker's
shop and there I received a crescent roll from
the baker's wife. I did not eat the roll but
carried it proudly in my hand. Only my mother
and the baker's wife were present, so I was the
only man." Such crescents are popularly called
"moon-teeth," and this symbolic allusion to the
moon underlines the dominating power of the
feminine—a power to which the little boy may
have felt exposed and which, as the "only
man," he was proud of being able to confront.

Another childhood memory came from his
fifth year. It concerned Henry's sister, who
came home after her examinations at school
and found him constructing a toy barn. The
barn was made with blocks of wood arranged
in the form of a square and surrounded with
a kind of hedge that looked like the battlements of a castle. Henry was pleased with his
achievement, and said teasingly to his sister:
"You have started school but you're already on
holiday." Her reply, that he was on holiday all
year, upset him terribly. He felt deeply hurt
that his "achievement" was not taken seriously.

Even years later Henry had not forgotten
the bitter hurt and injustice that he had felt
when his construction was rejected. His later
problems concerning the assertion of his masculinity and the conflict between rational and
fantasy values are already visible in this early
experience. And these problems are also to be
seen in the images of his first dream.

The initial dream

The day after Henry's first visit to me, he had the following dream:

I was on an excursion with a group of people I did not know. We were going to the Zinalrothorn. We had started from Samaden. We only walked about an hour because we were to camp and have some theatricals. I was not given an active part. I especially remember one performer—a young woman in a pathetic role wearing a long flowing robe.

It was midday and I wanted to go on to the pass. As all the others preferred to remain, I went up alone, leaving my equipment behind. However, I found myself right back in the valley and completely lost my orientation. I wanted to return to my party but did not know which mountainside I should climb. I was hesitant about asking. Finally, an old woman showed me the way I must go.

Then I ascended from a different starting point than our group had used in the morning. It was a matter of making a turn at the right altitude and then following the mountain slope to return to the party. I climbed along a cogwheel mountain railway on the right side. On my left little cars constantly passed me, each containing one hidden bloated little man in a blue suit. It is said they are dead. I was afraid of other cars coming from behind and kept turning around to look, so as not to be run over. My anxiety was needless.

At the point where I had to turn off to the right, there were people awaiting me. They took me to an inn. A cloudburst came up. I regretted that my equipment—my rucksack, and my motor bike—were not there, but I was told not to get them till next morning. I accepted the advice.

One of Henry's childhood memories involved a crescent roll, which he drew (top left). Center, the same shape on a modern Swiss bakery sign. The crescent shape has long been linked with the moon and thus with the feminine principle, as in the crown (left) of the goddess Ishtar of third-century B.C. Babylon.

Dr. Jung assigned great importance to the first dream in an analysis, for, according to him, it often has anticipatory value. A decision to go into analysis is usually accompanied by an emotional upheaval that disturbs the deep psychic levels from which archetypal symbols arise. The first dreams therefore often present "collective images" that provide a perspective for the analysis as a whole and can give the therapist insight into the dreamer's psychic conflicts.

What does the above dream tell us of Henry's future development? We must first examine some of the associations that Henry himself supplied. The village of Samaden had been the home of Jürg Jenatsch, a famous 17th-century Swiss freedom-fighter. The "theatricals" called up the thought of Goethe's *Wilhelm Meisters Lehrjahre*, which Henry liked very much. In the woman he saw a resemblance to the figure in a painting called *The Island of the Dead* by the 19th-century Swiss artist Arnold Böcklin. The "wise old woman," as he called her, seemed to be associated on the one hand to his analyst, on the other to the charwoman in J. B. Priestley's play *They Came to a City*. The cog-wheel railway reminded him of the barn (with battlements) that he had built as a child.

The dream describes an "excursion" (a sort of "walking tour"), which is a striking parallel to Henry's decision to undertake analysis. The individuation process is often symbolized by a voyage of discovery to unknown lands. Such a voyage takes place in John Bunyan's *Pilgrim's Progress*, or in Dante's *Divina Commedia*. The "traveler" in Dante's poem, searching for a way, comes to a mountain that he decides to climb. But because of three strange animals (a motif that will also appear in one of Henry's later dreams) he is forced to descend into the valley and even into hell. (Later he ascends again to purgatory and finally reaches paradise.) From this parallel one could deduce that

there might be a similar period of disorientation and lonely seeking in store for Henry. The first part of this life-journey, represented as climbing a mountain, offers ascent from the unconscious to an elevated point of view of the ego—i.e. to an increased consciousness.

Samaden is named as the starting point of the excursion. This is where Jenatsch (whom we may take as embodying the "freedom-seeking" sense within Henry's unconscious) started his campaign for the liberation of the Veltlin region of Switzerland from the French. Jenatsch had other characteristics in common with Henry: He was a Protestant who fell in love with a Catholic girl; and, like Henry, whose analysis was to free him from his mother-ties and from fear of life, Jenatsch also fought for liberation. One could interpret this as a favorable augury for the success of Henry's own fight for freedom. The goal of the excursion is the Zinalrothorn, a mountain in western Switzerland that he did not know. The word *rot* ("red") in Zinal*rot*horn touches on Henry's emotional problem. Red is usually symbolic of feeling or passion; here it points to the value of the feeling-function, which was insufficiently developed in Henry. And the word "horn" reminds one of the crescent roll in the baker's shop of Henry's childhood.

After a short walk, a halt is called, and Henry can return to a state of passivity. This also belongs to his nature. The point is underlined by the "theatricals." Attending the theatre (which is an imitation of real life) is a popular way of evading an active part in life's drama. The spectator can identify with the play, yet continue to pander to his fantasies. This kind of identification permitted the Greeks to experience catharsis, much as the psycho-drama initiated by the American psychiatrist J. L. Moreno is now used as a therapeutic aid. Some such process may have enabled Henry to undergo an inner development when his associations raised memories of *Wilhelm Meister*, Goethe's story of the maturing of a young man.

That Henry should have been impressed by the romantic appearance of a woman is also not surprising. This figure resembles Henry's mother and is at the same time a personification of his own unconscious feminine side. The connection Henry makes between her and Böcklin's *Island of the Dead* points to his depressive mood, so well expressed by the painting, which shows a white-robed priest-like figure steering a boat bearing a coffin toward an island. We have here a significant double paradox: The keel of the boat seems to suggest a contrary course, away from the island; and the "priest" is a figure of uncertain sex. In Henry's associations, this figure is certainly hermaphroditic. The double paradox coincides with Henry's ambivalence: The opposites in

his soul are still too undifferentiated to be clearly separated.

After this interlude in the dream, Henry suddenly becomes aware that it is noon and he must go on. So he again starts for the pass. A mountain pass is a well-known symbol for a "situation of transition" that leads from an old attitude of mind to a new one. Henry must go alone; it is essential for his ego to surmount the test unaided. Thus he leaves his kit behind —an action that signifies that his mental equipment has become a burden, or that he must change his normal way of going about things.

But he does not reach the pass. He loses his bearings and finds himself back in the valley. This failure shows that while Henry's ego decides on activity, his other psychic entities (represented by the other members of the party) remain in the old state of passivity and refuse to accompany the ego. (When the dreamer himself appears in a dream, he usually represents only his conscious ego; the other figures stand for his more or less unknown, unconscious qualities.)

Henry is in a situation where he is helpless, yet ashamed to admit it. At this moment he meets an old woman who indicates the right way to him. He can do nothing but accept her advice. The helpful "old woman" is a well-known symbol in myths and fairy tales for the wisdom of the eternal female nature. The rationalist Henry hesitates to accept her help because such acceptance requires a *sacrificium intellectus*—a sacrifice, or discarding, of a rational way of thought. (This demand will often be made of Henry in later dreams.) Such a sacrifice is unavoidable; it applies to his relationship with the analysis as well as with everyday life.

He associated the figure of the "old woman" to the charwoman in Priestley's play about a new "dream" city (perhaps an analogy to the New Jerusalem of the Apocalypse) into which the characters can enter only after a kind of initiation. This association seems to show that Henry had intuitively recognized this confrontation as something decisive for him. The charwoman in Priestley's play says that in the city "they have promised me a room of my own." There she will be self-reliant and independent, as Henry seeks to be.

If such a technically minded young man as Henry is consciously to choose the way of psychic development, he must be prepared for a reversal of his old attitudes. Therefore, on the advice of the woman, he must start his climb from a different spot. Only then will it be possible for him to judge at what level he must deviate to reach the group—the other qualities of his psyche—that he had left behind.

He climbs a cog-wheel railway track (a motif perhaps reflecting his technical education) and keeps to the right side of the track—which is the conscious side. (In the history of symbolism, the right side generally represents the realm of consciousness; the left, the unconscious.) From the left, little cars are coming down, and in each a little man is hidden. Henry is afraid that an unnoticed upward-bound car might hit him from the rear. His anxiety proves groundless, but it reveals that Henry is afraid of what, so to speak, lies behind his ego.

The bloated, blue-clothed men might symbolize sterile intellectual thoughts that are being brought down mechanically. Blue often denotes the function of thinking. Thus the men might be symbols of ideas or attitudes that have died on the intellectual heights where the air is too thin. They could also represent lifeless inner parts of Henry's psyche.

A comment on these men is made in the dream: "It is said they are dead." But Henry is alone. Who makes this statement? It is a voice—and when a voice is heard in a dream it is a most meaningful occurrence. Dr. Jung identified the appearance of a voice in dreams with an intervention of the Self. It stands for a knowledge that has its roots in the collective fundaments of the psyche. What the voice says cannot be disputed.

The insight Henry has gained about the "dead" formulas, to which he has been too committed, marks a turning point in the dream. He has at last reached the right place for taking a new direction, to the right (the conscious direction), toward the conscious and the outer world. There he finds the people he left behind waiting for him; and thus he can become conscious of previously unknown aspects of his personality. Since his ego has surmounted the dangers it confronted alone (an accomplishment that could make him more mature and stable), he can rejoin the group or "collective" and get shelter and food.

Then comes the rain, a cloudburst that relaxes tension and makes the earth fertile. In mythology, rain was often thought to be a "love-union" between heaven and earth. In the Eleusinian mysteries, for instance, after everything had been purified by water, the call went up to heaven: "Let it rain!" and down to

Left, the Greek maiden Danae, who was impregnated by Zeus in the form of a shower of gold (from a painting by the 16th-century Flemish artist Jan Gossaert). Like Henry's dream, this myth reflects the symbolism of the cloudburst as a sacred marriage between heaven and earth.

In another of Henry's dreams a doe appears—an image of shy femininity as is the fawn in the painting, right, by the 19th-century British artist Edwin Landseer.

earth: "Be fruitful!" This was understood as a sacred marriage of the gods. In this way rain can be said to represent a "solution" in the literal sense of the word.

Coming down, Henry again meets the collective values symbolized by the rucksack and motorcycle. He has passed through a phase in which he has strengthened his ego-consciousness by proving he can hold his own, and he has a renewed need for social contact. However, he accepts the suggestion of his friends that he should wait and fetch his things the next morning. Thus he submits for the second time to advice that comes from elsewhere: the first time, to the advice of the old woman, to a subjective power, an archetypal figure; the second time, to a collective pattern. With this step Henry has passed a milestone on the road to maturity.

As an anticipation of the inner development that Henry could hope to achieve through analysis, this dream was extraordinarily promising. The conflicting opposites that kept Henry's soul in tension were impressively symbolized. On the one hand, there was his conscious urge to ascend, and on the other his tendency to passive contemplation. Also, the image of the pathetic young woman in her white robes (representing Henry's sensitive and romantic feelings) contrasts with the bloated corpses in blue suits (representing his sterile intellectual world). However, to overcome these obstacles and bring about a balance between them would be possible for Henry only after the most severe trials.

Fear of the unconscious

The problems we encountered in Henry's initial dream showed up in many others—problems like vacillation between masculine activity and feminine passivity, or a tendency to hide behind intellectual asceticism. He feared the world, yet was attracted to it. Fundamentally, he feared the obligations of marriage, which demanded that he form a responsible relationship with a woman. Such an ambivalence is not unusual for someone on the threshold of manhood. Though in terms of age Henry had left that phase behind him, his inner maturity did not match his years. This problem is often met in the introvert, with his fear of reality and outer life.

The fourth dream that Henry recounted provided a striking illustration of his psychological state:

It seems to me that I have had this dream endless times. Military service, long-distance race. Alone I go on my way. I never reach the goal. Will I be the last? The course is well known to me, all of it *déjà vu*. The start is in a little wood, and the ground is covered with dry leaves. The terrain slopes gently to an idyllic little brook that invites one to tarry. Later, there is a dusty country road. It leads toward Hombrechtikon, a small village near the upper lake of Zurich. A brook bordered by willows similar to a painting of Böcklin's in which a dreamy female figure follows the course of the water. Night falls. In a village I ask for directions to the road. I am told the road leads on for seven hours over a pass. I gather myself together and go on.

However, this time the end of the dream differs. After the willow-bordered brook I get into a wood. There I discover a doe that runs away. I am proud of this observation. The doe has appeared on the left side and now I turn to the right. Here I see three strange creatures, half pig, half dog, with the legs of a kangaroo. The faces are quite undifferentiated, with large drooping dog ears. Maybe they are costumed people. As a boy, I once masqueraded in the circus costume of a donkey.

The beginning of the dream is conspicuously like Henry's initial dream. A dreamlike female figure again appears, and the setting of the dream is associated with another painting by Böcklin. This painting, called *Autumn Thoughts*, and the dry leaves mentioned earlier in the dream underline the autumnal mood. A romantic atmosphere also reappears in this dream. Apparently this inner landscape, representing Henry's melancholy, is very familiar to him. Again he is in a collective of people, but this time with military comrades on a long-distance race.

This whole situation (as the military service also suggests) might be regarded as a representation of an average man's fate. Henry himself said: "It's a symbol of life." But the dreamer does not want to adjust to it. He goes on alone—which was probably always the case with Henry. That is why he has the impression that everything is *déjà vu*. His thought ("I never reach the goal") indicates strong feelings of inferiority and a belief that he cannot win the "long-distance race."

His way leads to Hombrechtikon, a name that reminds him of his secret plans to break away from home (*Hom* = home, *brechen* = to break). But because this breaking away does not occur, he again (as in the initial dream) loses his sense of orientation and must ask for directions.

Dreams compensate more or less explicitly for the dreamer's conscious attitude of mind.

The romantic, maidenly figure of Henry's conscious ideal is balanced by the appearance of the strange, female-like animals. Henry's world of instincts is symbolized by something feminine. The wood is a symbol of an unconscious area, a dark place where animals live. At first a doe—a symbol of shy, fugitive, innocent womanliness—emerges, but only for a moment. Then Henry sees three mixed-up animals of a strange and repulsive appearance. They seem to represent undifferentiated instinctuality—a sort of confused mass of his instincts, containing the raw material for a later development. Their most striking characteristic is that they are all virtually faceless, and thus without the slightest glimmerings of consciousness.

In the minds of many people, the pig is closely associated to dirty sexuality. (Circe, for example, changed the men who desired her into swine.) The dog may stand for loyalty, but also for promiscuity, because it shows no discrimination in its choice of partners. The kangaroo, however, is often a symbol for motherliness and tender carrying capacity.

All these animals present only rudimentary traits, and even these are senselessly contaminated. In alchemy, the "prime material" was often represented by such monstrous and fabulous creatures—mixed forms of animals. In psychological terms, they would probably symbolize the original total unconsciousness, out of which the individual ego can rise and begin to develop toward maturity.

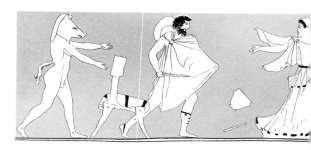

Left, Henry's drawing of the strange animals of his dream. They are mute and blind, unable to communicate, and so represent his unconscious state. The animal on the ground (which he colored green, the color of vegetation and nature, and in folklore a symbol of hope) hints at possibilities of growth and a chance of differentiation.

Henry's fear of the monsters becomes evident by his attempt to make them seem harmless. He wants to convince himself that they are only dressed-up people, like himself in a boyhood masquerade. His anxiety is natural. A man discovering such inhuman monsters in his inner self, as symbols of certain traits of his unconscious, has every reason to be afraid.

Another dream also shows Henry's fear of the depths of the unconscious:

I am a cabin boy in a sailing boat. Paradoxically, the sails are spread, though there is a complete calm. My task consists of holding a rope that serves to fasten a mast. Strangely enough, the railing is a wall covered with stone slabs. This whole structure lies exactly on the border between the water and the sailing boat that floats there alone. I hold fast to the rope (not to the mast) and I am forbidden to look into the water.

In this dream Henry is in a psychological borderline situation. The railing is a wall that protects him but at the same time obstructs his view. He is forbidden to look into the water (where he might discover unknown powers). All these images reveal his doubt and fear.

The man who fears the communications of his inner depths (like Henry) is as much afraid of the feminine element in himself as he is of real women. At one moment he is fascinated by her, at another he tries to escape; fascinated and terrified, he flees so as not to become her "prey." He does not dare to approach a beloved (and therefore idealized) partner with his animal-like sexuality.

As a typical result of his mother-tie, Henry had difficulty in giving both feeling and sensuality to the same woman. Again and again his dreams brought proof of his desire to free himself from this dilemma. In one dream he was a "monk on a secret mission." In another, his instincts tempted him into a brothel:

Together with a military comrade who has had many erotic adventures I find myself waiting in front of a house on a dark street in an unknown city. Entrance is permitted only to women. Therefore, in the hall, my friend puts on a little carnival mask of a woman's face and goes up the stairs. Possibly I did the same as he, but I do not remember clearly.

What this dream proposes would satisfy Henry's curiosity—but only at the price of a fraud. As a man he lacks the courage to enter the house, which is obviously a brothel. But if he divests himself of his masculinity, he might gain an insight into this forbidden world—forbidden by his conscious mind. The dream, however, does not tell us whether he decides to enter. Henry had not yet overcome his inhibitions—an understandable failure if we consider the implications of going into the brothel.

The above dream seemed to me to reveal a homoerotic strain in Henry: He appeared to feel that a feminine "mask" would make him

The pig-like animal of the dream connotes bestiality and lustfulness—as in the myth of Circe, who turned men into swine. Above left, from a Greek vase, a pig-man, Odysseus, and Circe. Right, in one of the cartoons by George Grosz attacking pre-war German society, a man (with a prostitute) is given a pig's head to show his vulgarity.

attractive to men. This hypothesis was supported by the following dream:

I find myself back in my fifth or sixth year. My playmate of those days tells me how he participated in an obscene act with the director of a factory. My friend laid his right hand on the man's penis to keep it warm and at the same time to warm his own hand. The director was an intimate friend of my father's whom I venerated for his broad and varied interests. But he was laughed at by us as an "eternal youth."

For children of that age homoerotic play is not unusual. That Henry still came to it in his dream suggests that it was loaded with guilt feelings, and therefore strongly repressed. Such feelings were linked to his deep fear about forming a lasting tie with a woman. Another dream and its associations illustrated this conflict:

I take part in the wedding of an unknown couple. At one in the morning the little wedding party returns from the festivities—the bridal couple, the best man, and the maid of honor. They enter a large courtyard where I await them. It seems that the newlyweds have already had a quarrel, as well as the other couple. They finally find the solution by having the two men and the two women retire separately.

Henry explained: "You see here the war of the sexes as Giraudoux describes it." And then he added: "The palace in Bavaria, where I remember seeing this dream-courtyard, has until lately been disfigured by emergency housing for poor people. When I visited there, I asked myself if it would not be preferable to eke out a poor existence in the ruins of classic beauty than to lead an active life surrounded by the ugliness of a great city. I also asked myself when I was a witness at the wedding of a comrade whether his marriage would last, for his bride made an unfavorable impression on me."

The longing to withdraw into passivity and introversion, the fear of an unsuccessful marriage, the dream's separation of the sexes—all these are unmistakable symptoms of the secret doubts hidden beneath Henry's consciousness.

The saint and the prostitute

Henry's psychic condition was most impressively depicted in the following dream, which exposed his fear of primitive sensuality and his desire to escape into a kind of asceticism. In it one can see the direction his development was taking. For this reason the dream will be interpreted at greater length.

I find myself on a narrow mountain road. On the left (going down) there is a deep abyss, on the right a wall of rock. Along the road there are several caves, shelters, cut out of the rock, as protection from the weather for lonely wanderers. In one of these caves, half hidden, a prostitute has taken refuge. Strangely, I see her from behind, from the rock side. She has a formless, spongy body. I look at her with curiosity and touch her buttocks. Perhaps, it suddenly seems to me, she is not a woman but a kind of male prostitute.

This same creature comes then to the fore as a saint with a short crimson coat thrown around his shoulders. He strides down the road and goes into another, much larger cave fitted with rough-hewn chairs and benches. With a haughty look he drives out all those already present, also me. Then he and his followers move in and establish themselves.

The personal association that Henry contributed to the prostitute was the "Venus of Willendorf," a little carved figure (from the paleo

lithic age) of a fleshy woman, probably a nature or fertility goddess. Then he added:

"I first heard that touching the buttocks is a fertility rite when I was on a tour through the Wallis [a canton in French Switzerland], where I visited ancient Celtic graves and excavations. There I was told that there was once a smooth sloping surface of tiles smeared with all kinds of substances. Infertile women had to slide down on their bare buttocks in order to cure their sterility."

To the coat of the "saint," Henry associated this: "My fiancée owns a jacket of similar shape, but it's white. On the evening before the dream we were out dancing, and she was wearing this white jacket. Another girl, who is her friend, was with us. She had a crimson jacket that I liked better."

If dreams are not wish-fulfillments (as Freud taught) but rather, as Jung assumed, "self-representations of the unconscious," then we must admit that Henry's psychic condition could hardly be better represented than in the description given in the "saint" dream.

Henry is a "lonely wanderer" on the narrow path. But (perhaps thanks to analysis) he is already on his way down from inhospitable heights. To the left, on the side of the unconscious, his road is bordered by the terrifying depths of an abyss. On the right side, the side of consciousness, the way is blocked by the rigid rock wall of his conscious views. However, in the caves (which might represent, so to speak, unconscious areas in Henry's field of consciousness) there are places where refuge can be found when bad weather comes—in other words, when outside tensions become too threatening.

The caves are the result of purposeful human work: cut into the rock. In a way they resemble the gaps that occur in our consciousness when our power of concentration has reached its limits and is broken, so that the stuff of fantasy can penetrate without restraint. At such times something unexpected can reveal itself and allow a deep insight into the background of the psyche—a glimpse into the unconscious regions where our imagination has free play. Moreover, rock caves may be symbols of the womb of Mother Earth, appearing as mysterious caverns in which transformation and rebirth can come about.

Thus the dream seems to represent Henry's introverted withdrawal—when the world becomes too difficult for him—into a "cave" within his consciousness where he can succumb to subjective fantasies. This interpretation would also explain why he seeks the female figure—

Left, Henry's drawing of the boat of his dream, with a stone wall for a railing—another image of his introversion and fear of life.

Right, the prehistoric sculpture known as the "Venus of Willendorf" —one of Henry's associations to the image of the prostitute in his dream. In the same dream, the saint is seen in a sacred cave. Many actual caves are holy places—like the Cave of Bernadette (far right) at Lourdes, where a vision of the Virgin Mary appeared to a girl.

a replica of some of the inner feminine traits of his psyche. She is a formless, spongy, half-hidden prostitute representing the repressed image in his unconscious of a woman whom Henry would never have approached in conscious life. She would always have been strictly taboo to him in spite of the fact that (as the opposite of a too-much-venerated mother) the prostitute would have a secret fascination for him—as for every son with a mother-complex.

The idea of restricting a relationship with a woman to a purely animal-like sensuality, excluding all feelings, is often enticing to such a young man. In such a union he can keep his feelings split off, and thus can remain "true" to his mother in an ultimate sense. Thus, in spite of everything, the taboo set by the mother against every other woman remains inflexibly effective in the psyche of the son.

Henry, who seems to have withdrawn totally to the background of his fantasy-cave, sees the prostitute only "from behind." He dares not look her in the face. But "from the back" also means from her least human side—her buttocks

(i.e. the part of her body that will stimulate the sensual activity of the male).

By touching the buttocks of the prostitute, Henry unconsciously carries out a kind of fertility rite, similar to the rites that are practiced in many primitive tribes. The laying on of hands and healing often go together; in the same way, touching with the hand can be either a defense or a curse.

Immediately the idea arises that the figure is not a woman after all but a male prostitute. The figure thus becomes hermaphroditic, like many mythological figures (and like the "priest" figure of the first dream). Insecurity concerning his own sex can often be observed in a pubescent individual; and for this reason homosexuality in adolescence is not considered unusual. Nor is such uncertainty exceptional for a young man with Henry's psychological structure; he had already implied this in some of his earlier dreams.

But repression (as well as sexual uncertainty) may have caused the confusion about the sex of the prostitute. The female figure that has

A coat can often symbolize the outer mask or *persona* that one presents to the world. The mantle of the prophet Elijah bore a similar meaning: When he ascended to heaven (left, in a Swedish peasant painting), he left the mantle behind for his successor Elisha. Thus the mantle represented the prophet's power and role, to be assumed by his successor. (In the painting the mantle is red, like the saint's coat in Henry's dream.)

both attracted and repelled the dreamer is transformed—first of all into a man and then into a saint. The second transformation eliminates everything sexual from the image, and implies that the only means of escape from the reality of sex lies in the adoption of an ascetic and holy life, denying the flesh. Such dramatic reversals are common in dreams: Something turns into its opposite (as the prostitute becomes a saint) as if to demonstrate that by transmutation even extreme opposites can change into each other.

Henry also saw something significant in the saint's coat. A coat is often a symbol of the protective cover or mask (which Jung called the *persona*) that an individual presents to the world. It has two purposes: first, to make a specific impression on other people: second, to conceal the individual's inner self from their prying eyes. The *persona* that Henry's dream gives the saint tells us something about his attitude to his fiancée and her friend. The saint's coat has the color of the friend's jacket, which Henry had admired, but it also had the shape of his fiancée's coat. This may imply that Henry's unconscious wanted to confer the quality of saintliness on both women, in order to protect himself against their womanly attractiveness. Also, the coat is red, which (as has been noted before) is traditionally the symbolic color of feeling and passion. It thus gives the saint figure a kind of eroticized spirituality—a

quality that is frequently found in men who repress their own sexuality and try to rely solely on their "spirit" or reason.

Such an escape from the world of the flesh, however, is unnatural in a young person. In the first half of life, we should learn to accept our sexuality: It is essential to the preservation and continuation of our species. The dream seems to be reminding Henry of just this point.

When the saint leaves the cave and walks down the road (descending from the heights toward the valley), he enters a second cave with rough-hewn benches and chairs, which reminds one of the early Christians' places of worship and refuge from persecution. This cave seems to be a healing, holy place—a place of meditation and of the mystery of transformation from the earthly to the heavenly, from the carnal to the spiritual.

Henry is not permitted to follow the saint, but is turned out of the cave with all those present (that is, with his unconscious entities). Seemingly, Henry and all the others who are not followers of the saint are being told that they must live in the outside world. The dream seems to say that Henry must first succeed in outer life before he will be able to immerse himself in a religious or spiritual sphere. The figure of the saint also seems to symbolize (in a relatively undifferentiated, anticipatory fashion) the Self; but Henry is not yet mature enough to stay in the immediate vicinity of this figure.

Henry's touching the prostitute can be related to the belief in the magical effect of a touch: Left, the 17th-century Irishman Valentine Greatrakes, famous for healing by laying on of hands.

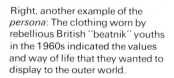

Right, another example of the *persona*: The clothing worn by rebellious British "beatnik" youths in the 1960s indicated the values and way of life that they wanted to display to the outer world.

How the analysis developed

In spite of an initial skepticism and resistance, Henry began to take a lively interest in the inner happenings of his psyche. He was obviously impressed by his dreams. They seemed to compensate for his unconscious life in a meaningful way and to give him valuable insights into his ambivalence, his vacillation, and his preference for passivity.

After a time more positive dreams appeared that showed that Henry was already "well on his way." Two months after his analysis had begun he reported this dream:

In the harbor of a little place not far from my home, on the shore of a lake in the neighborhood, locomotives and freight cars are being raised from the bottom of the lake where they had been sunk in the last war. First a large cylinder like a locomotive boiler is brought up. Then an enormous, rusty freight car. The whole picture presents a horrible yet romantic sight. The recovered pieces have to be transported away under the rails and cables of the nearby railway station. Then the bottom of the lake changes into a green meadow.

Here we see what a remarkable inner advance Henry has made. Locomotives (probably symbols of energy and dynamism) have been "sunk"—i.e. repressed into the unconscious—but are now being brought into the light of day. With them are freight cars, in which all kinds of valuable cargo (psychic qualities) can be transported. Now that these "objects" have again become available for Henry's conscious life, he can begin to realize how much active power could be at his disposal. The transformation of the dark lake bottom into a meadow underlines his potential for positive action.

Sometimes, on Henry's "lonely journey" toward maturity, he also received help from his

feminine side. In his 24th dream he meets a "humpbacked girl":

I am on the way to a school together with an unknown young lady of small and dainty appearance but disfigured by a hump. Many other people also go into the schoolhouse. While the others disperse to different rooms for singing lessons, the girl and I sit at a little square table. She gives me a private singing lesson. I feel an impulse of pity for her and therefore kiss her on the mouth. I am conscious, however, that by this act I am unfaithful to my fiancée—even though it may be excusable.

Singing is one of the immediate expressions of feelings. But (as we have seen) Henry is afraid of his feelings; he knows them only in an idealized adolescent form. Nevertheless, in this dream he is taught singing (the expression of feelings) at a square table. The table, with its four equal sides, is a representation of the "fourfoldness" motif, usually a symbol of completeness. Thus the relation between singing

As in the painting, left (by the 19th-century British artist William Turner), entitled *Rain, Steam, and Speed*, the locomotive is clearly an image of driving, dynamic energy. In Henry's dream (which he drew, below), locomotives are raised out of a lake—an expression of the release of a potential for valuable action that had previously been repressed into his unconscious.

and the square table seems to indicate that Henry must integrate his "feeling" side before he can achieve psychic wholeness. In fact, the singing lesson does move his feelings, and he kisses the girl on her mouth. Thereby he has, in a sense, "espoused" her (otherwise he would not feel "unfaithful"); he has learned to relate to "the woman within."

Another dream demonstrates the part that this little humpbacked girl had to play in Henry's inner development:

I am in an unknown boys' school. During the instruction period I secretly force my way into the house, I don't know for what purpose. I hide in the room behind a little square closet. The door to the corridor is half open. I fear being detected. An adult goes by without seeing me. But a little humpbacked girl comes in and sees me at once. She pulls me out of my hiding place.

Not only does the same girl appear in both dreams, but both appearances take place in a schoolhouse. In each instance Henry must learn something to assist his development. Seemingly, he would like to satisfy his desire for knowledge while remaining unnoticed and passive.

The figure of a deformed little girl appears in numerous fairy tales. In such tales the ugliness of the hump usually conceals great beauty, which is revealed when the "right man" comes to free the girl from a magic spell—often by a kiss. The girl in Henry's dream may be a symbol of Henry's soul, which also has to be released from the "spell" that has made it ugly.

When the humpbacked girl tries to awaken Henry's feelings by song, or pulls him out of his dark hiding place (forcing him to confront the light of day), she shows herself as a helpful guide. Henry can and must in a sense belong simultaneously to both his fiancée and the little humpbacked girl (to the first as a representative of the real, outer woman, and to the second as the embodiment of the inner psychic anima).

The oracle dream

People who rely totally on their rational thinking and dismiss or repress every manifestation of their psychic life often have an almost inexplicable inclination to superstition. They listen to oracles and prophecies and can be easily hoodwinked or influenced by magicians and conjurers. And because dreams compensate one's outer life, the emphasis such people put on their intellect is offset by dreams in which they meet the irrational and cannot escape it.

Henry experienced this phenomenon in the course of his analysis, in an impressive way. Four extraordinary dreams, based on such irrational themes, represented decisive milestones in his spiritual development. The first of these came about 10 weeks after the analysis began. As Henry reported the dream:

Alone on an adventurous journey through South America, I feel, at last, the desire to return home. In a foreign city situated on a mountain I try to reach the railway station, which I instinctively suspect to be in the center of the town at its highest level. I fear I may be too late.

Fortunately, however, a vaulted passage breaks through the row of houses on my right, built closely together as in the architecture of the Middle Ages, forming an impenetrable wall behind which the station is probably to be found. The whole scene offers a very picturesque aspect. I see the sunny, painted façades of the houses, the dark archway in whose shadowy obscurity four ragged figures have settled down on the pavement. With a sigh of relief, I hurry toward the passage—when suddenly a stranger, a trapper-type, appears ahead of me evidently filled with the same desire to catch the train.

At our approach the four gatekeepers, who turn out to be Chinese, jump up to prevent our passage. In the ensuing fight my left leg is injured by the long nails on the left foot of one of the Chinese. An oracle has to decide now whether the way could be opened to us or whether our lives must be forfeited.

I am the first to be dealt with. While my companion is bound and led inside, the Chinese consult the oracle by using little ivory sticks. The judgment goes against me, but I am given another chance. I am fettered and led aside, just as my companion was, and he now takes my place. In his presence, the oracle has to decide my fate for the second time. On this occasion it is in my favor. I am saved.

One immediately notices the singularity and the exceptional meaning of the dream, its wealth of symbols, and its compactness. However, it seemed as if Henry's conscious mind wanted to ignore the dream. Because of his skepticism toward the products of his unconscious it was important not to expose the dream to the danger of rationalization, but rather to let it act on him without interference. So I refrained at first from my interpretation. Instead I offered only one suggestion: I advised him to read and then to consult (as did the Chinese figures in his dream) the famous Chinese oracle book, the *I Ching*.

The *I Ching*, the so-called "Book of Changes," is a very ancient book of wisdom; its roots go back to mythical times, and it comes to us in its present form from 3000 B.C. According to Richard Wilhelm (who translated it into German and provided an admirable commentary), both of the main branches of Chinese philosophy—Taoism and Confucianism—have their common origin in the *I Ching*. The book is based on the hypothesis of the *oneness* of man and the surrounding cosmos, and of the complementary pairs of opposites Yang and Yin (i.e. the male and female principles). It consists of 64 "signs" each represented by a drawing made up of six lines. In these signs are contained all the possible combinations of Yang and Yin. The straight lines are looked upon as male, the broken lines as female.

Each sign describes changes in the human or cosmic situation, and each prescribes, in a pictorial language, the course of action to be followed at such times. The Chinese consulted this oracle by means that indicated which of the signs was relevant at a given moment. They did so by using 50 small sticks in a rather complicated way that yielded a given number. (Incidentally, Henry said that he had once read —probably in Jung's commentary on "The Secret of the Golden Flower"—of a strange game sometimes used by the Chinese to find out about the future.)

Today the more usual method of consulting the *I Ching* is to use three coins. Each throw of the three coins yields one line. "Heads," which stands for a male line, count as three; "tails," a broken female line, count as two. The coins are thrown six times, and the numbers that are produced indicate the sign or hexagram (i.e. the set of six lines) to be consulted.

But what significance has such "fortune telling" for our own time? Even those who accept the idea that the *I Ching* is a storehouse of wisdom will find it hard to believe that consultation of the oracle is anything more than an experiment in the occult. It is indeed diffi-

cult to grasp that more is involved, for the ordinary person today consciously dismisses all divining techniques as archaic nonsense. Yet they are not nonsense. As Dr. Jung has shown, they are based on what he calls the "principle of synchronicity" (or, more simply, meaningful coincidence). He has described this difficult new idea in his essay "Synchronicity: An Acausal Connecting Principle." It is based on the assumption of an inner unconscious knowledge that links a physical event with a psychic condition, so that a certain event that appears "accidental" or "coincidental" can in fact be psychically meaningful; and its meaning is often symbolically indicated through dreams that coincide with the event.

Several weeks after having studied the *I Ching*, Henry followed my suggestion (with considerable skepticism) and threw the coins. What he found in the book had a tremendous impact on him. Briefly, the oracle to which he referred bore several startling references to his dream, and to his psychological condition generally. By a remarkable "synchronistic" coincidence, the sign that was indicated by the coin-pattern was called MENG—or "Youthful Folly."

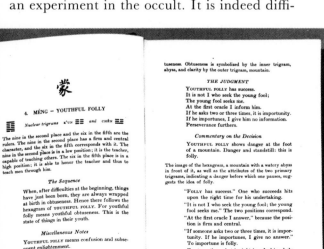

Left, two pages of the *I Ching* showing the hexagram MENG (which stands for "youthful folly"). The top three lines of the hexagram symbolize a mountain, and can also represent a gate; the bottom three lines symbolize water and the abyss.

Right, Henry's drawing of the sword and helmet that appeared to him in a fantasy, and that also related to a section of the *I Ching*—LI, "the clinging, fire."

In this chapter there are several parallels to the dream motifs in question. According to the text of the *I Ching*, the three upper lines of this hexagram symbolize a mountain, and have the meaning of "keeping still"; they can also be interpreted as a gate. The three lower lines symbolize water, the abyss, and the moon. All these symbols have occurred in Henry's previous dreams. Among many other statements that seemed to apply to Henry was the following warning: "For youthful folly, it is the most hopeless thing to entangle itself in empty imaginings. The more obstinately it clings to such unreal fantasies the more certainly will humiliation overtake it."

In this and other complex ways, the oracle seemed to be directly relevant to Henry's problem. This shook him. At first he tried to suppress its effect by willpower, but he could not escape it or his dreams. The message of the *I Ching* seemed to touch him deeply in spite of the puzzling language in which it was expressed. He became overpowered by the very irrationality whose existence he had so long denied. Sometimes silent, sometimes irritated, reading the words that seemed to coincide so strongly with the symbols in his dreams, he said, "I must think all this over thoroughly," and he left before our session was up. He canceled his next session by telephone, because of influenza, and did not reappear. I waited ("keeping still") because I supposed that he might not yet have digested the oracle.

A month went by. Finally Henry reappeared, excited and disconcerted, and told me what had happened in the meantime. Initially his intellect (which he had until then relied upon so much) had suffered a great shock—and one that he had at first tried to suppress. However, he soon had to admit that the communications of the oracle were pursuing him. He had intended to consult the book again, because in his dream the oracle had been consulted twice. But the text of the chapter "Youthful Folly" expressly forbids the putting of a second question. For two nights Henry had tossed sleeplessly in bed; but on the third a luminous dream image of great power had suddenly appeared before his eyes: a helmet with a sword floating in empty space.

Henry immediately took up the *I Ching* again and opened it at random to a commentary on Chapter 30, where (to his great surprise) he read the following passage: "The clinging is fire, it means coats of mail, helmets, it means lances and weapons." Now he felt that he understood why a second intentional consulting of the oracle was forbidden. For in his dream the ego was excluded from the second question; it was the trapper who had to consult the oracle the second time. In the same way, it was Henry's semi-unconscious action that had unintentionally asked the second question of the *I Ching* by opening the book at random and coming upon a symbol that coincided with his nocturnal vision.

Henry was clearly so deeply stirred that it seemed time to try to interpret the dream that had sparked the transformation. In view of the events of the dream, it was obvious that the dream-elements should be interpreted as contents of Henry's inner personality and the six dream-figures as personification of his psychic qualities. Such dreams are relatively rare, but when they do occur their after-effects are all the more powerful. That is why they could be called "dreams of transformation."

With dreams of such pictorial power, the dreamer seldom has more than a few personal associations. All Henry could offer was that he had recently tried for a job in Chile, and had been refused because they would not employ unmarried men. He also knew that some Chinese let the nails of their left hand grow as a sign that instead of working they have given themselves over to meditation.

Henry's failure (to get a job in South America) was presented to him in the dream. In it he is transported into a hot southern world—a world that, in contrast to Europe, he would call primitive, uninhibited, and sensual. It represents an excellent symbolic picture of the realm of the unconscious.

This realm was the opposite of the cultivated intellect and Swiss puritanism that ruled Henry's conscious mind. It was, in fact, his natural "shadow land," for which he had longed; but after a while he did not seem to feel too comfortable there. From the chthonic, dark, maternal powers (symbolized by South America) he is drawn back in the dream to the light, personal mother and to his fiancée. He suddenly realizes how far he has gone away from them; he finds himself alone in a "foreign city."

This increase in consciousness is symbolized in the dream as a "higher level"; the city was built on a mountain. So Henry "climbed up" to a greater consciousness in the "shadow land"; from there he hoped "to find his way home." This problem of ascending a mountain had already been put to him in his initial

dream. And, as in the dream of the saint and the prostitute, or in many mythological tales, a mountain often symbolizes a place of revelation, where transformation and change may take place.

The "city on the mountain" is also a well-known archetypal symbol that appears in the history of our culture in many variations. The city, corresponding in its ground plan to a mandala, represents that "region of the soul" in the middle of which the Self (the psyche's innermost center and totality) has its abode.

Surprisingly, the seat of the Self is represented in Henry's dream as a traffic center of the human collective—a railway station. This may be because the Self (if the dreamer is young and has a relatively low level of spiritual development) is usually symbolized by an object from the realm of his personal experience—often a banal object, which compensates the dreamer's high aspirations. Only in the mature person acquainted with the images of his soul is the Self realized in a symbol that corresponds to its unique value.

Even though Henry does not actually know where the station is, he nevertheless supposes it to be in the center of the city, on its highest point. Here, as in earlier dreams, he receives help from his unconscious. Henry's conscious mind was identified with his profession as an engineer, so he would also like his inner world to relate to rational products of civilization, like a railway station. The dream, however, rejects this attitude and indicates a completely different way.

The way leads "under" and through a dark arch. An arched gateway is also a symbol for a threshold, a place where dangers lurk, a place that at the same time separates and unites. Instead of the railway station that Henry was looking for, which was to connect uncivilized South America with Europe, Henry finds himself before a dark arched gateway where four ragged Chinese, stretched on the ground, block the passage. The dream makes no distinction between them, so they may be seen as four still undifferentiated aspects of a male totality. (The number four, a symbol of wholeness and completeness, represents an archetype that Dr. Jung has discussed at length in his writings.)

The Chinese thus represent unconscious male psychic parts of Henry that he cannot pass, because the "way to the Self" (i.e. to the psychic center) is barred by them and must still be opened to him. Until this issue has been settled he cannot continue his journey.

Still unaware of the impending danger, Henry hurries to the gateway, expecting at last to reach the station. But on his way he meets his "shadow"—his unlived, primitive side, which appears in the guise of an earthy, rough trapper. The appearance of this figure probably means that Henry's introverted ego has been joined by his extraverted (compensatory) side, which represents his repressed emotional and irrational traits. This shadow figure pushes itself past the conscious ego into the foreground, and, because it personifies the activity and autonomy of unconscious qualities, it becomes the proper carrier of fate, through whom everything happens.

The dream moves toward its climax. During the fight between Henry, the trapper, and the four ragged Chinese, Henry's left leg is scratched by the long nails on the left foot of one of the four. (Here, it seems, the European character of Henry's conscious ego has collided with a personification of the ancient wisdom of the East, with the extreme opposite of his ego. The Chinese come from an entirely different psychic continent, from an "other side" that is

still quite unknown to Henry and that seems dangerous to him.)

The Chinese can also be said to stand for the "yellow earth"; for the Chinese people are related to the earth as few people are. And it is just this earthy, chthonic quality that Henry had to accept. The unconscious male totality of his psyche, which he met in his dream, had a chthonic material aspect that his intellectual conscious side lacked. Thus the fact that he recognized the four ragged figures as Chinese shows that Henry had gained an increase of inner awareness concerning the nature of his adversaries.

Henry had heard that the Chinese sometimes let the nails of their left hand grow long. But in the dream the long nails are on the left foot; they are, so to speak, claws. This may indicate that the Chinese have a point of view so different from Henry's that it injures him. As we

Below, a drawing by a patient under analysis depicts a black monster (on the red or "feeling" side) and a Madonna-like woman (on the blue or spiritual side). This was Henry's position: over-emphasis on purity, chastity, etc. and fear of the irrational unconscious. (But note that the green, mandala-like flower acts as a link between the opposing sides.) Below left, another patient's painting depicting his insomnia—caused by his repressing too strongly his passionate, red, instinctual drives (which may overwhelm his consciousness) by a black "wall" of anxiety and depression.

know, Henry's conscious attitude toward the chthonic and feminine, toward the material depths of his nature, was most uncertain and ambivalent. This attitude, symbolized by his "left leg" (the point of view or "standpoint" of his feminine, unconscious side of which he is still afraid), was harmed by the Chinese.

This "injury," however, did not itself bring about a change in Henry. Every transformation demands as its precondition "the ending of a world"—the collapse of an old philosophy of life. As Dr. Henderson has pointed out earlier in this book, at ceremonies of initiation a youth must suffer a symbolic death before he can be reborn as a man and be taken into the tribe as a full member. Thus the scientific, logical attitude of the engineer must collapse to make room for a new attitude.

In the psyche of an engineer, everything "irrational" may be repressed, and therefore often reveals itself in the dramatic paradoxes of the dream-world. Thus the irrational appeared in Henry's dream as an "oracle game" of foreign origin, with a fearful and inexplicable power to decide human destinies. Henry's rational ego had no alternative but to surrender unconditionally in a real *sacrificium intellectus*.

Yet the conscious mind of such an inexperienced, immature person as Henry is not sufficiently prepared for such an act. He loses the turn of fortune, and his life is forfeit. He is caught, unable to go on in his accustomed way or to return home—to escape his adult responsibilities. (It was this insight for which Henry had to be prepared by this "great dream.")

Next, Henry's conscious, civilized ego is bound and put aside while the primitive trapper is allowed to take his place and to consult the oracle. Henry's life depends on the result. But when the ego is imprisoned in isolation, those contents of the unconscious that are personified in the shadow-figure may bring help and solution. This becomes possible when one recognizes the existence of such contents and has experienced their power. They can then become our consciously accepted constant companions. Because the trapper (his shadow) wins the game in his place, Henry is saved.

Facing the irrational

Henry's subsequent behavior clearly showed that the dream (and the fact that his dreams and the oracle book of the *I Ching* had brought him to face deep and irrational powers within himself) had a very deep effect on him. From then on he listened eagerly to the communications of his unconscious, and the analysis took on a more and more agitated character. The tension that until then had threatened the depths of his psyche with disruption came to the surface. Nevertheless, he courageously held to the growing hope that a satisfactory conclusion would be reached.

Barely two weeks after the oracle dream (but before it was discussed and interpreted), Henry had another dream in which he was once again confronted with the disturbing problem of the irrational:

Alone in my room. A lot of disgusting black beetles crawl out of a hole and spread out over my drawing table. I try to drive them back into their hole by means of some sort of magic. I am successful in this except for four or five beetles, which leave my table again and spread out into the whole room. I give up the idea of following them further; they are no longer so disgusting to me. I set fire to the hiding place. A tall column of flame rises up. I fear my room might catch fire, but this fear is unfounded.

By this time, Henry had become relatively skilful in the interpretation of his dreams, so he tried to give this dream an explanation of his own. He said: "The beetles are my dark qualities. They were awakened by the analysis and come up now to the surface. There is a danger that they may overflow my professional work (symbolized by the drawing table). Yet I did not dare to crush the beetles, which reminded me of a kind of black scarab, with my hand as I first intended, and therefore had to use 'magic.' In setting fire to their hiding place I, so to speak, call for the collaboration of something divine, as the upshooting column of flame makes me think of the fire that I associate with the Ark of the Covenant."

To go deeper into the symbolism of the dream, we must first of all note that these beetles are black, which is the color of darkness, depression, and death. In the dream, Henry is "alone" in his room—a situation that can lead to introversion and corresponding states of gloom. In mythology, scarab beetles often appear golden; in Egypt they were sacred animals symbolizing the sun. But if they are black, they symbolize the opposite side of the sun—something devilish. Therefore, Henry's instinct is quite correct in wanting to fight the beetles with magic.

Though four or five of the beetles remain alive, the decrease in the number of beetles is enough to free Henry from his fear and disgust. He then tries to destroy their breeding ground by fire. This is a positive action, because fire can symbolically lead to transformation and rebirth (as, for instance, it does in the ancient myth of the phoenix).

In his waking life, Henry now seemed full of enterprising spirit, but apparently he had not yet learned to use it to the right effect. Therefore, I want to consider another, later dream that throws an even clearer light on his problem. This dream presents in symbolic language Henry's fear of a responsible relationship with a woman and his tendency to withdraw from the feeling side of life:

An old man is breathing his last. He is surrounded by his relatives, and I am among them. More and more people gather in the large room, each one characterizing himself through precise statements. There are a good 40 persons present. The old man groans and mutters about "unlived life." His daughter, who wants to make his confession easier, asks him in what sense "unlived" is to be understood; whether cultural or moral. The old man will not answer. His daughter sends me to a small adjoining room where I am to find the answer by telling a fortune with cards. The "nine" that I turn up will give the answer, according to the color.

Above, an Egyptian relief (c. 1300 B.C.) shows a scarab beetle and the god Amon within the circle of the sun. In Egypt the golden scarab was itself a symbol of the sun. Below, a quite different kind of insect, more like the "devilish" beetles of Henry's dream: an engraving by the 19th-century artist James Ensor of humans with dark, repulsive insect bodies.

I expect to turn up a nine at the very beginning, but at first I turn up various kings and queens. I am disappointed. Now I turn up nothing but scraps of paper that don't belong to the game at all. Finally, I discover that there are no more cards in the deck but only envelopes and other pieces of paper. Together with my sister, who is also present, I look everywhere for the cards. Finally I discover one under a textbook or a notebook. It is nine, a nine of spades. It seems to me that this can only mean one thing: that it was moral chains that prevented the old man from "living his life."

The essential message of this strange dream was to warn Henry what awaited him if he failed to "live his life." The "old man" probably represents the dying "ruling principle"—the principle that rules Henry's consciousness, but whose nature is unknown to him. The 40 people present symbolize the totality of Henry's psychic traits (40 is a number of totality, an elevated form of the number four). That the old man is dying could be a sign that part of Henry's male personality is on the verge of a final transformation.

The daughter's query about the possible cause of death is the unavoidable and decisive question. There seems to be an implication that the old man's "morality" has prevented him from living out his natural feelings and drives. Yet the dying man himself is silent. Therefore his daughter (the personification of the mediating feminine principle, the anima) has to become active.

She sends Henry to discover the answer from the fortune-telling cards—the answer that will be given by the color of the first nine turned up. The fortune telling has to take place in an unused, remote room (revealing how far away such a happening is from Henry's conscious attitude).

He is disappointed when at first he uncovers only kings and queens (perhaps collective images of his youthful veneration for power and wealth). This disappointment becomes intense when the picture-cards run out, for this shows that the symbols of the inner world have also been exhausted. Only "scraps of paper" are left, without any images. Thus the source of pictures dries up in the dream. Henry then has to accept the help of his feminine side (this time represented by his sister) to find the last card. Together with her, he finally finds a card —the nine of spades. It is this card that must serve to indicate by its color what the phrase "unlived life" meant in the dream. And it is significant that the card is hidden under a textbook or notebook—which probably represents the arid intellectual formulas of Henry's technical interests.

The nine has been a "magic number" for centuries. According to the traditional symbolism of numbers, it represents the perfect form of the perfected Trinity in its threefold elevation. And there are endless other meanings associated with the number nine in various ages and cultures. The color of the nine of spades is the color of death and of lifelessness. Also, the "spade" image strongly brings to mind the form of a leaf, and therefore its blackness emphasizes that instead of being green, vital, and natural it is now dead. Furthermore, the word "spade" derives from the Italian *spada*, which means "sword" or "spear." Such weapons often symbolize the penetrating, "cutting" function of the intellect.

Thus the dream makes it clear that it was the "moral bonds" (rather than "cultural") that did not allow the old man to "live his life." In Henry's case, these "bonds" probably were his fear of surrendering fully to life, of accepting responsibilities to a woman and thereby becoming "unfaithful" to his mother. The dream has declared that the "unlived life" is an illness of which one can die.

Henry could no longer disregard the message of this dream. He realized that one needs something more than reason as a helpful compass in the entanglements of life; it is necessary to seek the guidance of the unconscious powers that emerge as symbols out of the depths of the psyche. With this recognition, the goal of this part of his analysis was reached. He now knew that he was finally expelled from the paradise of an uncommitted life and that he could never return to it.

كوكة آتش ومرغ سمندر

Above, a phoenix reborn in flames
(from a medieval Arabic manuscript)
—a well-known example of the
motif of death and rebirth by fire.
Below, a woodcut by the 19th-
century French artist Grandville
reflects some of the symbolic value
of playing cards. The Spades suit,
for instance, in French *Piques*, is
symbolically linked with the
"penetrating" intellect and, by its
black color, with death.

The final dream

A further dream came to confirm irrevocably
the insights Henry had gained. After some unimportant short dreams that concerned his
everyday life, the last dream (the 50th in the
series) appeared with all the wealth of symbols
that characterizes the so-called "great dreams."

Four of us form a friendly group, and we have
the following experiences: *Evening*: We are sitting
at a long, raw-lumber table and drinking out of
each of three different vessels: from a liqueur
glass, a clear, yellow, sweet liqueur; from a wine
glass, dark red Campari; from a large, classically
shaped vessel, tea. In addition to us there is also
a girl of reserved, delicate nature. She pours her
liqueur into the tea.

Night: We have returned from a big drinking
bout. One of us is the Président de la République
Française. We are in his palace. Walking out onto
the balcony we perceive him beneath us in the
snowy street as he, in his drunken condition,
urinates against a mound of snow. His bladder
content seems to be inexhaustible. Now he even
runs after an old spinster who carries in her arms
a child wrapped in a brown blanket. He sprays
the child with his urine. The spinster feels the
moisture but ascribes it to the child. She hurries
away with long steps.

Morning: Through the street, which glistens in
the winter sun, goes a Negro: a gorgeous figure,
completely naked. He walks toward the east,
toward Berne (that is, the Swiss capital). We are
in French Switzerland. We decide to go to pay
him a visit.

Noon: After a long automobile trip through a
lonely snowy region we come to a city, and into
a dark house where the Negro is said to have put up.
We are very much afraid that he might be frozen
to death. However, his servant, who is just as
dark, receives us. Negro and servant are mute.
We look into the rusksacks we have brought
with us, to see what each could give the Negro as a
gift. It must be some sort of object characteristic of
civilization. I am the first to make up my mind and
I take a package of matches from the floor and
offer it to the Negro with deference. After all have
presented their gifts, we join with the Negro in a
happy feast, a joyous revel.

Even at first glance the dream with its four parts makes an unusual impression. It encompasses a whole day and moves toward the "right," in the direction of growing consciousness. The movement starts with the evening, goes over into the night, and ends at noon, when the sun is at its zenith. Thus the cycle of the "day" appears as a totality pattern.

In this dream the four friends seem to symbolize the unfolding masculinity of Henry's psyche, and their progress through the four "acts" of the dream has a geometric pattern that reminds one of the essential construction of the mandala. As they first came from the east, then from the west, moving on toward the "capital" of Switzerland (i.e. the center), they seem to describe a pattern that tries to unite the opposites in a center. And this point is underlined by the movement in time—the descent into the night of the unconsciousness, following the sun's circuit, which is followed by an ascent to the bright zenith of consciousness.

The dream begins in the evening, a time when the threshold of consciousness is lowered and the impulses and images of the unconscious can pass across it. In such a condition (when the feminine side of man is most easily evoked) it is natural to find that a female figure joins the four friends. She is the anima figure that belongs to them all ("reserved and delicate," reminding Henry of his sister) and connects them all to each other. On the table stand three vessels of different character, which by their concave form accentuate the receptiveness that is symbolic of the feminine. The fact that these vessels are used by all present indicates a mutual and close relatedness among them. The vessels differ in form (liqueur glass, wine glass, and a classically formed container) and in the color of their contents. The opposites into which these fluids divide—sweet and bitter, red and yellow, intoxicating and sobering—are all intermingled, through being consumed by each of the five persons present, who sink into an unconscious communion.

The girl seems to be the secret agent, the catalyst who precipitates events (for it is the role of the anima to lead a man into his unconscious, and thus to force him to deeper recollection and increased consciousness). It is almost as though with the mixing of liqueur and tea the party would approach its climax.

The second part of the dream tells us more of the happenings of this "night." The four friends suddenly find themselves in Paris (which, for the Swiss, represents the town of sensuality, of uninhibited joy and love). Here a certain differentiation of the four takes place, especially between the ego in the dream (which is to a great extent identified with the leading thinking function) and the "Président de la République," who represents the undeveloped and unconscious feeling function.

The ego (Henry and two friends, who may be considered as representing his semi-conscious functions) looks down from the height of a balcony on the President, whose characteristics are exactly what one would expect to find in the undifferentiated side of the psyche. He is unstable, and has abandoned himself to his instincts. He urinates on the street in a drunken state; he is unconscious of himself, like a person outside civilization, following only his natural animal urges. Thus the President symbolizes a great contrast to the consciously accepted standards of a good middle-class Swiss scientist. Only in the darkest night of the unconscious could this side of Henry reveal itself.

However, the President-figure also has a very positive aspect. His urine (which could be the symbol of a stream of psychic libido) seems inexhaustible. It gives evidence of abundance, of creative and vital strength. (Primitives, for instance, regard everything coming from the body —hair, excrement, urine, or saliva—as creative, as having magical powers.) This unpleasant

President-image, therefore, could also be a sign of the power and plenty that often adheres to the shadow side of the ego. Not only does he urinate without embarrassment, but he runs after an old woman who is holding a child.

This "old spinster" is in a way the opposite or complement of the shy, fragile anima of the first part of the dream. She is still a virgin, even though old and seemingly a mother; in fact, Henry associated her to the archetypal image of Mary with the child Jesus. But the fact that the baby is wrapped in a brown (earth-colored) blanket makes it seem to be the chthonic, earth-bound counter-image of the Savior rather than a heavenly child. The President, who sprinkles the child with his urine, seems to perform a travesty of baptism. If we take the child as a symbol of a potentiality within Henry that is still infantile, then it could receive strength through this ritual. But the dream says nothing more; the woman hurries away with the child.

This scene marks the turning point of the dream. It is morning again. Everything that was dark, black, primitive, and powerful in the last episode has been gathered together and symbolized by a magnificent Negro, who appears naked—i.e. real and true.

Just as darkness and bright morning—or hot urine and cold snow—are opposites, so now the black man and the white landscape form a sharp antithesis. The four friends now must orient themselves within these new dimensions.

A drinking vessel from ancient Peru, in the shape of a woman, reflects the feminine symbolism of such containers, which occurs in Henry's final dream.

Their position has changed; the way that led through Paris has brought them unexpectedly into French Switzerland (where Henry's fiancée came from). A transformation has taken place in Henry during the earlier phase, when he was overpowered by unconscious contents of his psyche. Now, for the last time, he can begin to find his way forward from a place that was his fiancée's home (showing that he accepts her psychological background).

At the beginning he went from eastern Switzerland to Paris (from the east to the west, where the way leads into darkness, the unconsciousness). He has now made a turn of 180°, toward the rising sun and the ever-increasing clarity of consciousness. This way points to the middle of Switzerland, to its capital, Berne, and symbolizes Henry's striving toward a center that would unite the opposites within him.

The Negro is for some people the archetypal image of "the dark primal creature" and thus a personification of certain contents of the unconscious. Perhaps this is one reason why the Negro is so often rejected and feared by people of the white race. In him the white man sees his living counterpart, his hidden, dark side brought before his eyes. (This is just what most people try to avoid; they want to cut it off and repress it.) White men project onto the Negro the primitive drives, the archaic powers, the uncontrolled instincts that they do not want to admit in themselves, of which they are unconscious, and that they therefore designate as the corresponding qualities of other people.

For a young man of Henry's age the Negro may stand on the one hand for the sum of all dark traits repressed into unconsciousness; on the other hand, he may represent the sum of his primitive, masculine strength and potentialities, his emotional and physical power. That Henry and his friends intend consciously to confront the Negro signifies therefore a decisive step forward on the way to manhood.

In the meantime it has become noon, when the sun is at its highest, and consciousness has reached its greatest clarity. We might say that Henry's ego has continued to become more and more compact, that he has enhanced his capacity consciously to make decisions. It is still winter, which may indicate a lack of feeling and warmth in Henry; his psychic landscape is still wintry and apparently intellectually very cold. The four friends are afraid that the naked Negro (being accustomed to a warm climate) might be frozen. But their fear turns out to be groundless, for after a long drive through deserted snow-covered country they stop in a strange city and enter a dark house. This drive and the desolate country is symbolic of the long and wearisome search for self-development.

A further complication awaits the four friends here. The Negro and his servant are mute. Therefore it is not possible to make verbal contact with them; the four friends must seek other means to get in touch with the Negro. They cannot use intellectual means (words) but rather a feeling gesture to approach him. They offer him a present as one gives an offering to the gods, to win their interest and their affection. And it has to be an object of our civilization, belonging to the values of the intellectual white man. Again a *sacrificium intellectus* is demanded to win the favor of the Negro, who represents nature and instinct.

Henry is the first to make up his mind what to do. This is natural, since he is the bearer of the ego, whose proud consciousness (or *hybris*) has to be humbled. He picks up a box of matches from the floor and presents it "with deference" to the Negro. At first glance it may seem absurd that a small object lying on the floor and probably thrown away should be the proper gift, but this was the right choice. Matches are stored and controlled fire, a means by which a flame can be lit and put out at any time. Fire and flame symbolize warmth and love, feeling and passion; they are qualities of the heart, found wherever human beings exist.

In giving the Negro such a present, Henry symbolically combines a highly developed civilized product of his conscious ego with the center of his own primitivity and male strength, symbolized by the Negro. In this way, Henry can come into the full possession of his male sides, with which his ego must remain in constant touch from now on.

This was the result. The six male persons—the four friends, the Negro, and his servant—are now together in a gay spirit at a communal meal. It is clear that here Henry's masculine totality has been rounded out. His ego seems to have found the security it needs to enable him consciously and freely to submit to the greater archetypal personality within himself, which foreshadows the emergence of the Self.

What happened in the dream had its parallel also in Henry's waking life. Now he was sure of himself. Deciding quickly, he became serious about his engagement. Exactly nine months after his analysis had begun, he married in a little church of western Switzerland; and he left the following day with his young wife for Canada to take up an appointment that he had received during the decisive weeks of his last dreams. Since then he has been living an active, creative life as the head of a little family and holds an executive position in a great industry.

Henry's case reveals, so to speak, an accelerated maturation to an independent and responsible manliness. It represents an initiation into the reality of outer life, a strengthening of the ego and of his masculinity, and with this a completion of the first half of the individuation process. The second half—which is the establishment of a right relationship between the ego and the Self—still lies ahead of Henry, in the second half of his life.

Not every case runs such a successful and stirring course, and not every case can be handled in a similar way. On the contrary, every case is different. Not only do the young and the old, or the man and the woman, call for different treatment; so does every individual in all these categories. Even the same symbols require different interpretation in each case. I have selected this one because it represents an especially impressive example of the autonomy of the unconscious processes and shows by its abundance of images the untiring symbol-creating power of the psychic background. It proves that the self-regulating action of the psyche (when not disturbed by too much rational explanation or dissection) can support the development process of the soul.

In *Psychology and Alchemy* Dr. Jung discusses a sequence of over 1000 dreams produced by one man. The sequence revealed a striking number and variety of representations of the mandala motif—which is so often linked with the realization of the Self (see pp. 213 ff.). These pages present a few examples of mandala imagery from the dreams, to indicate the vastly different forms in which this archetype can manifest itself, even in one individual's unconscious. The interpretative meanings offered here may, because of their brevity, seem to be arbitrary assertions. In practice no Jungian would produce an interpretation of a dream without knowledge of the dreamer and careful study of his associations to the dream. These interpretative statements must be taken as hints toward possible meanings—nothing more.

Left: In the dream the anima accuses the man of being inattentive to her. A clock says five minutes to the hour. The man is being "pestered" by his unconscious; the tension thus created is heightened by the clock, by waiting for something to happen in five minutes.

Below: A skull (which the man tries in vain to kick away) becomes a red ball, then a woman's head. Here the man may try to reject the unconscious (kicking the skull), but it asserts itself by means of the ball (perhaps alluding to the sun) and the anima figure.

Left: In part of a dream, a prince places a diamond ring on the fourth finger of the dreamer's left hand. The ring, worn like a wedding ring, indicates that the dreamer has taken a "vow" to the Self.
Below left: A veiled woman uncovers her face, which shines like the sun. The image implies an illumination of the unconscious (involving the anima) —quite different from conscious elucidation.
Below: From a transparent sphere containing small spheres, a green plant grows. The sphere symbolizes unity; the plant, life and growth.

Below: Troops, no longer preparing for war, form an eight-rayed star and rotate to the left. This image perhaps indicates that some inner conflict has given way to harmony.

Conclusion: M.-L. von Franz

Science and the unconscious

In the preceding chapters C. G. Jung and some of his associates have tried to make clear the role played by the symbol-creating function in man's unconscious psyche and to point out some fields of application in this newly discovered area of life. We are still far from understanding the unconscious or the archetypes—those dynamic *nuclei* of the psyche—in all their implications. All we can see now is that the archetypes have an enormous impact on the individual, forming his emotions and his ethical and mental outlook, influencing his relationships with others, and thus affecting his whole destiny. We can also see that the arrangement of archetypal symbols follows a pattern of wholeness in the individual, and that an appropriate understanding of the symbols can have a healing effect. And we can see that the archetypes can act as creative or destructive forces in our mind: creative when they inspire new ideas, destructive when these same ideas stiffen into conscious prejudices that inhibit further discoveries.

Jung has shown in his chapter how subtle and differentiated all attempts at interpretation must be, in order not to weaken the specific individual and cultural values of archetypal ideas and symbols by leveling them out—i.e. by giving them a stereotyped, intellectually formulated meaning. Jung himself dedicated his entire life to such investigations and interpretative work; naturally this book sketches only an infinitesimal part of his vast contribution to this new field of psychological discovery. He was a pioneer and remained fully aware that an enormous number of further questions remained unanswered and call for further investigation. This is why his concepts and hypotheses are conceived on as wide a basis as possible (without making them *too* vague and all-embracing) and why his views form a so-called "open system" that does not close the door against possible new discoveries.

To Jung, his concepts were mere tools or heuristic hypotheses that might help us to explore the vast new area of reality opened up by the discovery of the unconscious—a discovery that has not merely widened our whole view of the world but has in fact doubled it. We must always ask now whether a mental phenomenon is conscious or unconscious and, also, whether a "real" outer phenomenon is perceived by conscious or unconscious means.

The powerful forces of the unconscious most certainly appear not only in clinical material but also in the mythological, religious, artistic, and all the other cultural activities by which man expresses himself. Obviously, if all men have common inherited patterns of emotional and mental behavior (which Jung called the archetypes), it is only to be expected that we shall find their products (symbolic fantasies, thoughts, and actions) in practically *every* field of human activity.

Important modern investigations of many of these fields have been deeply influenced by Jung's work. For instance, this influence can be seen in the study of literature, in such books as J. B. Priestley's *Literature and Western Man*, Gottfried Diener's *Fausts Weg zu Helena*, or James Kirsch's *Shakespeare's Hamlet*. Similarly, Jungian psychology has contributed to the study of art, as in the writings of Herbert Read or of Aniela Jaffé, Erich Neumann's examination of Henry Moore, or Michael Tippett's studies in music. Arnold Toynbee's work on history and Paul Radin's on anthropology have benefited from Jung's teachings, as have the contributions to sinology made by Richard Wilhelm, Enwin Rousselle, and Manfred Porkert.

Sound waves, given off by a vibrating steel disk and made visible in a photograph, produce a strikingly mandala-like pattern.

Of course, this does not mean that the special features of art and literature (including their interpretations) can be understood *only* from their archetypal foundation. These fields all have their own laws of activity; like all really creative achievements, they cannot ultimately be rationally explained. But within their areas of action one can recognize the archetypal patterns as a dynamic background activity. And one can often decipher in them (as in dreams) the message of some seemingly purposive, evolutionary tendency of the unconscious.

The fruitfulness of Jung's ideas is more immediately understandable within the area of the cultural activities of man: Obviously, if the archetypes determine our mental behavior, they *must* appear in all these fields. But, unexpectedly, Jung's concepts have also opened up new ways of looking at things in the realm of the natural sciences as well—for instance, in biology.

The physicist Wolfgang Pauli has pointed out that, due to new discoveries, our idea of the evolution of life requires a revision that might take into account an area of interrelation between the unconscious psyche and biological processes. Until recently it was assumed that the mutation of species happened at random and that a selection took place by means of which the "meaningful," well-adapted varieties survived, and the others disappeared. But modern evolutionists have pointed out that the selections of such mutations by pure chance would have taken much *longer* than the known age of our planet allows.

Jung's concept of synchronicity may be helpful here, for it could throw light upon the occurrence of certain rare "border-phenomena," or exceptional events; thus it might explain how "meaningful" adaptations and mutations could happen in less time than that required by entirely random mutations. Today we know of many instances in which meaningful "chance" events have occurred when an archetype is activated. For example, the history of science contains many cases of simultaneous invention or discovery. One of the most famous of such cases involved Darwin and his theory of the origin of species: Darwin had developed the theory in a lengthy essay, and in 1844 was busy expanding this into a major treatise.

While he was at work on this project he received a manuscript from a young biologist, unknown to Darwin, named A. R. Wallace. The manuscript was a shorter but otherwise parallel exposition of Darwin's theory. At the time Wallace was in the Molucca Islands of the Malay Archipelago. He knew of Darwin as a naturalist, but had not the slightest idea of the kind of theoretical work on which Darwin was at the time engaged.

In each case a creative scientist had independently arrived at a hypothesis that was to change the entire development of the science. And each had initially conceived of the hypothesis in an intuitive "flash" (later backed up by documentary evidence). The archetypes thus seem to appear as the agents, so to speak, of a *creatio continua*. (What Jung calls synchronistic events are in fact something like "acts of creation in time.")

Similar "meaningful coincidences" can be said to occur when there is a vital necessity for an individual to know about, say, a relative's death, or some lost possession. In a great many cases such information has been revealed by means of extrasensory perception. This seems to suggest that abnormal random phenomena may occur when a vital need or urge is aroused; and this in turn might explain why a species of animals, under great pressure or in great need, could produce "meaningful" (but *acausal*) changes in its outer material structure.

But the most promising field for future studies seems (as Jung saw it) to have unexpectedly opened up in connection with the complex field of microphysics. At first sight, it seems most unlikely that we should find a relationship between psychology and microphysics. The interrelation of these sciences is worth some explanation.

The most obvious aspect of such a connection lies in the fact that most of the basic concepts of physics (such as space, time, matter, energy, continuum or field, particle, etc.) were originally intuitive, semi-mythological, archetypal ideas of the old Greek philosophers—ideas that then slowly evolved and became more accurate and that today are mainly expressed in abstract mathematical terms. The idea of a particle, for instance, was formulated by the fourth-century B.C. Greek philosopher Leucippus and his pupil Democritus, who called it the "atom"—i.e. the "indivisible unit." Though the atom has not proved indivisible, we still conceive matter ultimately as consisting of waves and particles (or discontinuous "quanta").

The idea of energy, and its relationship to force and movement, was also formulated by early Greek thinkers, and was developed by Stoic philosophers. They postulated the existence of a sort of life-giving "tension" (*tonos*), which supports and moves all things. This is obviously a semi-mythological germ of our modern concept of energy.

Even comparatively modern scientists and thinkers have relied on half-mythological, archetypal images when building up new concepts. In the 17th century, for instance, the absolute validity of the law of causality seemed "proved" to René Descartes "by the fact that God is immutable in His decisions and actions." And the great German astronomer Johannes Kepler asserted that there are not more and not less than three dimensions of space on account of the Trinity.

These are just two examples among many that show how even our modern and basic scientific concepts remained for a long time linked with archetypal ideas that originally came from the unconscious. They do not necessarily express "objective" facts (or at least we cannot prove that they ultimately do) but spring from innate mental tendencies in man—tendencies that induce him to find "satisfactory" rational explanatory connections between the various outer and inner facts with which he has to deal. When examining nature and the universe, instead of looking for and finding objective qualities, "man encounters himself," in the phrase of the physicist Werner Heisenberg.

Because of the implications of this point of view, Wolfgang Pauli and other scientists have begun to study the role of archetypal symbolism in the realm of scientific concepts. Pauli believed that we should parallel our investigation of outer objects with a psychological investigation of the *inner origin* of our scientific concepts. (This investigation might shed new light on a far-reaching concept to be introduced later in this chapter—the concept of a "one-ness" between the physical and psychological spheres, quantitative and qualitative aspects of reality.)

Besides this rather obvious link between the psychology of the unconscious and physics, there are other even more fascinating connections. Jung (working closely with Pauli) discovered that analytical psychology has been forced by investigations in its own field to create concepts that turned out later to be strikingly similar to those created by the physicists when confronted with microphysical phenomena. One of the most important among the physicists' concepts is Niels Bohr's idea of *complementarity*.

Modern microphysics has discovered that one can describe light only by means of two logically opposed but complementary concepts: The ideas of particle and wave. In grossly simplified terms, it might be said that under certain experimental conditions light manifests itself as if it were composed of particles; under others, as

The American physicist Mrs. Maria Mayer, who in 1963 shared the Nobel prize for physics. Her discovery—concerning the constituents of the atomic nucleus—was made like so many other scientific discoveries: in an intuitive flash of insight (sparked by a colleague's chance remark). Her theory indicates that the nucleus consists of concentric shells: The innermost contains two protons or two neutrons, the next contains eight of one or the other, and so on through what she calls the "magic numbers"—20, 28, 50, 82, 126. There is an obvious link between this model and the archetypes of the sphere and of numbers.

if it were a wave. Also, it was discovered that we can accurately observe either the position or the velocity of a subatomic particle—but not both at once. The observer must choose his experimental set-up, but by doing so he excludes (or rather must "sacrifice") some other possible set-up and its results. Furthermore, the measuring apparatus has to be included in the description of events because it has a decisive but uncontrollable influence upon the experimental set-up.

Pauli says: "The science of microphysics, on account of the basic 'complementary' situation, is faced with the impossibility of eliminating the effects of the observer by determinable correctives and has therefore to abandon in principle any objective understanding of physical phenomena. Where classical physics still saw 'determined causal natural laws of nature' we now look only for 'statistical laws' with 'primary possibilities.' "

In other words, in microphysics the observer interferes with the experiment in a way that cannot be measured and that therefore cannot be eliminated. No natural laws can be formulated, saying "such-and-such will happen in every case." All the microphysicist can say is "such-and-such is, according to statistical probability, likely to happen." This naturally represents a tremendous problem for our classical physical thinking. It requires a consideration, in a scientific experiment, of the mental outlook of the participant-observer: It could thus be said that scientists can no longer hope to describe any aspects of outer objects in a completely "objective" manner.

Most modern physicists have accepted the fact that the role played by the conscious ideas of an observer in every microphysical experiment cannot be eliminated; but they have not concerned themselves with the possibility that the *total* psychological condition (both conscious and unconscious) of the observer might play a role as well. As Pauli points out, however, we have at least no *a priori* reasons for rejecting this possibility. But we must look at this as a still unanswered and an unexplored problem.

Bohr's idea of complementarity is especially interesting to Jungian psychologists, for Jung saw that the relationship between the conscious and unconscious mind also forms a complementary pair of opposites. Each new content that comes up from the unconscious is altered in its basic nature by being partly integrated into the conscious mind of the observer. Even dream contents (if noticed at all) are in that way semi-conscious. And each enlargement of the observer's consciousness caused by dream interpretation has again an immeasurable repercussion and influence on the unconscious. Thus the unconscious can only be approximately described (like the particles of microphysics) by paradoxical concepts. What it really is "in itself" we shall never know, just as we shall never know this about matter.

To take the parallels between psychology and microphysics even further: What Jung calls the archetypes (or patterns of emotional and mental behavior in man) could just as well be called, to use Pauli's term, "primary possibilities" of psychic reactions. As has been stressed in this book, there are no laws governing the specific form in which an archetype might appear. There are only "tendencies" (see p. 67) that, again, enable us to say only that such-and-such is likely to happen in certain psychological situations.

As the American psychologist William James once pointed out, the idea of an unconscious could itself be compared to the "field" concept in physics. We might say that, just as in a magnetic field the particles entering into it appear in a certain order, psychological contents also appear in an ordered way within that psychic area which we call the unconscious. If we call something "rational" or "meaningful" in our conscious mind, and accept it as a satisfactory "explanation" of things, it is probably due to the fact that our conscious explanation is in harmony with some preconscious constellation of contents in our unconscious.

In other words, our conscious representations are sometimes ordered (or arranged in a pattern) *before* they have become conscious to us. The 19th-century German mathematician Karl Friedrich Gauss gives an example of an experience of such an unconscious order of ideas: He says that he found a certain rule in the theory of numbers "not by painstaking research, but by the Grace of God, so to speak. The riddle *solved itself as lightning strikes*, and I myself could not tell or show the connection between what I knew before, what I last used to experiment with, and what produced the final success." The French scientist Henri Poincaré is even more explicit about this phenomenon; he describes how during a sleepless night he actually watched his mathematical representations colliding in him until some of them "found a more stable connection. One feels as if one could watch one's own unconscious at work, the unconscious activity partially becoming manifest to consciousness without losing its own character. At such moments one has an intuition of the difference between the mechanisms of the two egos."

As a final example of parallel developments in microphysics and psychology, we can consider Jung's concept of *meaning*. Where before men looked for causal (i.e. rational) explanations of phenomena, Jung introduced the idea of looking for the meaning (or, perhaps we could say, the "purpose"). That is, rather than ask *why* something happened (i.e. what caused it), Jung asked: What did it happen for? This same tendency appears in physics: Many modern physicists are now looking more for "connections" in nature than for causal laws (determinism).

Pauli expected that the idea of the unconscious would spread beyond the "narrow frame of therapeutic use" and would influence all natural sciences that deal with general life phenomena. Since Pauli suggested this development he has been echoed by some physicists who are concerned with the new science of cybernetics—the comparative study of the "control" system formed by the brain and nervous system and such mechanical or electronic information and control systems as computers. In short, as the modern French scientist Oliver Costa de Beauregard has put it, science and psychology should in future "enter into an active dialogue."

The unexpected parallelisms of ideas in psychology and physics suggest, as Jung pointed out, a possible ultimate *one-ness* of both fields of reality that physics and psychology study—i.e. a psychophysical one-ness of all life phenomena. Jung was even convinced that what he calls the unconscious somehow links up with the structure of inorganic matter—a link to which the problem of so-called "psychosomatic" illness seems to point. The concept of a unitarian idea of reality (which has been followed up by Pauli and Erich Neumann) was called by Jung the *unus mundus* (the one world, within which matter and psyche are not yet discriminated or separately actualized). He paved the way toward such a unitarian point of view by pointing out that an archetype shows a "psychoid" (i.e. not purely psychic but almost material) aspect when it appears within a synchronistic event—for such an event is in effect a meaningful arrangement of inner psychic and *outer* facts.

In other words, the archetypes not only fit into outer situations (as animal patterns of behavior fit into their surrounding nature); at bottom they tend to become manifest in a synchronistic "arrangement" that includes both matter and psyche. But these statements are just hints at some directions in which the investigation of life phenomena might proceed. Jung felt that we should first learn a great deal more about the interrelation of these two areas (matter and psyche) before rushing into too many abstract speculations about it.

The field that Jung himself felt would be most fruitful for further investigations was the study of our basic mathematical *axiomata*—which Pauli calls "primary mathematical intuitions," and among which he especially mentions the ideas of an infinite series of numbers in arithmetic, or of a continuum in geometry, etc. As the German-born author Hannah Arendt has said, "with the rise of modernity, mathematics do not simply enlarge their content or reach out into the infinite to become applicable to the immensity of an infinite and infinitely growing, expanding universe, but cease to be concerned with appearance at all. They are no longer the beginnings of philosophy, or the 'science' of Being in its true appearance, but become instead the science of the structure of the human mind." (A Jungian would at once add the question: Which mind? The conscious or the unconscious mind?)

As we have seen with reference to the experiences of Gauss and Poincaré, the mathematicians also discovered the fact that our representations are "ordered" before we become aware of them. B. L. van der Waerden, who cites many examples of essential mathematical insights arising from the unconscious, concludes: ". . . the unconscious is not only able to associate and combine, but even *to judge*. The judgment of the unconscious is an intuitive one, but it is under favorable circumstances completely sure."

Among the many mathematical primary intuitions, or *a priori* ideas, the "natural numbers" seem psychologically the most interesting. Not only do they serve our conscious everyday measuring and counting operations; they have for centuries been the only existing means for "reading" the meaning of such ancient forms of divination as astrology, numerology, geomancy, etc.—all of which are based on arithmetical computation and all of which have been investigated by Jung in terms of his theory of synchronicity. Furthermore, the natural numbers —viewed from a psychological angle—must certainly be archetypal representations, for we are forced to think about them in certain definite ways. Nobody, for instance, can deny that 2 is the only existing even primary number, even if he has never thought about it consciously before. In other words, numbers are not concepts consciously invented by men for purposes of calculation: They are spontaneous and autonomous products of the unconscious—as are other archetypal symbols.

But the natural numbers are also qualities adherent to outer objects: We can assert and count that there are two stones here or three trees there. Even if we strip outer objects of all such qualities as color, temperature, size, etc., there still remains their "many-ness" or special multiplicity. Yet these same numbers are also just as indisputably parts of our own mental set-up—abstract concepts that we can study without looking at outer objects. Numbers thus appear to be a tangible connection between the spheres of matter and psyche. According to hints dropped by Jung, it is here that the most fruitful field of further investigation might be found.

I mention these rather difficult concepts briefly in order to show that, to me, Jung's ideas do not form a "doctrine" but are the beginning of a new outlook that will continue to evolve and expand. I hope they will give the reader a glimpse into what seems to me to have been essential to and typical of Jung's scientific attitude. He was always searching, with unusual freedom from conventional prejudices, and at the same time with great modesty and accuracy, to understand the phenomenon of life. He did not go further into the ideas mentioned above, because he felt that he had not yet enough facts in hand to say anything relevant about them—just as he generally waited several years before publishing his new insights, checking them again and again in the meantime, and himself raising every possible doubt about them.

Therefore, what might at first sight strike the reader as a certain vagueness in his ideas comes in fact from this scientific attitude of intellectual modesty—an attitude that does not exclude (by rash, superficial pseudo-explanations and oversimplifications) new possible discoveries, and that respects the complexity of the phenomenon of life. For this phenomenon was always an exciting mystery to Jung. It was never, as it is for people with closed minds, an "explained" reality about which it can be assumed that we know everything.

Creative ideas, in my opinion, show their value in that, like keys, they help to "unlock" hitherto unintelligible connections of facts and thus enable man to penetrate deeper into the mystery of life. I am convinced that Jung's ideas can serve in this way to find and interpret new facts in many fields of science (and also of everyday life), simultaneously leading the individual to a more balanced, more ethical, and wider conscious outlook. If the reader should feel stimulated to work further on the investigation and assimilation of the unconscious— which always begins by working on oneself— the purpose of this introductory book would be fulfilled.

Notes

Approaching the unconscious   C. G. Jung

page 37   Nietzsche's cryptomnesia is discussed in Jung's "On the Psychology of So-called Occult Phenomena," in Collected Works vol. I. The relevant passage from the ship's log and the corresponding passage from Nietzsche are as follows:

From J. Kerner, *Blätter aus Prevorst*, vol. IV, p. 57, headed "An Extract of Awe-inspiring Import . . ." (orig. 1831-37): "The four captains and a merchant, Mr. Bell, went ashore on the island of Mount Stromboli to shoot rabbits. At three o'clock they mustered the crew to go aboard, when, to their inexpressible astonishment, they saw two men flying rapidly toward them through the air. One was dressed in black, the other in grey. They came past them very closely, in greatest haste, and to their utmost dismay descended into the crater of the terrible volcano, Mount Stromboli. They recognized the pair as acquaintances from London."

From F. Nietzsche, *Thus Spake Zarathustra*, chapter xl, "Great Events" (translated by Common, p. 180, slightly modified), orig. 1883: "Now about the time that Zarathustra sojourned on the Happy Isles, it happened that a ship anchored at the isle on which the smoking mountain stands, and the crew went ashore to shoot rabbits. About the noon-tide hour, however, when the captain and his men were together again, they suddenly saw a man coming toward them through the air, and a voice said distinctly: 'It is time! It is highest time!' But when the figure drew close to them, flying past quickly like a shadow in the direction of the volcano, they recognized with the greatest dismay that it was Zarathustra . . . 'Behold,' said the old helmsman, 'Zarathustra goes down to hell!'"

38   Robert Louis Stevenson discusses his dream of Jekyll and Hyde in "A Chapter on Dreams" from his *Across the Plain*.

56   A more detailed account of Jung's dream is given in *Memories, Dreams, Reflections of C. G. Jung*, ed. Aniela Jaffé, New York, Pantheon, 1962.

63   Examples of the state of subliminal ideas and images can be found in Pierre Janet's works.

93   Further examples of cultural symbols appear in Mircea Eliade's *Der Schamanismus*, Zurich, 1947.

See also The Collected Works of Carl G. Jung, vols. I-XVIII; London, Routledge & Kegan Paul; New York, Bollingen-Pantheon.

Ancient myths and modern man   Joseph L. Henderson

108   Concerning the finality of Christ's resurrection: Christianity is an eschatological religion, meaning it has a final end in view that becomes synonymous with the Last Judgment. Other religions, in which matriarchal elements of tribal culture are preserved (e.g. Orphism), are cyclical, as demonstrated by Eliade in *The Myth of the Eternal Return*, New York, Bollingen-Pantheon, 1954.

112   See Paul Radin, *Hero Cycles of the Winnebago*, Indiana University Publications, 1948.

113   Concerning Hare, Dr. Radin remarks: "Hare is the typical hero as we know him from all over the world, civilized and pre-literate, and from the most remote periods of world history."

114   The twin Navaho warrior gods are discussed by Maud Oakes in *Where the Two Came to their Father, A Navaho War Ceremonial*, New York, Bollingen, 1943,

117   Jung discusses Trickster in "On the Psychology of the Trickster Figure," Collected Works vol. IX.

118   The ego's conflict with the shadow is discussed in Jung's "The Battle for Deliverance from the Mother," Collected Works vol. V.

125   For an interpretation of the Minotaur myth, see Mary Renault's novel *The King Must Die*, Pantheon, 1958.

125   The symbolism of the labyrinth is discussed by Erich Neumann in *The Origins and History of Consciousness*, Bollingen, 1954.

126   For the Navaho myth of Coyote, see Margaret Schevill Link and J. L. Henderson, *The Pollen Path*, Stanford, 1954.

128   The emergence of the ego is discussed by Erich Neumann, *op. cit.*; Michael Fordham, *New Developments in Analytical Psychology*, London, Routledge & Kegan Paul, 1957; and Esther M. Harding, *The Restoration of the Injured Archetypal Image* (privately circulated), New York, 1960.

129   Jung's study of initiation appears in "Analytical Psychology and the Weltanschauung," Collected Works vol. VIII. See also Arnold van Gennep, *The Rites of Passage*, Chicago, 1961.

132   Women's trials of strength are discussed by Erich Neumann in *Amor and Psyche*, Bollingen, 1956.

137   The tale of "Beauty and the Beast" appears in Mme. Leprince de Beaumont's *The Fairy Tale Book*, New York, Simon & Schuster, 1958.

141   The myth of Orpheus can be found in Jane E. Harrison's *Prolegomena to the Study of Greek Religion*, Cambridge University Press, 1922. See also W. K. C. Guthrie, *Orpheus and Greek Religion*, Cambridge, 1935.

142   Jung's discussion of the Catholic ritual of the chalice is in "Transformation Symbolism in the Mass," Collected Works vol. XI. See also Alan Watts, *Myth and Ritual in Christianity*, Vanguard Press, 1953.

145   Linda Fierz-David's interpretation of Orphic ritual appears in *Psychologische Betrachtungen zu der Freskenfolge der Villa dei Misteri in Pompeji, ein Versuch von Linda Fierz-David*, trans. Gladys Phelan (privately printed), Zurich, 1957.

148   The Roman funeral urn from the Esquiline Hill is discussed by Jane Harrison, *op. cit.*

149   See Jung's "The Transcendent Function," edited by the Students' Association, C. G. Jung Institute, Zurich.

151   Joseph Campbell discusses the shaman as bird in *The Symbol without Meaning*, Zurich, Rhein-Verlag, 1958.

152   For T. S. Eliot's "The Waste Land," see his *Collected Poems*, London, Faber and Faber, 1963.

The process of individuation   M.-L. von Franz

160   A detailed discussion of the meandering pattern of dreams appears in Jung's Collected Works vol. VIII, p. 23 ff. and pp. 237-300 (especially p. 290). For an example see Jung's Collected Works vol. XII, part 1. See also Gerhard Adler, *Studies in Analytical Psychology*, London, 1948.

161   For Jung's discussion of the Self, see Collected Works vol. IX, part 2, pp. 5 ff., 23 ff.; and vol. XII, pp. 18 f., 41 f., 174, 193.

161   The Naskapi are described by Frank G. Speck in *Naskapi: The Savage Hunter of the Labrador Peninsula*, University of Oklahoma Press, 1935.

162   The concept of psychic wholeness is discussed in Jung's Collected Works vol. XIV, p. 117, and in vol. IX, part 2, p. 6, 190. See also Collected Works vol. IX, part 1, pp. 275 ff., 290 ff.

163   The story of the oak tree is translated from Richard Wilhelm, *Dschuang-Dsi; Das wahre Buch vom südlichen Blütenland*, Jena, 1923, pp. 33-4.

163 Jung deals with the tree as a symbol of the individuation process in "Der philosophische Baum," *Von den Wurzeln des Bewusstseins*, Zurich, 1954 (not yet translated).

163 The "local god" to whom sacrifices were made on the stone earth-altar corresponds in many respects to the antique *genius loci*. See Henri Maspéro, *La Chine antique*, Paris, 1955, p. 140 f. (This information is owed to the kindness of Miss Ariane Rump.)

164 Jung notes the difficulty of describing the individuation process in Collected Works vol. XVII, p. 179.

165 This brief description of the importance of children's dreams derives mostly from Jung's *Psychological Interpretation of Children's Dreams* (notes and lectures), E. T. H. Zurich, 1938-9 (private circulation only). The special example comes from an untranslated seminar, *Psychologische Interpretation von Kinderträumen*, 1939-40, p. 76 ff. See also Jung's "The Development of Personality," Collected Works vol. XVII; Michael Fordham, *The Life of Childhood*, London, 1944 (especially p. 104); Erich Neumann, *The Origins and History of Consciousness*; Frances Wickes, *The Inner World of Consciousness*, New York-London, 1927; and Eleanor Bertine, *Human Relationships*, London, 1958.

166 Jung discusses the psychic nucleus in "The Development of Personality," Collected Works vol. XVII, p. 175, and vol. XIV, p. 9 ff.

167 For fairy tale patterns corresponding to the sick king motif, see Joh. Bolte and G. Polivka, *Anmerkungen zu den Kinder- und Hausmärchen der Brüder Grimm*, vol. I, 1913-32, p. 503 ff.—i.e. all variations to Grimm's tale *The Golden Bird*.

168 Further discussion of the shadow can be found in Jung's Collected Works vol. IX, part 2, chapter 2, and vol. XII, p. 29 f., and idem: *The Undiscovered Self*, London, 1958, pp. 8-9. See also Frances Wickes, *The Inner World of Man*, New York-Toronto, 1938. A good example of shadow realization is given in G. Schmalz, *Komplexe Psychologie und Körperliches Symptom*, Stuttgart, 1955.

170 Examples of the Egyptian concept of the underworld appear in *The Tomb of Rameses VI*, Bollingen series XL, parts 1 and 2, Pantheon Books, 1954.

172 Jung deals with the nature of projection in Collected Works vol. VI, Definitions, p. 582; and Collected Works vol. VIII, p. 272 ff.

175 The Koran (Qur'an) has been translated by E. H. Palmer, Oxford University Press, 1949. See also Jung's interpretation of the story of Moses and Khidr in Collected Works vol. IX, p. 135 ff.

175 The Indian story *Somadeva: Vetalapanchavimsati* has been translated by C. H. Tawney, Jaico-book, Bombay, 1956. See also Henry Zimmer's excellent psychological interpretation *The King and the Corpse*, Bollingen series IX, New York, Pantheon, 1948.

176 The reference to the Zen master is from *Der Ochs und sein Hirte* (trans. by Kōichi Tsujimura), Pfullingen, 1958, p. 95.

177 For further discussion of the anima, see Jung's Collected Works vol. IX, part 2, pp. 11-12, and chapter 3; vol. XVII, p. 198 f.; vol. VIII, p. 345; vol. XI, pp. 29-31, 41 f., 476, etc.; vol. XII, Part 1. See also Emma Jung, *Animus and Anima, Two Essays*, The Analytical Club of New York, 1957; Eleanor Bertine, *Human Relationships*, part 2; Esther Harding, *Psychic Energy*, New York, 1948, passim, and others.

177 Eskimo shamanism has been described by Mircea Eliade in *Der Schamanismus*, Zurich, 1947, especially p. 49 ff.; and by Knud Rasmussen in *Thulefahrt*, Frankfurt, 1926, passim.

178 The Siberian hunter story is from Rasmussen, *Die Gabe des Adlers*, Frankfurt a.M., 1926, p. 172.

179 A discussion of the "poison damsel" appears in W. Hertz, *Die Sage vom Giftmädchen*, Abh. der k. bayr. Akad. der Wiss., 1 Cl. XX Bd. 1 Abt. München, 1893.

179 The murderous princess is discussed by Chr. Hahn in *Griechische und Albanesische Märchen*, vol. 1, München-Berlin, 1918, p. 301: Der Jäger und der Spiegel der alles sieht.

180 "Love madness" caused by an anima projection is examined in Eleanor Bertine's *Human Relationships*, p. 113 sq. See also Dr. H. Strauss' excellent paper "Die Anima als Projections-erlebnis," unpublished ms., Heidelberg, 1959.

180 Jung discusses the possibility of psychic integration through a negative anima in Collected Works vol. IX, p. 224 sq.; vol. XI, p. 164 ff.; vol. XII, pp. 25 sq., 110 sq., 128.

185 For the four stages of the anima, see Jung's Collected Works vol. XVI, p. 174.

186 Francesco Colonna's *Hypnerotomachia* has been interpreted by Linda Fierz-David in *Der Liebestraum des Poliphilo*, Zurich, 1947.

186 The quotation describing the role of the anima is from *Aurora Consurgens I*, translated by E. A. Glover (English translation in preparation). German edition by M.-L. von Franz, in Jung's *Mysterium Coniunctionis*, vol. 3, 1958.

187 Jung has examined the knightly cult of the lady in Collected Works vol. VI, p. 274 and 290 sq. See also Emma Jung and M.-L. von Franz, *Die Graalslegende in psychologischer Sicht*, Zurich, 1960.

189 For the animus' appearance as a "sacred conviction," see Jung's *Two Essays in Analytical Psychology*, London, 1928, p. 127 ff.; Collected Works vol. IX, chapter 3. See also Emma Jung, *Animus and Anima*, passim; Esther Harding, *Woman's Mysteries*, New York, 1955; Eleanor Bertine, *Human Relationships*, p. 128 ff.; Toni Wolff, *Studien zu C. G. Jung's Psychologie*, Zurich, 1959, p. 257 ff.; Erich Neumann, *Zur Psychologie des Weiblichen*, Zurich, 1953.

189 The gypsy fairy tale can be found in *Der Tod als Geliebter*, Zigeuner-Märchen. *Die Märchen der Weltliteratur*, ed. F. von der Leyen and P. Zaunert, Jena, 1926, p. 117 sq.

194 The animus as provider of valuable masculine qualities is dealt with by Jung in Collected Works vol. IX, p. 182 sq., and idem: *Two Essays*, Chapter 4.

196 For the Austrian tale of the black princess, see "Die schwarze Königstochter," *Märchen aus dem Donaulande*, *Die Märchen der Weltliteratur*, Jena, 1926, p. 150 sq.

196 The Eskimo tale of the Moon Spirit is from "Von einer Frau die zur Spinne wurde," translated from K. Rasmussen, *Die Gabe des Adlers*, p. 121 sq.

196 A discussion of the Self's young-old personifications appears in Jung's Collected Works vol. IX, p. 151 sq.

200 The myth of P'an Ku can be found in Donald A. MacKenzie's *Myths of China and Japan*, London, p. 260, and in H. Maspéro's *Le Taoisme*, Paris, 1950, p. 109. See also J. J. M. de Groot, *Universismus*, Berlin, 1918, pp. 130–31; H. Koestler, *Symbolik des Chinesischen Universismus*, Stuttgart, 1958, p. 40; and Jung's *Mysterium Coniunctionis*, vol. 2, pp. 160-61.

200 For discussion of Adam as Cosmic Man, see August Wünsche, *Schöpfung und Sündenfall des ersten Menschen*, Leipzig, 1906, pp. 8-9 and p. 13; Hans Leisegang, *Die*

Gnosis, Leipzig, Krönersche Taschenausgabe. For the psychological interpretation see Jung's *Mysterium Coniunctionis*, vol. 2, chapter 5, pp. 140-99; and Collected Works vol. XII, p. 346 sq. There may also be historical connections between the Chinese P'an Ku, the Persian Gayomart, and the legends of Adam; see Sven S. Hartmann, *Gayomart*, Uppsala, 1953, pp. 46, 115.
202 The concept of Adam as "super-soul," coming from a date palm, is dealt with by E. S. Drower in *The Secret Adam, A Study of Nasoraean Gnosis*, Oxford, 1960, pp. 23, 26, 27, 37.
202 The quotation from Meister Eckhart is from F. Pfeiffer's *Meister Eckhardt*, trans. C. de B. Evans, London, 1924, vol. II, p. 80.
202 For Jung's discussions of Cosmic Man, see Collected Works vol. IX, part 2, p. 36 sq.; "Answer to Job," Collected Works vol. XI, and *Mysterium Coniunctionis*, vol. 2, p. 215 sq. See also Esther Harding, *Journey into Self*, London, 1956, passim.
202 Adam Kadmon is discussed in Gershom Sholem's *Major Trends in Jewish Mysticism*, 1941; and Jung's *Mysterium Coniunctionis*, vol. 2, p. 182 sq.
204 The symbol of the royal couple is examined in Jung's Collected Works vol. XVI, p. 313, and in *Mysterium Coniunctionis*, vol. 1, pp. 143, 179; vol. 2, pp. 86, 90, 140, 285. See also Plato's *Symposium*, and the Gnostic God-man, the Anthropos figure.
205 For the stone as a symbol of the Self, see Jung's *Von den Wurzeln des Bewusstseins*, Zurich, 1954, pp. 200 sq., 415 sq., and 449 sq. (not yet translated).
206 The point where the urge to individuate is consciously realized is discussed in Jung's Collected Works vol. XII, passim, *Von den Wurzeln des Bewusstseins*, p. 200 sq.; Collected Works vol. IX, part 2, pp. 139 sq., 236, 247 sq., 268; Collected Works vol. XVI, p. 164 sq. See also Collected Works vol. VIII, p. 253 sq.; and Toni Wolff, *Studien zu C. G. Jung's Psychologie*, p. 43. See also, essentially, Jung's *Mysterium Coniunctionis*, vol. 2, p. 318 sq.
207 For an extended discussion of "active imagination," see Jung's "The Transcendent Function," in Collected Works vol. VIII.
207 The zoologist Adolf Portmann describes animal "inwardness" in *Das Tier als soziales Wesen*, Zurich, 1953, p. 366.
209 Ancient German beliefs concerning tombstones are discussed in Paul Herrmann's *Das altgermanische Priesterwesen*, Jena, 1929, p. 52; and in Jung's *Von den Wurzeln des Bewusstseins*, p. 198 sq.
210 Morienus's description of the philosophers' stone is quoted in Jung's Collected Works vol. XII, p. 300, note 45.
210 That suffering is necessary to find the stone is an alchemical dictum; compare Jung's Collected Works vol. XII, p. 280 sq.
210 Jung discusses the relationship between psyche and matter in *Two Essays on Analytical Psychology*, pp. 142-46.
211 For a full explanation of synchronicity, see Jung's "Synchronicity: an Acausal Connecting Principle," in Collected Works vol. VIII, p. 419 sq.
212 For Jung's views on turning to Eastern religion in order to contact the unconscious, see "Concerning Mandala Symbolism," Collected Works vol. IX, part 1, p. 335 sq., and vol. XII, p. 212 sq. (Of the latter, see also pp. 19, 42, 91 sq., 101, 119 sq., 159, 162.)
212 The excerpt from the Chinese text is from *Lu K'uan Yü*, Charles Luk, Ch'an and Zen Teaching, London, 1962, p. 27.
216 The tale of the Bath Bâdgerd is from *Märchen aus Iran, Die Märchen der Weltliteratur*, Jena, 1959, p. 150 sq.

217 Jung examines the modern feeling of being a "statistical cipher" in *The Undiscovered Self*, pp. 14, 109.
220 Dream interpretation on the subjective level is discussed in Jung's Collected Works vol. VIII, p. 266 and vol. XVI, p. 243.
220 That man is instinctively "in tune" with his surroundings is discussed by A. Portmann in *Das Tier als soziales Wesen*, p. 65 sq. and passim. See also N. Tinbergen, *A Study of Instinct*, Oxford, 1955, pp. 151 sq. and 207 sq.
221 El. E. E. Hartley discusses the mass unconscious in *Fundamentals of Social Psychology*, New York, 1952. See also Th. Janwitz and R. Schulze, *Neue Richtungen in der Massenkommunikationforschung*, Rundfunk und Fernsehen, 1960, pp. 7, 8 and passim. Also, *ibid*, pp. 1-20, and *Unterschwellige Kommunikation, ibid.*, 1960, Heft 3/4, p. 283 and p. 306. (This information is owed to the kindness of Mr. René Malamoud.)
224 The value of freedom (to create something useful) is stressed by Jung in *The Undiscovered Self*, p. 9.
224 For religious figures that symbolize the individuation process, see Jung's Collected Works vol. XI, p. 273 and passim, and *ibid.*, Part 2 and p. 164 sq.
225 Jung discusses religious symbolism in modern dreams in Collected Works vol. XII, p. 92. See also *ibid.*, pp. 28, 169 sq., 207, and others.
225 The addition of a fourth element to the Trinity is examined by Jung in *Mysterium Coniunctionis*, vol. 2, pp. 112 sq., 117 sq., 123 sq. (not yet translated), and Collected Works vol. VIII, p. 136 sq. and 160-62.
228 The vision of Black Elk is from *Black Elk Speaks*, ed. John G. Neihardt, New York, 1932. German edition: *Schwarzer Hirsch: Ich rufe mein Volk*, Olten, 1955.
228 The story of the Eskimo eagle festival is from Knud Rasmussen, *Die Gabe des Adlers*, pp. 23 sq., 29 sq.
228 Jung discusses the reshaping of original mythological material in Collected Works vol. XI, p. 20 sq., and vol. XII, Introduction.
229 The physicist W. Pauli has described the effects of modern scientific discoveries, like Heisenberg's, in *Die Philosophische Bedeutung der Idee der Komplementarität*, "Experientia," vol. VI/2, p. 72 sq.; and in *Wahrscheinlichkeit und Physik*, "Dialectica," vol. VIII/2, 1954, p. 117.

Symbolism in the visual arts   Aniela Jaffé

234 Max Ernst's statement is quoted in C. Giedion-Welcker, *Contemporary Sculpture*, New York, 1955.
234 Herbert Kühn's examination of prehistoric art is in his *Die Felsbilder Europas*, Stuttgart, 1952.
236 Concerning the No drama, compare D. Seckel, *Einführung in die Kunst Ostasiens*, Munich, 1960, figs. 1 e and 16. For the fox-mask used in No drama, see G. Buschan, *Tiere in Kult und Aberglauben*, Ciba Journal, Basle, Nov. 1942, no. 86.
237 For the animal attributes of various gods, see G. Buschan, *op. cit.*
238 Jung discusses the symbolism of the unicorn (one symbol of Christ) in Collected Works vol. XII, p. 415 ff.
240 For the myth of Brahma, see H. Zimmer, *Maya, der indische Mythos*, Stuttgart-Berlin, 1936.
240 The birth of Buddha appears in the Sanskrit *Lalita Vistera, c.* A.D. 600 to 1000; trans. Paris, 1884.
240 Jung discusses the four functions of consciousness in Collected Works vol. VI.
240 Tibetan mandalas are discussed and interpreted in Jung's Collected Works vol. IX.
242 The picture of the Virgin in the center of a circular tree is the central panel of the *Triptyque du*

Buisson Ardent, 1476, Cathédrale Saint-Saveur,
Aix-en-Provence.

242 Examples of sacred buildings with mandala
ground plans: Borobudur, Java; the Taj Mahal; the
Omar Mosque in Jerusalem. Secular buildings: Castel del
Monte, built by the Holy Roman Emperor Frederick II
(1194-1250) in Apulia.

242 For the mandala in the foundation of primitive
villages and sacred places, see M. Eliade, *Das Heilige
und das Profane*, Hamburg, 1957.

242 The theory that quadrata means "quadripartite"
was proposed by Franz Altheim, the Berlin classical
scholar. See K. Kerenyi, Introduction to Kerenyi-Jung,
Einführung in das Wesen der Mythologie, Zurich, p. 20.

242 The other theory, that the *urbs quadrata* referred
to squaring the circle, is from Kerenyi, *loc. cit.*

243 For the Heavenly City, see Book of Revelation, XXI.

243 The quotation from Jung is from his *Commentary
on the Secret of the Golden Flower*, London-New York,
1956, 10th edition.

243 Examples of the equilateral cross: crucifixion from
the *Evangelienharmonie*, Vienna, Nat. Bib. Cod. 2687
(Otfried von Weissenberg, ninth century); Gosforth
cross, 10th century; the Monasterboice cross,
10th century; or the Ruthwell cross.

245 The discussion of the change in ecclesiastical
building is based on information in Karl Litz's essay
Die Mandala, ein Beispiel der Architektursymbolik,
Winterthur, November 1960.

247 Matisse's *Still Life . . .* is in the Thompson
Collection, Pittsburgh.

247 Kandinsky's painting containing loose colored balls
or circles is entitled *Blurred White*, 1927, and is in the
Thompson Collection.

247 Paul Nash's *Event on the Downs* is in Mrs. C.
Neilson's collection. See George W. Digby, *Meaning and
Symbol*, Faber & Faber, London.

249 Jung's discussion of UFOs is in *Flying Saucers:
A Modern Myth of Things Seen in the Skies*, London-
New York, 1959.

250 The quotation from Bazaine's *Notes sur la peinture
d'aujourd'hui* (Paris, 1953) was quoted in Walter
Hess, *Dokumente zum Verständnis der modernen Malerei*,
Hamburg, 1958 (Rowohlt), p. 122. A number of
quotations in this chapter have been taken from this
extremely useful compilation, which will be referred to
hereafter as *Dokumente*.

250 Franz Marc's statement is from *Briefe, Aufzeichnungen
und Aphorismen*, Berlin, 1920.

250 For Kandinsky's book, see sixth edition, Berne,
1959. (First edition, Munich, 1912.) *Dokumente*, p. 80.

250 Mannerism and modishness in modern art is
discussed by Werner Haftmann in *Glanz und Gefährdung
der Abstrakten Malerei*, in *Skizzenbuch zur Kultur der
Gegenwart*, Munich, 1960, p. 111. See also Haftmann's
Die Malerei im. 20. Jahrhundert, second edn., Munich,
1957; and Herbert Read, *A Concise History of Modern
Painting*, London, 1959, and numerous individual studies.

251 Kandinsky's essay "Über die Formfrage" is in
Der blaue Reiter, Munich, 1912. See *Dokumente*, p. 87.

253 Bazaine's comments on Duchamp's bottle rack are
from *Dokumente*, p. 122.

253 Joan Miró's statement is from *Joan Miró*, Horizont
Collection, Arche Press.

254 The reference to Schwitters' "obsession" is from
Werner Haftmann, *op. cit.*

254 Kandinsky's statement is from *Selbstbetrachtungen*,
Berlin, 1913. *Dokumente*, p. 89.

254 The quotation from Carlo Carrà is from W.
Haftmann's *Paul Klee, Wege bildnerischen Denkens*, Munich,
1955, third edn., p. 71.

254 The statement by Klee is from *Wege des
Naturstudiums*, Weimar, Munich, 1923. *Dokumente*, p. 125.

254 Bazaine's remark is from *Notes sur la peinture
d'aujourd'hui*, Paris, 1953. *Dokumente*, p. 125.

254 The statement by de Chirico is from *Sull'Arte
Metafisica*, Rome, 1919. *Dokumente*, p. 112.

255 The quotations from de Chirico's *Memorie della mia
Vita* are in *Dokumente*, p. 112.

255 Kandinsky's statement about the death of God is
in his *Ueber das Geistige in der Kunst, op. cit.*

255 Of the 19th-century European poets alluded to,
see especially Heinrich Heine, Rimbaud, and
Mallarmé.

255 The quotation from Jung is from Collected Works
vol. XI, p. 88.

257 Artists in whose work *manichini* appear include
Carlo Carrà, A. Archipenko (1887-1964), and Giorgio
Morandi (1890-1964).

257 The comment on Chagall by Herbert Read is from
his *A Concise History of Modern Painting*, London, 1959,
p. 124, 126, 128.

257 André Breton's statements are from *Manifestes du
Surréalisme 1924-42*, Paris, 1946. *Dokumente*, p. 117, 118.

258 The quotation from Ernst's *Beyond Painting* (New
York, 1948) is in *Dokumente*, p. 119.

259 References to Hans Arp are based on Carola
Giedion-Welcker, *Hans Arp*, 1957, p. xvi.

259 Reference to Ernst's *Histoire Naturelle* is in
Dokumente, p. 121.

260 On the 19th-century Romantics and "nature's
handwriting," see Novalis, *Die Lehrlinge zu Sais*;
E. T. A. Hoffmann, *Das Märchen vom Goldnen Topf*;
G. H. von Schubert, *Symbolik des Traumes*.

260 Kassner's comment on Georg Trakl is from
Almanach de la Librairie Flinker, Paris, 1961.

262 Kandinsky's statements are, respectively, from
Rückblicke (quoted by Max Bill's Introduction to
Kandinsky's *Ueber das Geistige . . ., op. cit.*); from
Selbstdarstellung, Berlin, 1913 (*Dokumente*, p. 86);
and from Haftmann, *Malerei im. 20. Jahrhundert*.

262 Franz Marc's statements are respectively from
Briefe, Aufzeichnungen und Aphorismen, op. cit.;
Dokumente, p. 79 f.; and from Haftmann, *op. cit.*, p. 478.

262 Klee's statement is from *Ueber die moderne Kunst*,
Lecture, 1924. *Dokumente*, p. 84.

262 Mondrian's statement is from *Neue Gestaltung*,
Munich, 1925. *Dokumente*, p. 100.

263 Kandinsky's statements are respectively from
Ueber das Geistige . . ., op. cit., p. 83; from *Ueber die
Formfrage*, Munich, 1912 (*Dokumente*, p. 88); from
Ueber das Geistige . . . (*Dokumente*, p. 88); and from
Aufsätze, 1923-43 (*Dokumente*, p. 91).

263 Franz Marc's statement is quoted from Georg
Schmidt, *Vom Sinn der Parallele* in *Kunst und Naturform*,
Basle, 1960.

263 Klee's statements are respectively from *Ueber die
Moderne Kunst, op. cit.* (*Dokumente*, p. 84); *Tagebücher*,
Berlin, 1953 (*Dokumente*, p. 86); quoted from Haftmann,
Paul Klee, op. cit., p. 93 and p. 50; *Tagebücher*, (*Dokumente*
p. 86); and Haftmann, p. 89.

264 Reference to Pollock's painting is in Haftmann,
Malerei im 20. Jahrhundert, p. 464.

264 Pollock's statements are from *My Painting,
Possibilities*, New York, 1947. Quoted from Herbert Read,
op. cit., p. 267.

264 The quotation from Jung is from Collected Works vol. IX, p. 173.
265 Read's quotation of Klee is from *Concise History . . .* , *op. cit.*, p. 180.
265 Marc's statement is from *Briefe, Aufzeichnungen und Aphorismen. Dokumente*, p. 79.
265 The discussion of Marini is from Edouard Roditi, *Dialoge über Kunst*, Insel Verlag, 1960. (The conversation is given here in a very abbreviated form.)
268 The statement by Manessier is quoted from W. Haftmann, *op. cit.*, p. 474.
268 Bazaine's comment is from his *Notes sur la peinture d'aujourd'hui*, *op. cit. Dokumente*, p. 126.
270 The statement by Klee is from W. Haftmann, *Paul Klee*, p. 71.
270 For reference to modern art in churches, see W. Schmalenbach, *Zur Ausstellung von Alfred Manessier*, Zurich Art Gallery, 1959.

Symbols in an individual analysis   Jolande Jacobi

273 The Palace of Dreams: a 16th-century illustration to Book XIX of Homer's *Odyssey*. In the center niche stands the goddess of sleep holding a bouquet of poppy flowers. On her left is the Gate of Horn (with the head of a horned ox above it); from this gate come true dreams: on her right the Gate of Ivory with an elephant's head above; from this gate come false dreams. Top left, the goddess of the moon, Diana; top right, Night, with the infants Sleep and Death.
277 The importance of the first dream in an analysis is indicated by Jung in *Modern Man in Search of a Soul*, p. 77.
290 Regarding the section on the Oracle Dream, see the *I Ching or Book of Changes*, trans. Richard Wilhelm (with an introduction by C. G. Jung), Routledge and Kegan Paul, London, 1951, vols. I and II.
292 The symbolism in the three upper lines of the sign Meng—the "gate"—is mentioned in *op. cit.*, vol. II, p. 299, which also states that this sign ". . . is a bypath, it means little stones, doors and openings . . . eunuchs and watchmen, the fingers . . ." For the sign Meng, see also vol. I, p. 20 ff.
292 The quotation from the *I Ching* is in vol. I, p. 23.
292 Concerning a second consulting of the *I Ching*, Jung writes (in his Introduction to the English edition, p. x): "A repetition of the experiment is impossible for the simple reason that the original situation cannot be reconstructed. Therefore in each instance there is only a first and single answer."
292 For the commentary on the sign Li, see *op. cit.*, vol. I, p. 178; and a reference in vol. II, p. 299.
293 The motif of the "city on the mountain" is discussed by K. Kerenyi in *Das Geheimnis der hohen Städte*, *Europäische Revue*, 1942, Juli-August-Heft; and in *Essays on a Science of Mythology*, Bollingen Series XXIII, p. 16.
294 Jung's discussions of the motif of four appear, for instance, in his Collected Works, vol. IX, XI, XII, and XIV; but the problem of the four, with all its implications, is woven like a red thread through all his works.
297 For some of the symbolic meanings ascribed to playing cards, see *Handwörterbuch des Deutschen Aberglaubens*, vol. IV, p. 1015, and vol. V, p. 1110.
297 The symbolism of the number nine is discussed in (among other works) F. V. Hopper's *Medieval Number Symbolism*, 1938, p. 138.
299 Concerning the "night-sea-journey" pattern of this dream, see J. Jacobi, "The Process of Individuation," *Journal of Analytical Psychology*, vol. III, no. 2, 1958, p. 95.
300 The primitive belief in the power of bodily secretions

is discussed by E. Neumann in *Origins of Consciousness* (German edition), p. 39.

Science and the unconscious   M.-L. von Franz

304 The archetypes as *nuclei* of the psyche are discussed by W. Pauli in *Aufsätze und Vorträge über Physik und Erkenntnis-theorie*, Verlag Vieweg Braunschweig. 1961.
304 Concerning the inspiring or inhibiting power of the archetypes, see C. G. Jung and W. Pauli, *Naturerklärung und Psyche*, Zurich, 1952, p. 163 and passim.
306 Pauli's suggestion concerning biology appears in *Aufsätze und Vorträge*, *op. cit.*, p. 123.
306 For further explanation of the statement concerning the time required for mutation, see Pauli, *op. cit.*, pp. 123-25.
306 The story of Darwin and Wallace can be found in Henshaw Ward's *Charles Darwin*, 1927.
307 The reference to Descartes is expanded in M.-L. von Franz's "Der Traum des Descartes," in *Studien des C. G. Jung Instituts*, called "Zeitlose Dokuments der Seele."
307 Kepler's assertion is discussed by Jung and Pauli in *Naturerklärung und Psyche*, *op. cit.*, p. 117.
307 Heisenberg's phrase was quoted by Hannah Arendt in *The Human Condition*, Chicago Univ. Press, 1958, p. 26.
307 Pauli's suggestion of parallel psychological and physical studies appears in *Naturerklärung*, *op. cit.*, p. 163.
307 For Niels Bohr's ideas of complementarity, see his *Atomphysik und menschliche Erkenntnis*, Braunschweig, p. 26 ff.
308 "Momentum" (of a subatomic particle) is, in German, *Bewegungsgrösse*.
308 The statement quoted from Pauli was quoted by Jung in "The Spirit of Psychology," in Jos. Campbell's *Coll. Papers of the Eranos Year Book*, Bollingen Series XXX, 1, N.Y. Pantheon Books, 1954, p. 439.
308 Pauli discusses the "primary possibilities" in *Vorträge*, *op. cit.*, p. 125.
308 The parallels between microphysics and psychological concepts also appear in *Vorträge*: the description of the unconscious by paradoxes, pp. 115-16; the archetypes as "primary possibilities," p. 115; the unconscious as a "field," p. 125.
309 The quotation from Gauss is translated from his *Werke*, vol. X, p. 25, letter to Olbers, and is quoted in B. L. van der Waerden, *Einfall und Ueberlegung: Drei kleine Beiträge zur Psychologie des mathematischen Denkens*, Basel, 1954.
309 Poincaré's statement is quoted in *ibid.*, p. 2.
309 Pauli's belief that the concept of the unconscious would affect all natural sciences is in *Vorträge*, p. 125.
309 The idea of the possible one-ness of life phenomena was taken up by Pauli, *ibid.*, p. 118.
309 For Jung's ideas on the "synchronistic arrangement" including matter and psyche, see his "Synchronicity: An Acausal Connecting Principle," Coll. Works vol. VIII.
309 Jung's idea of the *unus mundus* follows some medieval philosophic ideas in scholasticism (John Duns Scotus, etc.): The unus mundus was the total or archetypal concept of the world in God's mind before he put it into actual reality.
309 The quotation from Hannah Arendt appears in *The Human Condition*, *op. cit.*, p. 266.
309 For further discussion of "primary mathematical intuitions," see Pauli, *Vorträge*, p. 122; and also Ferd. Conseth, "Les mathématiques et la réalité," 1948.
310 Pauli, following Jung, points out that our conscious representations are "ordered" before becoming conscious in *Vorträge*, p. 122. See also Conseth, *op. cit.*
310 B. L. van der Waerden's statement is from his *Einfall und Ueberlegung*, *op. cit.*, p. 9.

Index

Illustration credits

Key: (B) bottom; (C) center; (L) left; (M) middle; (R) right; (T) top; and combinations, e.g. (BR) (TL)

Academia de San Fernando, Madrid, 65(BR); © A.D. A.G.P., Paris, 216(BL), 271(ML)(BR); courtesy Administrationskanzlei des Naturhistorischen Museums, Wien, 285(BC); Aerofilms and Aero Pictorial, 218(BL), 243(TL); Signor Agnelli, 251(BR); Albertina, Vienna, 169(BL); Aldus Archives, 129(L), 220(TL); Alte Pinakothek, Munich, 87(BR), 115(BR), 280; American Museum of Natural History, 68(BL); courtesy the Archbishop of Canterbury and the Trustees of Lambeth Palace Library, 156(BL); Archives Photographiques, Paris, 204(TR); The Art Institute of Chicago, Potter Palmer Collection, 245(BR); Arts Council of Great Britain, 147; Ruth Berenson & Norbert Muhlen, *George Grosz 1961*, Arts Inc., New York, 283; Associated Press, 79(BL). Courtesy Miss Ruth Bailey, 52, 57, 198(TC); Collection Frau Dr. Lydia Bau, 220(MR); Bayreuther Festspiele, 192(MR); Berlin Staatl. Museen, Antikenabteilung, 51(BL); Bibliothèque de la Bourgeoisie, Berne, 188(BC); Bibliothèque Nationale, Paris, 99, 110(MR), 140, 145(BC), 189(BR), 215(BR), 222(TL), 298(TL); Peter Birkhäuser, 187(TR), 199; Black Star, 35(BL), 59(BR), 117(BL), 201(TL), 235(TR); *The Blue Angel* (director: Joseph von Sternberg), Germany, 1930, 179(M); Bodleian Library, Oxford, 176(B); The Bollingen Foundation, New York, 38(BC), 72(L), 107(BC); British Crown Copyright, 71(R), 120(TR); courtesy the Trustees of the British Museum, 21, 38(BL), 42(T), 53(BR), 54(M), 55(BL), (Natural History) 66, 105, 107(BL), 110(BL), 111(ML)(MC), 115(T), 124(BL), 125(BR)(BL), 133, 144(TR), 145(BR), 150(BR), 155(TL), 156(BR), 160, 165(BR), 171(TR), 186(BL), 188(BL), 190(BL), 192(BR), 195(TL), 197(TL), 198(TL), 209(BL), 216(BR), 259(T), 273, 281, 298(BL); Shirley Burroughs, 80(T). Cabinet des Médailles, Paris, 141(BL)(BR); Cairo Museum, 22(T); Camera Press, 47(TL), 97(B), 111(BR), 194(BL); Jonathan Cape Limited, London, from *Angkor Wat*, Malcolm MacDonald, 91(BR); Central Press, 50(TR); W. & R. Chambers Limited, from *Twentieth Century Dictionary*, 45; Church of England Information Office, 30(R); CIBA Archives, Basle, 239(MR); courtesy Jean Cocteau, 138, 139, 178(BL); Compagnie Aérienne Française, 242(TL); Contemporary Films Ltd., *Ugetsu Monogatari* (director: Kenji Mizoguchi), Japan, 1953, 182(T) and *Zéro de Conduite* (director: Jean Vigo), Franfilmdis Production, France, 1933, 116; Conzett & Huber, Zürich, 26(T), 166(BL), 188(MC), 265, 293; Cornell University Press, Ithaca, New York, 68(BR); *Crin Blanc* (director: Albert Lamorisse), France, 1953, 174(T) (BL). Daiei Motion Picture Company Ltd., 182(T); courtesy Madame Delaunay, 248(TR); Maya Deren, *The Living Gods of Haiti*, 35(TL)(TC)(TR); by courtesy of Walt Disney Productions, 110(BR); *La Dolce Vita* (director: Federico Fellini), Italy/France, 1959, 166(BR); courtesy Madame Trix Dürst-Haass, 263(TR); Collection Dutuit, 241(TL). Edinburgh University Library, 119(BR), 210(ML); Éditions Albert Guillot, Paris, 209(BR); Éditions d'Art, Paris, 271(ML); Éditions Hoa-Qui, Paris, 44; Éditions Houvet, 20; Education and Television Films Ltd., 112(BL); Esquire Magazine © 1963 by Esquire, Inc., 51(TR). Faber & Faber Ltd., London, *Dance and Drama in Bali*, by Beryl de Zoete and Walter Spies, 126; Jules Feiffer, permission of the artist's agent, 58; *Find Your Man*, Warner

Bros., 1924, 206(BL); W. Foulsham & Co. Ltd., London, 53(BL); courtesy M.-L. von Franz, 215(ML)(BL), 227; French Government Tourist Office, London, 127(BR), 232(T), 243(TR); artist Henrard, Frobenius-Institut an der Johann Wolfgang Goethe-Universität, Frankfurt a.M., 202. Gala Film Distributors Ltd., 192(T); Galerie de France, 271(ML); Galerie Stangl, Munich, 260(BR), 261(B); Germanisches National-Museum, Nuremberg, 181(TL); German Tourist Information Bureau, London, 237(BR); Giraudon, 86(MR), 99, 103(L), 112(BR), 154, 181(TR), 184(BL)(BR), 185(BR), 215(BR), 217, 223(BL), 225, 252(TL); *Godzilla* (directors: Jerry Moore & Ishiro Honda), Japan/U.S.A., 1955, 93(BR); Goethehaus, Frankfurt a.M., 63; courtesy Samuel Goldwyn Pictures Ltd., 65(BL); Göteborgs Konstmuseum, 266(TR); Granada TV, 173; Graphis Press, Zürich, 98(TL), 247(T); Solomon R. Guggenheim Museum, New York, 248(BL); © the artist, Hans Haffenrichter, 211; George G. Harrap, London, *Fairy Tales*, Hans Christian Andersen, 1932, 197(BL); by permission of the President and Fellows of Harvard College, 109(M); William Heinemann Ltd., London, *The Twilight of the Gods* by Ernest Gann, 178(BR); reproduced by gracious permission of Her Majesty The Queen, 245(BL); from Conze, *Heroen und Göttergestalten*, 155(BL); Museum Unterlinden, Colmar/photo Hans Hinz, 48(T); *Hiroshima mon Amour* (director: Alain Resnais), France/Japan, 1958–9, 221(TL); Ides et Calendes, Neuchâtel, *Faces of Bronze*, photo Pierre Allard & Philippe Luzuy, 88, 237(BL); Imperial War Museum, London, 121(BL); Inter Nationes, 54(B); Irish Tourist Board, 210(BR). Erhard Jacoby, 39, 229; Japan Council against Atomic and Hydrogen Bombs, 100(B); Dr. Emilio Jesi, Milan, 256(BR); The Jewish Institute of History, Warsaw, 94(BL); courtesy the family of C. G. Jung, 56; Karsh of Ottawa, frontispiece; Keystone, 108(BR), 157, 172(B), 210(MR), 235(TL); Christopher Kitson, 90; Kunsthaus, Zürich, 188(MC); Kunsthistorisches Museum, Vienna, 29, 188(TL), 244; Kunstmuseum, Basle, 219(BC), 248(BR), 258(TL), 279(TL); Kunstmuseum, Berne, 263(TL); Larousse, Éditeurs, Paris, from *La Mythologie* by Félix Guirand, 119(T), 179(BL), drawings by I. Bilibin; *Lascaux chapelle de la préhistoire*, F. Windels, 148; Leyden University Library, 31(T); Libreria dello Stato, Roma, *La Villa dei Misteri*, Prof. Maiuri, 142–3(T); London Express, 270; Longmans, Green & Co. Ltd., London, 1922, *Mazes and Labyrinths*, W. H. Matthews, 171(ML)(MC)(MR); Macmillan & Co. Ltd., London, *Alice's Adventures in Wonderland* (Sir John Tenniel drawing), 54(T); Magnum, 22(BL), 34, 146(BR), 172(T), 194(TMR), 198(B), 208(BL), 238(TL), 269; Mansell Collection, 46, 150(BL), 190(BR), 191, 197(R), 201(BL), 205, 209(BL), 220(TR), 239(MC); Marlborough Fine Art Gallery Ltd., London, 252(TR); © The Medici Society Ltd., 150(T); *The Medium* (director: Gian-Carlo Menotti), Italy/U.S.A., 1951, 177(BR); Metro-Goldwyn-Mayer Inc., 24, 182(BL); *Metropolis* (director: Fritz Lang), Germany, 1926, 223(BR); courtesy The Metropolitan Museum of Art, New York, 30(L) (The Cloisters Collections Purchase), 40(T) (gift of M. Knoedler & Co., 1918), 119(BR), 184(TR) (gift of William Church Osborn, 1949), 231 (Fletcher Fund, 1956); *Modern Times*, Charles Chaplin, United

Artists Corporation Ltd., 113(BR); The Pierpont Morgan Library, New York, 73, 201(BR); *Mother Joan of the Angels*, Film Polski, 1960, © Contemporary Films Ltd., 168; Mt. Wilson and Palomar Observatories, 23, 103(R); Prof. Erwin W. Müller, Pennsylvania State University, 22(BR); Musée de Cluny, Paris, 225; Musée Condé, Chantilly, 111(MR), 184(BL), 226; Musée Ensor, Ostend, 296(B); Musée Étrusque de Vatican, 114(BR); Musée Fenaille à Rodez, Aveyron, 233(BC); Musée Guimet, Paris, 97(T), 241(BL); Musée Gustave Moreau, Paris, 179(BR); Musée de l'Homme, Paris, 234(TC), 236(BL); Musée du Louvre, Paris, 103(L), 111(TL), 112(BR), 146(TR), 154, 184(BR), 185(BR), 223(BL), 276(B); Musée du Petit Palais, Paris, 241(TL); Musées de Bordeaux, 120(BR); Museo Nazionale, Napoli, 124(BR); Museo del Prado, Madrid, 75; The Museum of Navaho Ceremonial Art Inc., New Mexico, 71(TL), 114(BL), 214(BR); Museum für Völkerkunde, Basle, 127(L); Museum für Völkerkunde, Berlin, 177(BC), 300. Nasjonalgalleriet, Oslo, 87(BL); The National Gallery of Canada, 47(TR); National Gallery, London, 83, 122, 288; National Museum, Athens, 76; The National Museum, Copenhagen, 242(TR); © National Periodical Publications Inc., New York, 111(BC); National Portrait Gallery, London, 190(T), 207(BL); Dr. Neel & Univ. of Chicago Press, *Human Heredity*, Neel & Schull, © 1954, 31(B); Max Niehans Verlag, Zürich, 108(BL); *Newsweek*, 307; *The New York Times*, 134(BL); Nigeria Magazine, 43; *The Nun's Story* (director: Fred Zinneman), U.S.A., 1957–9, 134(TL); Ny Carlsberg Glyptotek, Copenhagen, 113(BC). Olympic Museum, Athens, 185(BC); *On the Bowery* (director: Lionel Rogosin), U.S.A., 1955, 62; Open Air Museum for Sculpture, Middelheim, Antwerp, 266(MR); Count Don Alfonso Orombelli, Milan, 256(ML); © Daniel O'Shea, 189(BL). Palermo Museum, 144(TL); *Paris Match*, 270; *Passion de Jeanne d'Arc* (director: Carl Dreyer), France, 1928, 91(BL); Paul Popper, 25(BL), 28(BL), 42(BR), 111(BL), 134(ML), 152, 200(TL), 210(BL), 236(BC), 285(BR); Pepsi-Cola Company, 50(TL); Planet News, 32, 169(BR); Le Point Cardinal, Paris, 233(BR); P & O Orient Lines, 151; courtesy H. M. Postmaster-General, 25(BR); Private Collection, London, 203(BL); Private Collection, New York, 256(BL); *Punch*, 33(L); Putnam & Co. Ltd., London, 1927, by permission, from *The Mind and Face of Bolshevism* by René Fulopp-Muller, 107(BR); G. P. Putnam's Sons, New York, 1953, & Spring Books Ltd., London, from *A Pictorial History of the Silent Screen* by Daniel Blum, 123. Radio Times Hulton Picture Library, 194(BML), 195(BR), 220(BR), 222(BC); Rapho, 153, (Izis) 165(BL); Rathbone Books Ltd., 194(TML); *Réalités*, 212(BL); Ringier-Bilderdienst AG., 218(BR); Routledge & Kegan Paul Ltd., London, 1951, The Bollingen Series XIX, 2nd. edn., New York, 1961, & Eugen Diederichs Verlag, Düsseldorf, 1951, the *I Ching or Book of Changes*, 291(BL); courtesy Miss Ariane Rump, 201(TR). Salvat Editores S.A., 275(BL); Sandoz Ltd., Basle, 259(B); Scala, 77, 118, 144(BL), 155 (BR), Slavko, 187(BR); *The Son of the Sheik* (director: George Fitzmaurice), U.S.A., 1926, 195(BL); Soprintendenza alle Antichità delle Province di Napoli, 266(BR); © S.P.A.D.E.M., Paris, 1964, 147, 167, 247(B), 252(ML), 263(TL); Staatliche Museen, Berlin-Dahlem, 144(BR); Staat Luzern, 189(BC); Staatsgemäldesammlungen, München, 111(TR); Städelsches Kunstinstitut, Frankfurt, 185(TR); Swedish National Travel Association, 80(BR), 111(TC), 286(BL). *Tarzan and his Mate* (director: Cedric Gibbons), U.S.A., 1934, 194(TL); Tate Gallery, London, 72(R), 186(R), 249(BL), 264(BR), 271(BR); *They Came to a City*, J. B. Priestley (director: Basil Deardon), Gt. Britain, 1944, 279(TR); © 1935 James Thurber © 1963 Helen Thurber, from *Thurber's Carnival* (orig. publ. in *The New Yorker*), 78(BR); © James Thurber 1933, 33(R); *Titanic* (director: Herbert Selpin), Germany, 1943, 121(BR); Topix, London, 59(BL), 200(TR); Toshodaiji Temple, Japan, 175(BL); Trianon Press, Jura, France, from the Blake Trust Facsimile of *Songs of Innocence and of Experience*, 219(TL). Uni-Dia-Verlag, 19; USAF Academy, 129(BC); U.S. Coast and Geodetic Survey, 100(T); United States Information Service, London, 221(R); Vatican Museum, 127(TR); Verlag Hans Huber, 27; Verlag Kurt Desch, München, 79(BR); Victoria and Albert Museum, London, 48(B), 109(T)(BL), 115(BL), 136, 163, 174(BR), 198(TC), 203(ML)(BR), 206(ML); Ville de Strasbourg, 70; Volkswagen Ltd., 36. Collection of Walker Art Center, Minneapolis, 260(BL); Wiener Library, © Auschwitz Museum, Poland, 94(BR); courtesy the Wellcome Trust, 69, 246(TL), 286(BR); Wide World, 117(BR); Gahan Wilson, 49(BL); *Wuthering Heights* (director: William Wyler), U.S.A., 1939, 190(T). Yale University Art Gallery, James Jackson Jarves Collection, 180(TL). Zentralbibliothek, Zürich, 249(BR); © Mrs. Hans Zinsser, from G. F. Kunz, *The Magic of Jewels and Charms*, 207(ML); Zentralbibliothek Zürich, 248(TR).

Cover photograph: Tibetan Mandala, photo L. Courteville Top

Photographers:

Ansel Adams, 208(BL); Alinari, 46; David G. Allen, Bird Photographs Inc., 68(T); Douglas Allen, 222(ML). Werner Bischof, 22(BL), 269; Joachim Blauel, 261(B); Leonardo Bonzi, 135(BL); Édouard Boubat, 212(BL); Mike Busselle, 28(BR), 93(BL), collages 121(BL)(BR), 135(BR), 180(TR), 181(B), 183(TR)(BR), montages 190(T), 207(TL), 212(BR), 219(BR); Francis Brunel, 239(TR). Robert Capa, 194(TMR), 198(B); Cartier-Bresson, 34, 172(T); Chuzeville, 276(B); Franco Cianetti, 264(BL); Prof. E. J. Cole, 258(BR); J. B. Collins, 35(ML)(MC); Ralph Crane, 117(BL). N. Elswing, 242(TR). John Freeman, 105, 107(BL), 171(TR), 195(TL), 197(TL), 259(MR), 281, 298(BL). Ewing Galloway, 82(BL); Marcel Gautherot, 213; Georg Gerster, 109(BR); Roger Guillemot, 89. Ernst Haas, 146(BR); Leon Herschtritt, 84; Hinz, Basle, 127(L), 219(BC), 258(T). Isaac, 35(BL). William Klein, 86(BL). Lavaud, 97(T), 159, 241(BL); Louise Leiris, 261(BL); Dr. Ivar Lissner, 149(BR); Sandra Lousada at Whitecross Studio, 175(BR); Kurt & Margot Lubinsky, 149(BL). Roger Mayne, 164(BR); Don McCullin, 287; St. Anthony Messenger, 143(B); Meyer, 29; John Moore, 72(R), 238(BL), 252(BL). Jack Nisberg, 256(TR). Michael Peto, 164(BL); Axel Poignant, 95, 128, 130, 131, 204(TMR). Allen C. Reed, 74, 214(T). Sabat, 65(BR); Prof. Roger Sauter, 243(BL); Kees Scherer, 35(BR); Émil Schulthess, 201(TC); Carroll Seghers, 98(TR); Brian Shuel, 55(BR), 129(BR); Dennis Stock, 238(T); David Swann, 21, 48(B), 53(BL), 54(M), 66, 109(T)(BL), 110(BL), 115(T)(BL), 133, 136, 155(T), 163, 174(BR), 186(BL), 188(BL), 190(BL), 198(TR), 203(BR)(ML), 206(ML), 264(BR), 302, 303. Felix Trombe, 234(TC). Villani & Figli Frl., 80(BL). Yoshio Watanabe, 232(B); Hans Peter Widmer, 305).